SOCIOLOGY
a new approach

Edited by
Michael Haralambos

Written by
Michael Haralambos, Frances Smith, James O'Gorman
and Robin Heald

C a u s e w a y   P r e s s

Dedication

Jane, Kate and Pauline
Ian, Timothy and Matthew
Jude
Ben

Acknowledgements

Cover design Caroline Waring-Collins (Waring-Collins Partnership)
Cover illustration Bruce Coleman
Page design Caroline Waring-Collins
Graphic origination Caroline Waring-Collins
Graphics Elaine M. Sumner (Waring-Collins Partnership)
Typing Ingrid Hamer
Photography Andrew Allen, Rob Harrison
Cartoons Brick, Tony Winterbottom
Advice Liz Roynayne, Martin Holborn, Vincent Farrell

Picture credits

Advertising Archives 22 (l), 138, 193 (tr); Allen Lane, Penguin Books Ltd 14, 15; Andrew Allen 185 (t), 221 (br), 260 (t, m and b); Blues and Rhythm 258; Boddingtons 193 (br); Bradford Education 271 (m and b); Camera Press 13, 52 (bl), 53, 71, 177, 193 (ml), 232, 244, 247; Brick 42, 68 (t and b), 69, 102, 126, 223, 227; Bruce Coleman 9 (b), 10; Conservative Central Office 67 (r); David Hoffman 23 (l and r), 47, 72 (br), 79 (l), 81 (t, m, b), 89 (l), 96, 106, 115 (t), (and Susie Martin) 121, 166, 189, 191; David King Collection 28 (l and r); Dover Publications Inc 48, 55, 197 (t), 207; Ethnological Museum, Berlin/World of Leather 269; Format (and Val Wilmer) 77, (and Jenny Matthews) 91, (and Melanie Friend) 92, (and Monique Cabral) 95, (and Brenda Prince) 105, 180, 181, 252, (and Sarita Sharma) 131 (br), (and Sheila Solloway) 140, (and Jacky Chapman) 142, 158, (and Maggie Murray) 172, 178 (m), 185 (b), 221 (tr), 267 (r), (and Raissa Page) 179 (b), 246, (and Joanne O'Brien) 221 (tl), (and Connie Treppe) 270; Frances Smith 33; Glenbow Archives (Calgary) 21; Guardian Newspapers 56; Hulton Deutsch 66, 86, 87 (b), 135 (b), 137, 150, 156, 178 (t), 198, 206, 213, 225 (tl), 251, 256, 273 (m); Institute of Agricultural History 217 (l); J.F. Batellier/Free Association Books 37, 210; James O'Gorman 39 (l and m); Joe Bloggs 74; Lancashire Library, Preston District 19; Library of Congress 26, 130; Manchester Studies Unit 133; Mansell Collection 87 (m), 98 (br), 103, 209 (t), 215; Margaret Thatcher's Office 67 (l); Mary Evans Picture Library 111, 148, 208; Mattel UK Ltd 187 (b); Mersey TV/Channel 4 149; Mike Haralambos 35, 41 (l and r); Museum of the American Indian 17 (b); National Museum of Labour History 135 (t); National Museums of Canada 43; Network 65 (l), 360, (and Mike Goldwater) 20 (r), 40, (and Sunil Gupta) 51 (m), 250, (and Harriet Logan) 60 (l), (and Michael Abrahams) 72 (bl), (and Roger Hutchings) 83 (r), (and Laurie Sparham) 108, (and Barry Lewis) 164, 275, (and Peter Jordan) 190, (and A. Koster/JB Pictures) 192, 254, (and Homer Sykes) 209 (b), (and Neil Libbert) 229, (and John Sturrock) 234, 254 (b), 266; Oxo 132; Peter Newark's American Pictures 45, 52 (br), 84 (br), 216 (tl and tr); Popperfoto 52 (t), 60 (r), 72 (t), 75, 89 (r), 145, 157, 167, 175, 204, 248 (l), 265; Rex Features 20 (l), 29 (l and r), 31, 51 (t), 76, 79 (r), 83 (l), 113, 160, 211, 216 (br), 226, 236, 240, 248 (r), 261, 262, 267 (l); Rob Harrison 39 (r); Royal Geographical Society 8 (m and b), 9 (t), 12, 257; Sally and Richard Greenhill 64, 217 (r); Smithsonian Institution 11; Times Newspapers 65 (r); Tony Winterbottom 17 (m), 32, 116, 122, 152, 153, 168, 224, 238; Topham Picturepoint 22 (r), 70, 100 (m), 115 (bl and br), 120, 124, 171, 174, 179 (t), 183; Tropix Photo Library 241; United Nations (and Ray Witlin) 195; Waring-Collins 228; White and Reed 245.

Statistical data

Central Statistical Office for figures and tables from various issues of *Social Trends, General Household Survey, Employment Gazette* and *Labour Market Trends*. Crown Copyright.
Reproduced by the permission of the Controller of HMSO and the Central Statistical Office.
Child Poverty Action Group for figure from C. Oppenheim *Poverty the Facts* (CPAG, London, 1993).

Text

For extracts from the following publications:
Animal Farm and *Nineteen Eighty-Four* by George Orwell. Copyright © The estate of the late Sonia Brownell Orwell and Martin Secker and Warburg Ltd.
Long Lance by Chief Buffalo Child Long Lance reproduced with permission from Corgi Books.
Uncle Tom's Children by Richard Wright. Copyright 1937 by Richard Wright. Renewed 1965 by Ellen Wright. By permission of Harper & Row, Publishers Inc.

British Library Cataloguing in Publication Data
A catalogue record for this book is available from the British Library.

ISBN 1 873929 55 2

Causeway Press Limited
PO Box 13, Ormskirk, Lancs L39 5HP

First edition 1983 (reprinted six times)
Second edition 1986 (reprinted eleven times)
Third edition 1996, reprinted 1997

© Michael Haralambos, Frances Smith, James O'Gorman, Robin Heald

Printed and bound by Cambus Litho Ltd, East Kilbride.

CONTENTS

Chapter 9 — The Family — 128

Chapter 10 — Education — 152

Chapter 11 — Age and generation — 174

Chapter 12 — Gender — 182

CULTURE AND SOCIALISATION

This chapter looks at some of the basic ideas or concepts that sociologists use to understand human behaviour. It begins with the idea of **culture**, the learned, shared behaviour of members of society. Comparisons are then made between human and non-human societies in order to develop an understanding of the importance of culture for human behaviour. Some of the main aspects of culture - values, norms, statuses and roles - are then examined. The chapter ends by showing the importance of **socialisation** - the process by which people learn the culture of their society. Throughout the chapter comparisons are made between Western and non-Western society in order to illustrate the variety of human behaviour.

CULTURE

PART 1

Human beings learn how to behave. They share much of their behaviour with other members of the society to which they belong. The learned, shared behaviour of members of a society is known as *culture*. The following passage examines the importance of culture for human society.

Many living creatures do not learn how to behave. They have not been taught by their parents, they have not copied older brothers and sisters or imitated adult members of their society. They do not have to learn their behaviour because their actions are directed by instinct. Instincts are instructions about how to behave which are biologically inherited. They guide the salmon's return from the sea to spawn and die in fresh water. They direct the migration of birds and organise the complex society of ants and bees.

The instinctive behaviour of creatures which belong to the same species is very similar. For example, blackbirds build similar nests at the same time of year. All human beings belong to the same species but studies of various human societies show considerable differences in behaviour. This suggests that the way of life of men and women is learned rather than biologically inherited. If their actions were based on instinct, human beings, as members of the same species, should behave in much the same way.

Tibetan nuns in 1904

The following examples of customs concerning marriage and family life indicate the variety of human behaviour. In traditional China, a woman's father or one of her brothers is responsible for finding a husband for her. If a woman does not marry, her entire family is disgraced. When unmarried female missionaries came to China from the West, they were thought to be escaping from the shame brought about by the failure of the men of their household to find them a husband. For a Koryak woman of Siberia, sharing a husband with other wives is an ideal system. It reduces her workload and provides her with company. She cannot understand how Western women could be so selfish as to restrict their husbands to a single wife. Amongst the Cheyenne Indians a son-in-law is expected to provide food for his mother-in-law. However, he must never speak to her. Should he find himself alone in her presence, he must cover his head with a buffalo robe.

Kikuyu women, Kenya

The above examples are taken from three societies which have different ways of life. Sociologists use the term culture to refer to the way of life of members of a society. Culture includes the values, beliefs, customs, rules and regulations which human beings learn as members of a society. People need culture to meet even the most basic of human needs. For example, they have no instincts to tell them what is edible and how to prepare

Russian women in 1890

chaos and confusion that would result in today's society if there were no road traffic regulations. Rules must be both learned and shared.

Culture then is the learned shared behaviour of members of a society. Without culture human society would not exist.

(adapted in part from 'Sociological Perspective' by Ely Chinoy, Random House, New York, 1968 and 'The Individual and Culture' by Mary E. Goodman, Dorsey, Homewood, 1967)

QUESTIONS

1. What is instinctive behaviour? (4)
2. How does behaviour based on instinct differ from behaviour based on culture? (4)
3. Why do the examples of different customs concerning marriage and the family and the different forms of dress shown in the pictures suggest that human behaviour is learned rather than instinctive? (5)
4. Human beings spend considerable time and effort teaching young people the culture of their society. Why do they do this? (7)

food and eat it. They learn these lessons from the culture of their society.

It is essential that culture is not only learned but also shared. Thus without a shared language members of society could not communicate and cooperate effectively. Without rules applying to everybody, there would be disorder in society. Imagine the

PART 2 — INSTINCT

Many living creatures apart from human beings live in social groups. An understanding of human behaviour can be developed by an examination of non-human societies. The following passage gives a brief description of the social life of honeybees. It shows how a society can be organised on the basis of *instinct* rather than culture.

Like human beings, the honeybee lives in societies. It is a social insect. A hive consists of one queen, a few hundred male drones and between twenty and sixty thousand female worker bees. Each honeybee has a part to play in the running of the hive. The queen specialises in the production of eggs. This is her only job and she lays up to 200,000 a year. The male drones have the sole task of fertilising the queen. They receive food from the worker bees and help themselves from the stores of honey in the hive. In the autumn, at the end of the breeding season, the workers refuse to feed them or allow them access to the stores of honey. The starving drones drop to the bottom of the hive and are pulled out by the workers and left to die.

The worker bees spend the first three weeks of their lives performing household tasks. They build and repair the honeycombs from their wax producing glands and feed the newly hatched youngsters from their food producing glands. They clear out the hive removing debris and dead bees which have collected at the bottom. For the remaining two weeks of their lives most worker bees become field bees, foraging for nectar and pollen.

Honeybees live a highly ordered and organised social life. Each bee specialises in particular tasks and has set duties to perform. However, they have *not* learned how to behave. They have not been taught by older members of the colony, they

A honeybee with yellow pollen sacs performing a dance

have not imitated other bees. Instead, their behaviour is directed by instinct, by instructions contained in the genes which they inherit from their parents. The behaviour of honeybees is therefore inborn. This can be shown by the ways in which honeybees communicate. When a worker bee discovers a source of food it passes this information on to other bees by dancing on its return to the hive. The dance indicates the distance and direction of the food from the hive. One study suggests that the distance is indicated by the speed at which the bee turns. If the food is 275 metres away it turns 28 times a minute. If it is 2,750 metres away it turns nine times a minute. Worker bees who have never had any contact with other workers can both perform and interpret the dance. These skills are therefore instinctive. Since the bees have had no opportunity to learn from others, their ability to understand and perform the dance must be inborn.

(adapted from 'Bees and Beekeeping' by A.V. Pavord, Cassell, London, 1975)

QUESTIONS

1. Name the three types of honeybees and briefly outline the tasks they perform. (6)
2. Explain why honeybees do not have to learn the parts they play in society. (4)
3. What evidence is given in the passage which can be taken as proof that the behaviour of honeybees is based on instinct? (4)
4. Without instinct the society of honeybees could not exist. Explain this statement. (6)

PART 3 — ANIMAL BEHAVIOUR

The closer we approach human beings in the animal kingdom, the less important instincts are for directing behaviour and the more important learned behaviour becomes. It was once thought that the behaviour of all creatures apart from human beings was based on *instinct*. A large number of studies, particularly of apes and monkeys, has shown that this view is incorrect. The following study of macaque monkeys illustrates this point.

Japanese macaques washing potatoes

For a number of years Japanese scientists have been studying the behaviour of macaque monkeys on islands in northern Japan. On one island the macaques lived in the forest in the interior. The scientists tried to discover whether they could change the behaviour of the monkeys. They began by dumping potatoes in a clearing in the forest. The macaques picked them up, sniffed them inquisitively and tasted them. Gradually they changed their eating habits and potatoes, a food previously unknown to them, became their main diet. The scientists then began moving the potatoes towards the shoreline and the macaques followed. The potatoes were regularly dumped on

the beach and the troupe took up residence there rather than in the forest. Then, without any encouragement from the scientists, a number of brand new behaviour patterns developed. Some of the macaques began washing potatoes in the sea before eating them, a practice which was soon adopted by the whole group. Some of the younger monkeys began paddling in the sea then took the plunge and learned how to swim. Their elders followed suit and swimming became normal behaviour for the whole troupe. Finally, some of the more adventurous youngsters began diving into the sea from rocks on the shoreline. Other members of the troupe imitated them but some of the older macaques

Paddling in the sea

decided that this time they would not follow the lead of the youngsters.

(adapted from 'Sociology: Themes and Perspectives', 4th edition, by Michael Haralambos and Martin Holborn, Collins Educational, London, 1995)

QUESTIONS

1. List three new behaviour patterns which developed in the macaque troupe. (3)
2. Give one similarity between the ways in which macaques and human beings learn their behaviour. Provide examples to illustrate your answer. (5)
3. Why did the Japanese scientists argue that much of the behaviour of macaque monkeys is learned rather than instinctive? (6)
4. The learned behaviour of monkeys and apes is simple and limited compared with that of human beings. Show briefly with examples that this is the case and suggest why it is so. (6)

4 PART CULTURE AND VALUES

Values form an important part of the culture of a society. A *value* is a belief that something is good and worthwhile. It defines what is worth having and worth striving for. Values often vary considerably from society to society. The following description of the major values of traditional Cheyenne society provides a sharp contrast with the values held today in the West.

The Cheyenne Indians lived on the Great Plains of the United States of America, west of the Mississippi River and east of the Rocky Mountains. The following account describes part of their traditional way of life which came to an end at the close of the last century when they were defeated by the US army and placed on reservations.

Cheyenne Indians photographed in 1889

The Cheyenne believe that wealth, in the form of horses and weapons, is not to be hoarded by the owner. Instead it is to be given away. Generosity is highly regarded and people who accumulate wealth and keep it for themselves are looked down upon. A person who gives does not expect an equal amount in return. The greatest gift they can receive is prestige and respect for their generous action.

Bravery on the battlefield is one of the main ways a man can achieve high standing in the eyes of the tribe. Killing an enemy, however, does not rank as highly as a number of other deeds. Touching or striking an enemy with the hand or a weapon, rescuing a wounded comrade or charging the enemy alone while the rest of the war party looks on are amongst the highest deeds of bravery. The Cheyenne developed war into a game. Killing large numbers of the enemy is far less important than individual acts of courage which bring great respect from other members of the tribe. The brave deeds of a warrior are recounted at meetings of the warrior societies and sung about by the squaws. They may lead to his appointment to the tribal council and to the position of war chief which means others will follow him into battle and respect his leadership.

The values of Cheyenne society provide goals for its members to aim for and general guidelines for their behaviour. Values, like culture in general, are learned and shared by members of society. Some sociologists argue that shared values form the basis for social unity or social solidarity. They help to bind people into a close knit group. Because they share the same values, members of society are likely to see others as 'people like themselves'. They will therefore have a sense of belonging to a social group, they will feel a part of the wider society. In this respect shared values form the basis for unity in society.

(adapted from 'The Cheyennes' by E. Adamson Hoebel, Holt, Reinhart and Winston, New York, 1960)

QUESTIONS

1. What are the two major values of Cheyenne society? (2)
2. Identify two major values from your own society. (2)
3. How do the Cheyenne express the values of their society in their behaviour? (4)
4. Give three rewards a Cheyenne warrior might receive for being successful in terms of the values of his society. (3)
5. How does the Cheyenne attitude towards wealth differ from that in your own society? (4)
6. a) Why are shared values beneficial to society? (2)
   b) How might it be harmful to society if people held a wide range of differing values? (3)

CULTURE AND NORMS

Values provide general guidelines for conduct. **Norms** are much more specific. They define appropriate and acceptable behaviour in particular situations. A society may value privacy but this value provides only a general guide to behaviour. Norms define how the value of privacy is translated into action in particular situations and circumstances. Thus in British society norms relating to privacy state that a person's mail must not be opened by other people and that their house must not be entered without their permission. A person's 'private life' is their own concern and others must not pry into their personal affairs. In this way a series of norms direct how people should behave in terms of the value of privacy.

Norms guide behaviour in all aspects of social life. There are norms of dress which define the types of clothing appropriate for members of each sex, age group and social situation. There are norms governing behaviour with family, friends, neighbours and strangers. There are norms which define acceptable behaviour in the home, classroom and workplace, at a party, wedding and funeral, in a cinema, supermarket and doctor's waiting room.

As a part of culture, norms are learned, shared and vary from society to society. This can be seen clearly from norms concerning food. Amongst the Bedouin of North Africa, sheep's eyes are regarded as a delicacy whereas in the West they are not even considered fit to eat. The Bedouin eat with their fingers and a loud and prolonged burp at the end of a meal is a compliment to the host. In the West such behaviour would be considered the height of bad manners. Or,

as a sociologist would say, it would not conform to Western norms of eating behaviour.

Norms provide order in society. Imagine a situation in which 'anything goes'. The result is likely to be confusion and disorder. This can sometimes be seen in the classroom if teacher and students fail to establish a set of rules for conducting a lesson. Norms help to make social life predictable and comprehensible. If there were no norms stating how people should express pleasure or irritation, warmth or hostility it would be difficult to understand how others felt, to predict their behaviour and respond to them in appropriate ways.

Bedouin eating, Syria 1923

Norms also provide practical solutions to everyday problems. Take an apparently simple operation like cooking, cracking open and eating a boiled egg. There are norms directing the whole operation. Social life would be much less efficient if such methods had to be constantly re-invented by trial and error.

Lacking instincts, human beings need norms to guide and direct their actions. In a thousand and one areas of social life norms define appropriate and acceptable behaviour.

(adapted in part from 'Sociology', by Leonard Broom and Philip Selznick, Harper and Row, New York, 1977)

QUESTIONS

1. It has often been claimed that a high value is placed on human life in Western society. Describe three norms which direct behaviour in terms of this value. (6)
2. Briefly outline the norms which define acceptable behaviour at a party and in a doctor's waiting room and indicate how they differ. (8)
3. Using your own examples, outline two ways in which norms are useful for the operation of human society. (6)

CULTURE, STATUS AND ROLE
PART 6

    All the world's a stage
    And all the men and women merely players.

In these lines Shakespeare makes the point that in society people have certain positions and play certain parts. In sociological terminology, they hold **statuses** and play **roles**.

For example in Western society there are occupational statuses such as bricklayer, nurse, clerk and solicitor and family statuses such as father, mother, brother and sister. A status can be ascribed or achieved. An **ascribed status** is largely fixed and unchangeable, the individual having little or no say in the matter. Many are fixed at birth such as the gender statuses of male and female. In preindustrial society status was often ascribed, a boy taking on the status of his father, a girl that of her mother. Thus most Cheyenne males automatically became hunters and warriors like their fathers before them while females became wives and mothers and gathered roots and berries as their mothers had done. In present day British society, aristocratic titles provide an example of an ascribed status. Prince Charles is heir to the throne simply because he is the eldest son of the reigning monarch. There are, however, occasions when an ascribed status can be changed. A monarch can abdicate as in the case of Edward VIII who was forced to give up the English throne in 1936 because he intended to marry an American divorcee.

An ascribed status is imposed upon a person. There is little he or she can do about it. An **achieved status**, on the other hand, involves some degree of choice and direct and positive action. A person chooses to get married and adopt the status of a husband or wife. There is often an element of choice in selecting an occupation in modern industrial societies. An achieved status, as the name suggests, results partly from individual achievement. To some extent a person achieves his or her job as an architect, librarian or joiner on the basis of ability and effort.

Each social status is accompanied by a role. Roles define the expected and acceptable behaviour for those occupying particular statuses. Thus the role of doctor states how a doctor is expected to behave. It is a collection of norms defining how the part of a doctor should be played. Roles are a part of culture and often differ considerably from society to society. In traditional Cheyenne society the role of women is mainly domestic - caring for children, preparing and cooking food and making clothing. Hunting is left to the men. However, hunting formed an important part of the female role amongst the Australian aborigines of Tasmania. The women hunted seals and

The Queen at the State Opening of Parliament, 1994

opossums (small tree-dwelling animals).

Roles are performed in relation to other roles. Thus the role of teacher is played in relation to the role of student, the role of husband in relation to the role of wife. Tasks can often be accomplished more effectively if those concerned adopt their appropriate roles. Thus a doctor can do his job more efficiently if he and his patients stick to their roles rather than also playing the part of old friends or courting couples. Roles provide social life with order and predictability. If teacher and student play their roles, they know what to do and how to do it. Knowing each others' roles they are able to predict and understand what the other is doing. Like other aspects of culture, roles guide and direct behaviour in human society.

(adapted from 'Sociological Perspective' by Ely Chinoy, Random House, New York, 1968 and 'Sociology: Themes and Perspectives', 4th edition, by Michael Haralambos and Martin Holborn, Collins Educational, London, 1995)

QUESTIONS

1. List your own statuses and identify which are ascribed and which are achieved. (2)
2. a) Give one example of an ascribed status that can be changed. (1)
   b) Briefly outline the difficulties that such a change might create for the individual concerned. (3)
3. Select one occupational status in modern industrial society and suggest how it is achieved on the basis of ability and effort. (4)
4. Roles are learned rather than instinctive. How do the roles of Cheyenne and Tasmanian women provide evidence to support this statement? (4)
5. Outline, with your own examples, two ways in which roles are useful for the operation of human society. (6)

PART 7 — SOCIALISATION (1)

In view of the importance of values, norms, statuses and roles, it is essential for the wellbeing of society that culture is effectively learned by its members. The process by which people learn the culture of their society is known as *socialisation*. Socialisation begins at birth and continues throughout a person's life. During its early years, the child learns many of the basic behaviour patterns of its society. This is the period of *primary socialisation*, the first and probably the most important part of the socialisation process. In practically every society the family bears the main responsibility for primary socialisation. As the child moves into the wider society, *secondary socialisation* begins. During this process the child learns from a wider range of people and institutions. Thus in modern industrial societies, schools play an important part in secondary socialisation.

Something of the importance of the socialisation process may be seen from the following extract. It describes the behaviour of two girls who, for a large part of their short lives, had been isolated from other human beings.

In 1920 two girls were reportedly discovered in a wolf den in Bengal, India. Aged about two and eight years, they were taken to an orphanage where they were looked after by the Reverend J. A. L. Singh and his wife. The younger child, Amala died soon after she arrived at the orphanage, the elder girl, Kamala, remained in the orphanage until 1929 when she too died. Despite the fact that Amala and Kamala were called 'wolf-children' and found in a wolf's den, there is no evidence that they were actually raised by wolves. The Reverend Singh wrote the following description of their behaviour in 1926.

At the present time Kamala can utter about forty words. She is able to form a few sentences, each sentence containing two, or at the most, three words. She never talks unless spoken to, and when spoken to she may or may not reply. She is obedient to Mrs Singh and myself only. Kamala is possessed of very acute hearing and evidences an exceedingly acute animal-like sense of smell. She can smell meat at a great distance. Never weeps or smiles but has a 'smiling appearance'. Shed a single tear when Amala died and would not leave the place where she lay dead. She is learning very slowly to imitate. Does not now play at all and does not mingle with other children. Once both

Kamala and Amala soon after they were brought to the orphanage

Kamala receiving a biscuit from Mrs Singh

talk. But one day they gave him such a biting and scratching that the infant was frightened and would never approach the wolf-children again. Amala and Kamala liked the company of Mrs Singh, and Kamala, the surviving one of the pair, is much attached to her. The eyes of the children possessed a peculiar glare, such as that observed in the eyes of dogs or cats in the dark. Up to the present time Kamala sees better at night than during the daytime and seldom sleeps after midnight. The children used to cry or howl in a peculiar voice neither animal nor human. Kamala still makes these noises at times. She is averse to all cleanliness, and serves the calls of nature anywhere, wherever she may happen to be at the time. Used to tear her clothes off. Hence a loin cloth was stitched to her in such a fashion that she could not open or tear it. Kamala used to eat and drink like a dog, lowering her mouth down to the plate, and never used her hands for the purpose of eating or drinking. She would gnaw a big bone on the ground and would rub it at times in order to separate the meat from the bone. At the present time she uses her hands for eating and walks straight on two legs but cannot run at all.

Amala and Kamala somewhat liked the company of an infant by the name of Benjamin while he was crawling and learning to

(letter quoted in 'Human Societies' edited by Geoffrey Hurd, Routledge & Kegan Paul, London, 1973, pp95-96)

QUESTIONS

1. The children had apparently spent much of their lives isolated from other human beings. Why did this prevent them from behaving in ways which would be considered normal in human society into which they were born? (4)
2. List four items of Kamala's behaviour which suggest that she was beginning to act in ways considered normal in human society. (4)
3. a) Briefly compare what Kamala had learned by the age of fourteen after six years in the orphanage with what most children have learned by the age of five. (3)
   b) Why does this suggest that primary socialisation is vital to effectively learn the culture of society? (3)
4. a) Give three possible reactions by people in the wider society to Kamala's behaviour which would make it difficult for
   • her to cope outside the orphanage. (3)
   b) Suggest why people would respond to her in these ways. (3)

8 PART — SOCIALISATION (2)

The socialisation of young people can be seen as a series of lessons which prepare them for their adult roles. During childhood people learn many of the basic skills they will require in adult life. This is clearly seen from the following description of children's games and activities in the society of the Mbuti pygmies.

The Mbuti pygmies live in the tropical rain forest in the northeast corner of Zaire in central Africa. They are hunters and gatherers, the men being mainly responsible for hunting and the women for gathering edible fruit, berries and roots. Nets are often used for hunting. They are stretched into a long arc and women and children drive game such as antelope into the nets where they are killed by the men with spears and bows and arrows. Arrows, usually tipped with poison, are also used to kill birds and monkeys. The pygmies' favourite food is honey. For two months of the year they spend considerable time and effort breaking into hives in the trees to extract honey. They are almost as much at home in the trees as they are on the ground. They take to the trees to avoid dangerous animals such as the forest buffalo and to chase game.

Women are mainly responsible for cooking. They roast plantains - a banana-like fruit - in hot ashes and make stews of meat, mushrooms and chopped leaves. They gather wood for the fire and carry water to the camp site. Women make the huts from a framework of saplings - young trees - thatched with broad leaves. They also make the carrying baskets which are used for transporting food and equipment.

Pygmy children enjoy their early years. They love climbing trees and swinging on vines. Some children actually begin climbing trees before they can walk. One of their favourite games involves half a dozen climbing to the top of a young tree and bending it over until the top touches the ground. Then they all jump off together. If anyone is too slow, they go flying upwards as the tree springs back. Their friends are highly amused and laugh and jeer as they swing in the air.

Like children in all societies, pygmy children like to imitate older people. Their parents encourage them to do this. Fathers make tiny bows for their sons with blunt arrows made of softwood. They may also give their sons a strip of hunting net. Mothers weave tiny carrying baskets for their daughters much to the enjoyment of all concerned. Boys and girls often 'play house', building a miniature house from sticks and leaves. The boys shoot their arrows at plantains and ears of corn and proudly carry them back to the play house. They are then cooked and eaten in a serious and solemn manner.

Hunting is a favourite childhood game. Boys stretch out their pieces of hunting net while girls beat the ground with bunches of leaves driving an old frog towards the net. If a frog cannot

Masalito shows his nephew Kelekome how to examine a piece of honeycomb to see if the hive is ready for raiding.

be found, a grandparent will be asked to imitate an antelope. He is chased round the camp and finally driven into the net. The children then jump on the unfortunate grandparent and playfully pound him with their fists.

(adapted from 'The Forest People' by Colin M. Turnbull, Jonathan Cape, London, 1961)

QUESTIONS

1. **What evidence does the extract contain to indicate the role of parents in the socialisation process? (4)**
2. **How do the games of pygmy boys help to prepare them for their adult roles? (6)**
3. **How do the games of pygmy girls help to prepare them for their adult roles? (6)**
4. **Select one children's game from your own society and suggest how it might prepare young people for adult life. (4)**

SOCIAL CONTROL

Every society has methods of making its members toe the line, of making sure that they stick to the straight and narrow. These methods are known as **mechanisms of social control**. They ensure that most of the people most of the time conform to society's norms and values. Chapter 1 indicated the importance of culture. It must be learned and shared for human society to operate effectively. But learning culture is one thing, acting in terms of it is another. Every society requires some mechanisms of social control to make sure its members follow the guidelines of their culture. For social order to exist norms and values are necessary and conformity to them must be enforced.

The ultimate and most obvious form of social control is physical force. In one form or another it exists in every known human society. Under certain circumstances some have the right to use physical force against others in an attempt to control their behaviour. The police and armed forces are obvious examples in modern industrial societies. Other forms of social control are less obvious. Few would regard the family, the peer group, religion and the mass media as powerful instruments of social control. Yet many sociologists would see them as far more important and effective than the whole state system of control which ranges from Parliament, which enacts the law, to the police, judiciary and prison service which enforce it.

THE FAMILY

The importance of the family in the socialisation process was discussed in Chapter 1. This point is now re-examined focusing on the family as an agency of social control.

Without the support of older members of its species, a newborn human baby could not survive. Alone it cannot meet basic human needs, such as the need for food, or learn the necessary knowledge and skills for living in human society. Most young people are raised in families. During its early years the child is largely dependent upon its immediate family and as a result its parents have considerable power to direct its behaviour. The child is at its most impressionable during infancy. This means that its behaviour can be more easily shaped and moulded than in later life. In view of these factors, the family can be a powerful mechanism of social control.

For society to operate effectively its members must learn social norms and values. But simply knowing the culture of their society does not necessarily mean that people will act in terms of it. There is much more likelihood of them doing so if they actually want to conform to their culture. During primary socialisation within the family many children not only learn the basic norms and values of their society but also become committed to them. They therefore feel that the norms and values are right and proper and experience guilt if they depart from them. In other words they develop a conscience which is rather like an 'inner policeman' preventing or punishing behaviour which deviates from accepted patterns with feelings of guilt and remorse. The child's behaviour will therefore be guided by internal controls - the voice of its conscience.

The family has often been seen as ideally suited to developing a conscience in new members of society. Once a deep emotional bond has been established between the child and its parents, any threat to that bond fills the child with anxiety. Rather than risk the loss of love, the child adopts the norms and values taught by its parents. It develops feelings of guilt and anxiety at the thought of deviating from the behaviour approved by its parents.

Parents use a wide variety of techniques for controlling the behaviour of their children. The Cheyenne do not tolerate babies crying, partly because it could give away the position of the camp to an enemy but also because they dislike anyone

Cheyenne women and children. Note the cradleboard on the right.

forcing their attention and demands on others. Infants are kept in cradleboards carried on their mothers' backs. When they cry they are taken away from the camp and the cradleboard is hung on a bush until the crying stops. After a few hours the squawling infant realises that its noisy behaviour leads to complete rejection by its parents and soon learns to change its tune. Cheyenne babies are never struck, scolded, or threatened for bad behaviour. However, good behaviour is consistently rewarded with praise, love and affection. Parents constantly encourage their children to be brave, generous, honest, hardworking and respectful to their elders.

A contrast to Cheyenne child training practices is provided by some of the methods used by many English working class parents. Threats and teasing are often used as the following statements from mothers indicate.

> I say, 'A policeman will come and take you away, and you'll have no Mummy and Daddy'.

> I tell her God will do something to her hand if she smacks me.

> I've told him I'll have to put him in a home if he's naughty.

> She picks her nose - I tell her it's dirty and her nose will fall off.

Children's behaviour is not simply shaped by responding to the rewards and punishments handed out by their parents. Much of the time they simply copy their mothers and fathers. They often identify with their parents and as a result want to be like them. Mothers provide role models for their daughters, fathers for their sons. The constant example provided by someone they want to be like is a powerful control over the child's behaviour.

Lessons learned during the child's early years often last a lifetime. As the following quotation suggests, this may well be essential for the wellbeing of human society.

'Every day society is submitted to a terrible invasion: within it a multitude of small barbarians is born. They would quickly overthrow the whole social order and all the institutions of society if they were not well disciplined and educated' (R. Pinot quoted in Goodman, 1967, p128).

(adapted from 'The Individual and Culture' by M.E. Goodman, Dorsey, Homewood, 1967; 'The Cheyennes' by E.A. Hoebel, Holt, Rinehart & Winston, New York, 1960; 'The Family and its Future' by J. and E. Newson, J.A. Churchill, Edinburgh, 1970)

QUESTIONS

1. Why do parents have considerable power to control the behaviour of their children? (5)
2. Why is the development of a conscience often seen as a far more effective means of social control than institutions such as the police and armed forces? (4)
3. Why is the method used by Cheyenne mothers to prevent their babies from crying so effective? (3)
4. The threats used by English mothers sometimes involve backing up the mother's authority with that of an outside authority figure. With reference to two of the outside authority figures mentioned, suggest why their use might be an effective means of controlling the child's behaviour. (4)
5. 'Like mother, like daughter, like father, like son.' What evidence is provided in the passage to explain how this might happen? (4)

RELIGION
PART 2

Religion may be defined as a belief in some form of supernatural power which influences or controls people's lives. Thus Melford Spiro defines religion as 'beliefs in superhuman beings and in their power to assist or harm man'. Religion promises rewards such as everlasting bliss to those who follow its teachings and punishments such as eternal damnation for those who do not. In this respect it can be seen as a mechanism of social control. Often religious teachings and commandments are similar to the values of society. This means that people are more likely to conform to social values. In such cases religion strengthens and reinforces the values of society. Religious beliefs may also help to maintain the structure of society. They may, for example, support the position of men and women and reinforce the power of princes and kings. In doing so religion acts as a mechanism of social control. The following extracts illustrate these points.

> You shall not kill.
> You shall not commit adultery.
> You shall not steal.

(Three of the Ten Commandments of the Christian religion)

QUESTIONS

1. Which social values do the above commandments support? (3)
2. How do religious commandments strengthen and reinforce social values? (5)

Neither was the man created for the woman; but
the woman for the man.
Wives, submit yourselves unto your own
husbands, as it is fit in the Lord.

(Saint Paul's interpretation of early Christian beliefs about the
relationship between men and women)

The divine right of kings - the church gives its blessing
to royal power.

In ancient Egypt from about 2700 to 2000 BC, the pharaohs or
kings were regarded as gods. State officials such as magistrates,
tax collectors and governors of the regions of Egypt were
directly responsible to the pharaoh. They were his
representatives. They voiced his wishes and commands and
therefore spoke with divine authority. After their lives as gods
and men ended, the pharaohs lived on as gods. They were
placed in pyramids, their eternal homes, whose grandeur
reflected their status.

(adapted from 'The Culture of Ancient Egypt' by John A. Wilson, Phoenix
Books, Chicago, 1956)

3 PART — THE PEER GROUP

A peer group is a group whose members share a similar status in society. Members of peer groups
are often of a similar age such as children's play groups and teenage gangs. They usually share a
similar social situation such as workers on the shopfloor and teachers in the classroom. Peer groups are important
agencies of social control. Because most people want to be accepted by members of their groups, they will usually
conform to peer group norms. If they do not they risk rejection by the group. The following passage indicates the
power of the peer group to control the behaviour of its members and to enforce group norms.

From 1927 to 1932, a famous study of workers' behaviour was
conducted at the Hawthorne works of the Western Electric
Company in Chicago. What follows is a small part of the findings
of this research. One work group, made up of fourteen men,
connected and soldered wires to terminals, which formed
components for telephone equipment. The men were paid a
basic wage plus a bonus if they produced more than a certain
number of completed units. The bonus was shared out equally
amongst all members of the group. The managers thought that
the bonus scheme would result in the men working as hard as
they could so as to earn as much money as possible. In practice
this did not happen.

Members of the work group established their own norm for
output. It was below the level that could have been reached if
each man worked as hard as he could. The men believed that if
they worked flat out then the supervisors would begin to expect
a much higher output. This might lead to the level at which
bonus was paid being raised. They also felt that if they reduced
their output too much it would give supervisors a reason to

'bawl them out'. To avoid these problems the workers produced
roughly the same amount from week to week.

The norm regulating the workers' output was enforced in
various ways. Anybody working too fast was ridiculed as a
'speed king' or a 'ratebuster'. Those producing too little were
called 'chiselers'. What the men called 'binging' was one way of
slowing people down or speeding them up. This involved
hitting a worker on the upper arm. As one man said to a 'speed
king', 'If you don't quit work I'll bing you'. He then struck his
workmate and chased him round the shopfloor.

The work group also developed a norm about relationships
between workers and their supervisors. It stated that a man
should not give information to supervisors which might get one
of his workmates into trouble. Anyone who did so was labelled
as a 'squealer'.

(adapted from 'The Management and the Worker' by F. J. Roethlisberger
and W. J. Dickson, Harvard University Press, Cambridge, 1939)

A Los Angeles gang

Miners in Nottinghamshire

QUESTIONS

1. Identify two ways in which workers were punished for failing to conform to the group norm for output. (2)
2. Suggest two further ways in which workers might have been punished for breaking the output norm. (2)
3. Suggest two rewards a worker might receive for conforming to the norms of the work group. (4)
4. Members of peer groups often insist on strong group loyalty and try to protect each other from outsiders. What evidence of this type of behaviour is contained in the passage? (4)
5. Why do the rewards and punishments of peer groups usually provide effective control over the behaviour of their members? (4)
6. Suggest why the peer groups in the pictures have particularly strong controls over their members. (4)

4 PART — SIGNIFICANT OTHERS

Significant others are people who matter to an individual. They usually include his or her immediate family, friends, neighbours and workmates. People are concerned about what significant others think about them. Their approval makes them feel good, their disapproval upsets them. Because the opinion of significant others is held so highly, they can play an important part in controlling the behaviour of an individual. People often conform to social norms in order to gain the approval of significant others and to avoid their disapproval. The following extracts illustrate these points. They are taken from the autobiography of Long Lance, a Blackfoot Indian.

1 The Blackfoot Indians lived on the plains of Western Canada. Children were taught the skills of horse riding from an early age. One of Long Lance's earliest recollections was falling off a horse. He was picked up by his eldest brother and planted firmly on the horse's back. His brother said, 'Now, you stay there! You are four years old, and if you cannot ride a horse, we will put girls' clothing on you and let you grow up a woman.'

QUESTION

1. Why was this remark effective in controlling the young boy's behaviour? Note in your answer the possible reactions of significant others to the boy if his brother's threat had been carried out. (5)

Blackfoot boys

2 Fathers were responsible for the physical training of the Blackfoot boys. They wanted to harden their bodies and make them brave and strong. Fathers used to whip their sons each morning with fir branches. Far from disliking this treatment, the youngsters proudly displayed the welts produced by the whipping. Sometimes they were whipped in public and they competed to see who could stand the most pain. Some would endure until all the branches were worn away. Their fathers would then 'hand them the stub, which we would keep and display with considerable pride during the rest of our young lives'.

3 When he was about six years old, Long Lance would play a game with his friends. They would place burning pine needles on the backs of their hands to see who could let them burn down to ashes. 'If there was anyone among us who could not stand the pain, we would ridicule him.'

4 Blackfoot mothers spent long hours telling their children the legends of the tribe. Long Lance recalls that, 'We had a legend for everything that was good, and the more we youngsters lived up to the legends which our mothers told us the more highly respected we were in the tribe.' Children were told stories about the 'great shame' befalling those who told lies and the prestige which results from courage and brave deeds. Long Lance states, 'We had no Bible as the white boys have; so our mothers trained us to live right by telling us legends of how all the good things started to be good'.

(adapted from 'Long Lance' by Chief Buffalo Child Long Lance, Corgi Books, London, 1956)

QUESTIONS

2. With some reference to extract 2, suggest how the desire for respect from significant others is an important factor in social control. (5)
3. The childhood peer group is one example of an individual's significant others. With some reference to extract 3, suggest how the peer group controls the behaviour of its members. (5)
4. Using information from extract 4, suggest the part played by significant others in reinforcing the message and moral of the legends and stories. (5)

PART 5 — THE MASS MEDIA

The mass media refers to means of communicating with large numbers of people without direct personal contact. It includes television, radio, newspapers, magazines, comics, books, films and advertising billboards. The mass media is a major source of information and ideas. These can shape people's attitudes and so to some degree direct their behaviour. Many researchers have seen the mass media in modern industrial society as a powerful instrument of social control. The following passage looks at some of the ways in which the media has represented women. (See also Chapter 18, Part 4.)

Most of the women who appear on television are well educated, young, of medium to high social status, and are under 40 years of age, according to research carried out by the Broadcasting Standards Council.

It also found that the BBC and ITV continue to sideline women in stereotyped roles, with far fewer women than men presenting or appearing in factual programmes. Heavyweight news and current affairs were dominated by men. On news programmes, 82% of those speaking were men, compared with 70% across a range of programmes in a sample week.

Where women were fronting news programmes and weather reports, they were very attractive, and, for weather reports, were always young. In comparison, the men who dominated news programmes were older. Eccentric male weather presenters were tolerated.

Lady Howe, who chairs the Broadcasting Standards Council, said yesterday: 'Hopefully broadcasters will notice, and do more to change the stereotyping of women. There is evidence that the portrayal of women is changing, but there are still far more men than women.'

Other areas of imbalance show that in factual programmes the ratio of men to women was 2:1, in light entertainment 7:3, sport 11:1, fiction 3:2 and children's programmes 1:1.

(adapted from 'Independent', 27.5.1994)

QUESTIONS

1. Women and men are not equal on television. Summarise the evidence for this view. (2)
2. Suggest reasons why men 'dominate' certain types of programmes. (4)
3. What evidence does the passage contain to support the view that television still stereotypes women? (3)
4. In what ways can the portrayal of women on television be seen as a means of social control? (3)
5. a) What images of women are presented in the advertisements? (3)
   b) How might these images influence women's behaviour? (5)

6 PART — THE POLICE

Some organisations are set up for the specific purpose of social control. The police force is an obvious example from industrial societies. In Britain the Metropolitan Police were established in London in 1829 by Sir Robert Peel. He felt that crime in the capital city was getting out of control and that something had to be done about it. Acts of Parliament in 1830 and 1856 established a nationwide police force. The following extract looks at different sociological interpretations of the role of the police in society.

Police arrest a demonstrator during the printers strike at Wapping against Rupert Murdoch's News International in 1986.

The industrial revolution resulted in widespread social upheaval. Large numbers of people moved from close-knit rural communities to work in the factories in towns and cities. This led to a breakdown in social order as traditional mechanisms of social control - the community, the peer group and the family - lost much of their power to maintain order. Some researchers argue that there was a breakdown in law and order which led to the creation of a new form of social control, the police.

The police have been seen as benefiting society as a whole. They enforce the law and maintain order. In particular, they protect the weakest sections of society - the poor and the powerless - who are the main victims of crime.

Others take a very different point of view. The police are seen as the agents of the rich and powerful. Their job is to keep the working class in its place, to maintain political control and provide a disciplined workforce. For example, the police prevent both demonstrations against the government and strikes against employers from getting out of control. Policing the working class in this way can be seen as protecting the property and privileges of the rich and powerful.

There is evidence to support both points of view. In recent years the police have made considerable efforts to reduce burglaries and street crime in inner city areas. These are crimes which particularly affect the poor and vulnerable. However, police action is sometimes seen very differently by those they define as likely lawbreakers. For example, Lord Scarman's report saw the Brixton riots of 1981 as 'a spontaneous act of defiant aggression by young men who felt themselves hunted by a hostile police force'.

Part of the job of the police is to maintain order in public places, particularly when large numbers of people are gathered together. For example, there is a police presence at all major sporting events. This aspect of policing has sometimes been seen as a means of controlling the working class. The police have been accused of siding with employers, as in the miners' strike of 1984-85 which saw pitched battles between police and striking miners. They have been accused of supporting landowners during the 1980s and 90s with their policing of hippy convoys heading for Stonehenge. And they have been accused of representing government interests in their policing of the poll tax demonstrations in 1990.

(adapted from 'The Politics of the Police' by Robert Reiner, Harvester Wheatsheaf, Hemel Hempstead, 1992)

QUESTIONS

1. Why are police forces a modern invention? (5)
2. a) Briefly outline the two main views of the role of the police in society. (5)
   b) How is it possible to support both points of view using evidence from the passage and pictures? (10)

⑦ PART TOTAL INSTITUTIONS

Total institutions are institutions in which people live and work, often cut off from the wider society for long periods of time. They include mental hospitals, boarding schools, army barracks, orphanages, monasteries, prisons and concentration camps. Life in total institutions is usually based on strict rules which enforce a rigid daily routine. To some extent those who live and work in such institutions are resocialised to lead a new way of life.

The following extract is taken from *Asylums* by Erving Goffman, a study of a mental hospital in Washington DC. Goffman argues that total institutions seek to change people's identity and behaviour - they are 'forcing houses for changing people'.

On admission to a total institution the individual is likely to be stripped of his usual appearance and of the equipment and services by which he maintains it, thus suffering personal defacement. Clothing, combs, needle and thread, cosmetics, towels, soap, shaving sets, bathing facilities - all these may be taken away or denied him.

Control in total institutions is based on a system of rewards and punishment. For example, a ward attendant in a mental hospital can give the patient privileges, and he can punish the patient. The privileges consist of having the best job, better rooms and beds, minor luxuries like coffee on the ward, a little more privacy than the average patient, going outside the ward without supervision, having more access than the average patient to the attendant's companionship or to professional personnel like the physicians, and such vital things as being treated with kindness and respect.

The punishments which can be applied by the ward attendant are suspension of all privileges, psychological mistreatment such as ridicule, vicious ribbing, moderate and sometimes severe physical punishment, or the threat of such punishment, locking up the patient in an isolated room, denial of access to the professional personnel, threatening to put, or putting, the patient on the list for electro-shock therapy, transfer of the patient to undesirable wards, and regular assignment of the patient to unpleasant tasks such as cleaning up after the soilers.

(adapted from 'Asylums' by Erving Goffman, Penguin, Harmondsworth, 1968)

The following passage provides an example of one type of total institution.

During the late 19th and first half of the 20th century, the United States government attempted to transform American Indians into 'American citizens'. In the words of Thomas Jefferson Morgan, Commissioner of Indian Affairs, 'The Indians must conform to the white man's ways'. Part of this policy involved transporting Indian children, despite objections from their parents, to white-run boarding schools often hundreds of miles from their homes. The intention, in the words of Captain Richard H. Pratt who founded the first of these schools, was to 'kill the Indian in him and save the man'.

At the Indian schools, children were stripped of all outward appearances that linked them to their Indian past. Their Indian clothing was taken away from them, their long hair was cut, and they were dressed in uniforms and Victorian garb. Under the frightening lash of 'loud, shrill voices' commanding them to obey, to cease speaking their tribal languages, and to model themselves on white society, the children were dazed. Buffeted by distorted images of their own people as 'evil', 'heathenish', and 'savage', most lost self-esteem and turned against, or came to doubt, their own identity. The school memories of Sun Elk, a Taos Pueblo Indian, were typical:

> 'We all wore white man's clothes and ate white man's food and went to white man's churches and spoke white man's talk. And so after a while we also began to say Indians were bad. We laughed at our own people and their blankets and cooking pots and sacred societies and dances.'

Mertha Bercier, a Chippewa student, tells how her Indian past slowly slipped away.

> 'The days passed by, and the changes slowly came to settle within me. Gone were the vivid pictures of my parents, sisters and brothers - only a blurred vision of what used to be. Desperately I tried to cling to the faded past which was slowly being erased from my mind.'

Some tried to resist. Lone Wolf, a Blackfoot Indian, describes his experiences.

> 'If we thought that the days were bad, the nights were much worse. This was the time when real loneliness set in. Many boys ran away but most of them were caught and brought back by the police. We were told never to talk Indian and if we were caught, we got a strapping with a leather belt.
>
> I remember one evening when we were all lined up in a room and one of the boys said something in Indian to another boy. The man in charge caught him by the shirt, and threw him across the room. Later we found out that his collar-bone was broken.
>
> The boy's father, an old warrior, came to the school. He told the instructor that among his people, children were never punished by striking them. That was no way to teach children; kind words and good examples were

'Before' and 'after' photographs of three Sioux pupils at the Carlisle Indian School in Pennsylvania

much better. Before the instructor could stop the old warrior he took his boy and left. The family then beat it to Canada and never came back.'

(adapted from 'Now that the Buffalo's Gone' by Alvin M. Josephy Jr., University of Oklahoma Press, Norman, 1984 and '500 Nations' by Alvin M. Josephy Jr., Hutchinson, London, 1995)

The 'broom brigade' at the Indian school in Riverside, California

QUESTIONS

1. Using examples from mental hospitals, prisons or monasteries, suggest why people are often stripped of their usual appearance on entry to a total institution. (5)
2. Why is the ward attendant in the above example of a mental hospital so powerful? (4)
3. a) Why did the US government focus its efforts on children in its attempt to resocialise American Indians? (4)
   b) Why did it use boarding schools? (3)
   c) Outline the methods used in the schools to change the behaviour and identity of the Indian children. (4)

PART 8 — RACIALISM AND SOCIAL CONTROL

Introductory sociology courses often present social control systems in a very positive light. They are seen as a good thing. Social control is said to be beneficial for society because it enables its members to work together and cooperate in relative peace and harmony. However there is another side to the picture. Many aspects of social control can be seen as harmful both to society and to its members. One such system which would probably be seen as unacceptable by most members of present day Western society is described in the following extract. It is taken from the autobiography of Richard Wright which was first published in 1937. Wright, a black American, describes how he experienced the 'Jim Crow system', in the southern states of the USA. This system of racial prejudice and discrimination kept the majority of black Americans on the lowest level of society. It employed a variety of mechanisms of social control to keep them 'in their place'. Often blacks encouraged other blacks to 'know their place' fearing that friends and relatives might be beaten up, jailed and even lynched for stepping out of line.

The back yard of Richard's house was paved with cinders. He and his friends used to have great fun throwing them at each other. One day Richard's gang got into a fight with a group of white boys. The black boys threw cinders but the whites replied with a barrage of broken bottles. One caught Richard behind the ear opening a deep gash which needed three stitches. He was furious. It wasn't fair to fight with broken bottles. All a cinder could do was leave a bruise. When Richard told his mother what had happened he was astonished at her reaction.

She grabbed a barrel stave, dragged me home, stripped me naked, and beat me till I had a fever of one hundred and two. She would smack my rump with the stave, and while the skin was still smarting, impart to me gems of Jim Crow wisdom. I was never to throw cinders any more. I was never to fight any more wars. I was never, never, under any conditions, to fight white folks again. And they were absolutely right in clouting me with the broken milk bottle. Didn't I know she was working hard every day in the hot kitchens of the white folks to make money to take care of me? When was I ever going to learn to be a good boy? She couldn't be bothered with my fights. She finished by telling me that I ought to be thankful to God as long as I lived that they didn't kill me.

All that night I was delirious and could not sleep. Each time I closed my eyes I saw monstrous white faces suspended from the ceiling, leering at me.

Richard got his first job with an optical company in Jackson, Mississippi. He recalls the interview. The morning I applied I stood straight and neat before the boss, answering all his questions with sharp yessirs and nosirs. I was very careful to pronounce my sirs distinctly, in order that he might know that I was polite, that I knew where I was, and that I knew he was a white man. I wanted that job badly.

'Boy, how would you like to learn something around here?' he asked me.

'I'd like it fine, sir,' I said, happy. I had visions of 'working my way up'. Even Negroes have those visions.

'All right,' he said, 'Come on.'

I followed him to the small factory.

'Pease,' he said to a white man of about thirty-five, 'this is Richard. He's going to work for us.' Pease looked at me and nodded. I was then taken to a white boy of about seventeen.

'Morrie, this is Richard, who's going to work for us.'

'Whut yuh sayin' there, boy!' Morrie boomed at me.

'Fine!' I answered.

The boss instructed these two to help me, teach me, give me jobs to do, and let me learn what I could in my spare time. My wages were five dollars a week.

I worked hard, trying to please. For the first month I got along O.K. Both Pease and Morrie seemed to like me. But one thing was missing. And I kept thinking about it. I was not learning anything and nobody was volunteering to help me. Thinking they had forgotten that I was to learn something about the mechanics of grinding lenses, I asked Morrie one day to tell me about the work. He grew red.

'Whut yuh tryin' t' do, nigger, get smart?' he asked.

'Naw; I ain' tryin t' git smart,' I said.

'Well, don't, if yuh know whut's good for yuh!'

I was puzzled. Maybe he just doesn't want to help me, I thought. I went to Pease.

'Say, are yuh crazy, you black bastard?' Pease asked me, his grey eyes growing hard.

I spoke out, reminding him that the boss had said I was to be given a chance to learn something.

'Nigger, you think you're *white*, don't you?'

'Naw, sir!'

'Well, you're acting mighty like it!'

'But, Mr Pease, the boss said ...'

Pease shook his fist in my face. 'This is a *white* man's work around here, and you better watch yourself!'

From then on they changed toward me. They said good-morning no more. When I was a bit slow performing some duty, I was called a lazy black son-of-a-bitch.

Richard's days at the optical company were now numbered. He had stepped over the line. Pease and Morrie made his life at work unbearable. Richard finally called it a day when they threatened to beat him up with a steel bar. He was surprised at his family's reaction. When I told the folks at home what had happened, they called me a fool. They told me that I must never again attempt to exceed my boundaries. When you are working for white folks, they said, you got to 'stay in your place' if you want to keep working.

This lesson was hammered home to Richard on his next job. He was slowly but surely learning how blacks were expected to behave.

My Jim Crow education continued on my next job, which was portering in a clothing store. One morning, while polishing brass out front, the boss and his twenty-year-old son got out of

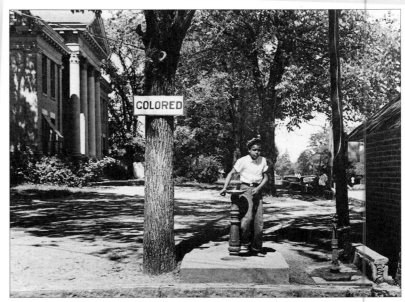

A drinking fountain on the county courthouse lawn for blacks only - Halifax, North Carolina, USA, 1938

their car and half dragged and half kicked a Negro woman into the store. A policeman standing at the corner looked on, twirling his night-stick. I watched out of the corner of my eye, never slackening the strokes of my chamois upon the brass. After a few minutes, I heard shrill screams coming from the rear of the store. Later the woman stumbled out, bleeding, crying, and holding her stomach. When she reached the end of the block, the policeman grabbed her and accused her of being a drunk. Silently, I watched him throw her into a patrol wagon.

When I went to the rear of the store, the boss and his son were washing their hands in the sink. They were chuckling. The floor was bloody and strewn with wisps of hair and clothing. No doubt I must have appeared pretty shocked, for the boss slapped me reassuringly on the back.

'Boy, that's what we do to niggers when they don't want to pay their bills,' he said, laughing.

His son looked at me and grinned. 'Here, have a cigarette,' he said.

Not knowing what to do, I took it. He lit his and held the match for me. This was a gesture of kindness, indicating that even if they had beaten the poor old woman, they would not beat me if I knew enough to keep my mouth shut.

'Yes, sir,' I said, and asked no questions.

After they had gone, I sat on the edge of a packing box and stared at the bloody floor till the cigarette went out. That day at noon, while eating in a hamburger joint, I told my fellow Negro porters what had happened. No one seemed surprised. One fellow, after swallowing a huge bite, turned to me and asked;

'Huh! Is tha' all they did t' her?'

QUESTIONS

1. What evidence does the extract contain to indicate that the status of blacks is lower than that of whites? (5)
2. How did Richard's family encourage him to accept his place in the Jim Crow system? (5)
3. How can the reaction of the black porters be seen as further encouragement to Richard to accept the situation? (5)
4. What evidence does the extract contain to show that whites worked together to keep blacks 'in their place'? (5)

9 PART TOTALITARIANISM (1)

Totalitarian societies lack many of the civil rights which are taken for granted in Western democracies. These include freedom of speech, freedom of assembly and equality under the law. Totalitarian societies are usually single party states in which organised political opposition is banned. Government control relies heavily on the police and army and on a network of spies and informants. Nazi Germany and the Soviet Union under Stalin are examples of totalitarian societies. The following passage comes from *Nineteen Eighty-Four* by George Orwell. It represents one man's vision of a totalitarian future.

People in the Records Department did not readily talk about their jobs. In the long, windowless hall, with its double row of cubicles and its endless rustle of papers and hum of voices murmuring into speakwrites, there were quite a dozen people whom Winston did not even know by name. He knew that in the cubicle next to him the little woman with sandy hair toiled day in day out simply at tracking down and deleting from the press the names of people who had been vaporised and were therefore considered never to have existed. And a few cubicles away a mild, ineffectual, dreamy creature named Ampleforth, with very hairy ears and a surprising talent for juggling with rhymes and metres, was engaged in producing garbled versions - definitive texts, they were called - of poems which had become ideologically offensive. And this hall, with its fifty workers or thereabouts, was only one sub-section, a single cell, as it were, in the huge complexity of the Records Department. Beyond, above, below, were other swarms of workers engaged in an unimaginable multitude of jobs. There were the huge printing shops with their sub-editors, their typography experts and their elaborately equipped studios for the faking of photographs. There was the telephone programmes section with its engineers, its producers and its teams of actors specially chosen for their skill in imitating voices. There were the armies of reference clerks whose job was simply to draw up lists of books and periodicals which were due for recall. There were the vast repositories where the corrected documents were stored, and the hidden furnaces where the original copies were destroyed. And somewhere or other, quite anonymous, there were the directing brains who coordinated the whole effort and laid down the lines of policy which made it necessary that this fragment of the past should be preserved, that one falsified, and the other rubbed out of existence.

And the Records Department, after all, was itself only a single branch of the Ministry of Truth, whose primary job was not to reconstruct the past but to supply the citizens with newspapers, films, textbooks, telescreen programmes, plays, novels - with every conceivable kind of information, instruction or entertainment, from a statue to a slogan, from a lyric poem to a biological treatise, and from a child's spelling book to a Newspeak dictionary.

Winston took the Newspeak dictionary from the shelf, pushed the speakwrite to one side, cleaned his spectacles and settled down to his main job of the morning. 'You haven't a real appreciation of Newspeak, Winston,' his fellow worker said almost sadly. 'Do you know that Newspeak is the only language in the world whose vocabulary gets smaller every year?' Winston did know that, of course. 'Don't you see that the whole aim of Newspeak is to narrow the range of thought? Every concept that can ever be needed will be expressed by exactly one word, with its meaning rigidly defined and all its subsidiary meanings rubbed out and forgotten. Every year fewer and fewer words, and the range of consciousness always a little smaller. By 2050 - earlier, probably - all real knowledge of Oldspeak will have disappeared. The whole literature of the past will have been destroyed. Chaucer, Shakespeare, Milton, Byron - they'll exist only in Newspeak versions, not merely changed into something different, but actually changed into something contradictory of what they used to be. Even the literature of the Party will change. Even the slogans will change. How could you have a slogan like 'freedom is slavery' when the concept of freedom has been abolished? The whole climate of thought will be different. In fact there will be no thought, as we understand it now.'

(adapted from 'Nineteen Eighty-Four' by George Orwell, Secker & Warburg, London, 1949, pp 32, 33, 40, 41)

Lenin, one of the founders of the Soviet Union, addressing troops in Moscow. On the right of the podium are Trotsky and Kamenev, two leaders of the Russian revolution.

When Stalin came to power he 'disposed' of Trotsky (who was murdered) and Kamenev (who was executed). In this picture they have been painted out.

QUESTIONS

1. Why should people who have been vaporised be removed from all records? (6)
2. What is the point of rewriting poems, faking photographs, imitating voices, recalling books and burning documents? (6)
3. How can Newspeak be seen as the ultimate mechanism of social control? (8)

10 PART — TOTALITARIANISM (2)

The Indonesian invasion of East Timor took place in 1975. No one knows how many people were killed but the figure is probably between a quarter and a third of the entire population - 100,000 to 200,000 people. The Indonesian rulers have imposed a blanket of control over the conquered population. The following extract is taken from a description of a visit to East Timor by Edward Thebarton.

Landing at Dili, the capital of East Timor, one senses immediately the dead hand of totalitarianism. An eerie stillness reigns despite the presence of many people. There is no life or spontaneity in their movement or faces, only suspicion, watchfulness and a deep mistrust.

Indonesian secret police torturing an East Timorese man

East Timorese freedom fighters posing for the camera

The authorities watch everyone. Ten photographers, one with a video camera, took my picture before I reached the terminal building. On almost every corner stands an Indonesian policeman or soldier. Without them, Indonesian rule in East Timor would collapse overnight.

People are frightened to speak but occasionally the truth emerges in single statements blurted out as if by a sudden, irresistible impulse. 'It is not good here.' 'My family was killed.' 'My sister was raped by many soldiers'. People have to be very careful. There are spies and informants everywhere. A young man explains why he spies for the authorities. 'I am a student and I attended a meeting. The Indonesians caught me. They tortured me. They let me go if I am a spy for them.'

Like all totalitarian rulers, the Indonesians attempt to rewrite history and to obliterate and deny people's memories. Any mention of the slaughter of the invasion is dangerous. People can 'disappear' for saying the wrong thing. Yet the memories live on. Travelling on buses in the countryside people will furtively point out the location of mass graves, unmarked but not forgotten.

Even in a totalitarian state, control is never total. On 12 November 1991, 3,000 people assembled at Santa Cruz cemetery in Dili. They were demonstrating for independence and paying their respects to a young man killed by Indonesian troops. They paid dearly for this show of resistance. Hundreds of soldiers surrounded the cemetery and opened fire with semi-automatic rifles. An estimated 200 people were killed and hundreds more injured.

(adapted from 'Amnesty', May/June 1994)

QUESTIONS

1. Why do totalitarian regimes make extensive use of spies and informants? (5)
2. Why do totalitarian regimes want to rewrite history and obliterate people's memories? (5)
3. Indonesian control in East Timor is not total. Give evidence to support this statement. (5)
4. Why are the army and the police necessary to maintain control in totalitarian societies? (5)

RESEARCH METHODS

Sociologists use a wide variety of information or data in their research. Some of this material comes from existing sources such as official statistics, newspapers and historical documents. These are known as secondary sources and are examined in the second part of the chapter. However sociologists themselves collect much of the data they use in their research. These types of sources are known as primary sources. The first part of the section deals with some of the more important methods of data collection.

1 PART — PARTICIPANT OBSERVATION (1)

Many sociologists claim that an effective study of human behaviour requires as full and complete a picture as possible of the life of a social group. Some argue that the best way to obtain such a picture is by directly observing people in their normal, everyday activities. A method known as *participant observation* has been developed for this purpose. It involves the observer directly participating in the activities of the group he or she is studying. For example, the observer may join a group of workers on the shopfloor or a group of unemployed men on the street corner.

Participant observation offers the sociologist an opportunity of seeing life as it is actually lived. However, as a research method, it has a number of disadvantages. It is very time consuming - many researchers spend a year or more studying a group. Also the number of people that can be directly observed is small - the researcher can only be at one place at a time and cannot watch and listen closely to large numbers of people. It is therefore not possible to generalise from the findings of participant observation studies. For example, the researcher would not be justified in making the generalisation that all factory workers are bored from a study of twenty men. In addition, there is a danger that the presence of an outsider will influence and change the behaviour of those he or she observes. This would reduce the possibility of obtaining a true picture of their way of life. Despite these disadvantages, participant observation does offer the opportunity to see life as it is lived and to appreciate the point of view of those who live it.

The following extract is taken from a study of an Italian American street corner gang in a low income district of south Boston. It was conducted by William Foote Whyte who spent three and a half years in the area as a participant observer. He gave the name 'Cornerville' to the area, the 'Norton Street gang' to the group and 'Doc' to the gang leader.

The spring of 1937 provided me with an intensive course in participant observation. I was learning how to conduct myself, and I learned from various groups but particularly from the Norton Street gang.

As I began hanging about Cornerville, I found that I needed an explanation for myself and for my study. As long as I was with Doc and vouched for by him, no one asked me who I was or what I was doing. When I circulated in other groups or even among the Nortons without him, it was obvious that they were curious about me.

I soon found that people were developing their own explanation about me: I was writing a book about Cornerville. This might seem entirely too vague an explanation, and yet it sufficed. I found that my acceptance in the district depended on the personal relationships I developed far more than upon any explanations I might give. Whether it was a good thing to write a book about Cornerville depended entirely on people's opinions of me personally. If I was all right, then my project was all right; if I was no good, then no amount of explanation could convince them that the book was a good idea.

Of course people did not satisfy their curiosity about me simply by questions that they addressed to me directly. They turned to Doc, for example, and asked him about me. Doc then answered the questions and provided any reassurance that was needed.

I learned early in my Cornerville period the crucial importance of having the support of the key individuals in any groups or organisations I was studying. Instead of trying to explain myself to everyone, I found I was providing far more information about myself and my study to leaders such as Doc than I volunteered to the average corner boy.

My relationship with Doc changed rapidly in this early Cornerville period. At first he was simply a key informant - and also my sponsor (a person who makes himself responsible for and supports another). As we spent more time together, I ceased to treat him as a passive informant. I discussed with him quite frankly what I was trying to do, what problems were puzzling me, and so on. Much of our time was spent in this discussion of ideas and observations, so that Doc became, in a very real sense, a collaborator in the research.

Doc found this experience of working with me interesting and enjoyable and yet the relationship had its drawbacks. He once commented: 'You've slowed me up plenty since you've been down here. Now, when I do something, I have to think what Bill Whyte would want to know about it and how I can explain it. Before, I used to do things by instinct.'

In my interviewing methods I had been instructed not to argue with people or pass moral judgements upon them. This fell in with my own inclinations. I was glad to accept the people and to be accepted by them. However, this attitude did not come out so much in the interviewing, for I did little formal interviewing. I sought to show this interested acceptance of the people and the community in my everyday participation.

I learned to take part in the street corner discussions on baseball and sex. This required no special training, since the topics seemed to be matters of almost universal interest. I was not able to participate so actively in discussions of horse racing. I did begin to follow the races in a rather general and amateur way. I am sure it would have paid me to devote more study to the *Morning Telegraph* and other racing sheets, but my knowledge of baseball at least insured that I would not be left out of the street corner conversations.

Whyte's research was carried out in the Italian American community of South Boston. Many east coast American cities have large Italian communities. This picture shows 'Little Italy' in New York.

Sometimes I wondered whether just hanging on the street corner was an active enough process to be dignified by the term 'research'. Perhaps I should be asking these men questions. However, one has to learn when to question and when not to question as well as what questions to ask.

I learned this lesson one night in the early months when I was with Doc in Chichi's gambling joint. A man from another part of the city was regaling us with a tale of the organisation of gambling activity. I had been told that he had once been a very big gambling operator, and he talked knowingly about many interesting matters. He did most of the talking, but the others asked questions and threw in comments, so at length I began to feel that I must say something in order to be part of the group. I said: 'I suppose the cops were all paid off?'

The gambler's jaw dropped. He glared at me. Then he denied vehemently that any policemen had been paid off and immediately switched the conversation to another subject. For the rest of that evening I felt very uncomfortable.

The next day Doc explained the lesson of the previous evening. 'Go easy on that "who", "what", "why", "when", stuff, Bill. You ask those questions, and people will clam up on you. If people accept you, you can just hang around, and you'll learn the answers in the long run without even having to ask the questions.'

I found that this was true. As I sat and listened, I learned the answers to questions that I would not even have had the sense to ask if I had been getting my information solely on an interviewing basis. I did not abandon questioning altogether, of course. I simply learned to judge the sensitiveness of the question and my relationship to the people so that I only asked a question in a sensitive area when I was sure that my

relationship to the people involved was very solid.

When I had established my position on the street corner, the data simply came to me without very active efforts on my part. It was only now and then, when I was concerned with a particular problem and felt I needed more information from a certain individual, that I would seek an opportunity to get the man alone and carry on a more formal interview.

(from 'Street Corner Society' by William F. Whyte, revised edition, University of Chicago Press, Chicago, 1955, pp 300-305)

QUESTIONS

1. How did 'Bill' (William Whyte) gain acceptance within the group? (5)
2. Whyte states, 'I tried to avoid influencing the group because I wanted to study the situation as unaffected by my presence as possible'. What evidence does the extract contain which suggests that a) he was successful and b) he was unsuccessful? (3,3)
3. Those involved in 'street life' are often suspicious of outsiders.
   a) What evidence for this is contained in the extract? (3)
   b) With some reference to the extract suggest why, particularly in this type of situation, participant observation is a more effective method of obtaining accurate data than interviews or questionnaires. (6)

PARTICIPANT OBSERVATION (2)

Social Relations in a Secondary School by David H. Hargreaves is a study of the behaviour of teachers and students in a secondary modern school in an industrial town in northern England. Part of the information came from participant observation. Hargreaves stayed for a year in the school and spent many hours observing the behaviour of teachers and students in the classroom. In the following extract he examines his role as a participant observer.

The method of participant observation leads the investigator to accept a role within the social situation he studies: he participates as a member of the group as well as observing it. In theory, this direct participation in the group life permits an easy entrance into the social situation by reducing the resistance of group members; decreases the extent to which the investigator disturbs the 'natural' situation; and permits the investigator to experience and observe the group's norms, values, conflicts and pressures, which (over a long period) cannot be hidden from someone playing an in-group role. The fact that I had three years' experience of teaching and that I was to spend a third of my time in the school teaching classes allayed (reduced) many of the fears teachers felt about my presence in the school. If I had been a teacher, the argument seemed to run, and I was going to do some teaching in the school, then surely I must be looking at the school from *their* point of view.

One aspect of my participant observation in the school was to sit at the back of a form during an ordinary lesson. Whereas initially most of the teachers happily ascribed a teacher role to me on the basis of my past experience and current teaching

within the school, to observe them within the confines of their own classrooms involved a disruption of their usual autonomy (freedom) and upset their ascription of a teacher role to me. In exceptional circumstances teachers do see their colleagues at work but for the most part the assessment any teacher may make of his colleagues' competency depends upon more indirect information, such as examination results, noise from the classroom, attitude of pupils outside the classroom and gossip.

As soon as I became an observer of the classroom situation, I could no longer be regarded as a teacher. Instead my role became more that of the Inspector. A few teachers reacted with some kind of withdrawal. Whenever I went into a lesson conducted by Mr H., he made the boys work quietly out of textbooks, talked in a whisper to boys at his desk so that I could not hear from the back and declined to speak to the class as a whole unless this became unavoidable. With other teachers, the changes my presence effected took more subtle forms. Mr O. usually set the form some written work and then joined me at the back of the room, where he chatted with me or told me jokes. Mr F. never refused to let me observe but if he could he decided to read a story to the form or directed a lesson in which the boys played a passive and silent role. Mr L. invariably sent boys to the back of the room with their books for me to examine and comment on, although when I had seen every book several times this practice declined. Many of the teachers appeared to behave quite naturally and act as if I was not in the room at all, and it is difficult to check on the extent of the changes my presence produced. Sometimes the teachers would themselves indicate the effects of my presence. In the lower streams in particular the boys are caned comparatively frequently, if the conversations over lunch and in the common room are any measure of this. But it was notable how very rarely a teacher caned a boy when I was in the room.

A further check came from conversation with the boys, who revealed changes which might otherwise have not been at all obvious.

'When you're in he tries to act calmly as though he's a little angel and all that.'
'Did you notice when you were in Mr M's - he called me by my first name. But when you're on the field (games) he calls you by your second name.'
'They put on a show for you. They put the good act on, smiles and all that, and when you've gone out ...'
'Like if Mr O's getting mad 'cos someone's ripped a book or something, but if you're in he seems to drop it. If you weren't there he'd get real mad.'

Initially my presence also caused changes in the boys' behaviour though I am convinced that these are of less importance, for once the boys became accustomed to me, they behaved normally.

(from 'Social Relations in a Secondary School' by David H. Hargreaves, Routledge & Kegan Paul, London, 1967, pp 193-4, 195-7)

QUESTIONS

1. In your own words outline two of the advantages of participant observation discussed by Hargreaves. (6)
2. If participant observation is to succeed, the observer must be accepted by the group.
   a) Why is this so? (2)
   b) Why was Hargreaves accepted, at least at first, by the teachers he was observing? (2)
3. Why did some of the teachers change their behaviour in the classroom when observed by Hargreaves? (5)
4. Why was Hargreaves worried about his presence as an observer in the classroom affecting the behaviour of teachers and students? (5)

PART 3 — INTERVIEWS (1)

Compared with participant observation, interviews are cheap and fast. As a result the number of people studied is usually larger than in research based on participant observation. However, interviews do not allow sociologists to directly observe people in their normal, everyday settings. What people say in an interview can be very different from what they actually do. Without other methods, sociologists are unable to adequately check the accuracy of interview data. In addition, the answers people give are often strongly influenced by the interviewer.

In the following extract, Hannah Gavron describes the way she conducted interviews for her book, *The Captive Wife*. She interviewed 96 mothers with one or more children under the age of five. Like many interviewers she was worried about directing the respondent - the person being interviewed. Often the interviewer expects or hopes for a certain answer and this can influence the respondent's reply. Sometimes interviewers ask 'leading questions' which direct the respondent to a particular answer. In the hope of avoiding these problems, Gavron used the technique of 'non-directive' interviewing which gives the respondent some freedom to direct the interview herself.

Each interview was allowed to develop naturally, enabling the respondent to direct the conversation along her own lines and filling in the schedule to suit her own order. This meant that the answers to many questions were obtained without any direct demand. For example, every wife said something about her methods of bringing up her children. This was then recorded in the appropriate section of the schedule, and *then* she was asked whether she found any difference between her own ideas and those of her husband, and those of her parents. In this way identical schedules were obtained from each person, which could then be compared, but at the same time each woman interviewed had been given a fair degree of freedom to express her own views in her own way. To some degree being one's own interviewer both increases and decreases the difficulties. There is no problem of misunderstanding or misinterpretation of the schedule, nor of different questions being given varying importance. Any bias is constant throughout so that the schedules, when complete, have a degree of uniformity. The main disadvantage,

A 'non-directive' interview

however, is that if the interviewer is also the author of the research, as in this case, the very expectations that led to the promotion of the research may determine some of the responses given. It is difficult to see how this can be avoided completely, but awareness of the problem plus constant self control can help. In circumstances such as these, it is probably best to employ the kind of 'non-directive' interviewing that has been used in this research.

(from 'The Captive Wife: Conflicts of Housebound Mothers' by Hannah Gavron, Routledge & Kegan Paul, London, 1966)

QUESTIONS

1. What is 'non-directive' interviewing? (4)
2. With some reference to the extract outline the advantages and disadvantages on 'non-directive' interviewing as a method of gathering information. (5)
3. What is the main problem of the author of the research being his or her own interviewer? (4)
4. What are the advantages of the author of the research being his or her own interviewer? (4)
5. Why did Gavron want 'identical schedules' from each person interviewed? (3)

PART 4 — INTERVIEWS (2)

One of the main disadvantages of interviews is the problem of 'interviewer bias'. This means that in some way the interviewer influences and directs the answer given by the respondent or interviewee. Thus the respondent may modify or change his or her answer depending on the age, sex, ethnicity or nationality of the interviewer. The interviewer may expect or hope for certain answers. This may be transmitted to the respondent and influence his or her reply. The following passages illustrate some of the effects of 'interviewer bias'.

In 1914, 2,000 destitute men ('down and outs' with no means of support) were questioned by two interviewers. They were asked, among other things to explain their situation. One of the interviewers was a strong supporter of prohibition - forbidding by law the manufacture and sale of alcoholic drinks. There was a strong tendency for the men he interviewed to blame their situation on alcohol. The second interviewer was a strong supporter of socialist political views. He believed that private industry should be brought into public ownership and that making a profit should take second place to the welfare of the workers. The men that he interviewed were much more likely to explain their misfortune in terms of the industrial situation.

(Discussed in 'On Errors in Surveys' by W. E. Deming in 'Research Methods' edited by B. J. Franklin and H.W. Osborne, Wadsworth, Belmont, 1971, p 347)

QUESTION

1. How can the idea of 'interviewer bias' be used to explain the different results obtained by the two interviewers? (6)

In the early 1960s a series of interviews were conducted with 840 black Americans in North Carolina. All the interviewers were women, thirteen were black and nine white. There were important differences between the results obtained by black and white interviewers. For example, a higher proportion of those interviewed by blacks as compared with those interviewed by whites, said that they approved of civil rights demonstrations and school desegregation (ending all-white and all-black schools). In addition, more respondents refused to give any answers to these questions when faced with a white interviewer.

(adapted from 'Interviewer - respondent Interaction' by J. Allan Williams Jr. in 'Research Methods' edited by B. J. Franklin and H.W. Osborne, Wadsworth, Belmont, 1971)

QUESTION

2. Suggest an explanation for the different results obtained by black and white interviewers. (8)

During the 1960s many black Americans rejected the idea that 'white is right' and stopped trying to copy white Americans. Being black became something to be proud of rather than ashamed. The author of the following research believed that this outlook was reflected in black American 'soul' music. The extract quotes a small part of an interview between the author, a young white researcher, and Jay Butler, a black disc jockey from Detroit.

Interviewer The song *Take me as I am* by Solomon Burke. What's it about?

Jay Butler It's just about a guy and his woman an' he's telling her not to try and change him, to take him as he is.

Interviewer But don't you think it could have a deeper meaning, that it's saying accept me as a black man, not as a poor substitute for a white man.

Jay Butler Yeah. You got a point there. The black community wants to be accepted as black American. I don't wanna be a white American, I wanna be a black American. It's like the Detroit Emeralds' song *I'm an ordinary man, take me the way I am*. There's a two-fold meaning in all these soul songs. Take Solomon Burke's *Take me as I am*. This song might be about a guy and his girl, but it means more at this period of time. Back in the 1950s we were trying to be accepted by white Americans on their terms. Now accept me as I am, accept my nappy hair, accept me period.

(from 'Right On: From Blues to Soul in Black America' by Michael Haralambos, Causeway Press, Ormskirk, 1994, p 146, with additional material from the author's unpublished notes)

The researcher interviewing blues singer Bobby Bland

QUESTION

3. How might the idea of 'interviewer bias' help to explain the development and result of this interview? (6)

5 PART

SAMPLING PROCEDURES (1)

Sociologists cannot study everybody. They have neither the time nor the money. They therefore select a sample of those they wish to study. The sample may be of the population as a whole, or of a particular section within the population such as the working class, women, teenagers, factory workers, managers and so on. The aim of sampling is to select a number of people who are representative of the particular section of the population under investigation. If, for example, a representative sample of 10% of the student population of a comprehensive school was taken, the sociologist would feel some justification in claiming that the results applied to all students in the school. In other words he or she would be able to generalise from the data obtained from the sample. One of the most frequently used sampling procedures is the *random sample*. A number is given to each individual in the group under investigation and a set of random numbers is then used to select the members of the sample. The nearest everyday equivalent is to give each individual in the group to be studied a number and then to pick these numbers out of a hat. By means of a random sample the researcher can predict with some assurance that the sample is representative of the group as a whole.

The following extract outlines the way in which Hannah Gavron selected the sample for her study entitled *The Captive Wife: Conflicts of Housebound Mothers*. The Group Practice mentioned refers to a health centre from which a group of doctors operate.

The working class wives were all drawn from the practice lists of the Caversham Centre, a Group Practice in Kentish Town in London. Selection was made as follows. An alphabetical list was taken from the files of all the wives who fell into the right categories, that is, (a) married (b) at least one child under five (c) born in or after 1930. 70 were selected at random from the list, but 20 had to be eliminated as being ineligible. The method of approach was to call at the address, explain my introduction from the doctor, and ask if they would be willing to assist in the work. In fact two refused and 48 agreed.

Selection of 48 middle class women proved more difficult. The practice at the Caversham Centre had very few middle class patients, and the doctors felt they were not in any way representative of the middle classes in general. It was decided that the advantages of an introduction such as the one obtained at the Caversham Centre were sufficiently great to try to repeat this with the middle class sample. However, it proved very difficult to find a doctor who had a large number of middle class patients in the right categories, and who was willing to assist in the research. Advice was sought from the College of

General Practitioners, and one doctor in West Hampstead offered to assist. In fact a study of his files revealed only 35 names which fulfilled all the right conditions. An initial introduction to the 35 women selected was obtained through a letter from the doctor explaining the purpose of my research. Subsequently I telephoned to ask their assistance and arranged a visit. In no case was there a refusal. The remaining 13 were selected from the London lists of the 'Housebound Wives' Register. This is an informal association, begun after a letter in the *Guardian*, of women with children. It has groups all over the country and discussion with the area organiser in North London revealed that its membership covered a wide variety of people. It is fully realised that to select from an organisation such as this involves a degree of bias, mainly due to the fact that the women have selected themselves, ie joined the group, and that this bias is probably a greater one than that incurred by selecting from a doctor's practice.

(from 'The Captive Wife: Conflicts of Housebound Mothers' by Hannah Gavron, Routledge & Kegan Paul, London, 1966)

QUESTIONS

1. The working class wives in the sample were selected randomly from doctors' lists. Why do researchers such as Gavron use random samples? (4)
2. Why was Gavron concerned about selecting part of her middle class sample from the 'Housebound Wives' Register? (4)
3. Gavron's sample was made up of 96 women. In view of this why does she state that 'large-scale generalisations' cannot be made from her study? (4)
4. Briefly suggest why Gavron selected both middle and working class wives for her sample. (4)
5. Gavron's selection of her sample was influenced by 'the advantages of an introduction'.
   a) Why might an introduction from a doctor be useful to a researcher? (2)
   b) What evidence is contained in the extract to suggest that such introductions were advantageous? (2)

SAMPLING PROCEDURES (2)
PART 6

The Family and Social Change: A Study of Family and Kinship in a South Wales Town by Colin Rosser and Christopher Harris is a study of family life in Swansea. Part of the information used in the research came from a random sample made up of 2% of the population of the County Borough of Swansea. In order to make sure that the sample was representative, it was compared with information from the census. Table 1 shows the age and sex distribution of the Swansea sample compared to that of the census which gives the percentage of males and females in various age groups for the nation as a whole. Table 2 compares the social class distribution of the sample with information from the census which shows the percentage of the national population in each social class.

Table 1 Age-sex distribution

Age Group	Sample Men %	Women %	Census Men %	Women %
20-29	11.9	14.8	18.8	16.4
30-39	20.5	19.0	21.0	18.2
40-49	22.1	20.2	20.2	19.2
50-59	21.6	18.0	19.2	18.8
60-69	14.7	15.7	13.0	15.2
70-79	7.8	8.8	6.3	9.1
80-89	1.3	3.2	1.5	2.9
90+	0.1	0.3	0.09	0.2
% of men and women	49	51	48	52

Table 2 Occupational class

Registrar - General's Occupational Class	Sample %	Census %
I	5.2	3.0
II	15.8	12.4
III	52.8	50.4
IV	13.2	13.0
V	12.3	21.2
Not known	0.7	-

(from 'The Family and Social Change: A Study of Family and Kinship in a South Wales Town' by Colin Rosser and Christopher Harris, Routledge & Kegan Paul, London, 1965, p 326)

A cross-section of society

QUESTIONS

1. Why did Rosser and Harris compare their sample with information from the census? (5)
2. In the age group 20-29 which gender group (men or women) in the sample appears more representative of the nation as a whole? Briefly explain your choice. (3)
3. Which two social classes in the sample appear least representative in terms of the social class distribution of the national population? Briefly explain your choices. (3)
4. Rosser and Harris state that it is 'likely that there was a slight exaggeration of occupational status by our informants' (ie those who made up the sample). How might this partly explain the differences between the social class distribution in the sample and the census? (4)
5. The sample was taken in 1960. The census was taken in 1951. Rosser and Harris state that 'there is a long-term trend away from unskilled to skilled and semi-skilled employment'. How might this help to explain some of the differences between the social class distributions in the sample and the census? (5)
(Class V - unskilled manual, Class IV - semi-skilled manual, Class III - skilled manual and clerical and minor supervisory occupations).

QUESTIONNAIRES

PART 7

A questionnaire is simply a list of questions. Questionnaires are often used for gathering data for social surveys. A social survey involves the collection of the same type of information from all members of the sample. Thus they may be given an identical set of questions and requested to answer them. Questionnaires provide a relatively cheap, fast and efficient method for obtaining large amounts of information from relatively large numbers of people. The data produced by questionnaires is often easily quantified which means it can be put into a numerical form. For example, a questionnaire completed by factory workers might show that 58% belonged to trade unions and 60% supported the Labour Party. When data is put into this form it is possible to measure the strength of the connection between different factors. Using the above example, it might be found that 90% of trade union members supported the Labour Party. Putting the data in the form of numbers makes it possible to measure the importance of the link between trade union membership and Labour Party support.

Those who support the use of questionnaires argue that they produce comparable data. Since everybody is answering exactly the same questions, it is claimed that different answers will indicate real differences between the respondents. Different answers in an interview, however, might reflect differences in the way a question is phrased or different reactions to the interviewer.

However there are a number of disadvantages involved with the use of questionnaires. The following passages examine some of the problems that have resulted from the use of questionnaires in social surveys.

Postal questionnaires are a relatively inexpensive method of obtaining information. The questionnaires are mailed to members of the sample who are asked to complete and return them. However, the response rate is frequently low. Often only a small per cent of the sample return postal questionnaires. Those who do may have a special reason for doing so and may therefore be untypical of the sample as a whole. In 1977 a nationwide survey of the sexual behaviour of American women known as the *Hite*

Report was published. 100,000 postal questionnaires were sent out but only 3,000 were returned. Thus only 3% of the sample replied.

(adapted from 'Scientific Method' by D. Crossland, R. Park and N. Lowe, National Extension College, Cambridge, 1978, p 33)

QUESTIONS

1. Suggest two reasons why the response rate in the Hite Report was low. (4)
2. Why should any generalisation about the sexual behaviour of American women based on the findings of the Hite Report be regarded with caution? (4)

Magazines sometimes produce questionnaires and invite their readers to complete them. For example in the mid-70s in Britain *Woman's Own* produced a questionnaire on love and marriage which was completed by some 10,000 women. However, as the following example shows, there are problems with making generalisations and predictions from this type of survey. In 1936 the *Literary Digest*, an American magazine with a mainly middle class readership, asked its readers a series of questions with the aim of predicting the results of the US presidential election. The survey forecast a Republican president whereas a Democrat was elected to the White House. In addition the number of votes predicted for each presidential candidate were substantially different from the election results.

(adapted from 'Research Methods' edited by B. J. Franklin and H.W. Osborne, Wadsworth, Belmont, 1971, p 162)

QUESTIONS

3. Suggest why the survey failed to predict the election results. (4)
4. Why would a random sample of the US voting population have been more likely to provide an accurate prediction? (4)

Great care must be taken with the wording of questionnaires. It is important that the questions have the same meaning for all members of the sample. It is also important that questions have the same meaning for the researcher who designed the questionnaire and those who answer it. The following example illustrates this point. A Gallup poll survey in 1939 found that 88% of a sample of the US population described itself as middle class, a result which surprised the researchers. Members of the sample were offered a choice of three alternatives, 'upper', 'middle' and 'lower class'. The survey was repeated shortly afterwards and the term 'lower class' was replaced by 'working class'. Now 51% of the sample described itself as working class.

(adapted from 'Introducing Sociology' by Peter Worsley, Penguin, Harmondsworth, 1977, p 428)

QUESTIONS

5. How can the large differences between the results of the two surveys be explained? (4)

8 PART — LONGITUDINAL STUDIES

Sociological research is often like a snapshot. It presents a picture of social life at one point in time. This view has its limitations. For example, one way of understanding social life in the present is to see it as a development from the past. And if we want to understand social change, we require a picture of social life over time.

The longitudinal study is one way of studying social life over time. It examines the same group of people at various times over a period of years. It is like a series of snapshots which show development and change. The following passage summarises a famous longitudinal study conducted by a team of researchers led by J.W.B. Douglas.

In 1947 the Population Investigation Committee carried out a survey of every mother who gave birth to a child in Britain between 3rd and 5th March 1946. This was followed by an examination of the children's health. Using the same sample J.W.B. Douglas studied the education of 5,362 children through primary school to the age of eleven. He then followed the progress of 4,720 members of his original sample through secondary school.

One of Douglas's main interests was educational attainment. He wanted answers to questions such as: Why do some children do better than others? Is there a link between how well a child does at primary school and their performance at secondary school? His findings indicate that in general the more encouragement a child received from its parents, the higher its educational attainment. And parental encouragement became increasingly important as the child grew older. Douglas also found that performance in the early years of primary school is often reflected throughout secondary school.

(adapted from 'The Home and the School' by J.W.B. Douglas, MacGibbon & Kee, London, 1964 and 'All Our Future' by J.W.B. Douglas et al, Peter Davies, London, 1968)

First Holy Communion

University five-a-side champion

Jim O'Gorman, one of the authors of this book, at age 7, 20 and 44

QUESTIONS

1. a) As with all longitudinal studies, Douglas's sample became smaller as time went on. What problems does this cause? (5)
   b) Suggest reasons why such samples become smaller. (5)
2. Using Douglas's findings, outline some of the advantages of longitudinal studies. (5)
3. Look at the pictures. Why might an interview at all three ages give a more rounded view than a single interview at age 44? (5)

CASE STUDIES

PART 9

A case study is a study of one particular example or instance of something. It may be a study of a particular school, factory or hospital, or a study of a single individual such as a manual worker, a mother with dependent children or a retired person.

Case studies have a number of advantages. They often give a richer and more detailed picture than research based on large samples. They can provide useful information for a larger research project. For example, the experiences of one retired person could be used in a questionnaire in order to discover how far they apply to other retired people. And there is a better chance of the questionnaire being relevant and meaningful if it is based, at least partly, on a case study.

Since they are one-off examples, case studies cannot be seen as representative. However, they guard against over confidence in research based on supposedly representative samples. A single case study can contradict the findings of a larger study and call into question conclusions drawn from those findings.

The following passage contains extracts from two case studies on bullying, the first from the point of view of a bully, the second from a victim of bullying.

The bully

It feels as if the teachers and bigger people only pick on you and you can't do anything to your own back. So instead, you take it out on someone. It really gets to you when someone grasses on you, so you get back at them some way or other.

I used to threaten them and give them a few nudges. After about a month they would get sick of it and would take a swing at you or say something about you. For instance, they would call you names by referring to the colour of your hair. As a result, you get mad so you do him in after the period or when school is finished.

It makes you feel shaky but good, because it's off your chest.

Sometimes, when its really bad, you have to do some vandalism to bus shelters or other things or join a group. The more vandalism you do, the better you feel, but that's only on the spur of the moment.

If you're like me, very emotional, you'll understand how I felt when someone said something about my mother or father or someone I was close to. I just felt as if I had to stop it by just smashing their head in and showing them who was boss.

The victim

When I started high school, I thought it was great. There were a lot of new friends to make. As time went on, however, I found that some people I thought to be my friends were really unkind.

The only thing that prevented me from enjoying my first year was one person in my class who started to bully me. This led to several other people following his example and my life became sheer misery. At first I was upset but able to cope with it, then I became angry and distressed. I couldn't sleep for worrying about the next day. It would be name-calling, stone-throwing and threatening. It all got too much and I decided to tell my Mum and Dad. We all agreed that I had to tell the teacher. The next day, though worried, I did.

The teacher was very sympathetic and said it must stop. We had lunch meetings to discuss the problems. The bullies were very surprised that they were included instead of being punished. We discussed my feelings at being bullied and we would agree on some plan of action so that I would get support from my friends. Once the bullies realised that they were being included, the bullying ceased.

(adapted from 'The Rights of the Child' edited by C. Donnellan, Independence, Cambridge, 1994)

QUESTIONS

1. a) How might the first case study be useful for writing a questionnaire designed to discover the causes of bullying? (6)
    b) Write three questions, based on the case study, for use in this questionnaire. (3)
    c) Why is it important to do a larger study on bullying? (3)
2. How does the case study of the victim show the power of the peer group as a mechanism of social control? (8)

Bullying often takes place in school playgrounds.

EXPERIMENTS

10 PART

Few sociologists use laboratory experiments in their research. Sociologists want to study people in 'real life' situations, in their normal, everyday settings. People are likely to see laboratories as artificial, abnormal and unusual. As a result their actions may be very different from those in their normal settings. One way round this problem is the *field experiment*, an experiment which takes place in everyday situations. The following passage looks at two field experiments. (For another example see Chapter 10, Part 8.)

What effect does social class have on the way strangers behave towards each other? An actor stood outside Paddington Station in London and asked passers-by for directions. For the first half of the experiment he was dressed as a businessman, for the second half as a labourer. The results showed that people were more helpful when he was dressed as a businessman. They were more likely to stop and to give fuller directions.

(adapted from 'The Psychology of Social Class' by M. Sissons, Open University Press, Milton Keynes, 1970)

Same man...

Different response

In 1984-85 the Policy Studies Institute conducted an experiment in London, Birmingham and Manchester to find out the extent of racial discrimination. The researchers wrote or telephoned in answer to advertisements for jobs. The applications made it clear that the person replying was either White, Asian or Afro-Caribbean. The applicants were similar in terms of age, sex and qualifications.

The replies from employers were divided into two groups. A *positive response* meant that an employer offered an interview, sent an application form or asked the applicant to telephone. A *negative response* meant that the employer didn't reply at all or rejected the application. The results of the experiment are shown in Table 1.

Table 1 Results of job applications

	Total	White	Asian	Afro-Caribbean
Positive response	72%	90%	63%	63%
Negative response	28%	10%	37%	37%
Number of applications	1005	335	335	335

(adapted from 'Racial Discrimination' by C. Brown and P. Gay, PSI, London, 1985)

QUESTIONS

1. Suggest an explanation for the results of the Paddington Station experiment. (6)
2. The Policy Studies researchers claimed that their experiment showed that racial discrimination is widespread. From the evidence given, do you agree? Give reasons for your answer. (6)
3. What are the advantages and disadvantages of using the experimental method in the above studies? (8)

11 PART — PILOT STUDIES

Many researchers begin with a *pilot study* before starting their main study. Often they obtain valuable information which can then be used in the main part of the research. The first extract describes the pilot study undertaken by Willmott and Young in their research on working class family life in the East End of London. The second extract describes what Hannah Gavron learned from the pilot study which preceded her investigation of the problems of housebound wives.

As well as taking care in choosing a sample, and trying to interview as many of the people selected, it is also important to ensure that one asks sensible and clear questions, of the kind which will produce meaningful answers. What people say in an interview may not correspond with what they actually do, as we warn the reader in the introduction to this book. Their memory may be faulty, they may be muddled, or they may for some reason deliberately mislead the interviewer, but in organising a survey one can reduce errors of this sort by framing the questions carefully, and by providing a number of opportunities to check on the consistency of people's answers, either in the course of the interview or by calling back later on for some fuller information. These problems help to explain why most investigators undertake a 'pilot' survey before proceeding to the main inquiry. In Bethnal Green and Greenleigh we carried out just over 100 'pilot' interviews, to help us decide upon the design of the inquiry, the questions to ask and how to put them.

(from 'Family and Kinship in East London' by Michael Young and Peter Willmott, Routledge & Kegan Paul, London, 1957)

The pilot study had revealed two things. Firstly that a considerable degree of rapport (understanding) was necessary for a satisfactory interview on this subject (which involved attitudes and emotions as well as facts), and secondly that if the

respondent was allowed to follow her own train of thought, many questions would be answered without the necessity of asking them specifically, although in some cases it might be valuable to check back later. For these reasons some time was spent at the beginning of each interview establishing a kind of relationship by exchanging small pieces of conversational information. Once some degree of rapport had been established the conversation ceased, leaving the respondent confident and at ease, and allowing the interview to develop.

(from 'The Captive Wife: Conflicts of Housebound Mothers' by Hannah Gavron, Routledge & Kegan Paul, London, 1966)

QUESTIONS

1. With reference to the first extract, briefly discuss the problems involved in constructing questions for an interview. (6)
2. a) What do Young and Willmott mean by checking on 'the consistency of people's answers'? (3)
   b) How is it possible to do this in the course of an interview? (3)
3. a) Gavron was investigating the problems and feelings of housebound mothers. Why did she feel that 'a considerable degree of rapport was necessary for a satisfactory interview on this subject'? (2)
   b) How did she achieve this rapport? (2)
   c) Once she achieved this rapport, what effect did it have on her respondents? (2)
4. How might a pilot study solve the problems illustrated in the cartoons? (2)

PART 12 — SECONDARY SOURCES

So far the extracts in this chapter have looked at ways in which sociologists collect their own information. These sources of information are known as *primary sources*; the material collected by means of participant observation, interviews and questionnaires is known as primary data. However, there is a vast range of existing information which is available for sociological research. It includes parish records, legal documents, letters, diaries, novels, autobiographies, official statistics, newspapers, books, television programmes, recorded music and films. These sources of information are known as *secondary sources*, the information itself as secondary data.

There are many examples of the use of modern secondary sources in this book. For example, extracts from autobiographies and novels are used to illustrate methods of social control - see Chapter 2, Parts 4, 8 and 9. Historical sources are also used throughout this book. Chapter 9, Part 3 shows how the use of historical documents provides a picture of family life in the past. It examines Peter Laslett's research on family life from 16th to the 19th century, which was based on parish records, and Michael Anderson's study of families in Preston based on the results of the 1851 census. Social change is one of the major concerns of sociologists. Without historical material they would be unable to document and explain how societies have changed, they would be unable to compare the present with the past.

However, there are a number of problems involved in using secondary sources for sociological research. As Part 15 shows, official statistics must be used with caution since it is often far from clear what they are actually measuring. Written material such as newspaper articles, novels and autobiographies cannot be taken at face value. They are written from a particular standpoint, to support an argument, make a point and reflect a political, religious or moral

belief. They cannot be seen as balanced, unbiased, objective accounts.

Despite these problems secondary sources are immensely valuable. In particular historical sources are all we have for understanding the past. Sociologists have only been around for some 150 years. The history of the human race stretches back well over a million years. Clearly we cannot rely on primary sources for understanding human society.

The following extract looks at an example of historical material. It is taken from *Long Lance*, the autobiography of Chief Buffalo Child Long Lance written in 1928. It is a unique record of the traditional way of life of the Blackfoot Indians who lived on the Canadian prairies - a way of life that has all but disappeared.

We youngsters were given daily lectures on how to live by twelve of the oldest men of the tribe. Because they had lived to such remarkable ages it was considered that they knew better how to live than anyone else. Every morning just before sunrise, while the camp still lay on their pallets in their teepees, one of these old men would take his turn in getting up early and walking through the camp shouting out his lecture on how to live to be old and his advice on morals, courage, and personal bravery. His voice would awake us, and we would lie still and listen intently to every word he said. At that time of the morning, just as we had awakened from a night's rest, his words seemed to pierce deep into us; we remembered every word he said, and all during the day his advice would keep coming back into our minds, and we would try to live up to it.

All of these men were great warriors who had many scalps to their credit, and we respected our old people above all others in the tribe. To live to be so old they must have been brave and strong and good fighters, and we aspired to be like them. We never allowed our old people to want for anything, and whenever any one of them would stop as he made his silent, dignified way through the camp, and put his arm across our shoulders and utter a little prayer for us to the Great Spirit, we would feel highly honoured. We would stand quietly, and when he was through we would remain in our tracks, respectful and silent, until he had disappeared. We looked upon our old people as demigods of a kind, and we loved them deeply; they were all our fathers.

*　　*　　*　　*　　*

When they received this news of the coming of the white missionary, all of the Indians painted their faces and put on all of their best medicine clothes. The medicine man got out his drum, and soon we were all ready to receive him.

When we saw the missionary coming, the medicine man started to beat his tom-tom and sing one of his medicine songs; for he thought that would please the visitor who represented the white man's 'medicine' and Great Spirit. Our chief went out and met the minister and shook his hand, and then he took him over to meet our minister, the medicine man.

After they shook hands, the missionary made a speech. He told our medicine man that he was preaching something not worthwhile. He said:
'I didn't mean for you people to fix up like this; I meant for you to wash the paint off your faces and put your medicine drums away. There is only one God in Heaven, and I am here to tell you about Him.'

Indians never interrupt anyone when he is talking, even if he should talk all day - that is an ancient courtesy among Indians - so everyone stood and listened to the minister while he told us of the white man's God. He made a long speech. He said that the Indians must lay down their arms and live peaceably alongside the white man who was coming into his country.

Blackfoot Indians performing a religious ceremony

When the missionary finished his speech, our chief arose and addressed him. He said:

'Why do you tell us to be good? We Indians are not bad; you white people may be, but we are not. We do not steal, except when our horses have been raided; we do not tell lies; we take care of our old and our poor when they are helpless. We do not need that which you tell us about.'

'But,' said the missionary, 'there is only one God, and you must worship him.'

'Then if that is true,' said our chief, 'we Indians are worshipping the same God that you are - only in a different way. When the Great Spirit made the world He gave the Indians one way to worship Him and He gave the white man another way, because we are different people and our lives are different. The Indian should keep to his way and the white man to his, and we should all work with one another for God and not against one another. The Indian does not try to tell you how you should worship God. We like to see you worship Him in your way, because we know you understand that way.'

'But the Great Spirit you speak of is not the same one that we worship,' said the missionary.

(from 'Long Lance' by Chief Buffalo Child Long Lance, Corgi Books, London, 1956, pp 41-42, 131-132)

QUESTIONS

1. Sociologists must use secondary sources if they are to understand human society. Briefly explain why. (4)
2. If you were studying present day Blackfoot society how might Long Lance's autobiography be useful for your research? (4)
3. Studying other societies helps us to understand our own.
   a) Briefly compare attitudes to the elderly in modern British society and traditional Blackfoot society. (3)
   b) Suggest why these attitudes differ. (3)
4. a) Why were there misunderstandings between the missionary and the Blackfoot? (3)
   b) What can we learn from this about how to approach people with cultures different from our own? (3)

NOVELS

13 PART

A good novel can bring a time, a place and the people who live there to life. It can offer a deep understanding of their world. Thus it has been claimed that George Orwell's novel, *The Road to Wigan Pier*, provides greater insight into working class family life than many sociological studies. Even science fiction, at first sight far removed from this world, can offer a great deal to the study of society. Ursula Le Guin's magnificent science fiction novel *The Dispossessed* presents one of the finest accounts of capitalism, communism and anarchism ever written. Read alongside some of the writings of Karl Marx, it would provide an excellent introduction to some of the main concerns of sociology.

Novelists do not often present balanced, objective accounts. However, this does not prevent their work from providing understanding and insight. This can be seen from the following extract from *Uncle Tom's Cabin* by Harriet Beecher Stowe, first published in 1852. At that time slavery was still legal in the United States. Ms Stowe tried to present a picture of slavery as a 'living dramatic reality', something more suited to a novel than a sociological report. She was passionately opposed to slavery and researched the novel by talking to escaped slaves in the anti-slavery headquarters in Boston.

The following extract is a conversation between Marie, the wife of St. Clare, a southern plantation owner and Miss Ophelia, a visiting relative from New England in the north. Mammy is Marie's lady's maid, she is black and a slave. The novel is set in the USA in the early 19th century.

'Now, Mammy has a sort of goodness,' said Marie; 'she's smooth and respectable, but she's selfish at heart. Now, she never will be done fidgeting and worrying about that husband of hers. You see, when I was married and came to live here, of course I had to bring her with me, and her husband, my father couldn't spare him. He was a blacksmith, and, of course, very necessary; and I thought and said, at the time, that Mammy and he had better give each other up, as it wasn't likely to be convenient for them ever to live together again. I wish now I'd insisted on it, and married Mammy to somebody else; but I was foolish and indulgent, and didn't want to insist. I told Mammy at the time that she mustn't ever expect to see him more than once or twice in her life again, for the air of father's place doesn't agree with my health, and I can't go there; and I advised her to take up with somebody else; but no - she wouldn't. Mammy has a kind of obstinacy about her that everybody don't see as I do.'

'Has she children?' said Miss Ophelia.

'Yes; she has two.'

'I suppose she feels the separation from them?'

'Well, of course, I couldn't bring them. They were little dirty things - I couldn't have them about; and, besides, they took up too much of her time; but I believe that Mammy has always kept up a sort of sulkiness about this. She won't marry anybody else; and I do believe now, though she knows how necessary she is to me, and how feeble my health is, she would go back to her husband tomorrow, if she only could. They are just so

Although slavery in the USA was abolished in 1865, many former slaves continued to serve their previous owners. This picture from 1899 shows servants at the Latimer household, Belton, South Carolina.

selfish, the best of them ... I hold to being kind to servants - I always am; but you must make 'em know their place. Eva [Marie's daughter] never does; there's no getting into the child's head the first beginning of an idea what a servant's place is! You heard her offering to take care of me nights, to let Mammy sleep! That's just a specimen of the way the child would be doing all the time, if she was left to herself.'

'Why,' said Miss Ophelia bluntly, 'I suppose you think your servants are human creatures, and ought to have some rest when they are tired?'

'Certainly, of course. I'm very particular in letting them have everything that comes convenient - anything that doesn't put one at all out of the way, you know. Mammy can make up her sleep, some time or other; there's no difficulty about that. She's the sleepiest concern that ever I saw; sewing, standing, or sitting, that creature will go to sleep, and sleep anywhere and everywhere. No danger but Mammy gets sleep enough. But this treating servants as if they were exotic flowers or china vases is really ridiculous,' said Marie, as she plunged languidly into the depths of a voluminous and pillowy lounge, and drew towards her an elegant cut-glass vinaigrette. 'You don't know what a provoking, stupid, careless, unreasonable, childish, ungrateful set of wretches they are.'

Marie seemed wonderfully supported, always, when she got upon this topic; and she now opened her eyes, and seemed quite to forget her languor.

'You don't know, and you can't, the daily, hourly trials that beset a housekeeper from them, everywhere and every way. But it's no use to complain to St. Clare. He talks the strangest stuff. He says we have made them what they are, and ought to bear with them. He says their faults are all owing to us, and that it would be cruel to make the fault and punish it too. He

says we shouldn't do any better, in their place; just as if one could reason from them to us, you know.'

'Don't you believe that the Lord made them of one blood with us?' said Miss Ophelia, shortly.

'No, indeed, not! A pretty story, truly! They are a degraded race.'

'Don't you think they've got immortal souls?' said Miss Ophelia, with increasing indignation.

'Oh, well,' said Marie, yawning, 'that of course - nobody doubts that. But as to putting them on any sort of equality with us, you know, as if we could be compared, why, it's impossible! Now, St. Clare really has talked to me as if keeping Mammy from her husband was like keeping me from mine. There's no comparing in this way. Mammy couldn't have the feeling that I should. It's a different thing altogether - of course, it is; and yet St. Clare pretends not to see it. And just as if Mammy could love her little dirty babies as I love Eva! Yet St. Clare once really and soberly tried to persuade me that it was my duty, with my weak health, and all I suffer, to let Mammy go back, and take somebody else in her place. That was a little too much even for me to bear. I don't often show my feelings. I make it a principle to endure everything in silence; it's a wife's hard lot, and I bear it. But I did break out, that time; so that he has never alluded to the subject since. But I know by his looks, and little things that he says, that he thinks so as much as ever; and it's so trying, so provoking!'

(from 'Uncle Tom's Cabin' by Harriet Beecher Stowe, J. M. Dent, London, 1961, pp 173, 176, 177, 178)

QUESTIONS

1. In view of Harriet Beecher Stowe's beliefs, why is Miss Ophelia presented as a much nicer person than Marie? (4)

2. Many slave owners saw blacks as a 'lower race' which could not be judged by the same standards as whites. What evidence does the extract provide to illustrate this point? (6)

3. Slavery as a system of social control was justified by a set of beliefs.
   a) What does this mean? (3)
   b) Briefly show how some of Marie's beliefs can be used to justify slavery. (3)

4. What are the problems of using the type of material in the extract as sociological data? (4)

CONTENT ANALYSIS

14 PART

Content analysis refers to the methods used to analyse a wide range of written and broadcast material including newspapers, novels, comics, diaries, letters, advertisements, posters, photographs and radio and television output. The following passage looks at various methods of content analysis and then provides material for you to analyse.

One of the simplest methods of content analysis is to count how often something occurs in printed or broadcast material. The Broadcasting Standards Council study of men and women on television is an example of this approach (see Chapter 2, Part 5). It shows, for instance, that 82% of those speaking on news programmes are men.

A second method is to examine the style and approach of what is written or spoken to see whether it encourages a particular interpretation. The following example is taken from a newspaper headline: GIRL GUIDE, 14, RAPED AT HELLS ANGELS CONVENTION. This is a typical trick of the journalist's trade. It is based on the two extremes of good and evil - the 'innocent victim' and the 'wicked perpetrator'. The reader is encouraged to make their mind up before even reading the article.

A third method is to look for bias. It usually seeks to discover which social group (if any) is being favoured at the expense of others. This approach was taken by the Glasgow University Media Group in their analysis of TV news presentation of disputes between management and workers. They claim to have found a strong pro-management, anti-union bias in the reporting of industrial disputes. For example, an interviewer's use of phrases such as 'acting irresponsibly' and 'cutting your own throats' when talking to union leaders gives the impression that unions rather than management are responsible for strikes.

(adapted in part from 'Methods of Content/Document/Media Analysis' by Ray Pawson, 'Developments in Sociology' vol 11, 1995)

BABY-FACED SEX BEAST SET TO KILL (Star)

Who will watch breakfast television when the BBC launches it next year? Some wives will watch it, of course, particularly if soap operas and feminine programmes are shown. The result will be many burnt offerings in the cooker, and holes scorched in shirts as the iron is forgotten during some dramatic screen moment. (Bristol Evening Post)

They lived happily ever after . . . After what?

"Look at these woollies. Shrunk to nothing. I washed them so carefully too." It was Gwen who was speaking.

"Bills, bills, bills" grumbled her father. "I should think the whole family subsists entirely on soap and soda by the amount we consume."

"Please Sir, the man's called to mend the burst pipes" announced Edith. "Says the old ones were full of scale."

"Dear, dear, dear. Troubles will never end" sighed Mother, and continued with her crossword.

The very next week some kind friend suggested that soft water might help. Whereupon the family clubbed together, bought a Permutit and lived happily and more economically ever after.

Permutits are available on H.P. terms for as little as 1½d a day

PERMUTIT
SOFTENED WATER

An advertisement from the 1930s

QUESTIONS

1. Analyse the content of the advertisement, the postcard, the newspaper headline from the *Star* and the extract from the *Bristol Evening Post*. (12)
2. The problem with a lot of content analysis is that researchers are influenced by their own values and prejudices. Discuss this statement. (8)

A postcard of former prime minister Margaret Thatcher

OFFICIAL STATISTICS

15 PART

Official statistics are one of the most important secondary sources available for sociological research. They are produced in ever increasing numbers by local and national government bodies. Each year Her Majesty's Stationery Office publishes the *Annual Abstract of Statistics* and *Social Trends* both packed with a mass of statistical information on births and deaths, marriage and divorce, income and wealth, employment and unemployment, health, crime, education and housing. These and many other areas contained in their pages make up a large part of the subject matter of sociology.

Although official statistics are widely used by many sociologists, they cannot be used uncritically, they cannot be taken at face value. Some of the problems of using official statistics are examined in the following passage.

To produce statistics you must first define what you are looking at and then measure it in terms of this definition. Take the case of unemployment. The unemployed are officially defined as those claiming unemployment benefit. Using this definition the Department for Education and Employment publishes monthly statistics which show the extent of unemployment. But if other definitions were used the figures might be very different. The unemployed could be defined as those wishing to find paid employment. This would include many people not entitled to unemployment benefit such as young people on training schemes and many married women. Measuring unemployment in terms of this definition would give a much higher figure than that provided by official statistics. (See Chapter 15, Part 11 for a discussion on defining unemployment.)

Poverty provides another example of this type of problem. The poor are sometimes defined as those receiving income support. This pays a minimum income to meet basic needs such as food, clothing and housing. However many researchers argue that people are poor if they are unable to afford a reasonable standard of living, not just the bare necessities. In terms of this definition many people whose incomes are well above the income support level would be poor. The extent of poverty would therefore be much greater than that measured by official statistics on income support (see Chapter 6, Parts 1-4).

Thus, before they can make use of official statistics sociologists need to know exactly what is being measured. Even with this knowledge official statistics must be used with caution since they may well be inaccurate. They may not even produce accurate figures in terms of their own definitions of what they are measuring. Each year the Inland Revenue publishes statistics on the distribution of income in the population. These figures are based on income tax returns. Yet the returns are sometimes falsified by people trying to evade income tax. Suicide provides another example of the problem of accuracy. Official figures are based on coroners' decisions that particular deaths are suicides. Often this involves a difficult judgement. Many deaths officially certified as accidental or due to natural causes may well be suicides.

Finally, sociologists need to know why official statistics are compiled and produced in certain ways. For example, why do governments define and measure unemployment in one way and not another? Why do coroners tend to define certain types of death (eg deaths in motor vehicle crashes) as accidental? Answers to these questions are needed before official statistics can be properly understood and used in sociological research.

(adapted in part from 'Demystifying Social Statistics' edited by J. Irvine, I. Miles and J. Evans, Pluto, London, 1979)

Training scheme for repairing computers in Camden. Should these people be counted as unemployed?

QUESTIONS

1. Are definitions of unemployment and poverty based on official statistics reasonable? Explain your answer. (6)
2. Suggest why governments have not adopted the alternative definition of unemployment given in the passage. (4)
3. a) Before they can use official statistics sociologists need to know exactly what is being measured. Briefly explain why. (5)
   b) Even with this knowledge, official statistics have to be treated with caution. Why? (5)

THE COMPARATIVE METHOD

16 PART

Comparative studies make comparisons between different societies, different groups within the same society and between societies and groups over time. For example, Duncan Gallie compared workers in oil refineries in Britain and France in order to discover whether the same kind of production technology produced the same kind of behaviour at work. He found important differences between British and French workers. For instance, there were far more strikes in the French refineries. Because the technology was the same, Gallie concluded that the differences in behaviour were due to differences in the culture and history of the British and French working classes.

The comparative method helps sociologists to pinpoint what causes what. In terms of Gallie's study, the behaviour of British and French workers could not be explained by their actual work - there was little difference in the way oil was produced in the two countries.

The following passage looks at one of the most famous studies in sociology, *Suicide* by Emile Durkheim, first published in 1895.

The suicide rate is the number of suicides per million of the population per year. Durkheim compared different European countries and different social groups within the same country. In each case he found differences in the rate of suicide. For example, the suicide rate in Denmark from 1866-1870 was over nine times higher than the rate in Italy over the same period. Denmark is a Protestant country, Italy a Catholic country. Did the difference in suicide rates have anything to do with religion?

Durkheim then compared Protestant and Catholic groups within the same society. Again he found the suicide rates for Protestants were higher than those for Catholics. Durkheim argued that Catholics form a close-knit religious community which provides strong moral and social support for its members. By comparison, Protestants are socially isolated and community support for the individual is much weaker. It is this isolation, Durkheim argued, which leads to higher rates of suicide.

If social isolation is the key to understanding suicide rates then it should show up in other comparisons. In addition to Protestants and Catholics, Durkheim compared the following groups.

City dwellers - Rural dwellers
Older adults - Younger adults
Unmarried - Married
Married without children - Married with children

In each case he found that the group on the left had a higher suicide rate than the group on the right. Durkheim argued that members of each group on the left are more socially isolated than those on the right. For example, married couples without children have fewer ties to bind them together than married couples with children.

(adapted from 'Suicide' by Emile Durkheim, Routledge & Kegan Paul, London, 1970)

QUESTIONS

1. Show how Durkheim used the comparative method. (3)
2. What are the strengths of the comparative method? (3)
3. Suggest how the first of each of the following pairs can be seen as more socially isolated than the second. (6)
   City dwellers : Rural dwellers
   Older adults : Younger adults
   Unmarried : Married
4. In what ways does the woman in the picture fit Durkheim's explanation of suicide? (2)
5. Durkheim used official statistics on suicide in his research. What problems might this produce? (See Part 15.) (6)

The Maniac Father and The Convict Brother Are Gone - The Poor Girl, Homeless, Friendless, Deserted, Destitute, and Gin Mad, Commits Self Murder.
(from a series of illustrations entitled 'The Drunkard's Children' drawn by George Cruikshank in 1848)

SOCIAL STRATIFICATION

People might be equal in the sight of God but they are far from equal in society. In every known human society there is some form of social inequality. In particular, some people have more wealth, power and prestige than others. In many societies there are fairly clearcut divisions between social groups. Thus in Western societies people can be divided into social classes. Class is one form of social stratification. Social stratification may be defined as a system in which social groups can be ranked, one above the other, usually in terms of wealth, power and prestige.

There are many forms of social stratification. This chapter concentrates on social class in Western society but it also considers the feudal system of medieval Europe, the caste system of traditional India, and slavery, both past and present.

Social class is a relatively 'open' system of social stratification. This means that there is a fairly high rate of social mobility or movement from one level or stratum to another. Thus it is by no means unusual for a person born into the working class to become upwardly mobile and spend his adult life as a member of the middle class. By comparison, feudalism, caste and slavery are 'closed'. There is relatively little social mobility and most people remain members of the stratum into which they were born.

THE FEUDAL SYSTEM

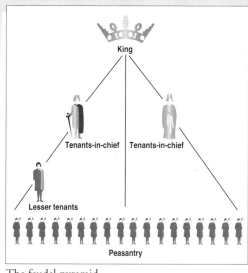

The feudal pyramid

By AD 1000, Europe was emerging from the upheavals of Dark Age migrations and Viking raids. But warfare among powerful families continued to form part of everyday life. Endless fighting created a need for two distinct social classes: highly trained warriors and a protected peasantry, whose chief duty was to keep the warriors well fed and clothed.

Thus arose the social order called feudalism. This pattern of society developed differently in different places, and it endured much longer in some areas than in others. (It survived, for instance, until the 20th century in much of Eastern Europe.) But it held its greatest sway during the Middle Ages.

The word 'feudalism' comes from the medieval Latin *feudum*, meaning a piece of land granted in return for services. Such grants date back to the years when Roman rule was collapsing. Because Roman law no longer protected small landowners from invading barbarians, the landowners sought protection from powerful neighbours. The neighbours supplied military aid in return for farm produce and services. In contrast, big landowners who needed military help paid for it by granting some of their land to knights-at-arms.

This practice also found favour with the Germanic peoples. By the 10th century, force of arms had raised many barbarian chiefs to kingship. Equipped with the powers of lawmaker, judge and general, they brought feudal government to wide areas of Western Europe - first France, then Germany, England and Scandinavia. Common to all systems was this main feature: the king, regarded as the owner of all land, granted estates ('fiefs') to his vassals. These were either nobles who inherited their estates, or people to whom the king actually granted land in return for a given number of soldiers. The greatest vassals were dukes, counts and abbots and these in turn were likely to have vassals of their own. At the base of the pyramid stood thousands upon thousands of peasants and serfs. There was little social mobility in the feudal system. Kings and nobles were usually succeeded by their eldest sons. Peasants and serfs had little opportunity to rise in the social hierarchy and most plodded on in their fathers' footsteps.

Ownership and control of land formed the basis of the feudal system. Land was the main form of wealth and the source of power and prestige. Medieval Europe was an agricultural society, therefore land formed the foundation of the economy. Its importance can be seen from the demands of the followers of William, Duke of Normandy, who conquered England in 1066. In the words of the historian, M. Bloch, 'We want lands', said the Norman lords who refused the gifts of jewels, arms and horses offered by their duke'.

Our most detailed knowledge of medieval feudal rule comes from England's *Domesday Book*, a census made by William I (1066-87). Though in name William owned all England, he kept only part of it for himself. He granted the rest to 1,500 chief nobles and churchmen, (known as tenants-in-chief), who swore loyalty and undertook to perform two important services for him. First, they advised him in his council. Second, they provided knights and men-at-arms for his army. To provide these troops the tenants-in-chief found it necessary to subdivide most of their lands among some 8,000 lesser tenants, notably knights-at-arms. In exchange for their land, the knights promised military service. In turn, the knights split some of their lands among peasant farmers.

Medieval law recognised two sorts of peasants: freemen and serfs. Freemen often held their land in return for part-time military service as men-at-arms. But it was the serfs who made up the vast majority - as much as 95% - of Europe's population. Unlike the freemen, serfs were not allowed to work or travel where they pleased. Oaths of life-long obedience tied them to their landholding. They and their descendants had to farm their lord's land and pay him special dues. They even required their lord's permission to marry.

In spite of these obligations, serfs were not slaves. They had rights dating back to the time when they first accepted serfdom in return for military protection. For example, they had a right to graze their cattle on common lands that - strictly speaking - belonged to the lord, and to send their pigs to feed in his forest.

In short, an intricate web of rights and duties bound serf, freeman, knight, noble and king to one another. Under this feudal system, everyone got some benefits. But the peasants benefited least. Though owed military protection in return for servitude, they often suffered from the nobles' quarrels; one lord was likely to annoy another by assaulting his peasants. So there were frequent peasant revolts. The lords feared such uprisings more than anything else. In fact, peasant revolt was often the only thing that could temporarily make the nobles stop fighting one another and close ranks.

(adapted from 'History: Civilisation from its Beginnings' edited by Alan Bullock, Macdonald, London, 1962, pp156-7)

Villagers paying taxes to the lord

QUESTIONS

1. Which of the following terms best describes status in the feudal system, a) ascribed, b) achieved? Briefly explain your choice. (2)
2. Which of the following terms best describes the feudal system of stratification, a) open, b) closed? Briefly explain your choice. (2)
3. Why was land so important in the feudal system? (4)
4. Why is land much less important in social class systems of stratification? (6)
5. What is the connection between military power, military service and land in the feudal system? (6)

2 PART CASTE

In India the caste system has existed for several thousand years. Even today its influence is still strong, particularly in rural areas, though in towns and cities it is tending to break down. The system is based in part on Hindu religious beliefs which provide justification and support for this form of social stratification. The following passage describes the caste system in Cochin, a state on the Malabar coast in southwest India.

1 The caste system

A caste is a group of families bearing a common name and claiming descent from a common ancestor. Each caste is divided into a number of sub-castes or jatis each of which specialises in a particular occupation - there are carpenter jatis, goldsmith jatis, potter jatis and so on. People's position in the system is fixed or ascribed at birth. They automatically belong to the same caste and usually follow the same occupation as their parents. Castes are endogamous social groups which means that a person must marry within his or her caste.

The castes of Cochin form a system of social stratification with those at the top having more wealth, power and prestige than those at the bottom. In Hindu society the higher castes are believed to be more pure in religious terms than the lower

castes. Members of the lowest stratum are defined as unclean, base and impure. These beliefs are reflected in the jobs people do and in the social relationships between members of different castes. For example, those at the base of the system perform unclean and degrading tasks such as the disposal of dead animals. Members of the higher castes regard contact with such people as polluting. They may even call out as they walk along the road so that low caste members will move to one side and not pollute the air they breathe.

The highest stratum in Cochin society is the Khshatriya caste. It is made up of members of the royal family who rule the state. They are relatively few in number but are extremely wealthy, owning large estates.

A Brahmin priest

Untouchables have been officially renamed Harijans in an attempt to remove the stigma attached to their former name. This picture shows a Harijan woman.

Members of the fourth caste perform personal services for the Brahmins and Nayars. This service caste includes teachers, barbers, washermen and weavers. They are able to approach members of higher castes without polluting them.

The Untouchables form the base of the caste system. They are the largest social grouping and include agricultural labourers, fishermen, potters and a wide variety of manual workers. Contact with Untouchables pollutes members of higher castes. Even if the shadow of an Untouchable falls across the food of a Brahmin it will render it unclean. Untouchables are despised by their social superiors and their occupations are considered degrading and impure.

The caste system is reflected in living arrangements. The magnificent palaces of the royal family stand in sharp contrast to the squalid huts of the Untouchables. In a typical settlement the houses of the Brahmins and Nayars are set apart in their own compounds. They are grouped around the temples and ceremonial baths. Members of the service caste live nearby. However, the Untouchables are segregated from other members of the caste system. They live on the outskirts of villages or in their own communities often in the middle of paddy fields.

(adapted from 'Habitat, Economy and Society' by C. Daryll Forde, Methuen, London, 1963)

QUESTIONS

1. What determines a person's caste position? (2)
2. Assuming that the rules of the caste system are strictly obeyed, how much social mobility would there be? Briefly explain your answer. (3)
3. What are the differences in the way a person obtains his or her occupational role in Hindu society and modern Britain? (3)
4. What advantages does an individual enjoy as a result of being born into a higher caste? (3)
5. What is the connection between religion and social status in the caste system? (3)
6. How does the location of people's homes reflect the caste system? Suggest possible similarities between this and the connection between housing location and social class in Britain. (6)

2 Caste conflict

The government of India led by V.P. Singh was determined to raise the status of the lower castes. In 1990 it reserved half of all government jobs for the Untouchables. Previously only members of the upper castes obtained these jobs. The upper castes felt they had no option: they must stand together and declare caste war.

Riots broke out in every city as high caste students fought police, disrupted traffic and derailed trains. Several high caste students doused themselves with petrol and set themselves ablaze in protest against government policy.

'In old times, these Untouchables were oppressed, but not today,' said Shyam Vyas, the students' leader. He shook his head

The Brahmin caste forms the second level of the caste system. The Brahmins are holy men whose high social standing comes from the belief that they are religiously pure. Many devote their lives to prayer and study and are regarded as the source of wisdom and truth. Because of this Brahmins act as advisers to the royal household.

The third caste is known as the Nayar. Traditionally members of this caste were the warriors of Cochin. They trained their sons in the use of the sword and the lance and served the royal family. Nowadays, they are usually landowners, earning their living by farming. Differences in prestige and purity are clearly seen from the way a Nayar addresses a Brahmin. He refers to his own house as a dung heap, to his clothes as spiders' webs and to his food as raw rice. But he refers to the Brahmin's house as a noble residence, to his food as ambrosia (food of the gods) and to his teeth as pearls.

A high caste student sets fire to himself.

with horror. 'If they get government jobs, everything will break down.'

'They will be wanting to marry high caste girls,' said his assistant, Arvind Chaudary.

'And anyway,' pointed out a third student, 'if there is no person to sweep the roads, where will the dust be going?'

(adapted from 'Caste Wars' by W. Dalrymple, 'Observer Magazine', 2.12.90)

QUESTIONS

1. Why did many members of the high castes violently oppose V. P. Singh's measures? (10)
2. The example of caste conflict has certain similarities with other attempts to break down stratification systems eg 'racial stratification' in the USA and Apartheid in South Africa. Suggest reasons for these similarities. (10)

PART 3 — SLAVERY

Slavery has existed in many societies. For example, in the final years of the Roman Empire the city of Rome contained some 200,000 slaves, one fifth of its population. Although there are different types of slavery, they have certain things in common. Slaves are not free, they are owned by other people. They are chattels - things that can be bought and sold. Their children are born into slavery and become the property of their masters. There is little chance to escape from slavery and become a free person. Thus a society based on slavery has a closed stratification system with very little social mobility. The status of slaves is ascribed.

The following passages look at slavery in the United States in the first half of the 19th century and slavery in Sudan in the mid-1990s. The first passage contains extracts from the autobiography of Frederick Douglass (1817-1895) who was born and raised a slave in the state of Maryland.

Slavery in the USA

My mother and I were separated when I was but an infant - before I knew her as my mother. Frequently, before the child has reached its twelfth month, its mother is taken away from it and hired out on some farm a considerable distance off, and the child is placed under the care of an old woman, too old for field labour.

My first master's name was Anthony. He was a cruel man

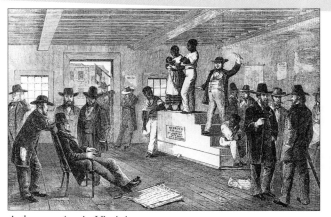

A slave auction in Virginia

Slaves on a Louisiana sugar plantation in the early 1860s

hardened by a long life of slaveholding. He would at times take great pleasure in whipping a slave. I have often been awakened at the dawn of day by the most heart-rending shrieks of an aunt of mine, who he would tie up to a joist, and whip her naked back until she was literally covered with blood.

Very soon I went to live with Mr and Mrs Auld. She very kindly commenced to teach me the A,B,C. After I had learned this, she assisted me in learning to spell words of three or four letters. Just at this point in my progress, Mr Auld found out what was going on, and at once forbade Mrs Auld to instruct me further, telling her that it was unlawful, as well as unsafe, to teach a slave to read. To use his own words, 'A nigger should know nothing but to obey his master - to do as he is told to do. Learning would *spoil* the best nigger in the world.'

(adapted from 'Narrative of the Life of Frederick Douglass, An American Slave', first published in 1845)

Slavery in Sudan

Alang Ajak's worst nightmare came true late one night when she was dreaming of her dead parents. It seemed that an intruder had grabbed her by the throat and was pressing burning hot metal on to her flesh.

As she opened her eyes, the terrified 10 year old realised it was no dream - she was the latest victim of slave branding, a practice adopted by some Sudanese Arabs who have revived slavery after more than 100 years.

The Sudanese trader who acquired her as a six year old decided to offer her as a gift to his son, Abdel Rahman, and his daughter-in-law, Zeinab. It was Zeinab who decided Alang should be branded 'in case you get lost among the other black bitches'. Displaying the scar that spreads above her knee, Alang, now 14, says of her former mistress: 'Zeinab was a very bad woman. She would make me work very long hours. If she ever found me crying for my real mother, she would take out a kitchen knife and shout, 'Shut up or I will slit your throat'.

According to Professor Ushari Ahmad Mahmoud, author of *Human Rights Violations in Sudan*: 'What usually happens is that Arab armed militia go into the southern villages or the Nuba mountains. They burn the villages, the men are killed if they don't escape, and the women and children are rounded up. These survivors are tied up and taken to the Arab North. They are divided into lots, and everyone takes his share to his town. He can then sell them. The women and children are put to work in the fields as shepherds and water carriers, doing domestic chores - all without pay.

Women and children are available as *khadam* - slave concubines (additional 'wives'). If they succeed in escaping and

Slavery in the 20th century. Villagers in the Nigerian bush captured by slave traders in 1972.

are caught, they could be killed. Slaves caught escaping are made to squat for hours on end, and the master's children are encouraged to ride them as if they were donkeys.

To prevent slaves from escaping, their masters will sometimes brand them; often it's a beta (the Greek letter B) or 8 sign on one of the ears.'

(adapted from 'Sudan Revives the Slave Trade' by Shyam Bhatia, 'Observer', 9.4.95)

QUESTIONS

1. Why were slaves in the USA often separated from their parents? (5)
2. Why did Frederick Douglass's master prevent him from learning to read and write? (5)
3. What does branding suggest about how owners see their slaves? (5)
4. Why do you think the master's children in Sudan are encouraged to 'ride' escaped slaves? (5)

4 PART — SOCIAL CLASS - THE REGISTRAR-GENERAL'S CLASSIFICATION

Class is the main system of social stratification in Western industrial society. There is no one accepted way of defining social class. Many researchers use occupation as the main indicator of a person's class position. Some use the economic rewards of different occupations as the basis for assigning them to

social classes. Some place more emphasis on the status or prestige of occupations and allocate them to classes on this basis. Others use occupational skill as the main indicator for social class.

The Registrar-General's social classification is the official UK classification of social class. It is widely used in government reports and surveys. For many years it was based on 'the general standing within the community of the occupations concerned'. In recent years increasing emphasis has been placed on occupational skill. By 1990 social classes were defined as groups of people 'with similar levels of occupational skill'. Despite these changes, the main outlines of the Registrar-General's classification have remained much the same over the past 60 years.

Table 1 The Registrar-General's social classification

		Examples of occupations in each class
Middle Class	**Class 1** Professional	Accountant, doctor, dentist, solicitor, university lecturer
	Class 2 Managerial and technical	Manager, teacher, librarian, nurse, farmer
	Class 3 (Non-manual) Clerical and minor supervisory	Clerk, shop assistant, policeman/woman, draughtsman/woman, sales representative
Working Class	**Class 3** (Manual) Skilled manual	Electrician, tailor, bus driver, printer, cook
	Class 4 Semi-skilled manual	Agricultural worker, postman/woman, telephone operator, fisherman/woman, bar staff
	Class 5 Unskilled manual	Railway porter, labourer, lorry driver's mate, window cleaner, office cleaner

QUESTIONS

1. Explain in your own words the two ways in which the Registrar-General has constructed his classification of social classes. (4)
2. Place the following occupations in the appropriate social classes using the guidelines provided by the Registrar-General in 1990. (5)
   a) bricklayer　　c) typist　　　　e) dishwasher
   b) architect　　　d) telephone supervisor
3. In view of the principles used by the Registrar-General for classifying occupations, why is the line dividing the middle and working classes drawn between Class 3 (Non-manual) and Class 3 (Manual)? (3)
4. The Registrar-General notes that occupation is linked to a number of social inequalities including education and economic factors. What does he mean by this? Give examples in your answer of links between occupation, education and economic factors. (8)

PART 5 — SOCIAL CLASS - A MARXIST VIEW

'Let the ruling classes tremble at a communist revolution. The proletarians have nothing to lose but their chains. They have a world to win. Working men of all countries unite.'

(from *Manifesto of the Communist Party* by Karl Marx and Friedrich Engels, 1848)

Karl Marx (1818-1883) provides a very different view of social class. He saw two main social classes in Western industrial societies, the ruling class or bourgeoisie made up of a minority of the population and the subject class or proletariat to which the majority belonged. The power of the ruling class comes from its ownership of the 'forces of production'. In an industrial society these include the factories and the machinery and raw materials used for manufacturing goods. Members of the proletariat own only their own labour which they hire out to the owners of industry in return for wages. The bourgeoisie is a non-producing class - it doesn't actually produce anything. Wealth in the form of manufactured goods is produced by the labour of the proletariat or working class. However, much of this wealth is taken from them by the owners of industry in the form of profits. Marx argued that the proletariat is exploited by the bourgeoisie. The bourgeoisie use them for their own benefit and harm the interests of the proletariat in the process.

Marx believed that members of the proletariat would eventually realise that they were being exploited and oppressed. They would then join together to overthrow the bourgeoisie either by force or by voting their own representatives into government. They would then set up a communist society which means that the forces of production would be communally owned, that is jointly owned by all members of society. Goods produced would be shared equally and everyone would work for the benefit of society as a whole.

Marx's views on class are part of his more general theory of the history of human society. Some sociologists argue that they are more appropriate to nineteenth century Europe and have little relevance today. However, Marx's ideas have had considerable influence within sociology.

The following extract presents some of Marx's ideas in the form of a conversation. A group of workmen sit drinking tea. One of them, a man named Owen, gives his explanation of the stark inequalities which he sees around him.

Employers, or rather exploiters of labour, profit-seeking shareholders, thieves, swindlers, bishops, financiers, capitalists, none of these people produce anything themselves, but by means of cunning and scheming they contrive between them to obtain possession of a very large proportion of the things produced by the labour of others.

The other class in society is those people who are engaged in useful work - the production of the benefits of civilisation, the refinements and comforts of life. These are the productive people, the working class.

Now we proceed to the 'share out' of those things produced. The people in division one are universally considered to be the most worthy and deserving, we give them two-thirds of the whole. The remainder is shared between the working people. You must not run away with the idea that in this class it is shared out equally between them. Some get more than their fair share, some get little, some get none at all. It is here that the 'battle of life' rages most fiercely.

And all those people in this class are so fully occupied in this dreadful struggle to secure a little that but few of them pause to enquire why there are not more of the things they are fighting for, or why it is necessary to fight at all.

(adapted from 'The Ragged Trousered Philanthropists' by Robert Tressall, Grant Richards Press, 1914)

Profits on their way to the bank. George Cruikshank's view of the exploitation of workers in the clothing industry in 1846.

QUESTIONS

1. With reference to Part 4, briefly compare Marx's view of class with the Registrar-General's social classification. (5)
2. Why does Owen talk about employers, thieves and swindlers in the same breath? (5)
3. Why do most members of the proletariat or working class tend to accept their position without question? (4)
4. How can the idea of 'divide and conquer' applied to the proletariat help to explain why the bourgeoisie rules successfully? (3)
5. Why does Marx urge working men of all countries to unite? (3)

CLASS, OCCUPATION AND INCOME

6 PART

Classifications of social class are often based on occupation, for example the Registrar-General's classification (see Part 4). There is a direct relationship between social class, defined in terms of occupation, and income from employment - in general, the higher a person's social class, the higher their occupational earnings.

Fringe benefits, sometimes known as 'perks', are a valuable addition to pay in many occupations. They include company pension schemes - a pension paid for by the employer and the employee which is additional to the state pension - company cars, meals and entertainment paid for by the employer. As a general rule, the higher a person's position in the class structure, the more fringe benefits they receive and the greater their value.

Figure 1 Average gross weekly earnings of full-time employees of different social classes (Great Britain, autumn 1994)

Class — Men, GB average: £388

Class	Occupation	Earnings
1	Professional occupations	£462
2	Intermediate occupations	£434
3 NM	Skilled occupations (non-manual)	£293
3 M	Skilled occupations (manual)	£276
4	Partly skilled occupations	£236
5	Unskilled occupations	£203

Women, GB average: £246

Professional occupations	£404
Intermediate occupations	£315
Skilled occupations (non-manual)	£207
Skilled occupations (manual)	£173
Partly skilled occupations	£163
Unskilled occupations	£159

0   £100   £200   £300   £400   £500   0   £100   £200   £300   £400   £500

Gross earnings are earnings before the deduction of income tax and national insurance contributions.

(adapted from 'Employment Gazette', June 1995, pLFS 32)

Table 1 Average gross weekly earnings of selected occupations

Full-time employees, Great Britain, April 1994

Waiter/waitress	£157
Bar staff	£165
Cleaner	£180
Receptionist	£182
Bricklayer/mason	£252
Carpenter/joiner	£261
Nurse	£316
Social worker	£332
Primary teacher	£394
Mechanical engineer	£511
Solicitor	£569
Medical practitioner	£746

(adapted from 'Social Trends', 1995, p87)

Opposite ends of the income scale

Table 2   Percentage of executives at each pay level having each of the following benefits

Salary band (£ a year)	Full use of company car %	Average list price of car £	Free fuel %	Help with house-buying %	At least 6 weeks holiday %	Enhanced pension %	Free medical insurance %	Profit sharing %	Tele-phone expense allowance %
20,000-25,000	51.2	12,815	26.6	4.4	3.1	4.7	51.0	17.6	19.7
25,000-30,000	72.7	13.526	35.1	5.1	3.4	4.8	54.6	13.9	23.7
30,000-35,000	84.2	15,101	46.1	6.5	4.4	9.4	62.0	15.1	25.7
35,000-40,000	90.7	16,270	51.5	4.6	7.4	16.1	64.8	13.5	30.0
40,000-45,000	90.0	17,641	59.7	4.8	12.1	26.7	64.0	15.9	37.1
45,000-50,000	92.8	19,032	60.9	5.4	16.9	34.2	66.5	19.3	41.6
50,000-60,000	94.3	19,801	67.6	9.4	16.1	41.1	69.5	19.6	40.9
60,000-70,000	95.0	21,513	69.2	8.2	14.7	52.5	70.6	22.5	42.7
70,000-80,000	93.3	23,490	72.0	12.9	16.5	48.4	68.0	22.7	36.9
80,000-90,000	94.9	26,360	79.0	10.9	16.8	60.1	68.1	33.3	43.5
90,000-100,000	93.9	27,823	77.6	8.2	23.2	54.1	65.3	34.7	48.0
100,000-120,000	92.4	27,631	74.5	11.5	23.7	60.5	67.5	29.3	38.2
Over 120,000	95.0	30,674	75.0	7.5	15.8	62.5	65.0	35.0	33.7
All ranks 1994	76.2	-	46.5	5.9	8.2	19.5	81.1	17.9	29.0

The above table is based on a survey carried out in July 1994 which covered nearly 9,000 executives, ranging from chairmen and managing directors to junior managers, employed by 662 companies.

(adapted from 'Financial Times', 7.12.1994)

QUESTIONS

1. a) Briefly summarise the link between social class and earnings shown in Figure 1. (2)
   b) What effect does gender (men and women) appear to have on earnings? (3)
2. Place the occupations in Table 1, on the basis of their earnings, in the classes shown in Figure 1. Decide which are primarily male and which primarily female occupations to help you make your choice. (7)
3. a) Briefly summarise the relationship between pay and fringe benefits indicated by Table 2. (4)
   b) Do they support the view that fringe benefits can provide a valuable addition to pay? (4)

7 PART   THE DISTRIBUTION OF INCOME

All researchers recognise that social class involves economic inequalities. Whereas Marxists give primary importance to inequalities in the distribution of wealth, particularly wealth in the form of ownership of the forces of production, other sociologists place equal if not more emphasis on income inequalities.

This part looks at the distribution of income in the UK. It uses three measures of income.

1. *Gross income* includes all income from wages, salaries, fringe benefits, pensions, investments and social security benefits such as income support and child benefit.

2. *Disposable income* is income after payment of income tax, national insurance contributions and local taxes (eg council tax). Disposable income is the amount of income people have available to spend or invest.

3. *Income after housing costs* is disposable income minus housing costs such as rent and mortgage payments.

Figure 1 and Table 1 are constructed in the following way. Households are divided into 5 groups of equal size (known as quintile groups). Those with the lowest income are placed at one end of the scale, through to those with the highest income at the other end.

Figure 1 Sources of gross household income: by income grouping, 1993 United Kingdom

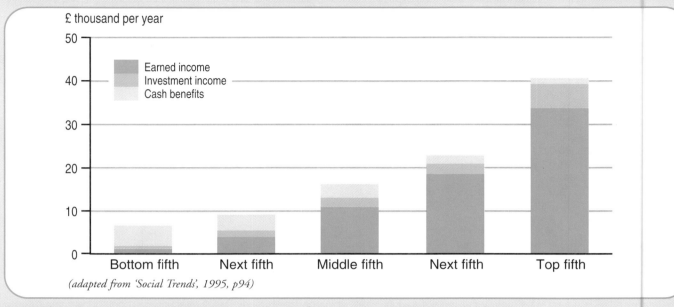

£ thousand per year

Earned income
Investment income
Cash benefits

Bottom fifth | Next fifth | Middle fifth | Next fifth | Top fifth

(adapted from 'Social Trends', 1995, p94)

Earned income includes wages and salaries and income from fringe benefits.
Investment income includes income from occupational pensions and shareholdings.
Cash benefits include income from social security payments such as income support.

Table 1 Household gross and disposable income

United Kingdom						£ per year
	Quintile groups of households					
	Bottom fifth	Next fifth	Middle fifth	Next fifth	Top fifth	All households
Gross income	£6,380	£9,370	£15,930	£22,780	£40,420	£18,980
Disposable income	£5,590	£8,170	£13,240	£18,250	£31,100	£15,270

(adapted from 'Social Trends', 1995, p93)

Figure 2 Income inequality, 1961-1991

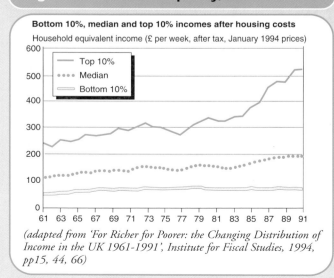

Bottom 10%, median and top 10% incomes after housing costs

Household equivalent income (£ per week, after tax, January 1994 prices)

Top 10%
Median
Bottom 10%

(adapted from 'For Richer for Poorer: the Changing Distribution of Income in the UK 1961-1991', Institute for Fiscal Studies, 1994, pp15, 44, 66)

Reasons for the growth of income inequality during the 1980s

- More people became dependent on state benefits, such as income support, due in part to higher unemployment and an increase in lone parent families.

- Occupational earnings rose more than prices. Since the early 1980s, benefit levels have been linked to prices. As a result benefits have grown more slowly than wages.

- Cuts in income tax from 1986 onwards have benefited those in higher income groups to a greater extent than those in middle and lower income groups.

- Between 1978 and 1992, salaries of higher income earners grew by 50% in real terms, those of middle groups by 35% while the wages of the low paid, in real terms, hardly changed at all.

(adapted from 'Inquiry into Income and Wealth' Volume 1, Joseph Rowntree Foundation, 1995, pp6-7)

'Pity the poor rich, crippled by taxation.' A cartoon from 1947

QUESTIONS

1. On the basis of Figure 1, would you describe the United Kingdom as an unequal society? Explain your answer. (2)
2. Using Figure 1 outline and suggest reasons for the differences between the bottom fifth and the top fifth in the proportion of income each derives from earnings, investments and benefits. (7)
3. Give reasons for the differences between gross and disposable income shown in Table 1. (2)
4. a) Briefly summarise the trend in income inequality indicated by Figure 2. (2)
   b) What could the government do to reduce this widening inequality? (7)

PART 8 — THE DISTRIBUTION OF WEALTH

The distribution of wealth is far more unequal than the distribution of income. The figures below are for *marketable wealth* owned by individuals. Marketable wealth is wealth that can be sold or cashed in. It includes land, company shares, houses, insurance policies and investments such as National Savings.

The most valuable item of marketable wealth for most people is the house they own and live in. However, if we look at the very rich, we find that many have large shareholdings in major companies. For example, the Cadbury and Sainsbury families own part of the companies which bear their names. Some of the very rich own vast areas of land. For example, around a third of the Scottish highlands is owned by less than 100 people.

Wealth inequalities have steadily narrowed for most of the 20th century but have stayed much the same since the early 1980s.

Table 1 Distribution of wealth, 1951-1992

United Kingdom						Percentages
	1951	1961	1971	1981	1991	1992
Marketable wealth						
Percentage of wealth owned by						
Most wealthy 1%	46	28	20	18	17	18
Most wealthy 5%	74	51	40	36	34	37
Most wealthy 10%	–	63	52	50	46	49
Most wealthy 25%	–	79	72	73	70	72
Most wealthy 50%	–	93	90	92	92	92
Total marketable wealth (£ billion)	–	55	113	565	1,801	1,811

– means no information available

(adapted from 'Distribution of Personal Wealth in Britain' by A.B. Atkinson and A.J. Harrison, University of Cambridge Press, Cambridge, 1978, p159; 'Social Trends', 1973, p111; 'Social Trends', 1995, p96)

The wealthy at play - grouse shooting in Scotland

'Hats for the Gentry', at the Royal Henley Regatta, an annual event frequented by the wealthy

Figure 1 Composition of marketable wealth, 1992

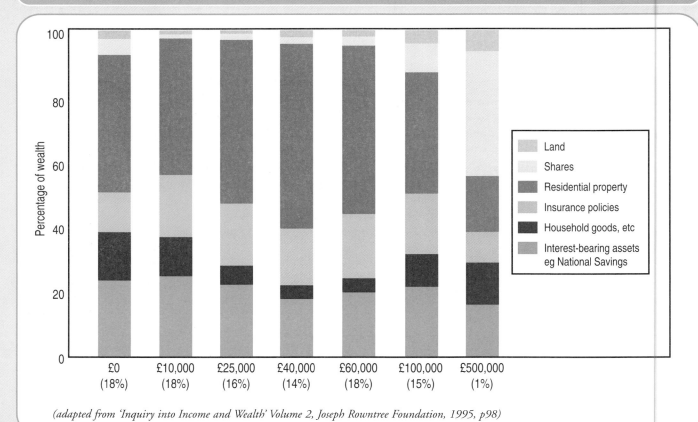

(adapted from 'Inquiry into Income and Wealth' Volume 2, Joseph Rowntree Foundation, 1995, p98)

The seven bars in the chart represent different levels of wealth holding, eg the first bar represents people with holdings under £10,000. The percentages in brackets are the percentage of the sample in each level, eg 1% of the sample owned wealth over £500,000. Each bar is divided into segments showing the composition of that group's wealth. For example, for those over £500,000, nearly 40% of their wealth is made up of shares.

QUESTIONS

1. a) From Table 1, what share of wealth in 1992 is owned by (i) the most wealthy 1%, (ii) the most wealthy 50%, (iii) the least wealthy 50%? (3)
   b) Briefly describe the trends in the distribution of wealth from 1951-1992. (4)
2. a) From Figure 1, what is the largest single source of wealth of (i) 99% and (ii) 1% of the population? (2)
   b) Suggest reasons for this difference. (4)
3. Use evidence from Table 1 and Figure 1 to assess the argument that Britain is a classless society. (7)

9 PART SOCIAL CLASS AND LIFE CHANCES

The German sociologist Max Weber (1864-1920) made the observation that a person's class position influences many areas of their life. In particular, class has an important effect on their *life chances*, that is their chances of obtaining those things defined as desirable and of avoiding those things defined as undesirable in society. According to Gerth and Mills, life chances include, 'Everything from the chance to view fine arts, the chance to remain healthy and grow tall, and if sick to get well again quickly, the chance to avoid becoming a juvenile delinquent and very crucially, the chance to complete an intermediary or higher education grade'. In general, the higher a person's class position, the better their life chances and the greater their opportunity to obtain and experience those things defined as desirable in their society. The relationship between social class and life chances is indicated in the following charts and tables.

Figure 1 Social class and unemployment, Great Britain, 1993

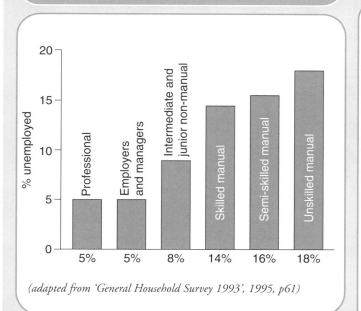

(adapted from 'General Household Survey 1993', 1995, p61)

Figure 2 Life chances

'Just dreaming, or do I have a real chance?'

Table 1 Social class and household goods, Great Britain, 1993

Percentage of households with:	Professional	Employers and managers	Intermediate non-manual	Junior non-manual	Skilled manual	Semi-skilled manual	Unskilled manual
Television							
colour	97	98	96	97	98	94	93
black and white	1	1	2	1	1	3	5
Video recorder	91	92	88	86	90	85	73
CD player	62	58	57	54	49	44	33
Home computer	51	41	38	26	29	24	17
Microwave oven	75	79	73	72	76	67	58
Deep freezer/fridge freezer	94	94	90	90	93	90	85
Washing machine	98	96	94	91	94	89	85
Tumble drier	65	68	60	51	58	53	43
Dishwasher	39	40	25	13	15	8	5
Telephone	99	98	97	91	90	84	72

(adapted from 'General Household Survey 1993', 1995 p24)

Table 2 Highest qualifications held by social class of their father, Great Britain, 1990-1991 (percentages)

	Professional	Employers and managers	Intermediate and junior non-manual	Skilled manual	Semi-skilled manual	Unskilled manual
Degree	32	17	17	6	4	3
Higher education	19	15	18	10	7	5
GCE A level	15	13	12	8	6	4
GCSE, grades A-C	19	24	25	21	19	15
GCSE, grades D-G	4	9	7	12	12	10
Foreign	4	4	4	3	2	2
No qualifications	7	19	18	40	50	60

Persons aged 25-59 not in full-time education

(adapted from 'Social Trends', 1994 p52)

Table 3 Social class and limiting longstanding illness, Great Britain, 1993

	Percentage who reported limiting longstanding illness	
	Males	Females
Professional	14	13
Employers and managers	17	18
Intermediate non-manual	16	21
Junior non-manual	18	25
Skilled manual	22	21
Semi-skilled manual	21	28
Unskilled manual	25	30

A limiting longstanding illness is a lengthy illness which limits people's activities.

(adapted from 'General Household Survey 1993', 1995, p87)

QUESTIONS

1. a) Briefly summarise the relationship between social class and unemployment indicated by Figure 1. (3)
   b) What effect might this have on class inequalities of income and wealth? (3)
2. Some items in Table 1 are more closely linked to social class than others. Briefly suggest reasons for this. (5)
3. Some people believe that there is equality of opportunity (everybody has an equal chance) in British society. Comment on this view in the light of Table 2. (5)
4. Some people argue that social class has little significance in today's society. Comment on this view in the light of Table 3. (4)

THE UNDERCLASS (1)

10 PART

In recent years a number of sociologists claim to have identified an *underclass* - a distinct class, below the working class, at the base of the class system. Other sociologists argue that the so-called underclass is simply the lowest level of the working class. They see no reason for identifying a new and distinct social class.

This part looks at the case for an underclass.

Members of the underclass are poor. They are often dependent on state benefits. Their numbers are growing and compared to the rest of society they are becoming poorer.

As Part 7, Figure 2 showed, the income gap between top and bottom steadily widened from 1961 to 1991. During this period the wages of the low paid hardly changed at all in real terms while those of higher paid groups grew steadily. At the same time social security benefits failed to keep up with the overall growth in wages. As a result, those dependent on state benefits fell further and further behind.

Figure 1 Individuals below half average income, 1961-1991

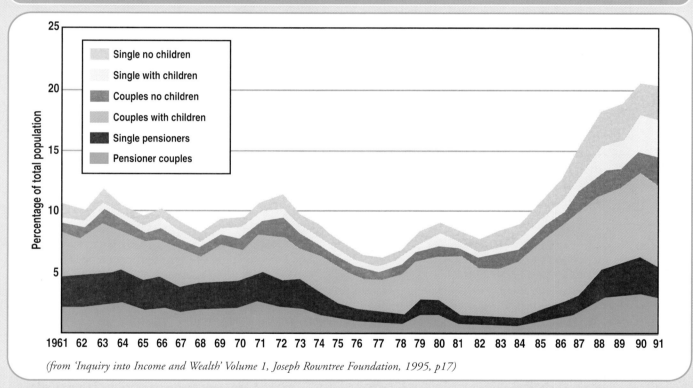

(from 'Inquiry into Income and Wealth' Volume 1, Joseph Rowntree Foundation, 1995, p17)

The number of people dependent on state benefits has grown rapidly in the 1980s and 1990s. Between 1979 and 1986 unemployment tripled to over three million people. Although the numbers have since gone down, they remain at very high levels compared to the 1960s and early 1970s, particularly for the young, ethnic minorities and the low skilled. The number of single parent families has risen sharply from 474,000 in 1961 to 1,400,000 (21% of all families with dependent children) in 1992. In 1993, 75% of single parent families were dependent on income support and a further 16% received family credit to top up low wages.

Two main reasons have been given for the emergence of the underclass - changes in government policy and changes in the economy. First, government policy. Many state benefits have declined in real value. They have failed to keep pace with the growth in wages of the higher and middle income earners. State benefits have been criticised as inadequate to meet the needs of the poor. In addition, government policy makes it difficult for many to take up employment. Paid employment can result in a reduction in income as benefits are reduced or removed. For single parents there is the additional cost of childcare which, if available, is often beyond their means.

Second, changes in the economy. These include the economic recession of the 1980s and early 1990s and the decline of manufacturing industry. This led to widespread unemployment, particularly in manual jobs. And there is no indication that lost manual jobs will return. The 'new jobs' of the 1980s and 1990s have tended to be in the service sector, often part time, temporary and low paid.

The above developments have led some sociologists to identify an emerging underclass whose members are trapped at the bottom of the class system. The direction of government policy and the economy suggests that the underclass will continue to grow.

(adapted from various sources including 'Sociology in Focus' by Paul Taylor et al, Causeway Press, Ormskirk, 1995)

Homelessness grew rapidly during the 1980s and 1990s. Those sleeping on the street are only the tip of the iceberg.

QUESTIONS

1. What is an underclass? (5)
2. Why is it seen as something new? (5)
3. Why is it seen as something which will continue to grow? (5)
4. Assuming an underclass exists, what might be done to reduce its numbers? (5)

PART 11

THE UNDERCLASS (2)

Some sociologists take a very different view of the underclass than that outlined in Part 10. One of the more extreme examples of an alternative view is given in the following passage. It is based on the writings of the American social scientist Charles Murray. (See Chapter 6, Part 6, for further discussion and criticism of Murray's views.)

For Charles Murray an underclass does not simply consist of those with the lowest income at the base of the class system. Instead, it consists of those with low income who behave in a certain way. In Murray's words, 'When I use the term *underclass* I am indeed focusing on a certain type of poor person defined *not* by his condition, eg long-term unemployed, but by his deplorable behaviour in response to that condition, eg unwilling to take the jobs that are available to him'.

Murray sees births outside marriage 'as the leading indicator of an underclass'. Such births often lead to single parent families, the majority of which are headed by women. When single parent families become widespread, they form the basis of and the 'breeding ground' for an underclass. And 'proof that an underclass has arrived is that large numbers of young, healthy, low-income males choose not to take jobs'. Many turn to crime (particularly violent street crime) and regular drug abuse. These are further characteristics of an underclass.

Many of these boys have grown up in a family without a father and male wage earner. As a result they lack the male role models of mainstream society. Within a female-headed family dependent on welfare benefits, the disciplines and responsibilities of mainstream society tend to break down. Murray believes that work must become the 'centre of life' for young men. They must learn the disciplines of work and respect for work. And they must learn to become 'real fathers', accepting the responsibilities of parenthood. However, 'Little boys don't naturally grow up to be responsible fathers and husbands. They don't naturally grow up knowing how to get up every morning at the same time and go to work. They don't naturally grow up thinking that work is not just a way to make money, but a way to hold one's head high in the world.' Murray believes that the socialisation and role models required to develop these attitudes are often lacking in female-headed, low-income families.

Although Murray appears to blame members of the underclass for their situation, he places most of the blame on government policy. It is the availability of overgenerous welfare benefits which have allowed the underclass to develop. Members of the underclass have become dependent on the state which has funded their unproductive lifestyles. Murray's solution is a sharp reduction or withdrawal of welfare benefits in order to force people to take responsibility for their own lives. Unless this is done, the underclass will tend to reproduce itself from generation to generation.

(adapted from 'Losing Ground' by Charles Murray, Basic Books, New York, 1984 and 'The Emerging British Underclass' by Charles Murray, Institute of Economic Affairs, London, 1990)

Sugar Daddy!

QUESTIONS

1. How, in Murray's view, is the underclass passed on from one generation to the next? (5)
2. Look at the picture and cartoon. To what extent, if at all, does each support Murray's view? (5)
3. Murray has often been criticised for blaming members of the underclass for their situation and for picturing them as irresponsible scroungers and layabouts. Is this a fair criticism of Murray? (5)
4. Do you agree that state benefits create an underclass? Give reasons for your answer using information from Part 10 and Part 11. (5)

12 PART SOCIAL MOBILITY

Social mobility refers to movement from one stratum to another in a system of social stratification. Social mobility can be either upward, for example moving from the working to the middle class, or downward. The most common way of measuring social mobility is to compare the status of sons with that of their fathers. Thus if the son of an unskilled manual worker becomes a labourer he is not socially mobile, but if he becomes an accountant he is upwardly mobile. In terms of the Registrar-General's classification he has moved from Class 5, the class into which he was born, to Class 1. The following passage examines some of the findings of a large scale study of social mobility in England and Wales.

In 1980, a group of sociologists at Nuffield College, Oxford, published the results of a study of social mobility in England and Wales. The 'Oxford Mobility Study' was conducted in 1972 and based on a sample of 10,000 men. Occupation was used to indicate a person's class with the main emphasis being given to the economic rewards of occupations. The authors identified seven classes which they then simplified into a three class system.

1. The Service Class: people with well paid jobs with career prospects in the professions, national and local government, senior management and higher technical jobs.

2. The Intermediate Class: people with routine non-manual jobs, clerks, sales personnel, self-employed with small businesses, supervisors, lower-grade technicians.

3. The Working Class: Skilled, semi-skilled and unskilled manual workers, including farm labourers.

One aim of the study was to discover whether Britain had become a more open society. Have, for example, the chances for a working class boy to reach the service class improved over the years. The study compared the social mobility rates of men born between 1908-1917 with those born between 1938-1947. Findings on the first group are shown in Figure 1 as 'then', those for the second group as 'now'.

The findings of the Oxford Mobility Study may be simply expressed as the 1:2:4 Rule of Relative Hope. This rule states that whatever the chance of a working class boy of reaching the service class, a boy from the intermediate class has twice the chance and a boy from the service class four times the chance.

The 1:2:4 rule applies to both groups of men in the survey (ie those born 1908-1917 and those born 1938-1947). Figure 1 compares the chances of the two groups of reaching the service class. Although the percentage of working class boys entering the service class has risen (from 14% to 18%) so has the percentage of those from the intermediate and service classes. The relative chances of children from each social class background has remained unaltered at approximately 1:2:4.

At first glance this might not make sense. How can considerably more people enter the service class over the years? This is due simply to a change in the occupational structure. During the period covered by the survey the number of service class occupations has nearly doubled. These changes are shown in Figure 2. As a result of changes in the occupational structure there is far more room at the top of the class system.

(adapted from 'The 1:2:4 Rule of Class in Britain' by P. Kellner and P. Wilby, 'Sunday Times', 13.1.1980, p13)

Figure 1

Your chance of ending up in service class
Then if your father was:

Working 14%
Intermediate 25%
Service 55%

Now if your father is:

Working 18%
Intermediate 30%
Service 62%

Figure 2

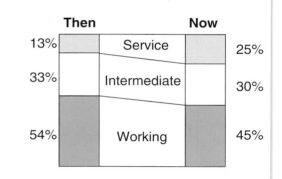

	Then		Now
Service	13%		25%
Intermediate	33%		30%
Working	54%		45%

There's more room at the top but the odds are still against the working class boy

QUESTIONS

1. Outline the changes in the occupational structure during the period covered by the study. (4)
2. What are the chances of those born into the intermediate class in a) 1908-17 and b) 1938-47 of reaching the service class? (2)
3. If Britain were a completely open society, would the chances of those born into the working class of entering the service class be, a) the same b) better or c) worse than those born into the service class? Briefly explain your answer. (4)
4. Why are more working class boys entering the service class in recent years? (2)
5. The relative chances of boys from each social class of reaching the service class has remained unchanged. Show that this is the case with reference to the figures in Figure 1. (4)
6. Briefly suggest why those born at the top have the greatest chance of obtaining service class jobs. (4)

TALKING ABOUT CLASS

The following quotations are from British Conservative Prime Ministers. They question some of the views put forward in this chapter.

'In the world in which we now live, divisions into class are outmoded and meaningless. We are all working people who basically want the same things.'

Margaret Thatcher, 1988

Margaret Thatcher

QUESTION

Comment on each of the quotations with some reference to material from this chapter. (20)

'I believe that in the next ten years we will have to continue to make changes that will genuinely produce across the whole of this country a genuinely classless society in which people can rise to whatever level that their own abilities and their own good fortune may take them from wherever they started.'

John Major, 1992

John Major

THINKING ABOUT INEQUALITY

The following passages look at the possibility of creating a fairer and more equal society. The first is taken from *The Road to Wigan Pier* by the English novelist George Orwell. Writing in the 1930s, he argues that class is so much a part of each and every one of us that to abolish class means changing part of ourselves.

The second passage is based on Michael Young's *The Rise of the Meritocracy* which imagines a society in the year 2034 based on meritocratic principles. In this society every individual achieves his or her position solely on the basis of merit. It is a completely open society with equality of opportunity for all its members.

The third passage is based on a short story entitled *Harrison Bergeron* by the American writer Kurt Vonnegut Jr. It pictures a completely equal society. Those with above average talents and attributes are penalised, those who are below average are compensated. Everybody is brought up or down until everybody is equal.

Class distinctions

The fact that has got to be faced is that to abolish class distinctions means abolishing a part of yourself. Here am I, a typical member of the middle class. It is easy for me to say that I want to get rid of class distinctions, but nearly everything I think and do is a result of class distinctions. All my notions - notions of good and evil, of pleasant and unpleasant, of funny and serious, of ugly and beautiful - are essentially *middle-class* notions; my taste in books and food and clothes, my sense of honour, my table manners, my turns of speech, my accent, even

the characteristic movements of my body, are the products of a special kind of upbringing and a special niche about half-way up the social hierarchy. When I grasp this, I grasp that it is no use clapping a proletarian on the back and telling him that he is as good a man as I am; if I want real contact with him, I have got to make an effort for which very likely I am unprepared. For to get outside the class-racket I have got to suppress not merely my private snobbishness, but most of my other tastes and prejudices as well. I have got to alter myself so completely that at the end I should hardly be recognisable as the same person.

(adapted from 'The Road to Wigan Pier' by George Orwell, first published in 1937)

A meritocratic society

It was the year 2034. Everybody in society had an equal chance to rise to the top or sink to the bottom. Status was achieved on

the basis of merit. Those who combined high intelligence with hard work rose to the highest positions. No longer did family connections or inherited wealth influence people's place in the stratification system. The ideal of equality of opportunity had become a reality.

But there were problems. In a meritocracy those at the bottom are clearly inferior. They have had the same chance as everybody else, so are unable to divert blame from themselves by pointing to an unfair system. Their failure is plain for all to see. As a result they become demoralised and lose their self-respect.

Those at the top have clearly earned their position. No longer can luck or accident of birth explain their high status. Recognising their superiority, they become arrogant and overbearing, despising those beneath them.

Resenting this, a protest movement develops in the lower strata. It calls for the meritocracy to be replaced by a truly classless society. This society would evaluate people not just according to their intelligence or education but also according to their kindliness and their courage, their imagination and sensitivity, their sympathy and generosity. It would encourage individual differences and it would respect the dignity of every human being.

(adapted from 'The Rise of the Meritocracy' by Michael Young, Penguin, Harmondsworth, 1961)

An equal society

The year was 2081, and everybody was finally equal. They weren't only equal before God and the law. They were equal every which way. Nobody was smarter than anybody else. Nobody was better looking than anybody else. Nobody was stronger or quicker than anybody else. All this equality was due to the 211th, 212th and 213th Amendments to the constitution, and the unceasing vigilance of agents of the United States Handicapper General.

George and Hazel Bergeron were watching television. Their fourteen year old son Harrison no longer lived with them. Hazel had a perfectly average intelligence, which meant she couldn't think about anything except in short bursts. And George, while his intelligence was way above normal, had a little mental handicap radio in his ear. He was required by law to wear it at all times. It was tuned to a government transmitter. Every twenty seconds or so, the transmitter would send out some sharp noise to keep people like George from taking unfair advantage of their brains.

'That was a real pretty dance, that dance they just did,' said Hazel, referring to the ballerinas on TV. 'Yup,' said George. He tried to think a little about the ballerinas. They weren't really very good - no better than anybody else would have been, anyway. They were burdened with sashweights and bags of birdshot, and their faces were masked, so that no one, seeing a free and graceful gesture or a pretty face, would feel like something the cat dragged in. George was toying with the vague notion that maybe dancers shouldn't be handicapped. But he didn't get very far with it before another noise in his ear radio scattered his thoughts.

The television program was suddenly interrupted for a news

bulletin. 'Harrison Bergeron, age fourteen,' the announcer stated, 'has just escaped from jail, where he was held on suspicion of plotting to overthrow the government. He is a genius and an athlete, is under-handicapped, and should be regarded as extremely dangerous.'

The shriek of a door being torn from its hinges interrupted the announcement. Harrison Bergeron filled the screen. He tore off his handicaps - the weights which bowed his seven foot frame, the tremendous pair of earphones which were his mental handicap, the spectacles with wavy lenses which made him half blind and the red rubber ball nose which offset his good looks.

'I am the Emperor!' cried Harrison. 'Do you hear? I am the Emperor! Everybody must do what I say at once!' He stamped his foot and the studio shook.

'I shall now select my Empress!' he said. 'Let the first woman who dares rise to her feet claim her mate and her throne!' A moment passed, and then a ballerina arose, swaying like a willow.

Harrison plucked the mental handicap from her ear, snapped

off her physical handicaps with marvellous delicacy. Last of all, he removed her mask.
She was blindingly beautiful.

'Now,' said Harrison, taking her hand, 'shall we show the people the meaning of the word dance? Music!' he commanded.

The musicians scrambled back into their chairs, and Harrison stripped them of their handicaps, too. 'Play your best,' he told them, 'and I'll make you barons and dukes and earls.' Harrison placed his big hands on the girl's tiny waist, letting her sense the weightlessness that would soon be hers.

And then, in an explosion of joy and grace, into the air they sprang!

It was then that Diana Moon Glampers, the Handicapper General, came into the studio with a double-barrelled ten-gauge shotgun. She fired twice, and the Emperor and the Empress were dead before they hit the floor.

It was then that the Bergerons' television tube burned out.
'You been crying?' George said to Hazel.
'Yup,' she said.
'What about?' he said.
'I forget,' she said. 'Something real sad on television.'
'What was it?' he said.
'It's all kind of mixed up in my mind,' said Hazel.
'Forget sad things,' said George.
'I always do,' said Hazel.

(adapted from 'Harrison Bergeron' in 'Welcome to the Monkey House' by Kurt Vonnegut Jr., Panther, St Albans, 1972)

QUESTIONS

1. Read the passage on class distinctions. Orwell was writing in the 1930s. Do you think his ideas are applicable today? Give reasons for your answer. (6)
2. Read the passage on a meritocratic society.
   a) Is a meritocracy desirable? (4)
   b) Is a meritocracy possible? (4)
3. Read the passage on an equal society. Is equality possible in a free society? Give reasons for your answer. (6)

RACE AND ETHNICITY

The previous chapter looked at various forms of social stratification - the feudal system, caste and social class. This chapter is concerned with ethnic stratification. It begins with the idea of race arguing that this idea is not particularly useful for understanding the position of non-white minority groups in society. Instead it argues that such groups are more usefully seen as ethnic groups and as the victims of racism. The chapter examines the idea of ethnicity and the case for and against ethnic subcultures. It looks at the various aspects of racism and the evidence for racism in British society. Ethnic stratification is analysed in terms of the life chances of members of ethnic minority groups. Ethnic conflict is examined in terms of the riots in English cities in the 1980s and 1990s, 'racial' attacks in Britain during the 1990s and 'ethnic cleansing' in the former Yugoslavia. The chapter closes with a case study on scapegoating - the Jews in Nazi Germany.

PART 1 · THE IDEA OF RACE

The following passage looks at some of the ways in which the term race has been used. From a sociological viewpoint race is a social definition, a social construction - a race is simply a group of people who see themselves, or are seen by others, as a race.

Human beings are all members of the same species. This means that if any male and female mate successfully they will produce offspring who are themselves human beings. However, not all human beings look alike and this has led to people being classified into types or 'races' in terms of physical appearance. One of the most commonly used classifications divides the human species into three groups, Mongoloid, Negroid and Caucasoid, as shown in Table 1.

This is a very broad classification. It is often subdivided - for example, the category Caucasoid is sometimes divided into 'whites', 'Asian Indians' and various other groups.

The idea of race, as summarised in Table 1, is based mainly on physical appearance. Large numbers of people are grouped together and called a race because they are said to look alike. However many biologists reject this view of race as unscientific. On the basis of people's outward appearance, it is possible to divide the human species into any number of races. For example, in Britain people with red hair, blue eyes and a pale skin could be classified as a

Ruins of Zimbabwe civilisation

separate race in terms of their physical appearance.

Many biologists reject the whole idea of different races. They argue that the genetic makeup of all human beings is basically the same. The minor variations that do exist are so small that it makes little sense to talk about different races.

From what has been said so far it can be argued that 'races' are simply social definitions or categories. A race is simply a

Table 1 · Classification of racial groups

Racial Group	Eyes	Hair	Skin	Face	Main location
Mongoloid	Black 'slanted'	Black straight	Yellow-reddish brown	Flat, high cheekbones, sparse beard	S & E Asia, N & S America, Pacific
Negroid	Brown	Black tightly curled	Dark brown-black	Broad nose, wide nostrils, thick lips, sparse beard	Sub-Saharan Africa
Caucasoid	Light blue to dark brown	Straight, wavy curly, balding more common	White to dark brown	Narrow nose, thin lips, more facial hair	Europe, M East, N Africa, India

group of people who see themselves as a race and/or are seen by other people as a race.

At different times and places all sorts of racial classifications have been devised. In Germany in the 1930s and 40s the Nazis divided Europeans into a number of racial groupings from blonde, blue eyed, white Aryans - the 'master race' - to dark haired brown eyed, olive skinned Mediterraneans. In South Africa today the main divisions are seen to be between whites, coloureds ('mixed races') and blacks.

Simply because race is a social definition does not mean it should be dismissed as unimportant. People make race important because, on the basis of supposed racial differences, they reject, discriminate against and kill each other. The idea of race is one of the main factors dividing the human species. This is partly because many people believe that each 'race' has certain inborn characteristics. These characteristics are often seen as undesirable. Thus Western 'whites' sometimes see themselves as superior to and more intelligent than other 'races'. Few, if any, sociologists would support this view. They point to the evidence of history to disprove it. Thus in Africa the Songhai, Ashanti and Zimbabwe civilisations flourished when Europe was in the Dark Ages. John Goldthorpe has argued that if we look at the world in the year 1600, China was probably the most advanced nation with India and Arabia close behind. This type of evidence strongly suggests that there is no basis to the claim that one so-called 'race' is superior to another.

(adapted in part from 'The Sociology of Race' by John Richardson and John Lambert, Causeway Press, Ormskirk, 1985)

The Great Wall of China, over 1,500 miles long, built in the 3rd century BC.

QUESTIONS

1. Classifications of races based on physical appearance are unscientific. Why? (3)
2. Why do some biologists reject the idea of different races? (3)
3. Race is simply a social definition.
   a) What does this mean? (2)
   b) Why is the idea of race important even though it may simply be a social definition? (6)
4. How can the evidence of history lead us to reject the view that some so-called races are superior to others? (6)

2 PART — THE IDEA OF ETHNICITY

The term race suggests that a group is in some way biologically different from the rest of the human species. The term ethnic group suggests that people are culturally different. Usually the term is used to refer to a group within a larger society - an ethnic minority group. The following passage looks at the idea of ethnicity.

An ethnic group can be defined as a group within a larger society whose members share a common origin, have a sense of belonging to the group, have a distinctive subculture - certain norms and values which differ from those of the mainstream culture - and who mix or interact regularly with each other. This view of ethnicity can be illustrated by looking at blacks in the USA.

1) They are a minority group in society - they make up around 12% of the population.

2) They share a common origin - they were transported as slaves from West Africa.

3) They have a sense of belonging to the group - phrases like 'I'm Black and I'm Proud' and 'Black is Beautiful' suggest a common identity, as does the term African-American.

4) They have certain distinctive aspects of culture, for example, black music and dialect.

5) Many interact regularly with other blacks as they often live in ghettoes which are largely separate from the wider society.

Turning to the United Kingdom, it is possible to identify a number of ethnic groups - Afro-Caribbeans (or West Indians), Chinese, Pakistanis, Cypriots, Punjabi Sikhs and so on. There has been considerable argument, however, about whether such groups have distinctive subcultures. This point will be examined later in the chapter.

(adapted in part from 'Right On: From Blues to Soul in Black America' by Michael Haralambos, Causeway Press, Ormskirk, 1994)

QUESTIONS

1. What is a minority group? (3)
2. What is meant by the following aspects of an ethnic group?
   a) a common origin (3)
   b) a sense of belonging to the group (3)
   c) a distinctive subculture (3)
   d) members interact regularly with each other. (3)
3. Briefly outline the difference between a racial group and an ethnic group. (5)

The 'Million Man March' in Washington DC, October 1995 - a demonstration by black Americans

 PART 3 — **THE BANGLADESHIS OF EAST LONDON**

The following passage looks at the life of the Bangladeshi community in the East End of London.

A Bangladeshi family in Tower Hamlets

Making chapatis

Some 35,000 Bangladeshi live in Tower Hamlets in the East End of London. They form a tight-knit community. Most come from Sylhet, a farming area in northeast Bangladesh.

Mrs Begum lives in a flat with her husband and children. She is dressed in a turquoise sari. Her two eldest boys sit at a table learning Arabic which they must know in order to read the

Koran (the Muslim bible). Cassette tapes of Bangladeshi music are on the table.

'We are very religious minded,' says Mrs Begum in Bengali - she speaks very little English. 'I pray five times a day.' The Bangladeshi are devout Muslims. Meals are cooked strictly in line with religious rules. 'We have two cooked meals a day, sometimes rice and curry, or fish which comes from Bangladesh.'

If Mrs Begum goes shopping, she will do so with her husband. If she meets a Bangladeshi male who is not a member of her family, she will put a veil on.

Marriages are arranged. Girls are only allowed to see a photograph of their fiancé before marriage - or possibly be allowed to watch him from a distance. Mrs Bibi, who lives near Mrs Begum, states, 'It would be very unusual for girls to want their own choice. They know our world isn't like the English world.'

The Bangladeshi keep to themselves. They have mixed feelings about living in Britain. As Mrs Bibi says; 'I am glad that we have come to live here because my children will have a better life. But I have my mother and father and in-laws in Bangladesh, our roots are there, and our hearts cry for it.'

(adapted from 'New Society', 22.8.1986)

QUESTIONS

1. The following have often been seen as the main characteristics of an ethnic group. In each case, does the Bangladeshi community of East London form an ethnic group?
   a) a common origin (3)
   b) a sense of belonging to the group (3)
   c) a distinctive subculture (4)
   d) members interact regularly with each other. (4)
2. Do you think the Bangladeshis will one day cease to be an ethnic group? Give reasons for your answer. (6)

PART 4 — ETHNICITY AND LIFE CHANCES

In general, members of ethnic minority groups do not share the same life chances as the rest of the population. They do not have the same opportunity of obtaining those things defined as desirable by the society in which they live, eg high status, well paid occupations and high quality housing, or of avoiding those things defined as undesirable, eg illness and unemployment. The following passage examines some of the life chances, of ethnic minorities in the United Kingdom compared to those of the white majority.

Occupation is probably the most important influence on a person's life chances. With a low status job, or no job at all, people's life chances will be limited. In all probability their income will be low, their housing below the standard of the population as a whole, their children will have less chance of obtaining high educational qualifications, they may well have a shorter life and suffer from more ill health than people in higher status jobs.

Table 1 Occupation and ethnicity

People aged 16 and over in employment (percentages), Great Britain 1989-91				
	White	Afro-Caribbean	Indian	Pakistani/Bangladeshi
Men				
professional	7	4	12	5
employers, managers	21	8	18	15
other non-manual	18	18	20	14
skilled manual	36	42	30	33
semi-skilled manual	13	20	14	27
unskilled manual	3	5	3	4
Women				
professional	2	0	5	0
employers, managers	11	9	9	4
other non-manual	52	51	42	48
skilled manual	8	5	12	14
semi-skilled	19	22	28	26
unskilled manual	6	9	2	1

(adapted from Labour Force Survey, 1990-91)

Table 2 Average earnings of full-time employees by ethnic group and sex; Great Britain, 1993/94

Ethnic origin	All	Men	Women
Average hourly pay			
White	£7.44	£8.00	£6.40
Black	£6.92	£7.03	£6.77
Indian	£6.70	£7.29	£5.77
Pakistani/ Bangladeshi	£5.39	£5.47	£5.15

Black includes Afro-Caribbeans and black Africans.

(adapted from 'Employment Gazette,' June 1995, p258)

Success stories

The dinner held at Kensington Palace was one of those occasions when businessmen pay dearly for the pleasure of socialising with the Prince of Wales. The two notable features about the businessmen were that they were all Asian and included some of the richest people in Britain. Many of the Asian millionaires came to Britain 20 years ago with virtually nothing and have built multi-million pound companies which employ thousands of people, mostly non-Asian. Though many from the first generation began with the corner shop, they have branched out into many fields - cash-and-carry stores, textiles, fashion, banking, newsagents, grocery and retail chains, electronics and manufacturing. One estimate is that Britain has at least 300 millionaires in its Asian community of 1.5 million.

(adapted from 'Sociology in Focus' by Paul Taylor et al, Causeway Press, Ormskirk, 1995, p113)

Shami Ahmad, founder and managing director of Joe Bloggs, the Manchester based clothing firm

Figure 1 Unemployment rates by ethnic group, Spring 1994

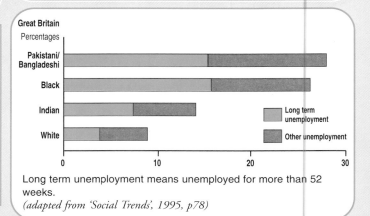

Long term unemployment means unemployed for more than 52 weeks.
(adapted from 'Social Trends', 1995, p78)

Figure 2 Households in worst housing: by ethnic group of head of household, 1991 (England)

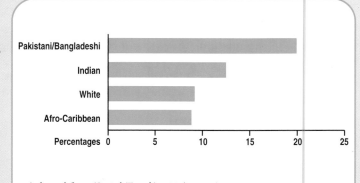

(adapted from 'Social Trends', 1994, p112)

QUESTIONS

1. Look at Table 1. What percentage of each group is working class? (3)
2. How might Table 1 help to explain the earnings differences in Table 2? (3)
3. Ethnic disadvantage in the labour market looks much greater when unemployment rates are taken into account. Explain using information from Figure 1. (3)
4. To what extent does the information from Tables 1 and 2 and Figure 1 help to explain Figure 2? (3)
5. Sociologists tend to emphasise ethnic disadvantage. Why is it important to highlight ethnic success? (8)

RACISM AND ETHNIC STRATIFICATION

PART 5

The previous part shows that members of ethnic minority groups are disproportionately represented in the lower levels of the class system. This means that a higher proportion of ethnic minority group members are working class than whites. Because of this it can be argued that ethnicity is an important aspect of social stratification - that there is an ethnic stratification system.

There are two main explanations for ethnic stratification in the UK. The first, known as the host-immigrant model, is the more optimistic. It begins with the observation that many members of ethnic minority groups are immigrants. Among other things, it argues that as they adapt to their new home, learn the British way of life and their children travel through the British educational system, they will become a part of the population as a whole. Ethnic stratification and ethnic disadvantage will disappear. The 'immigrants' will become like the 'hosts'.

The host-immigrant model has been strongly criticised. Evidence about the position of blacks in American society does not support it. Despite being resident in the United States for many generations, blacks as a group have still not entered the mainstream of American life and the majority remain in the lower levels of the US class system.

The second explanation for ethnic stratification argues that it is largely the result of racism. The idea of racism and some of its possible effects are considered in the following passage.

Racism is a general term used by sociologists to cover all the negative attitudes and practices directed towards groups seen as racially different. Racism can be divided into three main aspects 1) cultural racism 2) racialism 3) institutional racism. These will now be examined along with some of the evidence for racism in Britain.

Cultural racism

This is a set of beliefs and ideas which provides a false and mistaken picture of a so-called 'racial group'. Thus, simply because of the colour of their skin, a person may be seen as 'ignorant', 'primitive' and 'inferior'. Cultural racism is a form of prejudice whereby people are pre-judged to be a certain way simply because of their physical appearance.

Researchers have identified cultural racism in many areas of British life - in storybooks where 'Little Black Sambo' is still alive and well; in the media where blacks are often presented as 'outsiders' and portrayed as a problem with the spotlight on black crime; in history courses where the 'civilising' influence and conquests of the British over 'backward' peoples are used to justify Britain's colonial past. It is difficult to judge the extent of cultural racism in the UK, partly because attitudes are constantly changing. However, a number of surveys reveal its existence. When it is found in groups who work directly with ethnic minorities, it may well cause serious problems. Thus a report by the Policy Studies Institute in 1983 found that racial prejudice was widespread on the Metropolitan (London) Police Force and that terms of abuse such as 'nigger', 'coon' and 'wog' were widely used. And ten years later the 1993 Annual Report of the Chief Inspector of Constabulary noted 'unacceptable levels' of racial prejudice in the police forces of England and Wales.

Racialism

Racialism refers to racial discrimination - discrimination against people simply because they are seen as belonging to a particular racial group. It refers to actual behaviour rather than attitudes and beliefs. Examples of racialism include an employer refusing a job to someone simply because they are black, or a landlord refusing to rent a house to someone simply because of the colour of their skin.

Surveys from the 1960s to the 1990s show that racialism is widespread in the UK. It is found in employment, housing and services such as insurance, banking and building societies. Even with similar qualifications, occupations and income to whites, members of ethnic minority groups are less successful in applications for jobs, bank loans, mortgages, renting property and obtaining council houses, where they are often given inferior accommodation.

Institutional racism

This view sees racism as a basic part of the structure of society, as built into the institutions which form the foundations of the social system. Thus racism is seen to be entrenched in the political, legal and educational systems, in the labour market and the stratification system.

The following quotation makes clear the differences between racialism and institutional racism. Written by American authors, it refers to the city of Birmingham, Alabama in the Deep South of the USA.

'When white terrorists bomb a black church and kill five black children, that is an act of individual racism, widely deplored by most segments of the society. But when in the same city -

A young man prays on a glass littered sidewalk across from the Baptist church in Birmingham, Alabama, bombed by white racists in 1963.

Birmingham, Alabama - five hundred black babies die each year because of the lack of proper food, shelter and medical facilities, and thousands more are destroyed and maimed physically, emotionally and intellectually because of conditions of poverty and discrimination in the black community, that is a function of institutional racism. When a black family moves into a home in a white neighbourhood and is stoned, burned or routed out, they are victims of an overt act of individual racism which many people will condemn - at least in words. But it is institutional racism that keeps black people in dilapidated slum tenements, subject to the daily prey of exploitative slumlords, merchants, loan sharks and discriminatory real estate agents.'

(from 'Black Power' by S. Carmichael and C. Hamilton, Penguin, Harmondsworth, 1969)

Evidence from the UK provides some support for the existence of institutional racism. As Part 4 shows, the operation of the labour market results in ethnic disadvantage. Evidence from a range of life chances suggests that the structure of UK society denies opportunities to ethnic minorities.

The evidence of racism does not necessarily lead to a rejection of the host-immigrant model outlined in the introduction to this passage. Many blacks arrived in the UK with few paper qualifications or none at all. They were employed in low pay, low status jobs. Their children often started at the bottom of the class system. Even without racism it would have taken time for them to work their way up. However, whatever these disadvantages, they would be considerably less without the

barriers erected by racism.

(adapted from 'The Sociology of Race' by John Richardson and John Lambert, Causeway Press, Ormskirk, 1985 and 'Sociology Update 1995' by Martyn Denscombe, Olympus Books, Leicester, 1995)

QUESTIONS

1. Why is the host-immigrant model relatively optimistic from the point of view of ethnic minority groups? (3)
2. a) Briefly summarise the evidence which does not support the host-immigrant model. (2)
   b) Despite this evidence it can be argued that the model should not be completely rejected. Why not? (3)
3. Which of the following are examples of (i) cultural racism (ii) racialism (iii) institutional racism?
   a) A higher infant mortality rate for blacks compared to whites. (1)
   b) Blacks have a natural sense of rhythm. (1)
   c) Refusing a person a mortgage because of the colour of their skin. (1)
   d) Whites have civilised the 'coloured races'. (1)
4. Ethnic stratification will remain as long as racism is widespread in the UK. Briefly discuss this statement. (4)
5. There is no such thing as a black problem, only a white problem. Discuss in the light of evidence from the passage. (4)

6 PART — ETHNIC SUBCULTURES

The term ethnic group was defined earlier in this chapter (see Part 2). Part of this definition stated that it is a group within a larger society whose members have certain beliefs, attitudes and behaviour patterns which are different from those of the wider society - in other words a group with a distinctive subculture. The claim that ethnic subcultures exist has produced a number of questions. These questions are examined in the following passage.

Asian children at Drummond Middle School, Bradford

1) Do ethnic subcultures really exist? Are the differences in behaviour and attitudes which some researchers identify really important? Or are they simply superficial, surface differences in which case members of ethnic minority groups are, for all intents and purposes, no different from the rest of society? For example, if many Afro-Caribbeans listen to reggae music does this make them much different from mainstream white society? Are there just as many differences within white society as there are between whites and blacks?

2) If ethnic subcultures do exist, where do they come from? To answer this question it is necessary to look at a) the country from which the immigrants came, eg India or Jamaica b) the subculture that each group of migrants brought with them, eg Punjabi Sikhs and Punjabi Hindus each from the same part of India but with different religious beliefs and c) the subcultures which develop from adaptation to a new society, eg the second

generation youth cultures developed by the sons and daughters of the original migrants to the UK. All the above will probably have some input into ethnic subcultures.

3) How important are ethnic subcultures? Do they help to explain the position of ethnic minorities in society? Many sociologists would argue that racism is the main reason for ethnic disadvantage. Some would see ethnic subcultures as at least part of the explanation. From this viewpoint ethnic subcultures may lead to minority groups living apart from the wider society, jealously guarding their own customs, beliefs and cultural identity. This may prevent them from moving into the mainstream of society.

4) Do ethnic minorities choose to remain distinct from the wider society, do they choose to maintain separate subcultures? Or are they forced by hostility and racism to retreat into their own communities where they develop their own way of life? If this is the case then ethnic subcultures are not freely chosen, they are a response, a reaction to a racist society.

(adapted in part from 'The Sociology of Race' by John Richardson and John Lambert, Causeway Press, Ormskirk, 1985)

QUESTIONS

1. The fact that many members of ethnic minority groups had their origins outside the UK may result in ethnic subcultures. Why? (3)
2. Racism may help to create ethnic subcultures. Why? (3)
3. People may take steps to preserve their ethnic subcultures. Why? (3)
4. Ethnic subcultures may prevent the integration of minority group members into the wider society. Why? (3)
5. In Bradford there are some 40,000 Muslims of Asian origin. The Muslim Parents' Association has demanded separate schools for its children.
   a) In view of the history of religious schools in Britain, have they the right to make this demand? Give evidence to support your answer. (2)
   b) What does this demand suggest about their attitude towards their subculture? (3)
   c) Would you support their demand? Give reasons for your answer. (3)

PART 7 — AFRO-CARIBBEAN SUBCULTURE

Some of the questions raised in the previous passage will now be considered in terms of Afro-Caribbean subculture in Britain.

The sociologist Stuart Hall offers the following picture of the development of an Afro-Caribbean subculture. Many Afro-Caribbeans in the UK found themselves trapped in ghettoes and locked into the lower levels of the class structure. They shared experiences of disadvantage and discrimination. Being thrown together in similar circumstances provided the basis for a 'cultural revival', for the creation of 'an alternative black social life' based in part on Afro-Caribbean culture. It can be seen in the rise of 'Afro-Caribbean consciousness' which defines blackness in a positive way. It can be seen in the development of 'black' streets, neighbourhoods, cafés and pubs, in the growth of revivalist churches, gospel singing and mass baptisms in the local swimming baths. It can be seen in Caribbean fruit and vegetable stalls, in the shebeen and Saturday night blues party, in sound systems and black record shops selling ska and reggae.

Within this subculture there is diversity. Apart from Afro-Caribbean versions of Christianity, the Rastafarian religion, which developed in the 1930s among the Jamaican poor, became increasingly popular amongst young Afro-Caribbeans. Rastafarians are immediately visible with their rolled, uncut hair - dreadlocks - and their Ethiopian colours of red, gold and green and often heard with the Rastafarian inspired reggae of Bob Marley and others. Rastafarians see themselves as living in Babylon - the corrupt and evil white society which oppresses them but which will eventually crumble from its own

Rastafarian sound system, Notting Hill Carnival

77

corruption. They must find their 'true selves' and cleanse their minds of racist ideas of black inferiority imposed by white society. They are joined in brotherhood by the belief that Jah (God) is present in each of them and by the view that blacks are united in a common struggle. Rastafarians rejoice in blackness, they have a pride and self-respect based on their definition of what it means to be black.

On the one hand it is possible to paint a picture of an Afro-Caribbean subculture which appears different and distinctive. On the other hand a number of studies suggest that Afro-Caribbeans are little different from members of the wider society. What appears to be distinctive may simply be surface differences, a matter of style rather than anything basic. In the winter of 1979-80 Gaskell and Smith interviewed 240 blacks aged 16-25 living in London asking them to describe the way of life they most wanted. The answers stressed everyday ambitions - a good job, a decent home, a car, marriage and a happy family life. These results give no indications of a distinctive Afro-Caribbean subculture. What Gaskell and Smith did find, however, were feelings of hopelessness and despair - many blacks felt that their hopes had little chance of becoming reality.

(adapted from 'Policing the Crisis' by Stuart Hall et al, Macmillan, London, 1978 and 'Observer', 12.7.1981)

QUESTIONS

1. If a group has a subculture then some of its norms and values are distinctive, some are shared with the mainstream culture. In terms of this definition do Afro-Caribbeans have a subculture? Provide evidence in your answer. (4)
2. In terms of their major values Afro-Caribbeans share the culture of the wider society. Assess this view with reference to the passage. (4)
3. Suggest why some young blacks are attracted towards the Rastafarian religion. (4)
4. Some observers argue that Rastafarianism prevents its followers from seeking political solutions to their problems. Suggest why this might be so. (4)
5. Some Afro-Caribbeans see themselves as black rather than British. Why? (4)

ETHNICITY AND URBAN RIOTS

PART 8

Beginning with disturbances in the St Paul's district of Bristol in 1980, exploding in Brixton and Southall (London), Toxteth (Liverpool), Moss Side (Manchester), St Paul's (Bristol) and other English cities in 1981 and breaking out in Handsworth (Birmingham), Brixton, Tottenham (London) in 1985, urban riots became a feature of the inner cities in the first half of the 1980s. For the next 10 years things were relatively quiet until December 1995 when rioting broke out again in Brixton, though on a smaller scale than in the 1980s.

There is nothing new about riots in the UK. In 1919 there were 'race riots' in which black sailors were attacked by mobs of whites in many of the major ports. In the same year crowds in Luton burned the town hall with petrol and troops were called in. Again in 1919, after a police strike in Liverpool, rioting and looting broke out and tanks were used to restore order. Throughout the summer of 1919 crowds of young people fought with the police in various parts of London. There were unemployment riots in 1921 and much larger outbreaks in 1931 when the army was called out in Manchester to support the police.

So in one sense there is nothing new about the riots in the 1980s and 1990s. Some things are new, however. 1) The media coverage - via television the riots were brought into living rooms across the country. 2) The fact that Afro-Caribbean youths were the main participants. Some whites also took part, for example in Toxteth, but they were usually in the minority. Asian youths were rarely involved in any numbers except in Southall (1981) which saw a pitched battle between Asian youths and white skinheads with the police caught in the middle. The Asians saw themselves as defending their community against racist attacks. 3) A further new element in the 1980s riots was the first use of petrol bombs on the UK mainland.

The riots took place in deprived, low-income, inner city areas with large ethnic populations and against a background of high unemployment, bad housing and poor police/community relations. Many riots were triggered or sparked off by what the participants saw as 'police injustice', though it is generally agreed that the basic causes go far deeper. The following extracts look at various aspects of the 1980s and 1990s riots.

Many young blacks place the blame for the riots on the police who are sometimes seen as the 'enemy', as an army of occupation, as a racist force who harass and oppress them. Many riots were triggered by an incident seen by the participants as 'police injustice'. The Brixton riot of 1981 was preceded by 'Operation Swamp' in which the area was saturated with plain-clothes police in an attempt to control street crime. In the words of the Scarman Report (the official report on the Brixton riot of 1981) - 'the violence erupted from the spontaneous reaction of the crowds to what they believed to be police harassment ... the riots were essentially an outburst of anger and resentment by young black people against the

Brixton 1981

Brixton 1985

police'. Again in Brixton, in 1985, a new police strategy using armed raids to capture suspects led to heightened tension which sparked off a riot after the accidental police shooting of a black woman during a raid on her home. And in Brixton in 1995, the riot was triggered by the death of a young black man held in Brixton police station.

Some researchers claim that the attitudes, policies and practices of the police are racist. There is some evidence to support this claim. The 1983 Policy Studies Institute report found that racial prejudice was widespread in the Metropolitan (London) Police Force. And in 1993 the Chief Inspector of Constabulary noted 'unacceptable levels' of racial prejudice in the police forces of England and Wales. There is also evidence which may support black claims of harassment by the police. For example, blacks were over ten times more likely to be arrested by the Metropolitan police for 'sus'. (The 'sus' laws, abolished in 1981, gave police the right to arrest someone on suspicion of loitering with intent to commit an arrestable offence'. However, the police still have stop and search powers.) In 1995 Chief Superintendent David Gilbertson of the Metropolitan Police admitted that, 'Most people stopped and searched are from the lower social classes - they are young, they are unemployed and unfortunately black people are disproportionately affected'.

Other researchers take a rather different view. They admit that there are instances of police injustice against blacks but in general they believe there is equal treatment under the law. The reason that blacks are more likely to be stopped and searched and arrested is, they argue, that blacks are more likely to be involved in street crime. (See Chapter 16, Part 9.)

Many police forces responded to the 1981 riots with programmes of 'community policing'. Local 'bobbies', were put on the beat in ethnic minority areas. They were instructed to adopt a sensitive approach and to get to know the community. Despite such efforts - for example, Handsworth in Birmingham was held up as a model of community policing - riots still broke out in 1985.

(adapted from 'Race Relations in Britain' by Andrew Pilkington, University Tutorial Press, Slough, 1984, pp168-171; 'Guardian', 8.7.1995; 'Guardian', 15.12.1995; 'Independent', 15.12.1995)

The police do not create social deprivation, though unimaginative, inflexible policing can make the tensions which deprivation produces much worse. Conversely, while good policing can help diminish tension and avoid disorder, it cannot remove the causes of social stress which are deeply embedded in fundamental economic and social conditions.

(adapted from Scarman Report, 'The Brixton Disorders 10-12 April 1981', HMSO, London, 1981, p100)

Commander Alex Marnoch, head of the Brixton police force: 'What can we, the police, offer? We can talk to them, we can play cricket with them, we can go to their youth clubs. But we can't give them money and jobs.'

(quoted in 'Observer', 6.10.1985)

The statistics tell the story:

- Since the 1981 riots, unemployment had doubled in the borough of Lambeth, of which Brixton is a part, and now stands at 22%. In Brixton it is 33%.

- The rate of house building has fallen. In 1981, 1,022 new homes were completed. Last year, it was only 552. In 1981, the council spent £51 million on housing. This year it is spending £34 million.

- Central Government's contribution has fallen dramatically. Although Lambeth's spending on services has risen - from £91.6 million in 1980 to £114.3 million in 1984 - the central contribution has fallen from £56.4 million to only £39 million. In 1984, central Government gave the council £13 million aid from the urban programme - and took away £19 million in penalties for overspending.

A group of nine Brixton Anglican priests condemned the situation: 'We deplore the conditions of life which have persisted and worsened in Brixton since the 1981 riots. We deplore the fact that no effective steps have been taken by the Government in the past four years to alleviate unemployment.'

Since 1985 millions of pounds have been spent to regenerate Brixton - shopping arcades have been upgraded and a new business centre built. However, this has had little effect on black unemployment. In 1995, 61% of black males aged 16-24 in London were unemployed compared with 22% of the equivalent white group.

(adapted from 'Observer', 6.10.1985; 'Guardian', 8.7.1995; 'Financial Times', 15.12.1995)

Many blacks have been pushed into the margins of society. They are on the outside looking in. They have few organisations to represent their interests and through which to channel their grievances. Traditionally the white working class has been represented by trade unions and the Labour Party. Blacks as a group lack such organisations and political representation.

Riots can be seen in many different ways. One way is to see them as a political activity by those who are largely unrepresented in the wider society. In terms of this view, Jerry

White states, 'Riot has classically been a collective weapon of the politically powerless - to get those with power and wealth to share a little more or to take notice'. And, as the brother of a black man who died in police custody said after the Brixton riot of 1995, 'It took a riot to draw attention to the plight of black people dying in custody'.

(adapted from 'Urban Violence and Political Marginalisation' by J. Young and J. Lea, 'Critical Social Policy', Spring 1982; 'The Summer Riots of 1919' by Jerry White, 'New Society', 13.8.1981, pp260-261; 'Guardian', 15.12.1996)

QUESTIONS

1. What do researchers mean when they distinguish between the trigger and the causes of a riot? (4)
2. What evidence suggests that community policing is no solution to urban unrest? (4)
3. How can riots be seen as political activity? (4)
4. Using evidence from the above extracts and from the chapter as a whole, briefly outline your view of the causes of the riots. (8)

RACIAL ATTACKS

9 PART

Racial attacks are attacks on people because they are seen to be members of a racial group. They form part of a broader category - *racial incidents* - which covers crimes against property (eg vandalising houses) and crimes against the person, including murder, assault and threats, where the motive is racial.

The British Crime Survey is a national survey based on a representative sample of the population. It asks people whether they have been the victim of particular crimes during the previous year. It estimates that in 1992, 130,000 crimes involving some racial element were committed. This includes 32,250 racially motivated assaults. A large majority of the victims were from ethnic minority groups. Of the 130,000 estimated crimes, fewer than 8,000 were reported to the police. However, the level of reporting is increasing, eg from 28 in 1988 to 577 in 1993 to the Greater Manchester police. And the level of reporting in the press is also increasing. The following examples of racial attacks are drawn from newspaper reports.

On Wednesday evening, 8 September 1993, four Bangladeshi teenagers were set upon by seven white men and a woman in Stepney in London's East End. Without a word the whites kicked and punched the teenagers, one of whom was placed on a ventilator in the Royal London Hospital with three major wounds to his head. According to the Detective Superintendent in charge of the attempted murder inquiry, 'It was a particularly vicious assault which was totally unprovoked'. One of the boys stated, 'They just attacked us for no reason other than we are black'.

Asif is an Asian shopkeeper on a large housing estate in Derby described by the police as a 'problem area'. He has been terrorised by a teenage gang hurling bricks and bottles at his property and screaming racial abuse. For the last three years his house and business have been boarded up. He and his family

live in constant fear. Other shops on the estate, which are owned by whites, have had no problems.

Racial attacks are usually associated with inner city areas. However, around 200,000 people from ethnic minority groups live in small towns and villages in rural areas. And there is growing evidence of racial attacks in such areas. One of the highest rates of reported racial attacks in Britain occurs in the valleys of Mid-Glamorgan. One Neath shopkeeper, Mohan Singh Kullar, died after being beaten senseless. Another has had five cars stolen or burnt out in a single year. 'Some of those shops have had to be turned into semi-fortresses,' said Andrew Housley, regional officer for the Commission for Racial Equality.

Although most racial attacks appear to be whites attacking non-whites, this is not always the case. For example, young Bangladeshis in Somers Town in north London are fighting back and, according to the police, racial attacks on white people in the area are increasing. According to a local youth worker, 'Some attacks are retaliation, some are self-defence and very, very rarely, some Bangladeshis attack first. They have grown up in this area experiencing racist attacks. The older generation felt like visitors here, but the current generation feel they have got every right to be here.'

(adapted from 'Observer', 10.9.93; 9.4.95; 13.8.95)

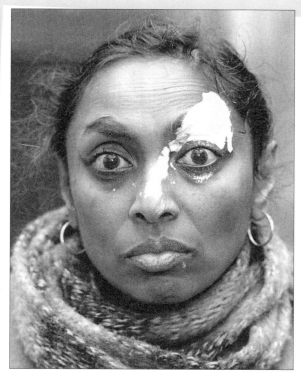

Leaving her flat in Hackney to go shopping, this Asian woman had white paint thrown in her face by a white youth.

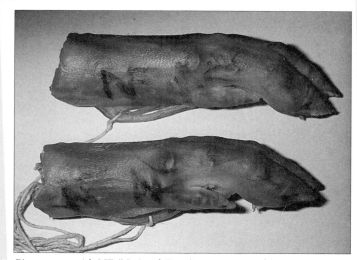

Pigs trotters with NF (National Front) written on in felt tip. They were nailed to the door of a flat in Tower Hamlets due to be occupied by a Muslim Bangladeshi family.

Five members of an Asian family were murdered in this arson attack on their home in Ilford. Petrol was poured through the letterbox and set alight.

QUESTIONS

1. a) Why do you think that relatively few racial incidents are reported to the police? (5)
   b) Suggest why the reporting of racial incidents to the police is increasing. (5)
2. Are racial attacks/incidents really 'racial'? Make judgements on the examples in the passage and pictures. (5)
3. Why, unlike their parents, are some members of the younger generation of ethnic minority groups fighting back? (5)

ETHNIC CLEANSING

Ethnic cleansing is a chilling phrase which was invented during the civil war in the former Yugoslavia. Although the phrase is new, the idea and practice are not. Ethnic cleansing means 'cleaning' or 'purifying' a population by driving out or killing ethnic minorities. Hitler did both. First Jews were driven out of Germany, then those that remained were rounded up into concentration camps and systematically slaughtered. The following passage looks at ethnic cleansing in the 1990s in the former Yugoslavia.

former Yugoslavia

The collapse of communism in Eastern Europe led to the break up of Yugoslavia. In 1991 Slovenia and Croatia declared their independence followed by Macedonia and Bosnia-Herzegovina in 1992. This left Serbia which attempted unsuccessfully to reunite Yugoslavia. The Serbian-Croatian war in 1991/92 led to the Serbian conquest of the Krajina region of Croatia. Krajina was reconquered by Croatia in 1995. In 1992 fighting broke out between Serbs, Croats and Muslims in Bosnia.

The former Yugoslavia is a patchwork of ethnic groups. Slovenia is 90% Slovene, Croatia had a Serb minority of 12% (mainly in Krajina) and Serbs make up 31% of Bosnia's population, Croats 17% and Muslims 44%. Each ethnic group has its own identity, its own history and its own customs and beliefs. For example, the Croats are Roman Catholics and the Serbs Orthodox Christians. The Muslims are descendants of Slavs converted to Islam after their conquest by the Turks in the 15th century.

Despite many years of harmony and intermarriage between the various ethnic groups, there have been many years of conflict. For example, during World War II the Croats sided with the Germans who occupied Yugoslavia. An estimated 1-2 million

Serbs were killed, many of them in the Jasenovac concentration camp. Standing on the site of the camp in 1991 Pero, a Serb policeman, says, 'My wife's parents were both killed here. The war with the Croats is a continuation of the Second World War. Our parents made the mistake of forgiving the Croats for what they did. We must never make the same mistake again.'

When Serbian forces conquered the Krajina region of Croatia in 1991/92 they were not forgiving. Serbs were in the majority in Krajina. The Serbian army drove out all the Croatian inhabitants 'cleansing' the area until it was ethnically 'pure'. This was justified in terms of the Serb's version of ethnic history. Father Starrofor Mrdjen explains, 'The Serbs were in this area 30 years before the Croats. Our Church of St Luke was built here in 872 AD. We have three monasteries here. The churches were built 600 years ago.'

All sides in the conflict in the former Yugoslavia have been responsible for atrocities. However, the ethnic cleansing of Muslims by Serbs in Bosnia is among the most vicious and horrific. Examples of rape, torture, murder and mass executions have been documented over and over again. In many towns all evidence of the presence of Muslims has been systematically wiped away - their houses have been occupied by Serbs and their mosques reduced to piles of rubble. For some Serbs this ethnic cleansing is almost like a holy war. They are defending the fatherland, purifying it of unclean Muslims and avenging their defeat by the Turks at the battle of the Field of the Blackbirds in the 14th century.

Jose Maria Mendiluce of the United Nations High Commission for Refugees (UNHCR) describes some of the horrors he witnessed. The small Bosnian city of Zvornic was occupied by Serbian mercenaries. 'I saw,' Mendiluce states, 'children placed under the wheels of tanks by upstanding men and then crushed by other men in full possession of their minds. These people have a coherent strategy. Their aim is to inflict the maximum terror on the civilian population, destroy the maximum property and exercise the maximum violence on women and children. As soon as the mercenaries have accomplished their mission, the established authorities - the police - arrive to restore order.'

In practice 'restoring order' means finishing the job - removing those Muslims who have not fled, been removed to concentration camps, or slaughtered. For example, in Banja Luka, a Serb held town in northern Bosnia, the remaining

Muslim community leaders were regularly beaten by Serbian police. A UNHCR report states that Muslims 'have been forced to crawl on their hands and knees to pick up wallets and documents while being kicked by police'.

By the close of 1995 ethnic cleansing in Bosnia was practically complete. Hundreds of thousands of people had fled their homes and untold thousands had died in the name of ethnic purity.

(adapted from 'The Times Atlas of European History', Times Books, London, 1994; 'Independent', 9.10.93, 20.6.94, 27.6.94; 'New Statesman and Society', 17.12.93; 'Observer', 8.10.95)

Muslims in a Serb prison camp

Muslim children in Bosnia. They have nicknamed the small boy Karadzic (after the Bosnian Serb leader) and threaten to shoot him with their imitation guns.

QUESTIONS

1. What evidence does the passage contain to show that (i) religion and (ii) history are important factors in ethnic identity? (8)
2. How can these factors lead to ethnic conflict? (4)
3. Can ethnic cleansing be seen as a solution to the conflict in the former Yugoslavia? (4)
4. Are there any parallels between the civil war in the former Yugoslavia and the 'troubles' in Northern Ireland? (4)

PART 11 — SCAPEGOATS

Prejudgement is a normal part of everybody's thinking. Without it we could not live our daily lives. Think about everyday routines such as cleaning your teeth - you prejudge that water will come out of the tap, that toothpaste will come out of the tube and that you will not be poisoned in the process.

Prejudgement becomes *prejudice* when it involves a judgement that something is good or bad. Part of this chapter has been concerned with racial prejudice, a negative prejudgement of people who are seen to belong to a racial group.

Prejudices involve *stereotypes*. A stereotype is a standardised view of what a person or thing is like. Social groups are often seen in terms of stereotypes. For example, there are stereotypes of Americans, Irish, the English upper class and so on.

Prejudices and stereotypes are important parts of a process known as *scapegoating*. All of us at some time have 'taken it out on the dog'. We've blamed someone else for our problems and misfortunes, for our wrongdoings and shortcomings. And we've taken out our anger and frustrations on them. In other words, we've found a *scapegoat*.

Certain social groups provide convenient scapegoats. It is much easier to blame a group for our problems and take out our frustrations on them if we are prejudiced against them and see them in terms of a negative stereotype. It is even easier if the group can be readily identified (eg by skin colour) and is weak and vulnerable and therefore not able to fight back effectively (eg witches in the Middle Ages). The following passage looks at an example of scapegoating from Nazi Germany.

Germany was defeated in World War I (1914-1918). The Germans were outraged and humiliated by the peace treaty of 1919. The victorious allies forced them to give up territory in Europe and their overseas colonies and to pay compensation to countries which had suffered damage during the war.

The German economy, badly damaged by the war, was hit by hyperinflation during the early 1920s. By 1923 the German mark was worthless. The price of a loaf of bread rose from 0.54 marks in 1918 to 201,000,000,000 marks in 1923. People were bitter and desperate as they saw their life savings wiped out.

In 1929 the price of shares on the US stock exchange collapsed and the USA was plunged into an economic depression. The 'Great Depression' spread rapidly to the rest of the world. By 1933, six million Germans were out of work including over half between the ages of 16 and 30.

Membership of the Nazi Party grew steadily in Germany throughout the 1920s and 30s. Adolf Hitler left the German army in 1919, bitter about its defeat. In 1920 he joined the Nazi Party and in 1933 he led them to power.

The Nazis blamed the Jews for just about every problem in Germany. They were blamed for Germany's defeat in World War I, despite the fact that 100,000 German Jews had fought and died alongside non-Jews in the German army. They were blamed for causing inflation in the 1920s and for causing unemployment in the 1930s.

In *Mein Kampf* ('My Story'), a book written by Hitler in 1925 which became a bestseller in Germany, Hitler wrote:

'Was there any form of filth or crime without at least one Jew involved in it? If you cut into such a sore, you find - like a maggot in a rotting body - a Jew. By defending myself against the Jew, I am fighting for the work of the Lord.'

To Hitler, the Jews were the *Untermenschen* - subhumans.

(adapted from 'Britain and the World: the 20th Century' by Tony and Steve Lancaster, Causeway Press, Ormskirk, 1995)

This 1935 cartoon from the magazine *Der Stürmer* ('The Stormer') shows a Jewish butcher making sausages out of rats.

This 1934 cartoon from *Der Stürmer* shows Jews draining the blood of innocent Germans.

Poster to advertise a German anti-Jewish film entitled *The Wandering Jew*

A poster in Dutch from 1941 for a German anti-Jewish film

This poster says, 'We peasants are clearing out the muck'. It shows a German peasant shovelling away Communists and Jews.

A beer mat from the 1930s. It reads, 'Whoever buys from a Jew is a national traitor'.

QUESTIONS

1. Using the extract and the pictures, outline the stereotype of the Jews portrayed by the Nazis. (6)
2. Why did the experience of the Germans from 1918 to 1933 encourage the creation of scapegoats? (7)
3. Hitler's 'final solution' to the 'Jewish problem' was the slaughter of six million Jews in concentration camps. How did the Nazi stereotype of Jews help to make this possible? (7)

POVERTY

This chapter is concerned with four main questions: 1) What is poverty? 2) How is it measured? 3) What is the extent of poverty? and 4) What are the causes of poverty? These questions are closely related. For example, if two researchers use widely differing definitions of poverty they will produce very different figures on the extent of poverty. The following extract looks at two views of poverty.

TWO VIEWS OF POVERTY

During the early years of this century a group of workers are having their lunch break. The conversation moves around to poverty.

'Poverty,' continued Jack after a short silence, 'consists in a shortage of the necessities of life. When things are so scarce or so dear that people are unable to obtain sufficient of them to satisfy their basic needs. Linden is poor. His family are actually starving. There is no food in the house and the children are crying for something to eat. All last week they have been going to school hungry for they had nothing but dry bread and tea every day and this week they don't even have that.'

For Owen, poverty was more than this. 'Yes Linden is poor,' he replied, 'but poverty should not be counted only as those who are starving. People are poor when they are not able to secure for themselves all the benefits of civilisation - not just the necessities but the comforts, pleasures and refinements of life, leisure, books, theatres, pictures, music, holidays, travel, good and beautiful homes, good clothes, good and pleasant food.'

Everyone laughed. It was so ridiculous. The idea of the likes of them wanting or having such things. Any doubts many of them had entertained as to Owen's sanity disappeared. The man was clearly as mad as a March hare.

(adapted from 'The Ragged Trousered Philanthropists' by Robert Tressall, Grant Richards Press, 1914)

Unemployed miner in Wigan, 1939

QUESTIONS

1. What does Jack mean by the 'necessities of life'? (2)
2. How does Jack decide whether or not a person is living in poverty? (2)
3. In terms of Jack's definition of poverty, has the extent of poverty a) increased b) stayed much the same or c) decreased in Britain during this century? Briefly give reasons for your answer. (4)
4. How does Owen's definition of poverty differ from Jack's? (5)
5. Name three 'comforts' or 'pleasures' from modern society without which people would be poor in terms of Owen's view of poverty. (3)
6. a) Why did the workmen doubt Owen's sanity? (2) b) Why would people be less likely to do so today? (2)

POVERTY IN YORK, 1899

2 PART One of the earliest systematic studies of poverty was conducted by Seebohm Rowntree in 1899 in the city of York. His view of poverty is similar to the one given by Jack in the previous extract. Rowntree calculated a minimum weekly sum of money which, in his opinion, was 'necessary to enable families to secure the necessities of a healthy life'. Those whose income fell below this sum were defined as poor. This concept of poverty is known as absolute or subsistence poverty. Rowntree admitted that it was 'on the side of stringency rather than extravagance' being 'the lowest standards which responsible experts can justify'. These experts included members of the British Medical Association who drew up a diet sheet which contained food with adequate nutritional value at the lowest possible cost. Presumably Rowntree expected the poor to be able to select and purchase cheap but highly nutritious food.

Early in 1899, with the aid of an interviewer and a secretary, Rowntree began a house-to-house inquiry, extending to the whole working class population of York. This involved 46,754 people, two-thirds of the total population. The keeping of servants was taken as the dividing line between the working classes and those of a higher social rank.

East End, London, 1900

East End, London, 1912. A mother and child crying because there is nothing for dinner.

Rowntree found 20,302 people living in a state of poverty. In other words, almost 28%, or two people in every seven, did not have enough food, fuel and clothing to keep them in good health. Since this was almost half of York's entire working class population, there could be no question but that the Victorian reformers had left a great deal of problems unsolved. Of those in poverty, about a third did not have enough money coming in each week to live a normal, healthy life even if they spent every penny wisely (Rowntree called this 'primary poverty'). All the traditional Victorian 'remedies' like thrift were no use to these people. You could not be expected to save money when you did not have enough for basic essentials. The remaining two-thirds had enough income to give them the bare necessities, but they spent some portion of it 'unwisely'. As a result, they were forced to go short on food or clothing, or both (Rowntree called this 'secondary poverty').

These figures were very close to those arrived at by Charles Booth. He found just over 30% in poverty in East London, working on roughly the same definition of poverty as Rowntree. Therefore it certainly seemed likely that almost a third of Britain's town dwellers were forced to go without some of the necessities of a civilised life. The terrible effect of this on the health and wellbeing of the people can be seen from the fact that a third of the men applying to join the army at this time were rejected as unfit. These conditions were not confined to the towns. A few years later, Rowntree found that agricultural labourers were even worse off.

What was it like living in poverty? Rowntree found that most of the families in this situation could afford nothing better than a damp, dark slum. Often one water tap supplied several houses and, in many cases, this was fixed to the wall of the W.C.! 'Midden privvies' were the general rule in the slums. In these the functions of lavatory and dustbin were combined in a brick-lined pit. Rowntree said: 'A large number of them are found inches deep in liquid filth, or so full of refuse as to reach above the cemented portions of the walls'. To make matters worse, they were often shared by several families.

Broken window panes were stuffed with rags or pasted over with brown paper. In the neighbourhood of these houses, the smell from dirt and bad air could be almost unbearable. This is a typical example of living conditions taken from a Sanitary Inspector's notebook: '2 rooms. In the lower one a brick floor is in holes. Fireplace without grate in bottom. Wooden floor of upper room has large holes admitting numbers of mice. Roof very defective, rain falling through on to the bed in wet weather.'

In these conditions, it was not surprising that one child out of every four born died before it was a year old and many of those that lived were stunted and deformed.

The diet of the poverty stricken slum dwellers was often seriously deficient. Many families could afford no butcher's meat at all. Although it may have contained enough bulk to fight off the feeling of hunger, it did not contain sufficient nourishment to keep the family in good health. Extras like clothing often had to be paid for by going short of food. One woman said: 'If there's anything extra to buy, such as a pair of boots for one of the children, me and the children goes without dinner'.

Taking those whose basic incomes were insufficient, ie those in primary poverty, Rowntree found two main reasons for their plight. In a quarter of these cases, the chief wage-earner of the family was out of action or dead. He might be ill or disabled, too old to work or unemployed. However, in over half the families in this category, the breadwinner was in regular work. His wages were simply too low to meet his family's needs. Unskilled labourers earned roughly 18-21 shillings a week in York at this time, yet Rowntree estimated that at least 21s 8d was needed to keep a family with three children out of poverty. The belief that a man could always provide for his family if he was thrifty and willing to work hard was shown to be false.

However hard he tried, he could not keep out of poverty if he was seriously underpaid.

In the case of those whose incomes were sufficient but who failed to spend every penny wisely, ie those in secondary poverty, it was more difficult to give definite reasons for their poverty. Drink and gambling - in that order - were seen to be the main causes. When father drank, the children often went supperless to bed. Rowntree deplored these vices but suggested that men often took to drink and gambling not from weakness of character but because of the terrible conditions under which they lived. 'Extravagant housekeeping' was another cause of unnecessary poverty. Housewives often spent unwisely through ignorance of what was the best value for money.

(adapted from 'The Making of the Welfare State' by R. J. Cootes, Longman, London, 1966, pp28-33)

QUESTIONS

1. What does Rowntree consider to be the 'necessities of a healthy life'? (2)
2. How does Rowntree define a) primary poverty and b) secondary poverty? (4)
3. Is it realistic to expect the poor to spend 'every penny wisely'? Give reasons for your answer. (3)
4. What was the extent of poverty in a) London and b) York? (2)
5. What evidence is provided in the extract to explain the high death rate amongst the poor? (3)
6. Why did Rowntree see a national minimum wage as one of the main solutions to poverty? (3)
7. Why doesn't Rowntree blame those in secondary poverty for their situation? (3)

3 PART — ABSOLUTE VS RELATIVE POVERTY

Rowntree conducted two further studies of York, one in 1936 and one in 1950. They revealed a steady reduction in the extent of poverty. By 1950 only 1.5% of the population of York lived in poverty. It appeared that the days of the poor were numbered. However, Rowntree's research was based on a concept of *absolute* or *subsistence poverty*. A very different picture of the extent of poverty will result from research based on the idea of *relative poverty*. In terms of this view people are poor if they lack the resources to afford what is generally considered to be an acceptable standard of living and a reasonable style of life. The following extract begins with a definition of relative poverty by Peter Townsend. It then compares the results of Rowntree's 1950 study with those of a study by Abel-Smith and Townsend entitled *The Poor and the Poorest*. This was the first major study of poverty in the UK based on a concept of relative poverty. It claimed that in 1960, 7.5 million people, that is 14.2% of the population, lived in poverty.

Individuals, families and groups in the population can be said to be in poverty when they lack the resources to obtain the types of diets, participate in the activities and have the living conditions and amenities which are customary, or at least widely encouraged or approved, in societies to which they belong. Their resources are so seriously below those commanded by the average individual or family that they are, in effect, excluded from ordinary living patterns, customs and activities.

(from 'Poverty as Relative Deprivation: Resources and Style of Living' by Peter Townsend in 'Poverty, Inequality and Class Structure' edited by D. Wedderburn, Cambridge University Press, Cambridge, 1974, p15)

Table 1   Two measures of poverty

Percentage of those in poverty Rowntree 1950	Cause of poverty	Percentage of those in poverty Abel-Smith and Townsend 1960
4.2	Inadequate wages and/or large families	40
68.1	Old age	33
6.4	Fatherless families	10
21.3	Sickness	10
Nil	Unemployment	7
1.5	Percent of sample population in poverty	14.2

(Wages are adequate or not depending on the number of dependent family members who require support.)

(adapted from 'Poverty: The Forgotten Englishmen' by K. Coates and R. Silburn, Penguin Books, Harmondsworth, 1970, p47)

Bangladeshi mother and child in decaying tenement block, Tower Hamlets, London

Mother and child suffering from malnutrition in Sierra Leone, West Africa

QUESTIONS

1. In terms of a relative concept, poverty in 1900 is very different from poverty today. Explain this statement. (4)
2. Why might people who cannot afford a refrigerator, washing machine and vacuum cleaner be defined as poor in terms of relative poverty but not in terms of absolute poverty? (3)
3. Briefly explain why the 1950 and 1960 estimates of poverty are so different. (3)
4. Give two reasons for the decline in absolute poverty from 1899 to 1950. (2)
5. Which is the largest group in poverty in a) 1950 and b) 1960? (2)
6. Suggest two measures the government might take to reduce the level of poverty among low wage earners. (2)
7. Use the idea of absolute and relative poverty to describe the situation of the women and children in the pictures. (4)

4 PART

POVERTY FROM THE 1960s TO THE 1990s

This part looks at changes in the extent of poverty from the 1960s to the 1990s. Statistics on the distribution of income show that from the late 1970s to the early 1990s the income gap between the top and bottom steadily widened. Reasons for this growth in income inequality are outlined on pages 58-59.

The Council of Europe defines poverty as below 50% of average national income. Using this definition, Figure 1 shows that poverty has doubled from the late 1970s to the early 1990s. Figure 2 shows that the income of the poorest 10% has fallen in real terms by 17% from 1979 to 1991/92. These statistics are based on income after housing costs.

Figure 1 Individuals below half average income, 1961-1991

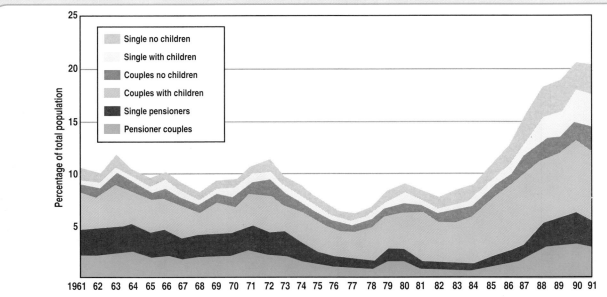

(from 'Inquiry into Income and Wealth' Volume 1, Joseph Rowntree Foundation, 1995, p17)

Figure 2 Changes in income, 1979-1991/92

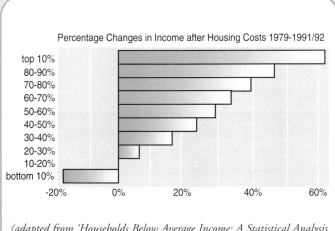

(adapted from 'Households Below Average Income: A Statistical Analysis 1979 to 1991-92', HMSO, London, 1994)

Figure 3 The changing composition of the poorest 10%, 1979-1988/89

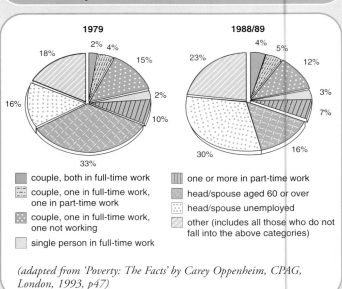

(adapted from 'Poverty: The Facts' by Carey Oppenheim, CPAG, London, 1993, p47)

Comments on the distribution of income.
These comments followed the publication of *Households Below Average Income* (from which Figure 2 is taken) in 1994.

Peter Lilley, Secretary of State for Social Security
'The results certainly do not show that the poor have become poorer, though they inevitably reflect changes in the number of unemployed people. But they do show how government policies have continued to increase the prosperity of the population as a whole.'

Donald Dewar, Labour's social security spokesman
'These figures back up the claim that Britain is more divided now than it has been for a generation. Poverty, like rising damp, creeps ever higher.'

Sally Witcher, director of Child Poverty Action Group
'Britain is a wealthy country. There is no excuse for this level of poverty and we should be deeply ashamed. Not even being in employment will mean staying out of poverty.'

(quotations from 'Independent', 15.7.1994)

QUESTIONS

1. Briefly explain why the Council of Europe's definition of poverty is a relative definition. (3)
2. Summarise the changing distribution of income shown in Figures 1 and 2. (4)
3. Summarise the changes in the groups in poverty shown in Figures 1 and 3. (4)
4. Use information from Figures 1, 2 and 3 to assess the comments on the distribution of income. (9)

5 PART — THE CULTURE OF POVERTY

There is a tendency for people who share similar circumstances and problems to develop a way of life which differs to some extent from that of the rest of society. In sociological terms they develop a subculture, that is certain norms, attitudes and values which are distinctive to them as a social group. A number of researchers have argued that the circumstances of poverty tend to produce a 'culture of poverty', that is a subculture shared by the poor. This idea was first introduced in the 1950s by the American anthropologist Oscar Lewis. It proved very influential forming the basis for the US government's 'war on poverty' during the 1960s. The following passage examines Lewis's ideas and their influence on the war on poverty.

Lewis developed the idea of a culture of poverty from his research among the urban poor in Mexico and Puerto Rico. He sees the culture of poverty as a 'design for living' which is transmitted from one generation to the next: 'By the time slum children are age six or seven, they have usually absorbed the basic values and attitudes of their subculture'.

The culture of poverty includes 'a strong present-time orientation with relatively little ability to defer gratification and a sense of resignation and fatalism'. As a result people tend to accept the situation believing that there is little or nothing they can do to change it. They tend to live from day to day, taking their pleasures when they find them with little thought for tomorrow. The culture of poverty also includes a feeling of helplessness and a 'strong feeling of marginality' - the poor feel they are on the outskirts of society, on the outside looking in. They rarely participate in the wider society and are unlikely to belong to trade unions or political parties.

According to Lewis the culture of poverty tends to perpetuate poverty, largely preventing the poor from escaping from their situation. In his words, they are 'not geared to take full advantage of changing conditions or increased opportunities which may occur in their lifetime'.

Collecting water in a Mexican shanty town

The idea of a culture of poverty formed the basis for government policy in the fight against poverty in the USA. In 1964 President Lyndon B. Johnson declared a 'war on poverty'. Its main strategy was to rid the poor of the culture of poverty. They would then be able to pull themselves up by their own bootstraps and seize the many opportunities which were supposed to be available.

The government set up a nationwide programme of pre-school education in low income areas known as 'Operation Headstart'. The idea was to nip the culture of poverty in the bud by teaching children middle class norms and values (see Chapter 10, Part 6). Programmes were also developed for older age groups. Unemployed youngsters were sent to residential camps in the wilderness with the aim of 'building character' and encouraging initiative and determination. Many work experience programmes were started to develop 'work habits'. The poor were encouraged to help themselves. Government money was provided to finance community self-help groups and small businesses.

By the late 1960s it was clear that the war on poverty had been lost. As one man on welfare put it, 'It's great stuff this war on poverty! Where do I surrender?' The poor, despite the billions of dollars expended on poverty programmes, remained stubbornly poor.

Ideas about the causes of poverty were beginning to change. Various studies of the poor in the United States and other societies found little evidence of a culture of poverty. Even if such a culture did exist, many now argued that it was not the major cause of poverty. The American sociologist Herbert J. Gans writing in the early 1970s reflects this change of viewpoint: 'The prime obstacles to the elimination of poverty lie in an economic system which is dedicated to the maintenance and increase of wealth among the already affluent'. But a war on poverty based on this view would be far harder to win, since victory would require considerable sacrifice by the rich and powerful.

The rich have been seen as the main obstacle to the elimination of poverty.

(adapted from 'Sociology: Themes and Perspectives' 4th edition by Michael Haralambos and Martin Holborn, Collins Educational, London, 1995, pp149-150; 167-168)

QUESTIONS

1. How is the culture of poverty transmitted from generation to generation? (3)
2. How might 'a sense of resignation and fatalism' help to keep the poor in poverty? (3)
3. How might lack of membership of trade unions, political parties and other organisations help to keep the poor in poverty? (3)
4. 'Work habits' are of little use without jobs. Explain this statement with reference to the situation of the unemployed. (3)
5. Briefly outline the two reasons suggested for the failure of the war on poverty. (4)
6. Why do many people argue that the type of war on poverty suggested by Gans's ideas is doomed to failure? (4)

6 PART — THE CULTURE OF DEPENDENCY

During the 1980s and 1990s a new version of the culture of poverty appeared - the culture of dependency. It's main supporter is the American social scientist Charles Murray whose views are examined in Chapter 4, Part 11. According to Murray an underclass has developed at the base of the class system in Western societies. It's members have developed their own way of life based on female-headed single parent families and a lack of respect for work, with large numbers of young men choosing not to take jobs. This way of life is passed on from one generation to the next as boys grow up without a father/wage earner role model. Their lifestyle is supported by welfare benefits on which they become dependent - hence the idea of a culture of dependency.

Murray's views have become extremely influential. This part looks at a British view on the culture of dependency followed by criticisms which argue that a culture of dependency does not exist.

The case for a culture of dependency

The British sociologist David Marsland argues that state welfare benefits have gone too far. They have created a population which has grown dependent on welfare. People expect the state to look after and provide for them. As a result they lose their self-reliance. Instead of encouraging them to struggle to improve their lives, state benefits lock the poor into dependency at the bottom of the pile.

Welfare pays people to stay unemployed. They grow used to the situation, they lose the incentive to work and with it their dignity and self-respect. Welfare makes possible the rapid growth of fatherless families, depriving children of the role models and discipline they need if they are going to stand on their own two feet and take responsibility for their lives. Growing up dependent on state benefits they are socialised into a culture of dependency.

(adapted from 'Universal Welfare Provision Creates a Dependent Population' by David Marsland, 'Social Studies Review', November 1989, p55)

The case against a culture of dependency

Growing up on welfare Charles Murray's views on the culture of dependency are based on studies of the black American poor. His conclusions are challenged by the experience of Rosemary Bray, a black American who grew up on welfare, raised by her mother along with two brothers and a sister. 'I know more than I want to know about being poor. I know that the welfare system is designed to be inadequate, to leave its constituents on the edge of survival. I know because I've been there.

My life on welfare ended on 4 June, 1976 - a month after my 21st birthday, two weeks after I graduated from Yale University. Before the decade ended, all of us had left the welfare rolls. The eldest of my brothers worked at the post office, assumed support of my mother (who also went to work, as a companion to an elderly woman) and earned his master's degree at night. My sister married and got a job at a bank. My baby brother parked cars and found a wife. Five people on welfare for 18 years had become five working, taxpaying adults. Three of us went to college, two of us finished; one of us has an advanced degree; all of us can take care of ourselves.'

Of black women considered 'highly dependent', that is on welfare for more than seven years, 81% of their daughters grow up to live productive lives off the welfare rolls, a 1992 Congressional report stated; the 19% who become second-generation welfare recipients can hardly be said to constitute an epidemic of welfare dependency.

(adapted from 'Observer Magazine', 2.1.1994)

Living on welfare A study based on interviews with 74 low income families in inner city areas in London, Manchester and the Midlands found no evidence of a culture of dependency. Elaine Kempson, one of the authors of the study, states 'There is no culture of dependency, no evidence that people prefer to stay on benefits rather than work. What they wanted above all else was work. Men wanted to earn their living and women wanted part-time jobs which they could combine with looking after children.'

(quoted in 'Guardian', 2.8.1994)

A study based on interviews with 140 income support claimants in Bradford rejects the idea that people choose to live on state benefits. It found just the opposite - people hated 'living off the state', they wanted to support themselves, they wanted work but the job vacancies weren't there.

A long-term unemployed man living in an area of high unemployment, and who could not get a job with a wage adequate to support his family, reflected: 'I don't like living off the state the way I am. I'd rather have a job. And the kids cop it because other kids say your dad's living off the state and all the rest of it, the taxpayers are paying your dinners.'

A woman talks about her unemployed husband: 'We don't feel good about it, but the problem is he can't get work. He used to work even for a low wage but now there isn't any work for him. No doubt those in work say "oh, they're claiming" but what can we do?' In fact her husband and many like him could do very little to find even low-wage employment. Textile companies, the main employers in Bradford, have been hit hard by competition and the recession of the early 1990s. This resulted in the loss of thousands of unskilled and semi-skilled jobs.

(adapted from 'Hardship Britain: Being Poor in the 1990s' by R. Cohen, J. Coxall, G. Craig and A. Sadiq-Sangster, CPAG, London, 1992, pp59-61)

QUESTIONS

1. David Marsland argues that welfare benefits can harm rather than help the poor. How can they be seen as harmful? (5)
2. It has been claimed that people are socialised into a culture of dependency.
   a) What does this mean? (5)
   b) Use Rosemary Bray's experience to criticise this view. (5)
3. It is a lack of jobs rather than a culture of dependency which keeps many people poor. Comment on this view. (5)

PART 7 — POVERTY AND CLASS (1)

From a Marxist point of view poverty is the result of the capitalist system found in Western industrial society. From this viewpoint the poor are poor because the rich are rich. This state of affairs is due to the economic system and the class system which it produces (see Chapter 4, Part 5 for an outline of a Marxist view of social class). The rich and powerful owe their position to ownership of the forces of production. They own capital which they invest in private industry and, if the company is successful, are rewarded with much of the profit.

The following extract continues the conversation between Owen and his workmates which began this chapter. It is set in the early years of this century.

Owen continued. 'The theory that drunkenness, laziness and inefficiency are the causes of poverty are so many devices fostered by those who are selfishly interested in maintaining the present state of affairs for the purpose of preventing us from discovering the real causes of our present condition.'

'Well what do you reckon is the cause of poverty?' demanded Easton.

'The present system of capitalism,' retorted Owen. 'It is not the poor themselves who are at fault but the way that wealth is divided. All the people in the working class are suffering and starving and fighting in order that the rich people, the capitalist class, can live in luxury and do nothing. These are the wretches that cause poverty. They produce nothing but exist on the work done by the people.'

'It can't never be altered,' interrupted old Linden. 'I don't see no sense in all this 'ere talk. There's always been rich and poor in the world and there always will be.'

'But that's where you're wrong,' shouted Owen. 'We can change all that. The rich are only rich because they rob the poor. They have got control of the land, the machinery, the tools and use that control to exploit us. We work all our lives and instead of being paid the real value of our work we are paid a pittance. The capitalist class keeps the rest as their profit and try to persuade us that it is rightfully theirs. But they have not worked for it - they have just sat and watched us. But we can change all that. If all the working men were to unite we

A bloated capitalist from a Soviet poster of 1919

would be too strong for them and they would be forced to give us what is rightfully ours. No one would own the land, the mines, the factories, they would belong to the whole community. We would *all* work and in return receive a just wage which would permit everyone to live a civilised life. Then there would be no poverty.'

The men started to shift uncomfortably and one or two of them on the edge of the group started to collect up their tools ready for the afternoon's labour.

(adapted from 'The Ragged Trousered Philanthropists' by Robert Tressall, Grant Richards Press, 1914)

QUESTIONS

1. What does Owen see as the main cause of poverty? (6)
2. Why does Owen argue that the view that drunkenness and laziness are the cause of poverty is beneficial to the capitalist class? (4)
3. Owen sees a communist system as the solution to poverty.
   a) What is communism? (3)
   b) How might it lead to the abolition of poverty? (3)
4. Why did the men 'shift uncomfortably' after listening to Owen? (4)

PART 8 — POVERTY AND CLASS (2)

It is not necessary to take a Marxist position in order to argue that the class system is the main cause of poverty. This is clear from the following extract based in part on the findings of an extensive survey conducted by Peter Townsend entitled *Poverty in the United Kingdom.*

Peter Townsend argues that poverty is an inevitable feature of the class system. The way the system operates produces both rich and poor. If we look at many of the factors linked to poverty - for example, unemployment, low wages, old age, longstanding illness and disability - those same factors are also linked to social class.

The unemployed are one of the largest groups in poverty (see Part 4, Figure 3). The lower a person's social class, the higher their chances of unemployment. For example, in 1993 unskilled manual workers were over 3 times more likely to be unemployed than professionals (see Figure 1, p61).

Disability and longstanding and chronic illness are also closely linked to both social class and poverty (see Table 3, p62). Manual workers and their families are more likely to be disabled or severely incapacitated than middle class people.

Poverty in old age is closely linked to social class. People with manual occupations are more likely to experience poverty in old age than those with non-manual occupations. They are less likely to be members of an occupational pension scheme or to earn enough to save for their retirement.

In these and many other ways, Townsend sees poverty as a result of the normal, everyday operation of the class system. However, he goes further arguing that poverty must also be seen as a consequence of 'actions by the rich to preserve and enhance their wealth and so deny it to others'. This can be illustrated by evidence from income tax and welfare benefits.

A number of researchers argue that the rich have far more influence over government policy than the poor. During the 1980s, changes in income tax considerably reduced the tax bills of the rich. At the same time the value of many of the benefits, on which the poor rely, went down (see Chapter 4, Part 7). Added to this there is evidence that there is one law for the rich and another for the poor

Two sides of the class system

when it comes to defrauding the Inland Revenue and the Department of Social Security. This is illustrated by the following figures. (See Chapter 7, Part 7 for a discussion of how the rich gain from state welfare benefits.)

Cost of social security fraud	£500 million
Number of prosecutions	14,000
Cost of tax fraud	£5,000 million
Number of prosecutions	20

(adapted from 'Observer', 23.10.1988)

(adapted in part from 'Townsend's 14 million Poor' by Mary Manning, 'Community Care', 25.10.1979, pp14-16)

QUESTIONS

1. Following Townsend's argument suggest reasons for the link between:
   a) injury at work, social class and poverty (2)
   b) low wages, social class and poverty (2)
   c) single parent families, social class and poverty. (2)
2. Use the information on social security and tax fraud to support the view that there is one law for the rich and another for the poor. (5)
3. Suggest further ways in which the rich 'preserve and enhance their wealth'. (4)
4. What solutions to poverty are suggested by Townsend's views? (5)

LIVING IN POVERTY

PART This part looks at two case studies of single mothers and their children. Case studies such as these provide a vivid impression of life in poverty.

Single mother in church crypt shelter for the homeless

Linda Jenkins is an unemployed single mother with three children living in Liverpool. She is 33, pale and careworn. She looks older. The only holiday she has had in years was a trip to a local seaside resort organised by Gingerbread, the single parent support group. Even then, she had to go collecting round the pubs to raise her contribution.

Life is a demeaning juggling act with the £103 a week she gets in benefit. Heating, hot water and electricity are turned on just before her children get back from school. Linda walks to the city centre markets to save a few pence on fruit and vegetables, and cuts off the ends of toothpaste tubes to squeeze out a little extra. Even her shoes are second hand.

Linda describes her situation, 'It's horrible. I just don't see any future round here. I'm pushing my kids hard at school so they'll have a chance. I pray to God that they have itchy feet and just get out of here. I want to work. I want to go to college. But the kind of work someone unqualified like me can get won't cover the child-minding fees and I won't be a latchkey mother. There've been times when I've wanted to kill myself. I try to keep how hard it is from the kids. But Lawrence, the oldest, said to me when he was seven: "We're poor, aren't we?".'

(adapted from 'Observer' 3.10.1993)

Pamela Benn, a single mother, and her baby Emma live in a battle-scarred hovel in north London, divided into eight bedsits on three floors. From the glassless front door to the rotting, carpetless stairs and cracked walls, the house exudes neglect and decay.

Pamela has few of the items most people would regard as essentials - no heating, no waterproof coat, no all-weather shoes. She comments on some other 'essentials'.

- An indoor toilet: 'There are three in the house but one is broken so we all have to share two. There's no light bulbs in the toilet or on the stairs. The last time I put one in it was stolen the same day.'

- An unshared bath: 'There's just one bath between the eight bedsits.'

- Three meals a day: 'Emma will have rice pudding for lunch and some mince and potatoes for dinner. I go without two or three days a week.'

We called at Pamela's bedsit, a small attic room at the top of six flights of stairs. Pamela has been lying huddled in her bed with Emma who wakes immediately. In the room there is a cot, a sofa, a coffee table and a sodden, filthy carpet.

Both Pamela and Emma have summer colds and the baby has thrush. 'The child is suffering from repeated ailments. The doctor says I have been using medicines which would be unnecessary if the accommodation was satisfactory.' Pest-control officers have recently called to spray the room and rid it of fleas and mice, but the vermin have returned.

The future holds little hope. Pamela has been on London's longest council housing list in Hackney for only a year. It is Emma's first birthday next Friday. Pamela intends to doubly neglect her diet to provide the child with a gift.

(adapted from 'Sunday Times', 21.8.1983)

QUESTIONS

1. People living in poverty often feel excluded from the wider society. With some reference to the case studies, explain why they feel this way. (7)
2. Research has indicated that the poor suffer more ill health than the population as a whole. With some reference to the case studies, suggest why this is so. (6)
3. People in poverty often experience a lack of self-confidence and a loss of self-respect. With some reference to the case studies, suggest why this is so. (7)

7 CHAPTER

THE WELFARE STATE

A welfare state is a state which provides social services for its citizens. These services are statutory - they are provided by law. This chapter examines the origins of the welfare state in Britain, its establishment after the Second World War and its development in the postwar years. It looks at the role of voluntary organisations in the provision of social welfare and the move from care in institutions to care in the community. It then takes a critical view of the welfare state by examining the argument that the rich gain more from the state's social policy than the poor. The chapter closes with a review of the debate over the future of the welfare state.

1 PART — THE ORIGINS OF THE WELFARE STATE

The following passage looks at the origins and development of the welfare state up to 1900. From one point of view this development represents progress towards a more humane and caring society. From another it represents increasing social control made possible by the growing power of the state. In this sense welfare is a means of 'gentling the masses', of controlling the 'dangerous classes'.

A wealthy man passes a beggar on a country road.

In 16th century Elizabethan England the wandering beggar had no security, only hope and desperation. Dragging himself from door to door he could appeal to pity and charity; roving in bands he could threaten and steal. Whipping and branding did little to control desperate people. The Elizabethan Poor Law required men to stay in their own communities where they could be disciplined but this would only be effective if they were provided for. Local parishes were obliged to set the able-bodied poor to work and provide for the sick, disabled and aged, the cost being met by ratepaying householders.

The origins of the welfare state can be traced back to the Elizabethan Poor Laws which provided minimum security for the destitute. They can be seen as a means of social control concerned with maintaining the Queen's peace and, to some extent, as an act of Christian charity.

The industrial revolution and rapid urbanisation in 19th century Britain created a new urban working class. Periodic

high levels of unemployment and low wages resulted in widespread absolute poverty. The 1834 Poor Law was based on the idea that unemployment was voluntary, that the unemployed were lazy and idle, that work was available for the able-bodied if they searched hard enough. Workhouses for the destitute poor were established. They were made harsh and degrading, the idea being that any job on the outside would be preferable to life inside. The theory was that relief should be less desirable than the condition of the lowest paid labourer. In practice the sick, disabled and aged often had to endure the same conditions as the able-bodied poor. The workhouse was feared and hated by those who might one day be forced to enter it.

During the last quarter of the 19th century attitudes began to change. Charles Booth's study of London and Seebohm Rowntree's study of York (see Chapter 6, Part 2) suggested that in many cases poverty was not the fault of the poor. Growing

Female ward in a workhouse, 1843

numbers of old people were now receiving poor relief in their own homes, those still in workhouses were provided with little 'luxuries' like tea and tobacco, workhouse hospitals (established during the late 1860s) were improved and ordinary members of the working class began to use them.

Throughout the nineteenth century the state accepted more and more responsibility for the welfare of its citizens. This can be seen from a series of Factory Acts aimed at improving working conditions, limiting hours of work and ending child labour. One result of these acts was that large numbers of children, excluded from the factories, were left to roam the streets. For example in Manchester in 1865, 6% of children between the ages of three and twelve were at work, 40% at school and 54% at neither work nor school. In 1870 a state system of primary education was introduced and made compulsory up to the age of ten in 1880. It was aimed mainly at working class children who were unable to find places in church schools and unable to afford places in fee-paying schools. State schools provided a minimal education based on the 3 Rs and strict classroom discipline.

Slowly the state was moving from providing relief for the poorest to a wider range of provisions for larger sections of the population.

(adapted from 'Social Security: A System Emerges' by E. P. Hennock 'New Society', 7.3.1968; 'Society and Education in England since 1800' by P. W. Musgrave, Methuen, London, 1968 and 'Introduction to the Social Services' by W.E. Baugh, 3rd edition, Macmillan, London, 1977)

QUESTIONS

1. The welfare state began as a means of controlling the poor rather than helping them. Briefly discuss this statement. (3)
2. The 1834 Act has been described as a deterrent poor law.
    a) What does this mean? (3)
    b) Why does a deterrent poor law fail to meet the needs of the sick and the elderly? (3)
3. How can present day attitudes towards 'welfare scroungers' be seen as reflected in the 1834 Poor Law? (4)
4. How can state education be seen as a means of social control? (4)
5. It would be wrong to assume that a desire to help the poor had no influence on social policy in the nineteenth century. Briefly discuss this view. (3)

2 PART — THE FOUNDATIONS OF THE WELFARE STATE

Before the establishment of the modern welfare state, social services were 'selective' - they were available only to those selected as being in the greatest need, in particular the poor. They were often subject to a 'means test' - a person's means (income and resources) were assessed and if they were below a certain level payments or services were provided. During the 20th century more and more services became 'universal' - available to everyone no matter what their income group or social class. Today, for example, state education and health services are provided for all members of society, not just those defined as being in special need. The move towards universal provision can be seen in the following passage which looks at the development of the welfare state during the first forty years of the 20th century.

The foundations of the modern welfare state were laid by the Liberal governments of 1905-1915. The 1908 Old Age Pensions Act provided pensions for people over 70. Whether or not they received a pension and its size was decided by a means test. They would be refused a pension if they had been convicted of drunkenness or any other crime in the previous 20 years, if they had recently claimed poor relief or if they had a record of 'habitual failure to work'. The 1911 National Insurance Act provided sickness benefit and payment of medical expenses for all manual workers and other workers below a certain income level. It also provided unemployment payments for workers in seven occupations which were subject to high levels of unemployment. Both schemes were paid for by contributions from workers, employers and government. Not everybody welcomed these reforms. Writing in 1916, the Russian communist leader Lenin called them 'sops for the obedient workers'.

In 1907 school medical examinations were made compulsory. This picture shows children being weighed and measured in Bradford in 1907.

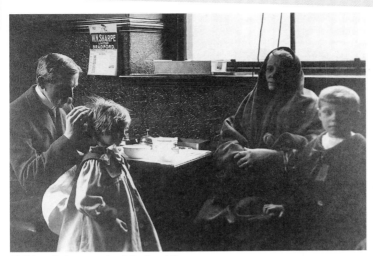

Children being examined for head lice.

of the insured worker any right to free treatment. Fees for dentists and opticians were too high for the poor. Thus people in the depressed areas were more likely to be ill and less likely to get proper treatment.

The government had done enough to prevent people living on the dole from starving to death. It did not believe it should spend more money partly because the country could not afford it and partly because it thought people would be deterred from genuinely seeking work if their dole were generous.

(adapted from 'The History of Social Welfare' by Pat Thane, 'New Society', 29.8.1974 ; 'Introduction to the Social Services' by W. E. Baugh, 3rd edition, Macmillan, London, 1977; 'The British Welfare State 1900-1950' by Sydney Wood, Cambridge University Press, Cambridge, 1982, pp33-34)

In the 1920s these provisions were widened and extended to larger sections of the population. For example, in 1920 unemployment insurance was extended to nearly all workers. However, it was not designed for the long-term unemployment brought about by the economic recession of the late 1920s and early 1930s. Unemployment benefit was only paid for a limited period and often ran out leaving workers destitute. Realising this and fearing working class unrest, the government introduced a series of 'transitional benefits' - often known as 'the dole' - to take over where unemployment payments left off. Sydney Wood gives the following description of how the dole operated.

The dole was only given after families had been checked to see if they had money of their own or other sources of income. Whether this was done by local authorities before 1934, or the Unemployment Assistance Board after 1934, it was strongly disliked. Children who earned a few shillings found that this amount would be knocked off their father's dole; a war-widow's pension or an old age pension could be reasons for cutting a family's payments. Until 1934 the dole might be cut off if officials found that a family had any savings; after that date they were allowed up to £200 of savings. The means test encouraged the breakup of families - where one of the younger members had a job officials cut the dole paid to the father of the household. Investigators working for the Carnegie Trust thought that 'weakening of family solidarity and disintegration of home life is perhaps the most serious and challenging aspect of the means test. The realisation that every cigarette smoked is paid for by the sacrifice of a brother or sister arouses bitterness, not against the regulations, but rather against the brother or sister who is fortunate enough to be able to help.'

Investigators found that people living in areas of high unemployment were more likely to be ill than those in better-off regions. Some ailments sprang from a poor diet, some from the mental depression of years of struggling to live on the dole. For people who were ill, the inter-war years saw little improvement. The 1911 health insurance scheme did not give the dependents

Mass protest in Trafalgar Square against the means test in 1932

QUESTIONS

1. **What is the difference between 'selective' and 'universal' benefits? (3)**
2. **What is a 'means test'? (3)**
3. **Why did Lenin describe the Liberal Party reforms as 'sops for the obedient workers'? (5)**
4. **How might the dole undermine the traditional role of the father and threaten family solidarity? (4)**
5. **The dole failed to meet the needs of the unemployed. Outline the evidence which supports this statement. (5)**

THE ESTABLISHMENT OF THE WELFARE STATE

PART 3

The aftermath of a war often brings changes. People have made great sacrifices, their lives have been disrupted and they are often not prepared to accept their old status - they want something better. This can be seen in the expansion of social services after the First World War (1914-18) when the then Prime Minister, Lloyd George promised the troops 'homes fit for heroes'. During the Second World War (1939-45) a committee chaired by Sir William Beveridge produced the famous *Beveridge Report on Social Insurance and Allied Services.* Published in 1942 it became an immediate bestseller. Popular support for its principles was widespread both at home and among the troops abroad. Its recommendations appeared to embody the very things being fought for - democracy, freedom and equality.

Before Beveridge social security provisions were largely selective - they were provided for certain occupational and income groups and directed towards the needs of particular individuals. With Beveridge the idea of universality was established - services should be provided for everyone as a matter of right. Thus the 1945 Family Allowance Act provided weekly cash payments for each child after the first. Every family in the land was entitled to those payments. This was very different from the idea of doling out money to selected individuals on the basis of a means test.

The following passage examines the Beveridge Report and the legislation that followed.

A *Punch* cartoon from 1942 shows the high hopes raised by the Beveridge Report.

The Beveridge Report aimed to provide for people's needs 'from the cradle to the grave'. It identified 'five giants on the road to social reconstruction and progress' - want, disease, ignorance, squalor and idleness - which had to be conquered. The Report's recommendations were put into effect by a series of Acts from 1944 to 1948. Together they created the modern welfare state in the UK.

Want The 1946 National Insurance Act extended, amongst other things, unemployment and sickness benefit and old age pensions. The 1948 National Assistance Act aimed to create a safety net for those who remained poor even with the benefits provided by the 1946 Act. It was based on a 'needs test' to make sure that claims were genuine. This was not as harsh as the old means test since it did not include a check on the earnings of members of the claimant's family.

Disease The 1946 National Health Service Act established a virtually free health service for all to be paid for out of taxation. The old health insurance scheme only covered employees who had paid contributions - neither their families nor the self-employed were covered. In 1946 Aneurin Bevan, the Minister of Health, introduced the new Bill with the words, 'This Bill provides a universal health service with no insurance qualifications of any sort. It is intended that there shall be no limitations on the kind of assistance given - general practitioners' service, specialists, hospitals, eye treatment, dental treatment, hearing facilities.'

'Just spots before the eyes.... Don't worry, we'll soon cure that!'

Health Minister Aneurin Bevan 'taking care' of a doctor. The British Medical Association campaigned against state control of medicine.

Ignorance The 1944 Education Act established the tripartite (three part) system of secondary education - grammar, technical and secondary modern schools. Education was free and in theory all children were given an equal chance to develop their talents in the type of school for which they were best suited (see Chapter 10, Part 14).

Squalor The postwar Labour government assumed responsibility for providing decent homes. Restrictions were put on private building and a large scale programme of building council houses for rent was undertaken.

Idleness The government committed itself to full employment basing its economic policy on the theories of the British economist John Maynard Keynes (1883-1946).

There have been many changes in the welfare state since the 1940s. However, the basic framework created by the postwar Labour government remains.

(adapted from 'Introduction to the Social Services' by W. E. Baugh, 3rd edition, Macmillan, London, 1977 and 'The British Welfare State 1900-1950' by Sydney Wood, Cambridge University Press, Cambridge, 1982)

QUESTIONS

1. Why does social change often follow a war? (3)
2. Identify three universal provisions established after 1945. (3)
3. Universality removes the stigma of means tested benefits. Explain this statement with reference to Part 2. (4)
4. The Beveridge reforms did not remove the means test. What evidence in the passage shows this? (2)
5. Why was the Beveridge Report met with public enthusiasm? Refer to Part 2 in your answer. (4)
6. Beveridge's 'five giants' have proved a lot harder to conquer than he hoped. Briefly discuss in terms of present day British society. (4)

4 PART — THE DEVELOPMENT OF THE WELFARE STATE

During the 1980s and 1990s there have been important changes to the welfare state. Since 1979 Conservative governments have argued that many parts of the welfare state are inefficient and wasteful. In other words the welfare state is not doing its job properly and is wasting money. Added to this is the view held by some that too much welfare is bad for people - it results in a culture of dependency which destroys initiative and self-help (see Chapter 6, Part 6). Finally, the question of whether the nation can afford a welfare state has been hotly debated. These views and concerns have influenced changes in the welfare state over the past 20 years.

Since 1979 Conservative governments have brought in a number of changes in welfare benefits and services. These include:

- **Increased selectivity and means testing** There has been a move away from universal benefits, free for all as a matter of right, to selective benefits based on means tests. For example, eyesight tests are no longer free for all but are means tested. Cuts in some universal benefits, such as unemployment benefit, have meant that more people have to rely on means tested benefits such as income support.

  It has been argued that selective, means tested benefits allow the welfare state to target those most in need. This will increase efficiency by directing resources only to those who really need help. It will also save money since those who can afford to pay will not receive benefits.

- **Privatisation** Before 1989 services such as refuse collection, and cleaning and catering in schools and hospitals were

One view of the future of the welfare state

performed by local authority employees. Since 1989 they must, by law, be put out to tender, which means that private companies can bid for contracts to perform such services. It has been argued that competition will increase efficiency and reduce costs.

The sale of council houses is another form of privatisation. It takes houses owned by local authorities from the public into the private sector. Since 1980 over 1.5 million council houses have been sold by local authorities.

- **Competition** During the 1980s and 1990s there have been moves to introduce competition within the welfare state itself. Again the aim is to increase efficiency and reduce costs. For example, many General Practitioners have been given budgets by Regional Health Authorities to buy services for their patients from hospitals. The idea is to encourage competition between hospitals as doctors shop around to get the best deal for their patients.

- **Community care** In recent years there has been a move from institutional care - care in institutions such as psychiatric and geriatric hospitals - to community care - care in the community. Large numbers of care institutions have been closed down and their former inmates - the elderly, disabled

and mentally ill - returned to the community where relatives, voluntary organisations and local authorities are expected to care for them. Care in the community is less expensive. One estimate suggests that support for a frail elderly person in their own home would be one third of the cost of a bed in a National Health Service geriatric ward. (Community care is examined in more detail in Part 6.)

(adapted from 'Sociology in Focus' by Paul Taylor et al, Causeway Press, Ormskirk, 1995, pp159-160; 167)

QUESTIONS

1. Using examples from the passage suggest how competition might a) increase efficiency and b) reduce costs. (8)
2. Suggest possible disadvantages of this emphasis on efficiency and cost-cutting. (6)
3. Suggest possible advantages and disadvantages of community care. (6)

VOLUNTARY ORGANISATIONS AND SELF-HELP

Voluntary welfare organisations are bodies outside the welfare state that provide social services. Their role is examined in the following passage.

During the 19th century voluntary organisations provided many of the services now administered by the state. They were the chief means of collective action for welfare outside the Poor Law. Many were based on ideas of Christian charity and duty. The church provided schools for those who otherwise could not afford them and homes for orphans, the disabled and the elderly. The Salvation Army (founded in 1865) provided for the poor and destitute combining board and lodging with a good dose of religion. Other voluntary groups were organised on a self-help basis. The Friendly Societies were formed by groups of workers who contributed to a common fund from which members could draw in times of hardship. In 1861 the Friendly Societies had around three million members and some £12 million capital.

The rise of the welfare state produced some changes in the voluntary welfare sector but by no

means ended it. After the Second World War much of the work of the Friendly Societies and voluntary hospitals was taken over by the state. But charity and self-help are still vital parts of

Evening service in a Salvation Army shelter, 1908

national welfare. Many 19th century organisations such as Dr Barnado's homes and the Salvation Army are alive and well. Self-help groups continue to thrive - housing associations build homes for joint ownership, squatters' groups organise their members to take over empty property for homes, mothers join together to form pre-school playgroups, widows, parents, alcoholics and drug addicts form associations to help themselves. One of the more recent developments in the voluntary sector is the formation of groups to put pressure on government to improve state services. Such groups include Shelter (the National Campaign for the Homeless) and the Child Poverty Action Group.

Supporters of voluntary organisations make the following points in their favour. They offer choice and specialist services so supplementing, supporting and filling gaps in state provision while at the same time saving public money. In some ways they may be better suited meeting certain needs. Groups such as Gingerbread for single parents and Cruse for widows are run by people in the same position as those they serve. They can often provide a more sensitive service because they share the problems and experiences of their members. It is important that some groups remain outside the state sector. Organisations such as Shelter and the Child Poverty Action Group can point to the failings in government policy and provide specialist advice for improving state welfare.

Critics of voluntary welfare argue that it is hit-and-miss, that it depends on the whims of private individuals. Services should be provided by the state, not left to chance. In addition, charity provided by voluntary groups can be patronising, it can degrade those who receive it. Needs should not be met by charitable gifts doled out by 'do-gooders'. They should be met by the state - welfare should be the right of every citizen.

(adapted from 'The Future of Voluntary Organisations', Report of the Wolfenden Committee, Croom Helm, London, 1978 and 'A National Perspective' by John Dearlove in 'Voluntary Action' edited by David Dickinson, BBC Publications, London, 1973)

QUESTIONS

1. a) Why were the Friendly Societies so important in the 19th century? (3)
   b) Why did their importance decline? (2)
2. What are the advantages of self-help groups staffed by people in the same position as those they serve? (4)
3. Why is it important that groups such as Shelter remain outside the state sector? (3)
4. How can charity be seen as degrading for those who receive it? (3)
5. If the welfare state did its job properly there would be no need for voluntary welfare organisations. Briefly assess this view. (5)

PART 6 — COMMUNITY CARE

Throughout the 1980s and 1990s there has been a move away from care in institutions to care in the community. Large numbers of institutions, such as geriatric hospitals for the elderly and psychiatric hospitals for the mentally ill, have been closed and replaced by care in the community.

Supporters of community care argue that it has a number of advantages. It is less expensive than institutional care. It allows people to lead a more normal life. Many prefer to be looked after by family and friends rather than care in an institution. And carers often value the opportunity to look after their relatives and contribute to the wider community. However, there is growing evidence that community care in practice is a long way from these optimistic claims. The case studies which follow look at some of this evidence.

Figure 1   Carers in the UK

Number of people in UK caring at home for sick, disabled or elderly relatives (last surveyed 1990): 6.8 million

Age group of carer	% of age group who are carers
16-29	8%
30-44	15%
45-64	24%
over 65	13%

What do they do?
- 22% of carers involved in personal care, such as washing, toilet, etc
- 16% administer medicines
- 79% give other practical help
- 23% care more than 20 hours per week
- 11% care over 50 hours per week
- Most care for only one person, but 3% care for more than one person
- 71% of carers care for someone with physical disability
- 5% care for those with mental disability

17% care for those with both
79% of those cared for are over 65
20% of those cared for are over 85

When carers were surveyed in 1992, it was discovered that:
47% of Carers' National Association members had suffered financial difficulty since becoming carers
65% say their health has suffered
20% have never had a break
33% get no help or support with their caring responsibilities

No practical help: In 1990, the General Household Survey showed that 55% of dependents received no regular visits from a doctor, nurse, social worker, home help or other source of support.

Child carers: A survey conducted by the Children's Society in 1994 estimated that as many as 40,000 young people in the UK, aged 17 and under, are caring for ill or disabled parents.

(adapted from 'Mums' and Dads' Army' by Roy Bainton, 'New Statesman & Society', 22.9.1995 and 'Children in Focus', Winter 1995)

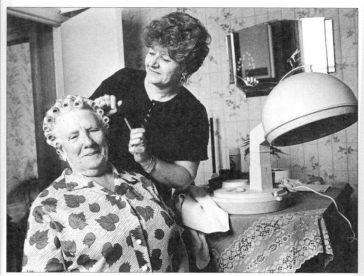

Helping an elderly neighbour

Caring for elderly relatives

My wife and I were looking forward to 1995. After 29 financially strapped years of marriage, with the kids now in their twenties, a rosy prospect beckoned for us to make some long overdue hay while our sun still shone.

At least, that was the scenario we'd imagined up until October 1994. Just after his 78th birthday, my father-in-law had his second stroke. This coincided with mother-in-law, aged 79, losing her ability to walk.

At first, we panicked; although we had a ground-floor room large enough to accommodate them, we could offer no toilet and washing facilities. Surely, there would be some way the state could care for the elderly and the infirm who wished to stay in their own homes?

A month of intense form filling and phone calls followed. It began to look as if we might just be able to keep them safely in their own home for the foreseeable future. With the Department of Social Security attendance allowance of £45.70 per week, we left our fragile relatives at the mercy of the visiting social services 'carers'.

Grandad remained unwashed for a week. We arrived on the Saturday morning to find him sad and rather soiled. Apparently, the breakfast visitor passed the buck for washing and hygiene to the afternoon visitor. The afternoon visitor claimed her breakfast colleague was responsible. Result - a dirty old man.

We kept a diary of the time spent on visits over a ten-day period. The total spent with the old folk was 2 hours and 50 minutes, an average of 13 minutes per day. For this they received a bill from the social services for £90.

We refused to pay. Additional help cost our in-laws dearly. A home help was hired at £4 per hour for ten hours per week. Another helper was taken on to do their shopping, and yet another to cash their pensions every Thursday. The garden needed tidying, the cat needed feeding. With grandma stranded in her chair, immobile, and granddad suffering with his impaired memory, we knew it was time. The experiment to allow the state to keep them at home had failed miserably.

Prior to being involved in caring, I was under the misguided impression that carers were adequately compensated for relieving the state of so much work. As a full-time worker outside the home, even though I devote around 20 hours per week to my in-laws' welfare, I am unable to claim any allowance.

The burden of the daily tasks falls to my wife. But the amount she receives is derisory. There is only one specific benefit carers can claim; the Invalid Care Allowance. This is one of the lowest of all social security benefits at £35.25 per week. Due to the strictness of the rules, only about 17.5% of full-time carers receive this benefit.

According to the Carers' National Association (1 March 1995), the true economic support given by carers in the UK shows that, if just one in ten carers threw in the towel, the cost of funding alternative care would add £2 billion annually to the social security budget.

(adapted from 'Mums' and Dads' Army' by Roy Bainton, 'New Statesman & Society', 22.9.1995)

Caring for the mentally ill

In December 1992, Christopher Clunis, a schizophrenic with a long history of mental instability and violence, walked up to Jonathan Zito, a complete stranger, and stabbed him to death. The murder took place in broad daylight, in front of horrified bystanders at Finsbury Park Tube Station. Clunis had passed through ten hospitals including psychiatric units at four major

Homeless man - covering the head is often a sign of mental illness.

London hospitals. His records were rarely passed on and there was little or no coordination between doctors, social workers and police. In the words of the official inquiry, 'Cluniss after-care plan was virtually non-existent. No one was coordinating his psychiatric care and treatment in the community.'

(adapted from 'Daily Telegraph' and 'Guardian', 25.2.1994)

QUESTIONS

1. a) According to Figure 1 which age group has the highest percentage of carers? (1)
   b) Suggest a reason for this. (1)
2. What evidence is given in Figure 1 to indicate that carers need more help and support? (4)
3. Community care is sometimes hopelessly inadequate. Use evidence from the first extract - 'Caring for elderly relatives' - to support this statement. (5)
4. One of the problems with community care is a lack of coordination between the various branches of the health and social services. Discuss this with reference to the second extract. (4)
5. In 1995, Health Secretary Stephen Dorrell stated with reference to community care, 'It is not the idea that is at fault'. Present an argument in favour of the idea of community care. (5)

7 PART — A CRITICAL VIEW OF WELFARE

High levels of unemployment and growing numbers of pensioners, single parent families and low wage earners have resulted in more and more people being dependent on state welfare. In the eyes of many critics the payments provided by the state are meagre and mean and the services it offers are often inadequate.

The welfare state has been seen by many as 1) mainly benefiting the poor and 2) as a means of redistributing income from the better to the worse off. The following passage rejects this view.

What is the value of the welfare state to the rich and the poor? If we look at education, the sons and daughters of those at the top are more likely to stay on at school beyond the minimum leaving age and continue into higher education. The cost of education steadily rises from primary to secondary school to university. Julian Le Grand calculates that families in the top 20% of income groups have nearly three times as much government money spent on their children's education than those in the bottom 20%. Health care provides a similar picture of unequal spending. Le Grand estimates that those at the top receive 40% more National Health Service expenditure per person reporting illness than those at the bottom.

Peter Townsend argues that government economic policy cannot be separated from its welfare policy. Decisions on investment, taxation and public expenditure will affect all members of society - some will be favoured, others will not.

There is evidence that during the 1980s and 1990s government policies contributed to the widening income gap between rich and poor. During these years there were a number of tax concessions to the rich - reductions in income tax and inheritance tax - while some of the welfare benefits relied on by the poor were reduced (see pages 58-59). There has also been a move away from direct taxation (taxing income, eg by income tax) to indirect taxation (taxing goods and services, eg by VAT - value added tax). Indirect taxes take up a greater proportion of the income of the poor than the rich.

Governments in recent years have mounted periodic campaigns against so-called 'welfare scroungers' - those who defraud the benefit system. Yet better-off 'scroungers' - those who defraud the Inland Revenue - do not appear to receive similar treatment. One estimate states that for every person prosecuted for tax fraud, some 700 are prosecuted for social

One view of social security fraud

security fraud. This despite the fact that the cost of tax fraud is estimated to be 10 times higher than social security fraud (see page 96). Thus it appears that even when both rich and poor steal from the government, the rich are still favoured.

(adapted from 'Society' by Peter Townsend, 'New Socialist', Sept/Oct 1981; 'Observer', 23.10.1988; 'Sociology: Themes and Perspectives' 4th edition by Michael Haralambos and Martin Holborn, Collins Educational, London, 1995, pp160-163)

QUESTIONS

1. a) Summarise the evidence which indicates that more money is spent on the education of the children of the rich than the poor? (3)
   b) Should the rich have to pay for higher education? (4)
2. a) What does Townsend mean when he says that economic policy cannot be separated from welfare policy? (4)
   b) Provide evidence to support this view. (4)
3. Government campaigns should be directed more at tax fraud than social security fraud. Discuss this view. (5)

8 PART THE FUTURE OF THE WELFARE STATE

Can we afford a welfare state? Is spending on social security out of control? Are there realistic alternatives to the welfare state? These kinds of questions have been raised with increasing frequency in recent years. The following passages look at the case for and against the modern welfare state in Britain.

The case against the welfare state

What costs more than £90 billion a year - five times its level in 1979 - and extracts £15 a day from every working taxpayer? What is clearly failing in the task of lifting the disadvantaged out of their vicious circle of unemployment and relative poverty? The answer, of course, is that bloated, ever-expanding monster known as the welfare state and its ballooning social security budget. An ageing population combined with the creation of a dependency culture, means that social security spending will soon lift already high taxation to punishing levels. The result will be the destruction of initiative and enterprise.

It is self-evident that the welfare state must be hacked back. It is not sensible for the middle classes to pay taxes with one hand and get them back as benefits with the other. In an age of private insurance, the state pension should only go to those in genuine need. Those who can afford it should take out private insurance policies to support themselves in their old age. The same applies to sickness and unemployment - those who can afford it should insure against such misfortunes. The state will then provide a means tested minimum safety net for those genuinely in need. This will reduce taxation, encourage self-reliance and initiative, and discourage the dependency culture.

(adapted from 'Sunday Times', 21.5.1995)

Figure 1 Social security spending, 1979-1995

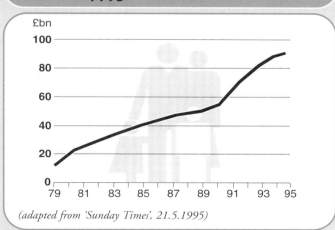

(adapted from 'Sunday Times', 21.5.1995)

One view of the future of welfare - homeless, jobless and begging but fending for himself

The case for the welfare state

Will Hutton attacks the view of a welfare state 'in crisis' with the social security budget running 'out of control'. First, he notes that Britain's social spending is low by international standards (see Figure 2). Despite an ageing population and advances in health care - which have led to increasing demands on the health service - growth in the health budget has been modest. And the education budget, despite the rapid growth in further and higher education, has not changed significantly in recent years. True, the social security budget has risen by 9.5% of GDP (gross domestic product - national output) in 1979 to over 12% in 1994-95, but this is hardly 'out of control'.

Part of this rise is due to higher levels of unemployment and growing numbers of people of pensionable age. The rise in housing benefit, which has doubled over the past five years, is due almost entirely to the government decision to increase council house rents. These three factors account for more than half the rise in social security spending. The growth in income support and invalidity benefit accounts for much of the rest. And benefits are far from generous. Britain expects its social security claimants to live on less, in relation to average income, than any other large European country.

Many reject the argument that taxes should be raised to adequately fund the welfare state. However, Will Hutton notes that the 36.75% of national output that the government will claim in the 1995/6 financial year is the second lowest in Europe. And the alternative of private insurance is beyond the means of over half the population which includes the unemployed, low paid, part-time workers and single parent families. If their needs are not met by an improved welfare state then the gap between the haves and the have-nots will widen to a chasm.

Figure 2 Social spending

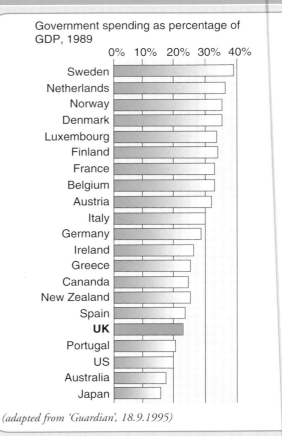

Government spending as percentage of GDP, 1989

(adapted from 'Guardian', 18.9.1995)

Given the scale of need and demand, Britain's social security budget is modest and growing slowly. The question is not whether we can afford a welfare state. The real question is whether the country is prepared to pay the price for social cohesion.

(adapted from 'A State of Decay' by Will Hutton, 'Guardian', 18.9.1995)

QUESTIONS

1. a) What is an ageing population? (1)
    b) How does it lead to an increase in welfare spending? (2)
2. How might higher taxes reduce initiative and enterprise? (2)
3. a) How might a move from state welfare to private insurance discourage a dependency culture? (2)
    b) How might it lead to a welfare state which targets the poor and those in real need? (2)
    c) Outline the case against private insurance. (3)
4. What evidence is there that Britain can afford to increase funding for the welfare state? (4)
5. What does Will Hutton mean when he states that, 'The real question is whether the country is prepared to pay the price for social cohesion'? (4)

POWER AND POLITICS

Politics is about power. Power is the ability of an individual or group to realise their aims even if others resist. The chapter begins with an examination of different ways of looking at power and measuring power. The focus then moves to Britain and asks who holds power, how is power distributed in society and how is it used. It starts with the view that power is widely distributed in Western democracies and rests ultimately with the electorate, those who have the right to vote. The role of pressure groups - groups which represent sectional interests in society - is then examined. This is followed by a Marxist view of power in Britain which presents a very different perspective, arguing that power is concentrated in the hands of a small minority, the ruling class.

A large body of research has been concerned with the social influences on the way people vote in general elections. This research is examined in terms of the influence of social class, age, gender and ethnicity on voting behaviour. This is followed by a discussion of why large numbers of people fail to use their right to vote. The possible effects of opinion polls on voting behaviour is then considered. Social influences on political behaviour are returned to with an examination of the social background of MPs.

The chapter closes with a view of democracy and totalitarianism from George Orwell's *Animal Farm*.

FORMS OF POWER

Sociologists often make a distinction between two forms of power - authority and coercion.

Authority is a form of power which is regarded as right and legitimate. For example, Parliament has authority if members of British society accept that it has the right to pass laws which must then be obeyed. *Coercion* is a form of power which is not regarded as right and legitimate. Thus the power of Parliament may be regarded as coercion by certain groups in British society.

The German sociologist Max Weber identified three types of authority - charismatic, traditional and rational-legal authority.

Charismatic authority is based on the personal qualities of leaders. There is something special about them which gives them authority over others. Sometimes they are seen to have supernatural or superhuman powers or exceptional courage, honesty, goodness or other valued characteristics. These personal qualities inspire devotion and loyalty from their followers. Examples of leaders with charismatic authority include Jesus, Alexander the Great and Mother Theresa.

Traditional authority is based on a belief in longstanding customs and traditions. Often these traditions are regarded as sacred and are backed by supernatural power, eg they are right because God says so. Those in authority hold power on the basis of their traditional status which is usually inherited. Those who obey them do so because of feelings of loyalty, duty and obligation. The feudal system of medieval Europe is an example of traditional authority (see Chapter 4, Part 1).

Rational-legal authority is based on legal rules. Those who obey rational-legal authority do so because they accept the laws and rules on which it is based. The rules are 'rational' because they are designed to achieve a particular goal. For example, the legal system is designed to achieve the goal of 'justice'. Examples of rational-legal authority include a judge, a tax inspector and an officer in the armed forces. Each is obeyed because others accept the laws and rules which give them power.

Weber saw rational-legal authority as the main type of authority in modern industrial societies.

Authority and coercion

A wallpainting in Londonderry in Northern Ireland which includes the city's coat of arms.

A wallpainting in Twinbrook, near Belfast, in Northern Ireland

Medieval monarchs

The coronation of King Edward I at Westminster, 19 August 1274. He is anointed by churchmen and crowned by an archbishop.

Nobles take an oath of loyalty to the King. This was known as doing homage. They promised to fight for the King when he asked.

The King grants a knighthood. This was an honour to reward service and obedience and to ensure the loyalty of followers.

Adolf Hitler

Listening to Hitler in 1922, an admirer said, 'I was held under a hypnotic spell. The will of the man seemed to flow into me. It was like a religious conversion'.

More than a hundred thousand people had paid to squeeze inside the Gruenwald Stadium in July 1932. Another hundred

Adolf Hitler at a Nazi Party rally in 1934

thousand packed a nearby race-track where loud-speakers had been set up to carry Hitler's words. And at home millions were waiting by the radio.

Suddenly a word was tossed from man to man: Hitler is coming! Hitler is here! A blare of trumpets rent the air, and a hundred thousand people leaped to their feet in tense expectancy. All eyes were turned towards the stand, awaiting the approach of the Fuehrer. There was a low rumble of excitement and then, releasing its pent-up emotion, the crowd burst into a tremendous ovation, the 'Heils' swelling until they were like the roar of a mighty cataract.

Vivian Ogilvie, a British teacher in Germany in the 1930s recalls: 'The religious lessons consisted for the most part of talks about Herr Hitler and the glories of Germany. Children told me that the teacher had said that Hitler was the second Jesus but greater than the first. The teacher asks leading questions such as 'Who at the present day reminds us most strongly of Jesus by his love of the people and self-sacrifice?' to which the answer is 'Herr Hitler', and 'Who reminds us by their loyalty and devotion of the Disciples?' The answer: 'General Goring and Dr Goebbels'.

(adapted from 'Britain and the World: the 20th Century' by Tony and Steve Lancaster, Causeway Press, Ormskirk, 1995, p45; 'Germany 1919-1945' by Maria McKay, Longman, Harlow, 1989, p54; 'The Rise and Fall of Hitler's Germany' by Simon Williams, Nelson, Walton-on-Thames, 1992, p35)

The Health and Safety Inspector

The Health and Safety at Work Act of 1974 lays down legally binding standards for health and safety in the workplace. Health and Safety Inspectors are employed to enforce the Act. They visit workplaces to check that employers are obeying the law. For example, they check that first aid equipment is available for all employees, that fire equipment is in place and ready for use, that substances hazardous to health are safely contained and stored and that safety guards on machines are in place and adequate for the purpose.

Inspectors have a number of powers. These include the right to enter business premises without permission; the issue of a prohibition notice which forbids work on equipment they regard as unsafe; the right to prosecute an employer who breaks health and safety regulations. Prosecution can lead to a fine and/or imprisonment.

(adapted from 'Essential Facts: Premises, Health and Safety' edited by Alastair Alexander and Clive Lampard, Gee, London, 1994)

QUESTIONS

1. Look at the pictures of wallpaintings in Northern Ireland. Which sees the power of the British government as authority and which as coercion? Give reasons for your answer. (8)
2. Which of the three types of authority (charismatic, traditional and rational-legal) best fits a) medieval monarchs, b) Adolf Hitler, c) Health and Safety Inspectors? Give evidence to support your answers. (12)

FACES OF POWER

Stephen Lukes identifies three *faces of power*. By this he means that power has three aspects or dimensions, that power can be exercised in three different ways.

1. Decision making This is the first face of power. It can be seen from decisions. For example, if Parliament makes decisions which consistently favour the demands of private industry, despite opposition from others such as trade unions and conservation groups, then this would indicate that private industry has considerable power. Power is measured in terms of who wins decisions.

2. Non-decision making This is the second face of power. It is the power to prevent things from ever reaching the point of decision making. For example, it has been argued that the monarchy in Britain has considerable power because the question of whether or not it should be abolished does not reach the point of decision making. In other words it is a non-decision.

3. *Shaping desires* This is the third face of power. It sees power as the ability to shape the wishes and desires of others. In this way a dominant group can persuade others to accept, or actually desire, their subordinate position. For example, it has been argued that men have power over women because many women accept and even desire their roles as housewives.

The following passage looks at the three faces of power in the classroom

The students liked Mrs Bentley. She had a good sense of humour, she listened to them and let them have their say. Take last week. She set her Chemistry class some homework and was greeted with a chorus of complaints that they already had far too much homework. 'OK, let's take a vote on it,' she said. 'I'd rather you did your homework this week, but you can leave it and do double next week.' The class voted for next week and Mrs Bentley's popularity was assured.

But nobody asked whether or not homework should be abolished altogether. And it is doubtful whether the democratic Mrs Bentley would have let her class vote on this matter. Nor did the students question the whole idea of going to school. In fact they never even thought about it.

(developed from an idea in 'Sociology: Themes and Perspectives' 4th edition, by Michael Haralambos and Martin Holborn, Collins Educational, London, 1995, p503)

QUESTIONS

1. Show how the three faces of power are illustrated in the passage. (12)
2. A study which uses only the decision making approach is unlikely to discover who has power in society. Discuss. (8)

3 PART — DEMOCRACY IN BRITAIN

This part looks at power in terms of the decision making - the first face of power. In terms of this approach, can Britain and other Western industrial societies be described as democratic?

A democracy is a political system which is based on government by the people. It has been argued that it is not practical or even possible for people in large complex societies to be directly involved in every decision which affects their lives. In practice the only way government by the people can work is in the form of *representative democracy* whereby a few represent the wishes and interests of the many. The two main institutions of a representative democracy are *political parties* and *pressure groups*. In theory political parties represent the nation as a whole. To be elected in the first place, they must reflect public opinion in their election promises. To gain re-election they must reflect the wishes of the people during their terms of office.

Pressure groups represent sectional interests, that is the wishes and concerns of sections of society. Thus trade unions represent the interests of workers, the Confederation of British Industry (CBI) represents large, privately owned manufacturing industries, the RAC and AA represent motorists and Friends of the Earth represent those concerned with conservation. Pressure groups aim to put pressure on governments to further their members' interests. In a democracy governments do not consistently favour any one pressure group but take account of a variety of pressure groups when passing legislation.

By means of political parties and pressure groups both the public in general and particular sectional interests in society are represented. This is the way, at least in theory, that a representative democracy works. The following extract from a study by Christopher J. Hewitt examines a representative democracy in action.

Hewitt's study examines 24 policy issues that arose in the British Parliament between 1944 and 1964. Such issues include Britain's bid to enter the Common Market (now the European Union), air pollution and the debate leading to the 1944 Education Act. Hewitt looked at the various organisations and pressure groups that attempted to influence the government on these issues. Thus stricter controls on pollution were supported by the National Smoke Abatement Society backed by some business interests but opposed by the cotton and chemical industries and the Federation of British Industries (later the CBI)

which wanted less stringent controls. Hewitt then looked at the outcome of these policy issues, that is the decisions taken by government, and examined which pressure groups were favoured by the government. Thus, in the case of air pollution, the wishes of the National Smoke Abatement Society were reflected in the Clean Air Act of 1956. Hewitt found that no one pressure group consistently got its own way. Often government decisions took account of all the pressure groups involved and the final decision was a compromise between their demands. Hewitt also looked at available public opinion polls on the various issues to see whether or not governments reflected the wishes of the public.

The following table looks at some of the findings of Hewitt's research. It lists 1) the issue, 2) the policy outcome, ie the decision taken by the government, and 3) whether or not the decision reflected the views of business interests, trade unions and the public. A dash indicates that business interests or unions were not involved in the issue or that information on public opinion was unavailable. Divided means that the group involved was divided over the issue.

The Houses of Parliament

Table 1   Policy issues and outcomes

Issue	Policy outcome	Government reflects views of		
		a) Business	b) Unions	c) Public
India	Independence for India	-	-	Yes
Russia	Hard-line policy to Russia	-	Yes	-
Abadan	Sanctions against Iran	Yes	-	-
Suez	Military intervention	-	No	Divided
Nuclear deterrent	Independent deterrent policy	No	Divided	-
Central Africa	Federation	-	-	-
US loan	Loan negotiated	-	-	-
Road haulage	Nationalisation	No	Yes	-
Steel	No effective nationalisation	Yes	No	Yes
Resale price maintenance (RPM)	Abolition of RPM	No	-	Yes
Common Market	No entry	No	Yes	-
Railways	Beeching's rationalisation policy	Yes	No	Divided
Education	1944 Education Act	Yes	Yes	Yes
National Health	National Health Service	-	-	Yes
National Insurance	National Insurance Act	No	Yes	Yes
Rent Act	Rent decontrol	Yes	No	-
Comprehensives	No support for comprehensives	-	-	-
Motorways	Motorway programme	Yes	Yes	Yes
Town and country	Town and Country Planning Act	No	Yes	Yes
Divorce	No change in divorce laws	-	-	-
Capital punishment	Abolition of capital punishment	-	-	No
Television	Commercial Television	Divided	No	Divided
Immigration	Immigration control	-	-	Yes
Clean Air	Clean Air Act	Divided	-	Yes

(from 'Elites and the Distribution of Power in British Society' by Christopher J. Hewitt in 'Elites and Power in British Society' edited by P. Stanworth and A. Giddens, Cambridge University Press, Cambridge, 1974, p59)

QUESTIONS

1. From the above evidence, do governments reflect the wishes of the people? (6)
2. Is there any evidence in the extract to support or reject the view that there is a ruling class made up of business interests in Britain? (6)
3. On the basis of Hewitt's study, is Britain a democratic society? (8)

4 PART — PRESSURE GROUPS

Pressure groups come in all shapes and sizes. They range from Greenpeace - its mission 'to save the natural environment' - with offices in over 30 countries, 1,000 staff worldwide and 4 million members, to Struggle Against Financial Exploitation with 1,000-2,000 members in the UK - its mission to campaign against financial institutions on behalf of customers. The following passage looks at some of the ways pressure groups try to influence decision makers.

Most people only hear about pressure groups when they hit the headlines. Examples from 1995 include the arrest of the Greenpeace ship *Rainbow Warrior II* for entering the French nuclear testing zone in the Pacific and the mass protests by animal rights groups against the export of veal calves from English ports. Such events are often designed to grab media attention in order to broadcast the concerns of the pressure groups involved.

Pressure groups often make use of the media. For example, Amnesty International, a human rights organisation which campaigns against the imprisonment, torture and killing of political activists, regularly places full page advertisements in newspapers. Organisations such as the Child Poverty Action Group and Shelter (which campaigns on behalf of the homeless) conduct their own research. The results of this research are often published in newspapers such as the

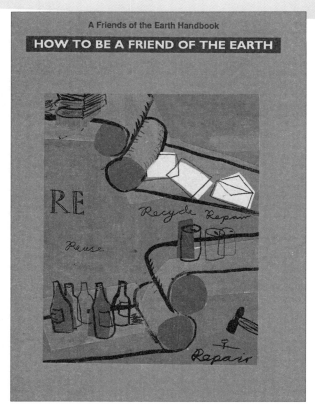

Many pressure groups aim to educate people as in this guide to waste disposal and recycling.

This advert was produced by UNISON, the trade union for workers in the public service and essential industries.

Guardian and reported on radio and TV.

Many pressure groups attempt to make direct contact with politicians. For example, the World Wide Fund for Nature (WWF) organised a mass card writing campaign. Over 30,000 people signed cards produced by WWF and sent them to their MPs. As a result the WWF was invited to a series of meetings with Lynda Chalker, the Minister for Overseas Development. This led to changes in government policy towards the World Bank and deforestation.

Pressure groups usually have specialised and expert knowledge of the areas with which they are concerned. As a result some groups are regularly consulted by government. For example, experts from MENCAP and MIND (groups which campaign on behalf of people with mental disabilities) are often invited to give information to government departments. In return, these groups are able to influence decisions and some receive financial contributions. About one fifth of MIND's funds comes directly from government.

Decision makers are more likely to listen to pressure groups if they think they have widespread public support. Large scale demonstrations, petitions and mass letter writing can indicate such support. For example, Greenpeace managed to get nearly half a million people to write letters protesting about whaling. Members of Amnesty International write letters to governments across the world, protesting about human rights abuses.

Members of the Women's Environmental Network block a road in Highbury, London, in protest at pollution caused by traffic.

Consumer boycotts have proved a very effective weapon for a number of pressure groups. The German airline Lufthansa agreed to stop transporting animals for laboratory testing 10 days after European anti-vivisectionist groups urged travellers to use other airlines. Anti-apartheid groups boycotted Barclays

Surfers against Sewage outside the Houses of Parliament with Liberal Democrat MP Simon Hughes

A Greenpeace protest against the killing of seals. The dead seal in the picture was washed up on the Norfolk coast. It was later taken to Downing Street.

Bank for 15 years in protest against its operations in South Africa. This was one factor contributing to the bank's withdrawal in 1986. In 1995 sales of Shell petrol slumped across Europe in response to a Greenpeace campaign to prevent the company from dumping an oilrig at sea. Shell bowed to the pressure and shelved the planned dumping.

Pressure groups can be divided into **insider** and **outsider** groups based on how the groups are treated by the government. Insider groups are consulted by government and asked to contribute their views. Insider groups include the National Farmers Union, the British Medical Association and the Automobile Association. Outsider groups have far less or no access at all to government departments. Some, like the Animal Liberation Front, are excluded because they use illegal methods such as bombings and break-ins. Others such as the Campaign for Nuclear Disarmament and Greenpeace oppose or are highly critical of government policy. Many outsider groups value their independence from governments and political parties. For example, Greenpeace proclaims that it 'maintains complete independence from all political parties anywhere in the world'.

(adapted from 'British Politics in Focus' edited by David Roberts, Causeway Press, Ormskirk, 1995, pp277-306 and 'Sunday Times', 10.9.1995)

QUESTIONS

1. Outline the main methods used by pressure groups to influence decision makers. (8)
2. What are the advantages and disadvantages of being an outsider pressure group? (6)
3. Democracy needs pressure groups. Discuss. (6)

5 PART

POWER IN BRITAIN - A MARXIST VIEW

This part looks at the second and third faces of power - *non-decision making*, the power to prevent things from reaching the point of decision and *shaping desires*, the power to shape the wishes and desires of others.

Part 3 presented a picture of a democratic society in which governments represent the interests of the people. However, this is only one point of view. Karl Marx, writing in the nineteenth century, saw the state as 'but a committee for managing the common affairs of the whole bourgeoisie'. He believed that the state represented the interests of a ruling class made up of those who own and control industry. The Marxist view therefore rejects the idea that governments are democratic and represent the people. It is examined in the following passage. (See also Chapter 4, Part 5 for a Marxist view of social stratification.)

From a Marxist viewpoint those who own private industry form a ruling class. Ownership of a successful company can bring high rewards - those profits which are not re-invested in the business are received by the owners. There are sometimes spin-offs for the workers - these may include higher wages, improved fringe benefits, better working conditions and more secure employment. However such spin-offs are small compared with the large sums of money often received by the owners.

Governments support private industry and particularly big business in a number of ways. Firstly, they take the position that the success of the nation depends in large part on the success of private industry. If ICI, GEC, BICC, BT and the major banks make big profits, this is good for Britain. It means, say successive government spokespersons, higher employment, higher wages, higher living standards and money from taxes, paid by private industry, for schools, hospitals and the whole range of public services. Governments do not support and advocate the alternative view - that workers have produced the profits by their labour and should therefore receive them. From a Marxist viewpoint, governments should support this policy, if they claim to

Power - a Marxist view

represent the majority of the population. Not supporting it means they represent a small minority - the ruling class.

Next, governments attempt to provide a framework in which private industry can grow and prosper. This was the stated objective of the Thatcher governments of the 1980s. They aimed to produce a fitter and leaner British industry and an end to what they saw as overmanning, restrictive practices and the abuse of union power. The result, they hoped, would be a more dynamic and competitive private sector which would once again make Britain great. In the area of foreign policy governments have always borne in mind the need to protect and secure markets abroad for British goods. They provide assistance to firms wishing to export their products. Again it is stated that such policies are in the national interest. However, if these efforts to help private industry succeed, the owners rather than the workforce stand to gain most.

During this century, however, the state has introduced a wide range of reforms which appear to benefit the mass of the population. These include legislation to improve health and safety in the workplace, social security benefits such as old age pensions and unemployment benefit, a national health service and free education for all. People as a whole have probably benefited considerably from these measures. But it is the people who have paid for them. The welfare state is largely paid for from taxes on the wages of those who use it. Governments have not acted like Robin Hood, taking from the rich to pay the poor.

Marx believed that workers were exploited and oppressed because a large part of the wealth they produced was taken from them. If this is the case then there is always a danger of conflict and rebellion. One way of keeping people in their place is to give them the impression that those in power represent their interests and act on their demands. This is what the state in modern Western societies has done. It has provided a range of benefits for workers so giving them the impression that their

interests are being represented. These measures can be seen as 'sops' to keep the masses happy, or at least quiet, and to damp down their frustration and resentment. This in turn produces a fairly quiet and passive workforce to earn profits for the owners of private industry. Thus governments help the poor a little and in doing so help the rich a lot.

From a Marxist point of view power must be seen in terms of 'non-decisions' and 'shaping desires'. The most important issues in Britain have remained non-decisions - Should there be private industry? Should a large part of the wealth produced by workers go to a small minority? The power of the ruling class can therefore be seen from its ability to keep such issues from reaching the point of decision. And it can also be seen from shaping wishes and desires. Most workers accept their situation as workers. They want higher wages and better living standards which, for much of the 20th century, they have received. But this is the extent of their desires. They do not look forward to the day when the ruling class is overthrown.

(based in part on 'Class in a Capitalist Society' by John Westergaard and Henrietta Resler, Penguin, Harmondsworth, 1975)

QUESTIONS

1. If private industry prospers, who gains most? Give reasons for your answer. (4)
2. a) Why do workers present a threat to the owners of private industry? (4)
   b) How do governments reduce this threat? (4)
3. From a Marxist viewpoint why will the decision making approach fail to reveal who has power? (4)
4. The view of Britain as a democracy is rejected from a Marxist viewpoint. Why? Use evidence from the passage in your answer. (4)

SOCIAL CLASS AND VOTING BEHAVIOUR

PART 6

Voting in general elections takes place in secret. The voter is alone when he or she places a cross on the ballot paper. Voting, at first sight, is an individual act. Looked at another way, however, voting is a social act - it is influenced by social factors. Sociologists have identified a number of links between the way people vote in general elections and their social background. This part looks at the relationship between social class and voting behaviour.

Traditionally the Labour Party has been seen as the party of the working class with its support for social welfare policies, nationalisation (public ownership) and a more equal distribution of income and wealth. By comparison the Conservative Party has been seen as the party of the middle and upper classes. With most of its Parliamentary candidates drawn from the ranks of the well-to-do, it has traditionally been regarded as the defender of wealth and privilege.

Table 1 shows how members of different social classes voted in the 1992 general election.

Table 1 Social class and voting in the 1992 general election (percentages)

Social class	Con	Lab	Lib Dem
Professional and managerial	56	20	22
White collar	52	25	19
Skilled manual	38	41	17
Semi & unskilled	30	50	15

(based on a Mori poll of 22,727 voters)

Table 2 shows the percentage of non-manual (middle class) and manual (working class) people who voted for each of the three main parties in general elections from 1964 to 1992. 'Class voters' refers to the percentage voting for their 'class party', ie manual workers voting Labour and non-manual workers voting Conservative.

Table 2 Social class and party choice, 1964-1992

	1964		1966		1970		1974 (Feb)		1974 (Oct)		1979		1983		1987		1992	
	N/M	M	N/M	M	N/M	M	N/M	M	N/M	M	N/M	M	N/M	M	N/M	M	N/M	M
Conservative	62	28	60	25	64	33	53	24	51	24	55	36	51	35	49	37	49	35
Liberal	16	8	14	6	11	9	25	19	24	20	19	17	31	28	31	23	25	20
Labour	22	64	26	69	25	58	22	57	25	57	26	46	18	37	20	40	26	45
class voters	63		66		60		55		54		51		45		44		47	

N/M = non-manual M = manual All figures in percentages

(adapted from 'Mrs Thatcher's Electoral Success' by J. Benyon and D. Denver, 'Social Studies Review', January 1990 and 'The Changing Basis of Party Choice, 1979-1992' by I. Crewe, Politics Review, February 1993)

Table 2 indicates that the link between social class and voting behaviour has weakened between the 1960s and the 1990s. This process has been termed class dealignment. Two explanations for **class dealignment** will now be examined.

Changes in the occupational structure

Since the 1960s, there has been a decline in traditional industries such as mining, shipbuilding and steel manufacture. Workers in these industries were highly unionised (most belonged to trade unions), they often lived in occupational communities (eg mining villages) and they had strong loyalties to their trade union, to the working class and the Labour Party.

Since the 1960s, there has been a steady decline in the numbers of people employed in manufacturing and a growth in employment in the non-manufacturing or service industries. This process accelerated in the 1980s and 90s (see Figure 1). At the same time there has been a decline in trade union membership from 13.3 million (53% of the workforce) in 1979 to 8.5 million (30% of the workforce) in 1994. These changes have weakened the link between manual workers, trade unions and the Labour Party.

Many former manual workers now have non-manual jobs. The increase in non-Conservative voting in the middle class may be due to these 'new recruits' retaining their loyalty to Labour.

The traditional and new working classes

Ivor Crewe claims that the working class has two main parts. He calls one the **traditional working class** which consists of manual workers who live on council estates, work in the public sector (employed by the government, local authorities and in nationalised industries), belong to trade unions and live mainly in the North of England and Scotland. They are the strongest supporters of the Labour Party. The second part, which Crewe calls **new working class**, are manual workers who own their own homes, are employed by private industry, do not belong to trade unions and live mainly in the South.

Figure 1 Employment in service and manufacturing industries, Great Britain 1981-1994

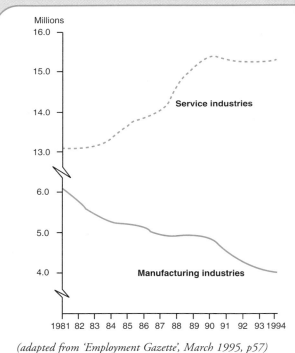

(adapted from 'Employment Gazette', March 1995, p57)

Table 3 shows how members of each group voted in the 1987 and 1992 elections (the figures are percentages and rounded up or down). Ivor Crewe argues that voters with traditional working class characteristics are declining and that this is a major reason for class dealignment.

Table 3 The traditional and new working class and the general elections of 1987 and 1992

1987 general election

The new working class

Party	Lives in South	Home owner	Non-union member	Private sector worker
Con	46	44	40	38
Lab	28	32	38	39
Lib/SDP	26	24	22	23

The traditional working class

Party	Lives in Scotland or North	Council tenant	Union member	Public sector worker
Con	29	25	30	32
Lab	57	57	48	49
Lib/SDP	15	18	22	19

1992 general election

The new working class

Party	Lives in South	Home owner	Non-union member	Private sector worker
Con	40	40	37	32
Lab	38	41	46	50
Lib Dem	23	19	17	18

The traditional working class

Party	Lives in Scotland or North	Council tenant	Union member	Public sector worker
Con	26	22	29	36
Lab	59	64	55	48
Lib Dem	15	13	16	16

(adapted from 'Why Did Labour Lose (Yet Again)?' by I. Crewe, 'Politics Review', September 1992)

(adapted from 'Sociology Update 1993' by Martyn Denscombe, Olympus Books UK, Leicester, 1993 and 'British Politics in Focus' edited by David Roberts, Causeway Press, Ormskirk, 1995)

QUESTIONS

1. Briefly summarise the relationship between social class and voting behaviour shown in Table 1. (5)
2. a) Provide evidence from Table 2 which indicates that the link between social class and voting behaviour is weakening. (4)
   b) What evidence is provided by trends in the occupational structure to suggest that the link will continue to weaken? (4)
3. What evidence does Table 3 provide to support Ivor Crewe's view that the growth of the new working class will weaken the link between manual workers and the Labour Party? (7)

PART 7 AGE, GENDER, ETHNICITY AND VOTING BEHAVIOUR

Apart from social class, a number of other social factors have been linked to voting behaviour. These include age, gender and ethnicity. They are examined in the following passage.

Age

Survey data from general elections usually shows a tendency for younger people to vote Labour and older people to vote Conservative. For example, in the October 1974 election 42% of new voters voted Labour compared to 24% who voted Conservative. Although in 1983 and 1987 the Conservatives gained more votes than Labour from the young, by 1992 the traditional pattern re-emerged with Labour winning a majority of first-time votes.

Traditionally the Labour Party has been seen as the party of change. Certainly in the past its policies on the welfare state and nationalisation have produced major changes in British society.

By comparison, the Conservative Party has been seen as the party which conserves the status quo, maintains things the way they are, though this view changed somewhat in the 1980s under Margaret Thatcher's leadership.

The young have less commitment to the status quo, less of a stake in the existing social order. They are more likely to support policies which offer change and a new direction. They are therefore more likely to vote Labour. By comparison the elderly tend to be more cautious and less likely to take the risks that policies for change might involve. They are therefore more likely to vote Conservative.

Table 1 Age and voting in the 1992 general election

	Con	Lab	Lib Dem
First-time voters	35	40	25
Aged 22-29	43	41	16
Aged 30-44	39	39	21
Aged 45-64	44	35	21
Aged 65 and over	48	37	14

(adapted from 'Why Did Labour Lose (Yet Again)?' by I. Crewe, 'Politics Review', September, 1992)

Gender

Table 2 Gender and voting on the 1992 general election (percentages)

	Conservative	Labour	Liberal Democrat
Men	41	40	19
Women	45	36	19

(adapted from 'Why Did Labour Lose (Yet Again)?' by I. Crewe, 'Politics Review', September, 1992)

In most general elections since 1945 more women voted for the Conservatives than for other parties. A number of reasons have been suggested for this. Firstly, women are less likely to be exposed to pro-Labour ideas as they are less likely to work outside the home and join trade unions. By 1994 the numbers of men and women in employment were roughly equal, but

Polling station, 1992 general election

women are much more likely to be in part-time, non-unionised jobs. Secondly, because women's traditional role has been in the home, they are more likely to be influenced by appeals to the family. 'Family values' often form a part of Conservative election campaigns. Also, given their domestic roles, women may be more concerned with security and less prepared to accept the risks to their families that change might bring. Thirdly, because the life expectancy of women is higher than men's, there are more women in the older age groups. Since older people are more likely to vote Conservative, age rather than gender may partly explain the higher Conservative vote amongst women as a whole.

Ethnicity

Opinion poll data indicates that Afro-Caribbean and Asian voters strongly support the Labour Party. For example, a Harris ITN poll showed that 90% of Afro-Caribbean voters and 71% of Asians voted Labour in the 1992 election. Most say they vote Labour because of its support for the working class (members of these ethnic groups are more likely to be working class than the white majority). However, non-manual voters from these ethnic groups are more likely to vote Labour. This suggests that Labour is seen as more sympathetic towards ethnic minorities.

(adapted from 'British Politics in Focus' edited by David Roberts, Causeway Press, Ormskirk, 1995 and 'Sociology in Focus' by Paul Taylor et al, Causeway Press, Ormskirk, 1995)

Table 3 Ethnic voting by social class in the 1987 general election

	Conservative	Labour	Alliance*
Professional and managerial	33	54	13
White collar	30	52	17
Skilled manual	14	78	9
Semi-skilled and unskilled	10	84	5

*the Liberal/SDP Alliance later became the Liberal Democrats

(adapted from 'Black Tribunes: Black Political Participation in Britain' by T. Sewell, Lawrence & Wishart, London, 1993)

QUESTIONS

1. Explain the possible connection between age, risk and voting behaviour. (7)
2. Gender equality will probably eliminate gender differences in voting behaviour. Discuss. (6)
3. Look at Table 3 and compare it with Table 1 in Part 6. Suggest an explanation for the difference. (7)

NON-VOTING

Large numbers of adults in the UK do not vote in general elections. Some are not registered to vote - they are not on the electoral register. Some who are on the electoral register are either unable to vote or choose not to do so. Some are not allowed to vote. In the 1992 general election 77.7% of those registered to vote actually voted. It has been argued that large numbers of non-voters means that a democracy is not functioning effectively. If people don't vote, their votes don't count. The following passage looks at some of these missing voters.

In 1992 the Office of Population Censuses and Surveys estimated that 1.8 million people in England and Wales had disappeared from official records, many of them to avoid paying the Poll Tax. The Poll Tax (or Community Charge) was replaced by the Council Tax in 1991. Large numbers of people refused to pay the Poll Tax either on principle, or because they could not afford it, or both. To avoid prosecution many did not enter their names on the electoral register, so losing their right to vote. Many of these 'lost' people are thought to be poor. This supports the view that the Poll Tax drove poor voters off the electoral register so helping the Conservative Party to win the 1992 general election. According to Labour MP David Blunkett, 'this could well have had a substantial effect on the outcome of the general election'.

Once a year each household receives a form to be filled in with the names of all people eligible to vote. As Figure 1 shows, it is the young who are most likely not to register (or not to be registered) to vote. This may indicate that many young people have little or no interest in party politics. Or they may feel that their vote will make no difference. Or they may feel cut off and alienated from the wider society and older generations. David Denver suggests that the lower the degree of social involvement in the community the less likely people are to register for a vote, and if registered, to vote. The typical non-voter is young, single, living in privately rented accommodation and residentially mobile. Some 20% of young people, 24% of

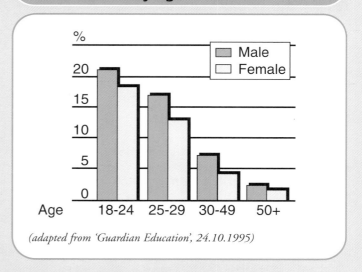

Figure 1 Those not registered to vote in 1991 by age

(adapted from 'Guardian Education', 24.10.1995)

Afro-Caribbeans and 15% of Asians, are not registered to vote.

There are many other reasons why people either choose not to or are unable to vote. Some refuse to vote on principle or as a protest. They may regard the whole political system as immoral and therefore refuse to participate. Others don't vote because they live in a 'safe seat' and feel their vote will make no difference to the outcome of the election. And some people are unable to vote. It has been estimated that one third of the UK's six million people with disabilities are unable to get into polling stations - many literally can't get their wheelchairs into the polling station and so cannot vote. Finally, some people are not allowed to vote. These include prisoners and homeless people.

(adapted from 'Independent', 13.9.1992; 'Nursing Times', June 1994; 'Guardian Education', 24.10.1995; 'British Politics in Focus', edited by David Roberts, Causeway Press, Ormskirk, 1995)

The underpass, Charing Cross to Strand, London. The homeless are not allowed to vote.

QUESTIONS

1. Non-voting can threaten democracy. Discuss. (7)
2. Non-voting can indicate a lack of social cohesion or social unity. Discuss. (7)
3. Look at Figure 1. Suggest reasons for the increase in electoral registration as people grow older. (6)

OPINION POLLS

PART 9

In the run up to a general election the results of opinion polls are presented regularly in the press and on television. The main concern of the pollsters is to predict the election result. The most common question is therefore, 'How do you intend to vote?' Polls are conducted by professional organisations which specialise in surveys of public opinion. They are usually based on a representative sample or cross-section of the population. The following passage looks at the methods, purposes and problems of opinion polls.

Often the first question people ask about opinion polls is, 'Are they any good?' In the case of elections, are they an accurate measure of intended voting behaviour? Up to 1970 the polls had a reasonably good record, but after 1970 they failed to predict the result in 5 of the following 7 elections. Despite this they weren't that far away from the actual results.

The polls really came unstuck in the 1992 general election. On average, the five major poll organisations gave Labour a 1.3% lead over the Conservatives but the actual result was a 7.6% win for the Conservatives. The opinion poll companies gave the following reasons for their failure to predict the result.

- **Non-voters** Some people who give their voting intention do not actually vote on election day.
- **Switchers** Some people change their mind at the last moment.
- **Late deciders** Some people have yet to make up their minds and are put down as 'don't knows'.
- **Secret voters** Some people are unwilling to say which way they intend to vote and are put down as 'won't says'.

According to the Market Research Society, these factors account for about a third of the error in the 1992 predictions. The rest is put down to 'fundamental problems' in the way polls are conducted.

The methods used in opinion polls have often been criticised. People are suddenly confronted with a list of questions which they often answer rapidly, off the top of their head. According to Conrad James, polls provide 'opinion that chokes off the opportunity to hear arguments pro and con, to consult a neighbour, to read up, to ask a question, to answer back; opinion so half-hearted it is hard to take seriously'. In addition there is the problem of sampling, of obtaining a representative sample. Some polls are conducted by telephone - a method that is unlikely to reach a cross-section of the population.

Perhaps the most serious problem is what to do with the 'refusers' (sometimes up to 45% of the sample) who refuse to or are unavailable to answer questions. The 'don't knows' (late deciders) or 'won't says' (secret voters) are recorded in opinion poll results. The 'refusers' are usually ignored and the interviewer finds replacements who a) fit the requirements of the sample and b) will answer the questions. One survey, the 1992 British General Election Survey, would not take no for an answer. If people were out or too busy, the interviewers went back again and again until they got answers. The results indicated that amongst those who would not or could not answer the first time, the Conservatives gained 6% more support than amongst those who answered first time.

In recent years there has been concern about the possible effects of opinion polls. Do poll results influence people particularly in terms of which party to vote for and whether or not to vote at all? These questions have become more relevant with the growth in support for the Liberal Democrats. Polls in one constituency may show Labour in the lead with the Liberal Democrats and Conservative candidates neck and neck in second place. This may lead to 'tactical voting' with, for example, Conservatives switching their votes to the Liberal Democrats in order to beat Labour, their least favourite candidate. In this case the polls, far from simply reflecting voting

'I'm a "don't know"! "Don't know" whether to smash your face in or not.'
(adapted from a cartoon by Edward McLachlan in 'Private Eye')

intentions will actually influence them.

There is no firm evidence about the influence of polls on voting behaviour. Despite this some countries have taken steps to reduce their possible effects. For example, the publication of poll results is banned in France and Germany during the last week of an election campaign.

(adapted from 'Sociology Update, 1993' by Martyn Denscombe, Olympus Books UK, Leicester, 1993 and 'British Politics in Focus' edited by David Roberts, Causeway Press, Ormskirk, 1995)

QUESTIONS

1. a) Why do pollsters attempt to obtain a representative sample of the population? (4)
   b) Why are telephone polls unlikely to provide a representative sample? (4)
2. Interviewers should not simply find replacements for those who refuse to answer or are unavailable to answer. Why not? (7)
3. Should opinion polls be banned for all or part of an election campaign? Give reasons for your answer. (5)

THE SOCIAL BACKGROUND OF MPs

PART 10

Despite its claim to represent the nation, the membership of the House of Commons is far from representative of the population as a whole. Whether MPs would represent the people more effectively if their backgrounds reflected the social composition of the nation as a whole is debatable. The following extract examines the social background of MPs elected to the House of Commons in 1992.

Occupation and education

Most MPs are middle aged, middle class, university educated, white and male. Table 1 shows the occupations of MPs elected in the 1992 general election. The proportion of Labour MPs from manual occupations has steadily fallen from 72% between the wars to 36% in the 1950s to 22% in 1992. The social distance between Labour and Conservative MPs has gradually narrowed.

Table 2 shows the educational background of MPs elected in 1992. The proportion of Labour MPs with university degrees has risen from 17% between the wars to 40% in the 1950s to 61% in 1992. And the proportion of Conservative MPs who went to public schools is decreasing - 75% in the 1950s down to 62% in 1992. Again the social distance between Labour and Conservative MPs has narrowed.

Table 1 The occupation of MPs, 1992

Occupation	Conservative	Labour	Liberal Democrat		Conservative	Labour	Liberal Democrat
Professions				Management/clerical	4	11	-
Barrister	39	9	5	General business	3	1	-
Solicitor	21	8	1	**Total**	**128**	**22**	**2**
Doctor/dentist	4	2	-		**(38%)**	**(8%)**	**(10%)**
Architect/surveyor	3	-	-				
Civil/chartered engineer	3	-	-	**Miscellaneous**			
Civil servant/local government	10	16	-	White collar	9	36	1
Armed services	14	-	1	Politican/political organiser	20	24	2
University teachers	4	14	1	Publisher/journalist	28	13	3
Polytechnic/college teachers	2	24	-	Farmer	10	2	-
School teachers	16	38	3	Housewife	6	-	-
Other consultants	2	-	1	**Total**	**73**	**75**	**6**
Scientific/research	1	2	-		**(22%)**	**(28%)**	**(30%)**
Total	**131**	**115**	**12**				
	(39%)	**(42%)**	**(60%)**	**Manual workers**			
				Miner	1	12	-
Business				Skilled worker	3	43	-
Company director	37	1	-	Semi/unskilled worker	-	4	-
Company executive	75	8	2	**Total**	**4**	**59**	**0**
Commerce/insurance	9	1	-		**(1%)**	**(22%)**	**(-)**
				Grand total	**336**	**271**	**20**

(adapted from 'The British General Election 1992' by D. E. Butler and D. Kavanagh, Macmillan, London, 1992)

Table 2 The educational background of MPs, 1992

Type of education	Con	Lab	Lib Dem
State School	19	34	2
State school + poly/college	28	61	2
State school + university	81	127	6
Public school	28	0	0
Public school + poly/college	16	2	1
Public school + university	164	38	9
Total	**336**	**271**	**20**
Oxford	83	28	4
Cambridge	68	16	2
Other universities	94	122	9
All universities	245	166	15
(% attending university)	(73%)	(61%)	(75%)
Eton	34	2	0
Harrow	7	0	0
Winchester	3	1	0
Other public schools	164	37	10
All public schools	208	40	10
(% attending public school)	(62%)	(14%)	(50%)

(adapted from 'The British General Election 1992' by D. E. Butler and D. Kavanagh, Macmillan, London, 1992)

Gender

Between 1918 and 1992, just 1,721 women have stood as parliamentary candidates (around 2,000 candidates stand in a general election and there were 21 general elections between 1918 and 1992). During this period there have been 166 women MPs. In 1992, 60 women were elected (out of a total of 651 MPs), compared to 41 in 1987 and 23 in 1983.

The House of Commons has often been described as 'the best men's club in Europe', and it is still very much a male domain. The hours - afternoon and evening sittings with often late-night, and sometimes all-night debates - do not suit women with children and other family commitments. MP Emma Nicholson argues for changes: 'In order to attract more women there will have to be an improvement in the hours, so that work does not demolish family life, and a more welcoming approach from the men instead of sexist comments'.

Janet Anderson won her seat for Labour at the 1992 general election. She spent six years fighting a seat whilst bringing up three children. She had to take out a second mortgage. 'Money is the biggest hurdle for female candidates. It is for men, too. But, women also have to think about getting childcare and cleaning and are more concerned about using valuable housekeeping money for travel expenses and accommodation,' she says.

Age

The typical MP is in his late 40s. Although the voting age was reduced from 21 to 18 in 1969, the minimum age at which a person can stand as an MP remains 21, but only one MP under the age of 30 was elected in 1992 (the Liberal Democrat MP, Matthew Taylor).

Ethnicity

In 1987, four black MPs were elected - the first since 1924. In 1992 they retained their seats and the total number of black MPs rose to six (one Conservative and five Labour). The main reason given for the small number of black MPs is the belief that they lose votes. However, the four black MPs elected in 1987 all retained their seats in 1992 with increased majorities, with an average swing to Labour well above the national average.

(adapted from 'Black Tribunes' by Terri A. Sewell, Lawrence & Wishart, London, 1993; 'British Politics in Focus' edited by David Roberts, Causeway Press, Ormskirk, 1995)

31 of the record number of 37 women Labour MPs who took their seats in the House of Commons in 1992.

QUESTIONS

1. In terms of their social background, MPs are not representative of the population as a whole. Provide evidence to support this statement. (6)
2. Would MPs represent the people more effectively if their backgrounds reflected the nation as a whole? Give reasons for your answer. (6)
3. Briefly suggest reasons for the small numbers of
   a) working class, b) women, c) young and d) ethnic minority MPs. (8)

11 PART FROM DEMOCRACY TO TOTALITARIANISM

The leaders of the Russian revolution in 1917 looked forward to a communist society in which power and wealth would be returned to the people. Eventually the state would 'wither away' as people learned to govern themselves for the benefit of society as a whole.

The reality of the Soviet Union under the dictator Joseph Stalin made a mockery of these hopes. By the late 1930s, the Soviet Union was a totalitarian state with Stalin in complete control (see Chapter 2, Parts 8 and 9 for material on totalitarianism). Anyone who was seen as a threat to Stalin's power was imprisoned, tortured or executed. Some were publicly tried and confessed to all sorts of 'crimes' they had never committed. For example, one man 'admitted' that, 'in 1932 we took measures to spread plague among pigs which resulted in a high pig mortality'. Millions of people were rounded up by the secret police and sent to slave labour camps.

Stalin was glorified. His portraits were everywhere - in offices, shops, on buildings, in public places. He was known as 'Man of Steel', 'Universal Genius' and 'Shining Sun of Humanity'. Films, plays, poems and novels celebrated every detail of his life.

The following extract is taken from *Animal Farm* by George Orwell. Published in 1945, it portrays the evils of Stalin's Soviet Union in a society of farm animals. They overthrow their oppressor, Mr Jones the farmer, and set up a new society. The extract begins with a speech by Major, a wise old pig, who died peacefully in his sleep three days later.

When Major saw that all the animals had all made themselves comfortable and were waiting attentively he cleared his throat and began:

'Now, comrades, what is the nature of this life of ours? Let us face it, our lives are miserable, laborious and short. We are born, we are given just so much food as will keep the breath in our bodies, and those of us who are capable of it are forced to work to the last atom of our strength; and the very instant that our usefulness has come to an end we are slaughtered with hideous cruelty. No animal in England knows the meaning of happiness or leisure after he is a year old. No animal in England is free. The life of an animal is misery and slavery: that is the plain truth.

Why then do we continue in this miserable condition? Because nearly the whole of the produce of our labour is stolen from us by human beings. There, comrades, is the answer to all our problems. It is summed up in a single word - Man. Man is the only real enemy we have. Remove Man from the scene, and the root cause of hunger and overwork is abolished for ever.

What then must we do? Why, work night and day, body and soul, for the overthrow of the human race! That is my message to you, comrades: Rebellion! And remember also that in fighting against Man, we must not come to resemble him. Above all, no animal must ever tyrannise over his own kind. Weak or strong, clever or simple, we are all brothers. No animal must ever kill any other animal. All animals are equal.'

One morning in June the farmworkers went out rabbiting, without bothering to feed the animals. Mr Jones got back drunk from his lunchtime visit to the Red Lion and fell asleep on the sofa. That evening the hungry animals broke into the store-shed and began to help themselves from the food-bins. Jones and his men rushed in with whips in their hands, lashing out in all directions. This was more than the hungry animals could bear. They attacked the men and drove them from the farm. Manor Farm was now theirs.

All through that summer the work of the farm went like clockwork. The animals were happy as they had never conceived it possible to be. The pigs did not actually work, but directed and supervised the others. With their superior knowledge it was natural that they should assume the leadership.

On Sundays there was no work. After the hoisting of the flag all the animals trooped into the big barn for a general assembly which was known as the Meeting. Here the work of the coming week was planned out and resolutions were put forward and debated. It was always the pigs who put forward the resolutions. The other animals understood how to vote, but could never think of any resolutions of their own.

Food was shared amongst the animals but after a time milk and apples disappeared from their diet. Some murmured complaints but it was no use. Squealer, one of the pigs, explained.

'Comrades!' he cried. 'You do not imagine, I hope, that we pigs are doing this in a spirit of selfishness and privilege? Many of us actually dislike milk and apples. I dislike them myself. Our sole object in taking these things is to preserve our health. Milk and apples (this has been proved by Science, comrades) contain substances absolutely necessary to the well-being of a pig. We pigs are brainworkers. The whole management and organisation of this farm depend on us. Day and night we are watching over your welfare.'

Many meetings were held in the big barn, and the pigs occupied themselves with planning out the work. It had come to be accepted that the pigs, who were manifestly cleverer than the other animals, should decide all questions of farm policy, though their decisions had to be ratified by a majority vote. This arrangement would have worked well enough if it had not been for the disputes between Snowball and Napoleon, the leaders of the pigs. These two disagreed at every point where disagreement was possible. At one meeting they disagreed as

Napoleon

demanded whether any other animal had anything to confess.

The three hens who had been the ringleaders in the attempted rebellion over the eggs now came forward and stated that Snowball had appeared to them in a dream and incited them to disobey Napoleon's orders. They too were slaughtered. Then a goose came forward and confessed to having secreted six ears of corn during the last year's harvest and eaten them in the night. Then a sheep confessed to having urinated in the drinking pool - urged to do this, so she said, by Snowball - and two other sheep confessed to having murdered an old ram, an especially devoted follower of Napoleon, by chasing him round and round a bonfire when he was suffering from a cough. They were all slain on the spot. And so the tale of confessions and executions went on, until there was a pile of corpses lying before Napoleon's feet and the air as heavy with the smell of blood, which had been unknown there since the expulsion of Jones.

Napoleon was now never spoken of simply as 'Napoleon'. He was always referred to in formal style as 'our Leader, Comrade Napoleon', and the pigs liked to invent for him such titles as Father of All Animals, Terror of Mankind, Protector of the Sheepfold, Ducklings' Friend, and the like. In his speeches Squealer, one of the pigs, would talk with the tears rolling down his cheeks of Napoleon's wisdom, the goodness of his heart, and the deep love he bore to all animals everywhere, even and especially the unhappy animals who still lived in ignorance and slavery on other farms.

About this time, too, it was laid down as a rule that when a pig and any other animal met on the path, the other animal must stand aside: and also that all pigs, of whatever degree, were to have the privilege of wearing green ribbons on their tails on Sunday.

One day, returning to the farmyard after working in the fields, the animals could not believe their eyes. It was a pig walking on his hind legs. Yes, it was Squealer. A little awkwardly, as though not quite used to supporting his considerable bulk in that position, but with perfect balance, he was strolling across the yard. And a moment later, out from the door of the farmhouse came a long file of pigs, all walking on their hind legs. Some did it better than others, one or two were even a trifle unsteady and looked as though they would have liked the support of a stick, but every one of them made his way right round the yard

usual and it was clear the vote was going to go against Napoleon. But just at this moment Napoleon stood up and, casting a peculiar side-long look at Snowball, uttered a high-pitched whimper of a kind no one had ever heard him utter before.

At this there was a terrible baying sound outside, and nine enormous dogs wearing brass-studded collars came bounding into the barn. They dashed straight for Snowball, who only sprang from his place just in time to escape their snapping jaws. In a moment he was out of the door and they were after him. Too amazed and frightened to speak, all the animals crowded through the door to watch the chase. Snowball was racing across the long pasture that led to the road, never to be seen again.

Napoleon, with the dogs following him, now mounted onto the raised portion of the floor where Major had previously stood to deliver his speech. He announced that from now on the Sunday-morning Meetings would come to an end. They were unnecessary, he said, and wasted time. In future all questions relating to the working of the farm would be settled by a special committee of pigs, presided over by himself. These would meet in private and afterwards communicate their decisions to the others. The animals would still assemble on Sunday mornings to salute the flag, sing 'Beasts of England' and receive their orders for the week; but there would be no more debates.

Then came the slaughter. Napoleon called on the four pigs who had protested when he had abolished Sunday Meetings to confess their crimes. They all confessed to a string of crimes they had never even committed. When they had finished the dogs promptly tore their throats out, and in a terrible voice Napoleon

successfully. And finally there was a tremendous baying of dogs and a shrill crowing from the black cockerel, and out came Napoleon himself, majestically upright, casting haughty glances from side to side, and with his dogs gambolling round him.

He carried a whip in his trotter.

There was a deadly silence. Amazed, terrified, huddling together, the animals watched the long line of pigs march slowly round the yard. It was as though the world had turned upside-down. And then they noticed what had been written on the big barn.

ALL ANIMALS ARE EQUAL
BUT SOME ANIMALS ARE MORE EQUAL
THAN OTHERS.

(adapted from 'Animal Farm' by George Orwell, Martin Secker and Warburg, London, 1945)

QUESTIONS

1. Briefly outline the events which indicate the decline of democracy and the development of a totalitarian dictatorship. (4)
2. a) What are the similarities between Stalin and Napoleon? (3)
   b) Why do dictators often glorify themselves? (3)
3. Why do people sometimes confess to crimes they did not commit? (4)
4. a) How did the pigs symbolise their power and their presumed superiority? (3)
   b) Are there any similarities between their methods and those used in human society? (3)

THE FAMILY

Many sociologists have seen the family as the cornerstone of human society. They find it difficult to imagine how society could operate without it. Part of their argument runs as follows. Without socialisation there would be no culture and without culture there would be no society. In every society the family is largely responsible for primary socialisation, the first and most important part of the socialisation process. Thus the family is essential for society since its major role or function is to transmit culture from one generation to the next.

This chapter looks at the family in a range of societies - small scale, large scale, preindustrial and industrial. It considers the functions of the family, that is the contribution the family makes to the maintenance and wellbeing of society. It also looks at the negative side of family life - the harm the family might cause both to its members and the wider society.

FAMILIES AND MARRIAGE

PART 1

There is no single blueprint for the family which applies to all societies. Families come in all shapes and sizes. This is shown in the following passage which examines different forms of marriage.

Monogamy is a marriage with one husband and one wife. It is the form of marriage found in Western industrial society and in many other societies, past and present.

Polygamy is a marriage with more than one husband or wife. It takes two forms: **polyandry** - two or more husbands and one wife - and **polygyny** - two or more wives with one husband.

Polyandry

The Nyinba people of Nepal practice fraternal polyandry - two or more brothers are married to one wife. They inherited this custom from their Tibetan ancestors who migrated to Nepal centuries ago. They also inherited a love for trading and herding which, together with cultivating the meagre soil, make up the traditional Nyinba economy. Polyandry suits this economy. 'With one or two husbands always on herding or trading trips, one husband will always be at home to care for the wife,' explained Maila Dai, a trader from the village of Bargaau. 'We think polyandry is just like insurance for the wife. If one husband is no

Polyandry among the Nyinba of Nepal. The 12 year old girl on the right is engaged to five brothers, three of whom are pictured here.

good or leaves his wife, there's always another brother.'

Polyandry has been explained as a way of preventing land from being divided up into less profitable units when a family of sons inherits from the previous generation. It also concentrates the wealth of each household by maintaining a large population of working adult males under one roof.

To the Nyinbas, its advantages are obvious. Both men and women talk about the wealth polyandry provides and the way it distinguishes them from their poorer Hindu neighbours. In the words of one mother, 'If my sons partition the land, we will become as poor as the Hindu village of Tey'.

'All our brothers work together,' explained Dawa Takpa, 'so we can be wealthy people. If we all go our own way, how can we survive? We have to study, do agricultural work, take care of animals and trade, so we have to work together.' 'For me,' said Tsering Zangmo, who at 21 is the wife of three brothers (the youngest of whom is seven), 'polyandry is fine. If I had only one husband, I would be very poor.'

Husbands are expected to do nothing that would cause a rift big enough to bring about the partitioning of the family land. Younger brothers have to ask the eldest brother in the morning for permission to sleep with the wife that night, but he would be unwise to refuse: if a younger brother becomes dissatisfied, he might take a new wife and settle independently on his share of land.

An ideal polyandrous wife is obedient to all her husbands' wishes, never shows sexual favouritism and does nothing to cause conflict between them. She should also have at least one child from each father - otherwise one of the husbands might accuse her of favouritism. (The mother always announces who the father is.)

When asked about jealousy between her husbands, Tsering Zangmo replied, 'But they are brothers. They are never jealous.' However when pressed she giggled and blushed, admitting, 'Well, they only have a very little jealousy. If you like one husband very much, you have to be secret so the others don't know. We make love in the middle of the night, lying naked in sheepskins. We'd never do it just before going to sleep or just before waking up as the others might hear us.'

Polygyny

Adama is a wealthy man. He lives in a village called Sobtenga in Burkina Faso, a country in northwest Africa. Ten years ago he had two wives.

Zenabou, his first wife, thought polygyny was a good idea. It provided her with a 'sister' to share the burdens of domestic work and childcare. Now she is not so sure. Adama has taken two more wives, the youngest of whom, Bintu, is only 16. He is besotted with Bintu and she clearly enjoys the attention. Despite grumbling, his other wives accept the situation. For marriage is seen primarily as an economic affair and Adama's 12 oxen are proof that he can provide security for his wives and children.

Polygyny is much more common than polyandry. It is found in many small scale traditional societies, particularly in Africa. As the example of Adama suggests, polygyny is a privilege of the wealthy. Not every man can afford two or more wives and in any case there aren't enough women for this. Census figures from 1911 for the Pondo of South Africa show that 10% of men had two wives and only 2% had more than two.

In some societies polygyny is a way of cementing alliances between different groups. For example, a Gisu chief in Uganda stated that he couldn't do his job if he was a monogamist. By having several wives, he was related by marriage to different groups and this strengthened his position as chief.

(adapted from 'Marriage' by Lucy Mair, Penguin, Harmondsworth, 1971; 'Brotherly Love' by Carroll Dunham, 'Observer Magazine', 18.10.1992; 'African Village' by Chris Brazier, 'New Internationalist', June 1995)

Adama's wives - Zenabou, Bintu, Meryam and Barkissou

QUESTIONS

1. Judging from the extract, what are the advantages and disadvantages of (i) polyandry and (ii) polygyny? (10)
2. Do you think that polyandry or polygyny will ever develop in Western societies? Give reasons for your answer. (5)
3. Marriage and the family are shaped by culture. Discuss. (5)

2 PART — THE FAMILY IN PREINDUSTRIAL SOCIETY

Many sociologists have argued that the family in industrial society has lost many of its functions. For example, in preindustrial society parents were mainly responsible for the health, welfare and education of their children. Now these functions have been largely taken over by the state in the form of specialised organisations such as hospitals, schools and a widespread system of social security.

The view that the family has lost many of its functions in industrial society is presented in the following extract. It is taken from an interview with a Pomo Indian man well over one hundred years of age. He vividly recalls the role of the family in his society and compares it with what he has seen of the family in white American society. The Pomo Indians live in northern California. Their traditional way of life came to an end in the nineteenth century after they were herded on to reservations by the white man.

What is a man? A man is nothing. Without his family he is of less importance than that bug crossing the trail. A man must be with his family to amount to anything with us. If he had nobody else to help him, the first trouble he got into he would be killed by his enemies. No woman would marry him because her family would not let her marry a man with no family. He would be poorer than a newborn child; he would be poorer than a worm, and the family would not consider him worth anything. He would not bring renown or glory with him. He would not bring support of other relatives either. The family is important. If a man has a large family and a profession (a specialised occupation such as deer hunter or doctor which requires years of training)

A Pomo Indian in a reed canoe

and upbringing by a family that is known to produce good children, then he is somebody and every family is willing to have him marry a woman in their group. It is the family that is important. In the white ways of doing things the family is not so important. The police and soldiers take care of protecting you, the courts give you justice, the post office carries messages for you, the school teaches you. Everything is taken care of, even your children, if you die; but with us the family must do all of that.

Without the family we are nothing, and in the old days before the white people came the family was given the first consideration by anyone who was about to do anything. That is why we got along. We had no courts, judges, schools, and the other things you have, but we got along better than you. We were taught that we would suffer from the devil, spirits, ghosts, or other people if we did not support one another. The family was everything, and no man ever forgot that. Each person was nothing, but as a group joined by blood the individual knew that he would get the support of all his relatives if anything happened. He also knew that if he was a bad person the head man of his family would pay another tribe to kill him so that there would be no trouble afterwards and so that he would not get the family into trouble all the time.

With us the family was everything. Now it is nothing. We are getting like the white people, and it is bad for the old people. We had no old people's homes like you. The old people were important. They were wise. Your old people must be fools.

(from 'An Indian's Soliloquy' by Burt W. Aginsky, 'American Journal of Sociology', 46 (1940), pp43-44)

QUESTIONS

1. What evidence does the extract contain which suggests that the social control function of the family in Pomo society was more widespread than that of the family in modern Britain? (6)
2. Why would a woman in Pomo society not marry a man without a family? (4)
3. What evidence does the passage contain to suggest that the family has fewer functions in modern industrial society compared with small scale, preindustrial societies such as the Pomo? (7)
4. Why does the Pomo Indian state, 'Your old people must be fools'? (3)

PART 3 — CHANGING FUNCTIONS OF THE FAMILY

Not all sociologists take the view that the family in modern industrial society has lost many of its functions. For example, the British sociologist Ronald Fletcher claims that not only has the family retained its functions but those functions have actually 'increased in detail and importance'. State education, for instance, has assisted parents rather than removed their responsibility for secondary socialisation. In Fletcher's words, 'Parents are expected to do their best to guide, encourage and support their children in their educational and occupational choices and careers'. In the same way the state has not removed the family's responsibility for the physical welfare of its members. Fletcher argues that, 'The family is still centrally concerned with maintaining the health of its members, but it is now aided by wider provisions which have been *added* to the family's situation since preindustrial times'. State health and welfare services have provided additional support for the family and made its members more aware of the importance of health, childcare, proper diet and hygiene in the home.

A nineteenth century view of the family's childcare function

Although he believes that the functions of the family have not been reduced in industrial society, Fletcher does recognise some important changes. This is particularly true of the family's economic function. In many preindustrial societies the family was the basic unit of production. Families were the main social groups that produced goods and services. The family therefore had an important economic function in society. This is illustrated in the first of the following extracts which describes a day in the life of a farming family in Manupur, a village in India.

In industrial societies the family is no longer the main production unit. The majority of adults are wage and salary earners. They do not produce goods and services as members of family groups. Although the family has largely lost its function as a unit of production, some sociologists argue that it has developed an important economic function as a unit of consumption. Goods and services are increasingly bought and consumed in the name of the family - houses, family cars and so on. From this viewpoint, examined in the second extract, the family still has an important economic function in society.

The family as a unit of production

The day begins early for a farmer in Manupur, around four in the morning. He must first feed the animals (oxen, cows, buffalo) and give them water.

The oxen are tied to the cart at around five o'clock in the morning and the men are ready to go to the fields and work. Work lasts until seven in the evening, interrupted only for 'fuelling oneself' (as the farmers are fond of saying) - that is, for breakfast in mid-morning (15 minutes around 10:00), lunch (from 12:00 to 1:00), and tea (from 4:00 to 4:15). If it is a hot summer day, lunch might last for two hours instead of one. Meals are brought to the field by the son, or, if necessary, by the daughter. The distance between the house and the farm is sometimes over a mile, and it would be a waste of precious time to go home.

When it begins to get dark - and in the summer this is usually around seven in the evening - oxen are reharnessed to the cart and everybody proceeds home. During sowing and harvest times, work may go on as late as 10:00 pm. Once home, the animals must be tended. If the farmer has a young son, grass has already been cut; if not, he must employ someone to do it. It remains for him to prepare the fodder, and to feed, wash, and clean the animals.

The farmer's wife has an even greater burden of work. She must prepare the meals (breakfast, lunch, and dinner) and tea (early morning, mid-afternoon, and late night). Meals are made for the husband and the children and, if there are few children, for the labourers who have to be hired. The work is hard. Flour must be mixed with water and made into dough, and dough into wheat or corn cakes - usually six cakes per person per

Harvest time in India

meal. The buffalo must be milked twice a day, morning and evening. The milk is used to make *lassi*, a yoghurt drink for warm mornings, and to make butter late in the evening. Dishes must be washed after every meal.

There is more. Animal dung must be collected and put in a pit to dry out. She must build a dungcake fire, which provides a slow and gentle heat over which to simmer a lentil curry. While it is cooking, she attends to other tasks. Firewood must also be cut, gathered, and carried to the house. The buffalo must be given drinking water and fed grass if the husband is in the fields at night. Clothes must be washed every day. Cleaning a dirty piece of clothing - and there is a lot of dirt in the fields - means soaking it in soapy water and then beating it with a wooden stick. The use of simple tools requires both time and effort. Younger children have to be tended to, fed, and washed. In the midst of all this, the wife must somehow find time to feed herself.

The farmer's children can be of considerable assistance, even while they are young. A son or daughter can bring grass and water for the cattle before going to school at eight in the morning, can help in the fields in the afternoon if necessary, and can graze the cattle in the evening. In fact, primary responsibility for the cattle can be left to the children and the adult's load lightened a little.

If a farmer's wife has no young children, it would mean intolerable hardship. She would then have to walk to the fields to deliver two meals and one tea every day. The walk over and back, the wait while everybody eats - so the utensils can be taken back, washed, and cleaned for the next meal - can take as much as four hours.

(from 'The Myth of Population Control', 'New Internationalist', May 1974, pp18- 19)

The family as a unit of consumption

The family in Britain remains an important economic unit from the viewpoint of consumption - goods and services are bought for the family as a unit. The expenditure of family income is still patterned not solely on 'individual preferences' but also on the needs of the family as a whole and the preferences of the family as a group. Advertisers are clearly aware of this, and sometimes play upon it to a rather nauseating extent, as may be seen by watching television advertisements for some foodstuffs, soap powders, holiday arrangements, and the like. Furthermore, it is probable that there is still, to some extent, a 'pooling' of proportions of family incomes for the upkeep of the family as a

A shot from an Oxo commercial

whole, and for the improvement of the home. Indeed, if one is to judge from the present concentration upon schemes of furnishing, schemes of interior decoration, 'do-it-yourself' techniques with appropriate tool-kits, and from the extent to which families devote themselves to improving their 'homes and gardens' along these lines, the present-day concern for the improvement of the family's household must be held to be very considerable indeed.

(adapted from 'The Family and Marriage in Britain' by Ronald Fletcher, Penguin Books, Harmondsworth, 1966, pp183-4)

QUESTIONS

1. How do members of the Indian farming family combine to form a unit of production? (6)
2. The main unit of production in industrial society is the factory. Briefly explain why the family is *not* an important part of this unit. (4)
3. What does Fletcher mean when he states that family income is not spent 'solely on "individual preferences" but also on the needs of the family as a whole'? (5)
4. Why is the family in industrial society beneficial to the economy? Make reference to the extract from Fletcher in your answer. (5)

FAMILY STRUCTURE IN EARLY INDUSTRIAL SOCIETY

4 PART

The family unit often seen as typical of modern industrial society is known as the *nuclear family*. It consists of a husband and wife and their children. Many sociologists consider this to be the smallest and most basic form of family structure. In many preindustrial societies the family contained relatives or kin beyond the nuclear family. This type of family structure is known as the *extended family*. It may include the parents of the married couple, their brothers and sisters or any kin beyond the nuclear family related by blood or marriage.

It has often been argued that the nuclear family is ideally suited to industrial society. Modern industry needs a geographically mobile workforce - people are required to move to areas where their skills and labour are in demand. The extended family is unsuited to geographical mobility, being a large and bulky unit. By comparison the nuclear family is a small, streamlined unit which is not tied down by binding loyalties and obligations to a wide range of kin. It was once argued that industrialisation produced a change in family structure from extended to nuclear. This does appear to have happened in some societies but certainly not in Britain.

Research by the historian Peter Laslett suggests that the nuclear family was the norm in preindustrial England. He found that from 1564 to 1821 only about 10% of households contained kin (relatives) beyond the nuclear family. This is roughly the same as the figure for England and Wales in 1966. However, research by Michael Anderson suggests that the early years of industrialisation encouraged the development of extended families. From a sample of households listed in the 1851 census for Preston, Lancashire, Anderson found that 23% of households contained kin other than members of the nuclear family. His research is examined in the following passage.

In 1851 between a quarter and a third of the adult male population of Preston worked in factories. Preston was one of the main centres of the cotton industry and women and children were widely employed in the mills. Times were hard for members of the working class. Unemployment was high and families struggled to make ends meet on low wages. Housing conditions were appalling, overcrowding was widespread and rents expensive. Families were large, fertility was high and birth control techniques, if they were used, were largely ineffective. By today's standards, disease was rampant and the death rate

unacceptably high. Organised social welfare was woefully inadequate. Social security provision for the old, sick, unemployed, the pregnant mother and the large family was practically non-existent.

Extended families in Preston were found mainly among the poor. They often included old people living with their children. The following table shows the domestic situation of people over 65 in Preston in 1851 and compares it with Britain in 1962.

Table 1 Household composition of the over sixty-fives (%)

	Married		Widowed, single and separated	
	Preston 1851	Britain 1962	Preston 1851	Britain 1962
Living with:				
Married child(ren)	16	6	41	27
Unmarried child(ren)	47	26	29	27
Spouse only	37	68	-	-
Other kin only	-	-	8	4
No related person	-	-	22	42
All (percentage)	100	100	100	100

Men and boys in Holmes Mill, Clitheroe, near Preston

'Parentless' children formed a major source of additions to the nuclear family. Some were the sons and daughters of unmarried women living with their parents. Others were orphans, their parents being part of the high death rate statistics. Apart from the elderly and children, families were extended by the addition of in-laws, siblings (brothers and sisters of the head of the household), uncles, aunts and cousins.

Anderson suggests that extended families will tend to develop if the advantages of this type of social unit outweigh its disadvantages. He argues that in Preston extended families provide an insurance policy for their members against hardship and crisis. They operate as mutual aid organisations, each member providing benefits and gaining support from the others.

(adapted from 'Family, Household and the Industrial Revolution' by Michael Anderson, in 'The Comparative History of Family and Household', edited by P. Laslett, Cambridge University Press, Cambridge, 1971)

QUESTIONS

1. What percentage of married couples over 65 lived with their children
   a) in Preston in 1851? (1)   b) in Britain in 1962? (1)
2. How might parents living with their married children benefit all concerned in Preston in 1851? (4)
3. How might taking in orphaned children provide benefits for all concerned in Preston in 1851? (4)
4. How might rising living standards discourage the development of extended families? (4)
5. How might the welfare state discourage the development of extended families? Give details of the provisions of the welfare state in your answer. (6)

PART 5 — THE WORKING CLASS EXTENDED FAMILY

The working class extended family has continued well into the present century. This can be seen from the famous study conducted by Michael Young and Peter Willmott from 1953 to 1955 in the borough of Bethnal Green, a traditional working class community in the East End of London. Young and Willmott define the extended family as a 'combination of families who to some large degree form one domestic unit'. Members of the extended family do not need to share the same dwelling as long as their lives are intertwined sufficiently for the household to be 'to some extent merged'. Young and Willmott see three main reasons for the continued existence of the extended family in Bethnal Green. Firstly, tradition - often families have lived in the same area for three or more generations and a practice begun in the last century has been handed down from one generation to the next. Secondly, proximity of kin - many relatives live near each other and so links can be easily maintained. Thirdly, the common experience of women - the mother-housewife role is shared by female members of the extended family. This provides a common experience which links them together. The extended family is largely organised by women and has sometimes been called 'the trade union of women'.

Most people in Bethnal Green want to live near their parents. Mr Sykes who lives near his mother-in-law said, 'This is the kind of family where sisters never want to leave their mother's side'. Table 1 shows the extent to which married couples live near their parents.

Table 1 Proximity of married children to parents

Parents' residence	Married men	Married women
Bethnal Green	50%	59%
Adjacent borough	18%	16%
Elsewhere	32%	25%
Total	100%	100%
Number	195	174

The link between mother and daughter in Bethnal Green is often strong. The following example shows how much their lives are sometimes woven together. Mrs Wilkins is in and out of her mother's all day. She shops with her in the morning and goes round there for a cup of tea in the afternoon. Then any time during the day, if I want a bit of salt or something like that, I go round to Mum to get it and have a bit of a chat while I'm there.' If the children have anything wrong with them, 'I usually go round to my Mum and have a little chat. If she thinks it's serious enough I'll take him to the doctor.' Her mother looked after Marilyn, the oldest child, for nearly three years. 'She's always had her when I worked; I worked from when she was just a little baby until I was past six months with Billy. Oh, she's all for our Mum. She's got her own mates over there and still plays there all the time. Mum looks after my girl pretty good. When she comes in, I say, "Have you had your tea?", and she says as often as not, "I've had it at Nan's."'

Table 2 shows the frequency of contact between married men and women with their parents.

A nurse visits a working class family in Bethnal Green in the 1890s. In an era of widespread poverty families such as this looked to their relatives for support.

The mother is the head and centre of the extended family, her home its meeting place. 'Mum's is the family rendezvous,' as one wife said. Her daughters congregate at the mother's, visiting her more often than she visits any one of them: 68% of married women last saw their mother at her home, and only 27% at their own. When there, they quite often see their other sisters, and brothers too, particularly if they are still living at home, but even if they live elsewhere, the sisters may call there at the usual time in the afternoon for a cup of tea, or just happen to drop in for a chat on their way to the shops. Regular weekly meetings often supplement the day-to-day visiting.

'All my family,' said Mrs Shipway, 'gather at Mum's every Saturday afternoon. We sit jawing, and get amused with the children when all of them get together, play cards, and listen to the wireless. No one leaves until tenish at night. It always happens on a Saturday.'

In Bethnal Green the old proverb often applies:

> My son's a son till he gets him a wife,
> My daughter's a daughter all her life.

The daughter continues to live near her mother. She is a member of her extended family. She receives advice and support from her in the great personal crises and on the small

Table 2 Contacts of married men and women with parents

	Fathers		Mothers	
	Number with father alive	Percentage who saw father in previous 24 hours	Number with mother alive	Percentage who saw mother in previous 24 hours
Men	116	30%	163	31%
Women	100	48%	155	55%

Table 3 examines the link between the number of contacts between married women and their mothers and the distance between their homes.

Table 3 Contacts of women according to distance of mothers

Residence of mother	Number of married women	Women who saw their mothers in previous 24 hours
Same street or block of flats	23	23
Elsewhere in Bethnal Green	49	33
Adjacent borough	25	4
Elsewhere	36	3

Passing the time of day in 1954

domestic occasions. They share so much and give such help to each other because, in their women's world, they have the same functions of caring for home and bringing up children.

Less than 20 miles away from Bethnal Green, the automatic doors of the tube train open on to the new land of Greenleigh. On one side of the railway are cows at pasture. On the other, the new housing estate. Greenleigh is fairly typical of the council estates to which many Bethnal Greeners have been moved. The changes in frequency of contact with relatives after moving to Greenleigh are outlined in Table 4.

Table 4 Changes in weekly contacts with relatives after moving to Greenleigh

Average number of contacts per week with own and spouse's parents and siblings

	Before leaving Bethnal Green	Greenleigh 1953	Greenleigh 1955
Husbands	15.0	3.8	3.3
Wives	17.2	3.0	2.4

In summer the most popular time for visiting is, of course, the weekend. On a Sunday morning in the summer dozens of people can be seen coming out of the station, many carrying bags of fruit and flowers, as one person said 'quite like hospital on a visiting day'. 'Last August Bank Holiday,' said Mrs Hall, 'we had fourteen relatives down here.' Visitors do not necessarily stay for only one day. Greenleigh is suitable for holidays as well as day excursions. Sometimes people told us, as Mrs Lowie did,

'Mum comes down to stay two or three times a year'. In Bethnal Green, relatives are at hand every day of the week. At Greenleigh the family has to wait for summer, for weekends, for holidays, before they appear.

(adapted from 'Family and Kinship in East London' by Michael Young and Peter Willmott, Routledge & Kegan Paul, London, 1957)

QUESTIONS

1. What percentage of a) married men and b) married women in Bethnal Green saw their mothers within the previous twenty-four hours? (See Table 2.) (2)
2. 'My son's a son till he gets him a wife,
   My daughter's a daughter all her life.'
   What evidence does the extract contain to support this proverb? (4)
3. Members of the extended family often provide each other with support and exchange services.
   a) Outline the evidence given in the extract which illustrates this point. (3)
   b) Suggest two services not mentioned in the extract which members of the extended family might provide for each other. (2)
4. What evidence does the extract contain to show the importance of distance for maintaining contacts with kin beyond the nuclear family? (5)
5. How might the changing role of women in society serve to weaken the extended family? (4)

6 PART THE SYMMETRICAL FAMILY

The Bethnal Green study was conducted from 1953 to 1955. In the early 1970s Young and Willmott conducted a large scale survey of family life in London based on a sample of nearly 2,000. They found that the nuclear family was now the typical form of family structure for members of all social classes. The extended family, found in their earlier study of Bethnal Green, had all but disappeared. They also found important changes in conjugal roles - the roles of husband and wife. Young and Willmott use the term *symmetrical family* to describe the type of nuclear family found in their research. The following passage presents an outline of the symmetrical family and the reasons for its development.

The symmetrical family is a largely self-contained and self-reliant unit. No longer do husbands and wives expect and receive the kind of help and support from relatives that was typical of Bethnal Green in the 1950s. Their leisure activities have also changed since the 50s. Husbands are much less likely to be down at the pub with their mates. Typical remarks include, 'My family is my hobby', 'My wife and family are my leisure time'. Compared to the Bethnal Green study, wives are less likely to spend time with their mothers and other female relatives. Leisure for both wives and husbands is centred on the home with watching television, gardening and playing with the children being the main leisure activities.

The roles of husband and wife in the symmetrical family have become increasingly similar. In the home, 'They shared their work; they shared their time'. Husbands increasingly help with domestic chores such as washing up and cleaning the house. They also help more with raising children though this still remains the main responsibility of the wife. Decisions about family life are now largely shared. The days of the Victorian husband laying down the law are rapidly disappearing.

Young and Willmott use the term symmetrical family to describe the typical nuclear family unit revealed by their research. Symmetry refers to an arrangement in which the parts are similar. In the symmetrical family, conjugal roles, though not the same, have become increasingly similar.

Young and Willmott give the following reasons for the development of the symmetrical nuclear family. Living standards have steadily improved. The value of wages has risen and many more wives are now working in paid employment. Family allowances (now child benefit), sickness and unemployment benefits and various other provisions of the welfare state have helped to reduce the extent of absolute poverty. There has been a steady reduction in family size from an average of five or six children per family in the nineteenth century to just under two in 1970. People are becoming more geographically mobile moving to new council house developments and new locations when changing jobs. The home has become a more attractive place. Better housing, less overcrowding, improved plumbing and heating facilities, home entertainment in the form of radio and television, fitted carpets, three-piece suites and household technology such as vacuum cleaners and washing machines have produced a more comfortable home environment.

A symmetrical family?

(adapted from 'The Symmetrical Family' by Michael Young and Peter Willmott, Penguin, Harmondsworth, 1975)

QUESTIONS

1. Why do Young and Willmott use the term 'symmetrical family'? Give two examples in your answer of symmetry in the family unit described in their research. (4)
2. a) Name the three main leisure activities of husbands and wives. (1)
   b) How might these forms of leisure limit contact with kin beyond the nuclear family? (3)
3. What evidence does the extract provide which suggests that husband and wife will be less likely to rely on relatives for assistance and support than in the past? (4)
4. How might the fact that growing numbers of wives are working outside the home result in decision making being increasingly shared between husband and wife? (3)
5. Why are husbands spending more time at home? (2)
6. Suggest one connection between the reduction in the numbers of children and the development of the symmetrical family. (3)

7 PART — CONJUGAL ROLES

A somewhat different picture of conjugal roles is provided by research conducted by Ann Oakley in the early 1970s (the same time as the symmetrical family research). The main aim of her study was to investigate women's attitudes to housework. The research was based on a sample of 40 women, with at least one child under five, who were each given a long, detailed, in-depth interview.

The following passage looks at Oakley's research then examines evidence from the 1980s and 1990s on the division of household tasks between husbands and wives.

With the emancipation of women has come the virtual equality of the sexes - or so many people believe. They also believe that one sign of equality is the increasing employment of married women, while another is the greater readiness of husbands to help in the home. In this small study I tried to find out firstly how much help husbands actually give in the home and secondly what was thought to be the ideal or proper roles of the sexes.

In thinking about the proper roles of the sexes we must ask if 'he' actually believes in the domestication of the male? Also does his wife? Is there really a change in the old dogma that a woman's place is in the home and a man's place is outside it?

The women in the sample were asked which household and childcare tasks their husbands regularly help with - ranging from shopping, general housework and washing up to putting children to bed, buying children's clothes and supervising their play. They were also asked about what they believed should be the roles of husband and wife in the home.

The most usual pattern was for husbands to share more in childcare than in housework. However, the childcare tends to involve playing with children rather than doing jobs like changing nappies and bathing them.

Not one of the housewives questioned their primary duty as being that of looking after the home and the physical needs of the family. Housework was spoken of as 'my work'. Even where husbands help with childcare, the housewife described this as an activity done 'for' her: 'Sometimes he'll help me to bath them'. Fathers are, therefore, at best, only aids to the mother who retains full responsibility for, and control over, what is done in the home. 'He's a very good father - he plays with the children' was a comment often voiced by both working class and middle class housewives. To play with the children in the evenings and at weekends; to take them off the mother's hands on a Sunday morning; to be interested in their welfare; and to act as a mother substitute in times of illness or childbirth - this defines the father's role for these husbands and wives.

There was little or no support for sex equality. 'I don't agree with men doing housework. I don't think it's a man's job ... I certainly wouldn't like to see my husband cleaning a room up.' 'I don't think it's mannish for a man to stay at home. I like a man to be a man.' Husbands are not regarded as domesticated creatures, nor is domestication set up as ideal.

One of the most important developments since Oakley's research in the early 1970s is the growth in women's employment. The proportion of women who are part of the labour force (working full time, part time or unemployed) increased from 44% in 1971 to 53% in 1994. This obviously reduces the amount of time these women have for household tasks. Table 1 shows the division of household tasks between

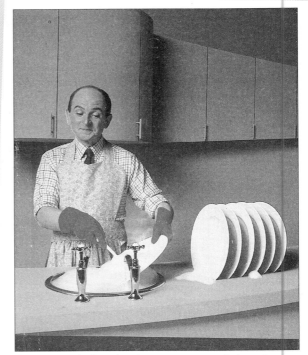

From a British Gas advertisement - an untypical man?

married and cohabiting men and women in 1983 and 1991. (Cohabiting is living together with a partner but not married.) Table 1 also gives figures for 1991 on how those in the survey felt household tasks should be divided. The figures in Table 1 are based on answers from both men and women.

Sociologists such as Ann Oakley argue that the growth of female employment has resulted in a **dual burden** for many women. The traditional burden of housework and childcare is combined with that of paid employment.

(adapted in part from 'Are Husbands Good Housewives?' by Ann Oakley, 'New Society', 17.2.1972)

Table 1 Division of household tasks, 1983 and 1991

Great Britain									Percentages
	Actual allocation of tasks						How tasks should be allocated		
	1983			1991			1991		
	Mainly man	Mainly woman	Shared equally	Mainly man	Mainly woman	Shared equally	Mainly man	Mainly woman	Shared equally
Household shopping	5	51	44	8	45	47	1	22	76
Makes evening meal	5	77	17	9	70	20	1	39	58
Does evening dishes	17	40	40	28	33	37	12	11	76
Does household cleaning	3	72	24	4	68	27	1	36	62
Does washing and ironing	1	89	10	3	84	12	-	58	40
Repairs household equipment	82	6	10	82	6	10	66	1	31
Organises household money and bills	29	39	32	31	40	28	17	14	66
Child rearing									
Looks after sick children	1	63	35	1	60	39	-	37	60
Teaches children discipline	10	12	77	9	17	73	8	4	85

(from 'Social Trends', 1995, p32)

QUESTIONS

1. What does the term sex roles (or gender roles) mean? (3)
2. What evidence is there in the extract to show that women still regard housework and childcare as *their* responsibility? (5)
3. What traditional images of masculinity do the women in the sample hold? (3)
4. What factors in the wider society reinforce traditional roles in the family? (6)
5. a) Briefly outline the changes from 1983 to 1991 indicated by Table 1. (1)
   b) On the basis of Table 1, how symmetrical is the family in 1991? (1)
   c) According to those in the survey, should it be more or less symmetrical? (1)

PART 8 — FAMILY DIVERSITY

From watching the ads on television there appears to be little doubt that the typical British family consists of mum, dad and the kids. The nuclear family is presented as alive and well, fit and healthy and enjoying life to the full. This picture of the nuclear family as typical is not confined to advertisements. It is the ideal presented to us all. It is the model on which governments usually base their policies and it is accepted by many sociologists. In recent years some sociologists have rejected the view that there is such a thing as the 'typical British family'. They see diversity and variation influenced by social class, ethnicity and region. They recognise an increasing variety of family types, in particular the growth of the lone parent family. This diversity has led the social historian Peter Laslett to argue that we should get rid of the phrase 'the British family' as soon as possible. The following passage examines this view.

Official statistics in the UK use the following definition of the family. 'A **family** is defined as a married or cohabiting couple with or without children, or a lone parent with children. People living alone are not normally considered a family.' **Households** consist of people living alone or groups of people living together as a unit. Most households consist of one family. Table 1 shows family and household types in Britain.

Table 1 Households

Great Britain				Percentages
	1961	1971	1981	1994-5
One person households				
Under pensionable age	4	6	8	12
Over pensionable age	7	12	14	15
Two or more unrelated adults	5	4	5	6
One family households				
Married couple with:				
No children	26	27	26	25
1-2 dependent children	30	26	25	20
3 or more dependent children	8	9	6	5
Non-dependent children only	10	8	8	6
Lone parent with:				
Dependent children	2	3	5	7
Non-dependent children only	4	4	4	3
Two or more families	3	1	1	1
Number of households				
(=100%)(millions)	16.2	18.2	19.5	23.1

(adapted from 'Social Trends', 1996, p51)

Table 2 looks at people rather than households. It shows the percentage of people living in different types of households and families.

Table 2 People in households

Great Britain				Percentages
	1961	1971	1981	1994-5
One family households				
Living alone	4	6	8	11
Married couple				
No children	18	19	20	21
Dependent children	52	52	47	41
Non-dependent children only	12	10	10	8
Lone parent	3	4	6	11
Other households	12	9	9	7
All people in private households				
(=100%)(millions)	-	53.4	53.9	55.9
People not in private households (millions)	-	0.9	0.8	0.9
Total population (millions)	51.4	54.4	54.8	56.8

(adapted from 'Social Trends', 1996, p52)

If we define a nuclear family as a married or cohabiting couple with children then Table 1 shows that nuclear families form only a minority of households. However, Robert Chester argues that such figures can be misleading. We get a rather different picture if we consider people rather than households. Table 2 shows that in 1994-5, 49% of people lived in parents-plus-children households. A further 21% of people are couples who mostly had, or will have, children. Given this, Chester argues that living in a nuclear family is a phase which is still experienced by most of us. He concludes that the evidence 'does not mean that the nuclear family has been abandoned as a normal experience'.

(adapted from 'The Rise of the Neo-conventional Family' by Robert Chester, 'New Society', 9.5.1985 and 'Social Trends', 1996)

9 PART ETHNICITY AND THE FAMILY

Studies of ethnic minority families support the view that we can no longer talk about 'the typical British family'. They show a wide variety of family structures and relationships. The following passage provides a brief and simplified outline of South Asian families before and after migration to Britain.

The South Asian population of Britain numbers around a million and a half people, more than half of whom were born here. Migration began in the 1950s from three main areas - Punjab (about three-quarters came from this region) Gujerat and Bengal. Most migrants came from peasant backgrounds. In Britain they formed communities based on religion, area of origin, caste and, most importantly, kinship.

In South Asia the basic family unit consists of a man, his sons, and grandsons together with their wives and unmarried daughters. At marriage daughters leave the group and become members of their husband's family. Family members hold land or a business or the right to perform a craft (eg weaving). They live and work together, sharing domestic, agricultural and other production tasks (see Part 2 in this chapter and Part 1 in Chapter 13).

Family membership involves a series of binding obligations and duties. Relationships within the family are hierarchical, with males having more power and status than females, the old having more power and status than the young. Those at the top are expected to support and care for those lower down, who in turn are expected to obey and respect them. However, few heads of households make important decisions without consulting every member of their family, women as well as men. Males keep close control over the female members of their families. For a woman to challenge her father's or husband's

authority in public shames his honour. Parents arrange marriages for both their sons and daughters.

Many migrants found their ideas of honour and family loyalty almost entirely absent in Britain. They made great efforts to maintain the unity of their family and traditional family relationships. Housing proved a problem. The large Victorian houses where many migrants first settled could accommodate large families but they were often in poor, run-down areas. Moving up-market often meant moving into smaller houses.

Indian sweetshop, Chapeltown, Leeds

Some bought adjoining houses and knocked through a connecting door. Others split the family into several nearby dwellings and constant visiting, sharing meals and leisure activities maintained the family unit.

South Asian children born in Britain are exposed to two very different cultures. At home parents expect conformity to the norms of cooperation, respect and family loyalty. Group membership is more important than individual self-interest. At school they are expected to achieve as individuals, they are judged in terms of individual effort rather than as members of a group. Many are multicultural - they switch their behaviour to fit the particular cultural setting. Most choose to organise their domestic and personal lives in terms of the ethnic subculture. They value group loyalty and the warm, secure personal relationships which come from traditional family life. However, exposure to British culture has brought changes. Young men, though still paying their fathers respect, insist on a greater say in decision making. Young people of both sexes are demanding either greater consultation in the arrangement of their marriages, or the right to choose marital partners for themselves.

Family loyalty has proved a valuable economic resource in the establishment of small businesses - corner shops, restaurants, market stalls, small clothing workshops. Family members work together as cooperative units producing goods and providing services. Often they work long hours for low wages building up businesses for the group as a whole. Only a minority of South Asian families in Britain own their own businesses. For those that do, the traditional economic function of the family in South Asia has been recreated in Britain.

(adapted from 'South Asian Families' by Roger Ballard in 'Families in Britain' edited by R. N. Rapoport, M. P. Fogarty and R. Rapoport, Routledge & Kegan Paul, London, 1982)

QUESTIONS

1. Outline the main norms and values of traditional South Asian family life. (6)
2. Housing in Britain is often designed for small nuclear families. (2)
   a) What problems did this present for some Asian families?
   b) How did they solve these problems? (3)
3. British born Asian children are often multicultural. Explain with examples what this means. (5)
4. A minority of Asian families in Britain run their own businesses. How has their family organisation helped them in this respect? (4)

10 PART — LONE PARENT FAMILIES

Lone parent families, also known as one parent or single parent families, have increased rapidly over the past 25 years. This can be seen as evidence of increasing family diversity (see Part 8). Some see the lone parent family as an alternative to the nuclear family. Others see it as a nuclear family gone wrong, as a poor substitute for a two parent family. These views are examined in the following passage.

Figure 1 Families headed by lone parents as a percentage of all families with dependent children

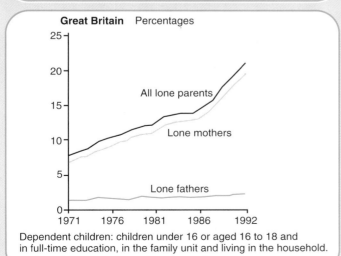

Dependent children: children under 16 or aged 16 to 18 and in full-time education, in the family unit and living in the household.

(adapted from 'Social Trends', 1995, p34)

Figure 2 Marital status of lone parents

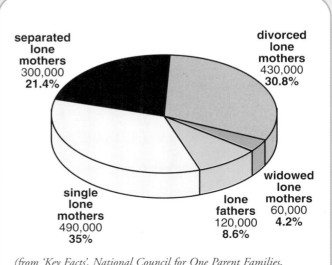

(from 'Key Facts', National Council for One Parent Families, London, 1995, p2)

One in five children lived in a lone parent family in 1994. Less than 4% of lone mothers were under 20, the largest proportion being in their late 20s. Lone parents are usually poor (see Chapter 6, Part 9). Out of 1.4 million lone parent families in Britain in May 1993, 75% received income support and 16% received family credit (designed to top up low wages). In 1993, 15% of lone mothers with dependent children worked full time and 24% part time. This compares with 21% and 42% of married mothers with dependent children. Surveys indicate that most lone parents would like to work but the lack of affordable child care and the 'benefits trap' prevent them from doing so - some benefits are withdrawn when they start work which can result in their wages being less than their former benefits.

Lone parents have had a bad press in recent years. They have been accused of being married to the state, of living off state benefits at the expense of the rest of society. They have been stereotyped as teenage girls engaging in casual sex without a thought for the consequences. They have been labelled as irresponsible by failing to conform to the 'normal' and 'natural' two parent family and harming their children in the process. (See also Chapter 4, Part 11.)

This negative view of lone parents is based on a number of beliefs.

- A two parent family is seen as better than a one parent family. For example, Conservative MP John Redwood believes that, 'The natural state should be the two adult family caring for their children'. And Home Secretary Michael Howard states, 'We must emphasise our belief that the traditional two parent family is best. Best for parents, best for society and above all best for children.'

- There is concern that social security spending is getting out of hand and this is partly due to benefits paid to lone parents.

- State benefits are sometimes seen as causing the 'problem' of lone parent families. For example, James Bartholomew states, 'The truth is the money does not help. It harms.' The state, by providing benefits, has made lone parenthood financially possible. As a result lone parenthood has been encouraged or, at best, people make less effort to avoid it. The solution - reduce or remove state support.

- Lone parent families harm children. A number of studies indicate that the children of lone parents do less well at school and are more likely to be unemployed and to break the law than children from two parent families.

Each of the points made by those who take a negative view of lone parent families can be countered.

- Rather than seeing the lone parent family as second rate, as a poor substitute for the nuclear family, it is simply an alternative family structure. It is not better or worse, it is not unnatural or abnormal, it is just different.

- The benefits paid to lone parents could be reduced considerably if government and employers provided more help with child care, so allowing many lone parents to return to work.

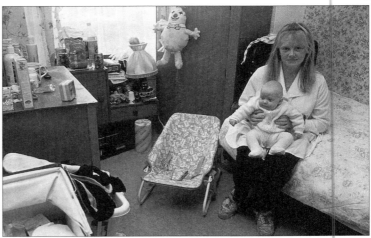
A single mother living in bed and breakfast accommodation

- A reduction or removal of state benefits would do considerable harm to lone parent families, many of whom are already living on the breadline.

- The supposed harmful effects on children are far from certain. For example, Jon Bright of Crime Concern states, 'Our research suggests that it's better to bring children up with one stable, loving parent than in a two parent family where there's violence or conflict'. Research by Joan McCord in the USA found that where parents were caring and loving, crime was no more common among those raised by one parent than among those from two parent homes.

And even if the children of lone parent families are disadvantaged, this may have little or nothing to do with lone parent families as such. It may have far more to do with the policies of government and employers and with the stigma attached to lone parent families. As one lone parent remarked, 'When you tell them you're a single parent, it's as if you've committed a crime'.

(adapted from 'Don't Take Single Parents for Granted: Stop the Hand-Outs' by James Bartholomew, 'Daily Telegraph', 16.8.95; 'Key Facts', National Council for One Parent Families, London, 1995; 'Crime and the Family' by David Utting, Jon Bright and Clem Henricson, Family Policy Studies Centre, London, 1993)

QUESTIONS

1. Briefly describe the trends shown in Figure 1. (3)
2. According to Figure 2, what percentage of lone mothers were formerly married? (2)
3. a) Lone parent families are largely caused by irresponsible teenage girls. Is this true? (2)
   b) Why are teenage girls often singled out for blame? (4)
4. Is the two parent nuclear family the 'natural state'? (5)
5. Find evidence in the extract which challenges the view that lone parent families are second best. (4)

COHABITATION

**11
PART**

In recent years many couples whether married or unmarried, refer to their 'other half' as their partner. This term reflects the steady rise in cohabitation - couples who live together but are not married. Some sociologists see this trend as evidence of increasing family diversity. Others are not so sure, since many couples see cohabitation as a prelude rather than an alternative to marriage.

Cohabitation and marriage

Figure 1 Percentage of non-married women aged 18-49 cohabiting, Great Britain, 1979-1993

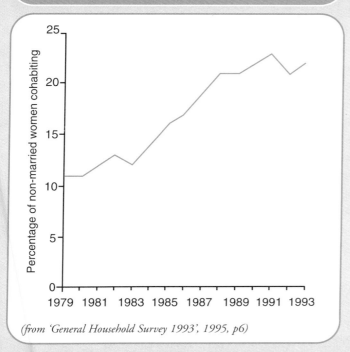

(from 'General Household Survey 1993', 1995, p6)

Figure 2 Percentage of non-married men and women cohabiting by age, Great Britain 1993

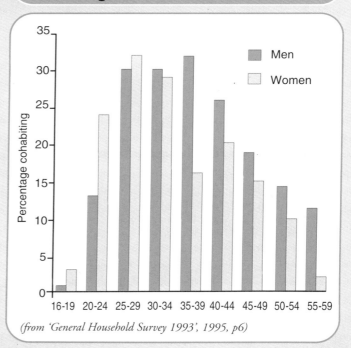

(from 'General Household Survey 1993', 1995, p6)

In 1979, 11% of non-married women aged 18-49 were cohabiting, by 1993 this figure had risen to 22%. Cohabitation tends to be shortlived, averaging around 32 months. Usually it either converts into marriage or breaks up. Only in 18% of cases does cohabitation last for 7 years or more.

The number of marriages in Britain has fallen steadily from 459,000 in 1971 to 299,000 in 1993. Part of this fall is due to the fact that people are delaying marriage. In 1983 the average age for a first marriage was 25.7 for men and 23.4 for women which compares with 28.2 and 26.2 in 1993. This is partly due to the increase in cohabitation. By the early 1990s over 50% of marriages and 7 out of 10 remarriages (marriages in which one or both partners have previously been married) were preceded by cohabitation. But part of the reduction in the number of

marriages may be due to couples choosing not to marry. In these cases cohabitation is seen as an alternative rather than a prelude to marriage.

Children

There has been a steady rise in births outside marriage from 8% of all births in 1971 to 31% in 1992. In 1992, three-quarters of these births were registered to both parents compared to 45% in 1971..This may indicate that a higher proportion of births outside marriage were occurring within stable relationships. Figure 3 shows the rise of births outside marriage from 1971 to 1992. Sole registration means that only the mother's name appears on the birth certificate, joint registration both mother and father.

Figure 3 Live births outside marriage as percentage of all births: by registration

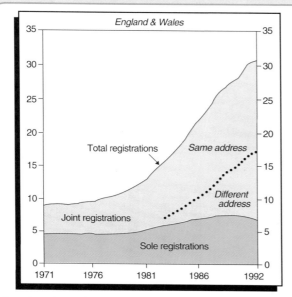

(from 'Social Trends', 1994, p40)

Attitudes towards cohabitation

Table 1 is taken from the 1989 British Social Attitudes Survey. People were asked what advice they would give to the young about cohabitation.

Table 1 Advice on cohabitation

Age of those asked	Cohabit before marriage %	Cohabit only %	Total %
18-24 years	59	9	68
25-34	58	5	63
35-44	55	7	62
45-54	37	3	40
55-59	25	0	25
60-64	29	1	30
65 or older	19	1	20

Like the public, the Church is divided about cohabitation. A Church of England report entitled *Something to Celebrate* (June, 1995) argued that the phrase 'living in sin' should be dropped and that some forms of cohabitation should be recognised as marriages in all but name. However, the Archbishop of Canterbury, George Carey, rejected these recommendations stating that, 'Cohabitation is not, and cannot be, marriage in all but name. Marriage, not cohabitation, is the institution which is at the heart of the good society, and let us not be reluctant to say so.'

Case studies

Victoria and Patrick are 38 and have lived together for five years. They have a two-year-old daughter and every intention of being together 'until death do us part'. They are not married. Victoria, a university lecturer, explains: 'We never got round to it and I don't like the idea of the state intervening in my private affairs. But I suppose the real truth is that I was worried about being a "wife", about the symbolism of it, the loss of identity.'

Woman's Hour presenter Jenni Murray describes marriage as 'a trap'. 'You can try to ignore it,' she says, 'but centuries of tradition are pushing you into a preordained role - a submissive one of helpmate, carer, servant. Women can find independence in or out of a relationship if they choose to avoid that band of gold.'

(adapted from 'Cohabitation' by K.E. Kiernan and V. Estaugh, Family Policy Studies Centre, London, 1993; 'Family Values: Issues for the 90s' edited by C. Donnellan, Independence, Cambridge 1994; 'General Household Survey 1993', HMSO, London, 1995; 'Guardian', 1.12.1995)

QUESTIONS

1. Briefly describe the trend shown in Figure 1. (3)
2. a) Describe the relationship between age and cohabitation indicated in Figure 2 and Table 1. (4)
   b) Suggest reasons for this relationship. (4)
3. Can cohabitation be seen as a rejection of marriage? Give reasons for your answer. (5)
4. How representative are the case studies of cohabiting couples? (4)

12 PART MARITAL BREAKDOWN

The divorce rate is steadily rising in every Western society. Whether or not this means that more marriages are breaking up is not at all clear. Marital breakdown can be divided into three categories: 1) *divorce* - the legal termination of a marriage 2) *separation* - the physical separation of husband and wife (they no longer live together) 3) *'empty shell' marriages* - the couple live together, remain legally married, but their marriage exists in name only.

Accurate figures on the extent of divorce are readily obtainable from court records. Some couples who separate apply for a legal separation order and again accurate figures are available from court records. Other couples, however, separate without obtaining a separation order. There are no figures available for people in this category. The same applies to empty-shell marriages. There is little or no information on the extent of this form of marital breakdown.

Simply because the divorce rate is rising does not necessarily mean that marital breakdown is increasing. It may be that people who in previous years separated are now obtaining a divorce. Some researchers believe that the overall rate of marital breakdown is increasing though they admit that this conclusion is based partly on guesswork.

There are probably as many explanations for the increase in divorce as there are people researching the subject. However, all researchers agree that at least part of the increase can be accounted for by changes in the law. The following extract provides figures on the divorce rate and examines some of the more important Acts of Parliament which are related to divorce.

Figure 1 Divorce: decrees absolute in England and Wales, 1901-1994

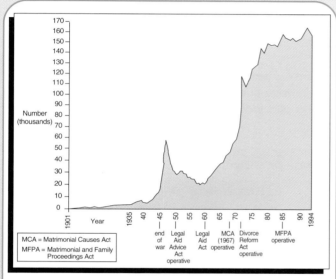

(adapted from 'Family' by Adrian Wilson, Tavistock, London, 1985, p84 and various issues of 'Social Trends')

Marital breakdown affects all social strata.

Before 1857 a private Act of Parliament was required to obtain a divorce in Britain. This was an expensive and complicated procedure beyond the means of all but the most wealthy. In 1857 the Matrimonial Causes Act set up a new court for divorce. The grounds for divorce included adultery, cruelty and desertion. At least one partner had to be proven guilty of one of these 'matrimonial offences'. Although the costs of obtaining a divorce were now reduced, they were still beyond the reach of most people. For the 10 years following the 1857 Act an average of nearly 150 divorces a year were granted rising to an annual average of nearly 600 from 1890-1900.

Beginning with the Matrimonial Causes Act of 1878, a series of Acts gave Magistrates Courts the power to grant separation and maintenance orders. From 1897-1906 around 8,000 separation orders a year were granted compared to an annual average of 700 divorces for the same period. By 1971, however, only 94 separation orders were granted compared to over 74,000 divorces.

Throughout the first half of this century a series of Acts simplified divorce proceedings, reduced the costs involved and widened the grounds for divorce. The financial burden of divorce was eased for the less well-off by the Legal Aid and Advice Act of 1949 which provided free legal advice and paid solicitors' fees for those who could not afford them.

The Divorce Reform Act of 1969 involved a major change in the grounds for divorce. Before this Act a 'matrimonial offence' had to be proven, a 'guilty party' had to be found. However, many people who wanted a divorce had not committed adultery, been guilty of cruelty and so on. The 1969 Act defined the grounds for divorce as 'the irretrievable breakdown of the marriage'. It was no longer necessary to prove guilt but simply to show that the marriage was beyond repair. The Act came into force in January 1971.

The Matrimonial Family Proceedings Act of 1984 came into effect in 1985. This Act reduced from three years to one the time a couple had to be married before they could petition for a divorce.

Changes in the law have made divorce a lot easier. The grounds for divorce have been widened, the procedure has been simplified and the expense reduced. As David Morgan comments, divorce, like foreign holidays, is now available to a growing proportion of the population rather than being confined to a wealthy minority.

(adapted from 'When Marriage Ends' by Nicky Hart, Tavistock, London, 1976, pp70-71; 'A Textbook of Sociology', 2nd edition, by Graham Sergeant, Macmillan, London, 1979, pp189-200; 'The Family' by D.H.J. Morgan, 'Developments in Sociology', Vol 11, 1990)

QUESTIONS

1. Describe the trends shown in Figure 1. (3)
2. a) Briefly explain why a rise in the number of divorces does not necessarily mean an increase in marital breakdown. (3)
   b) What evidence is there in the passage to suggest that the increase in marital breakdown may not be as great as the figures on divorce make it appear? (3)
3. How did the 1969 Divorce Reform Act differ from all previous legislation? (3)
4. a) Using evidence from Figure 1, suggest the possible effect of the 1969 Act on the extent of divorce. (The Act came into force in 1971.) (2)
   b) Why might it have had this effect? (3)
5. The rise in the number of divorces after 1971 does not simply represent a backlog of couples waiting for the Act to come into force. Discuss. (3)

PART 13 · REASONS FOR DIVORCE

The fact that divorce is now simpler and less expensive does not in itself explain why more and more married couples are choosing to divorce. This part looks at some of the explanations which have been given for the rise in divorce.

Changes in the family

Some researchers see the nuclear family in Western society as increasingly isolated from the wider kinship network. This means that problems within families are less likely to be shared with relatives. This can lead to an emotional overload. Under such circumstances there is a greater likelihood of conflict which can result in families breaking under the strain (see Part 14).

Other researchers argue that the family has lost many of its functions and as a result there are fewer bonds to unite its members. For example, the family is no longer a production unit with its members joined by the production of goods and services. Most people today marry for love rather than economic reasons. And if love goes out of the window there may be little else to hold the couple together.

The value placed on marriage

It has been suggested that marriage today is not as highly regarded as in the past. If this is so, then there will be less pressure to keep a marriage together. Others, however, take the opposite point of view. They believe that people set higher standards for marriage, they want and expect more from marriage than in the past. Because of this people are less likely to put up with unsatisfactory marriages. The growing number of remarriages is seen as evidence to support this view. Remarriages have increased from 14% of all marriages in 1961 to 38% in 1992. It has been argued that remarriage shows that people are not rejecting the institution of marriage but instead, attempting to find a marriage which lives up to their hopes and expectations.

Women and divorce

Table 1 **Proportion of petitions for divorce filed by husbands and wives 1946-1989**

Year	Husbands' petitions %	Wives' petitions %
1946	63	37
1948	50	50
1950	46	54
1954	45	55
1961	44	56
1971	40	60
1976	30	70
1980	29	71
1984	27	73
1989	27	73

1989 was the last year in which these statistics were made available.

(adapted from 'A Textbook of Sociology' by Graham Sergeant, 2nd edition, Macmillan, London, 1979, p196 and various issues of 'Social Trends')

By the 1980s nearly three-quarters of divorce proceedings were started by women. A number of researchers believe that the changing situation and expectations of women are the main reasons for the rising divorce rate. Women are entering the labour force in increasing numbers - 44% of all women in 1971, 53% in 1994. Nicky Hart has suggested that the increase in female employment 'undermines the traditional division of labour in the home'. This may cause domestic conflict and in particular threaten the traditional authority of the husband as head of the household.

As Part 7 indicated, many married women have the dual burden of paid employment and the main responsibility for housework and childcare. This may result in further pressure on their marriage.

According to Polly Toynbee, paid employment gives married women a new sense of independence and often leads to demands for more equality within the home. They are less likely to tolerate men who expect to dominate and order them around, while contributing little more than part of their wage packet to the family. Women's expectations of marriage have changed but men's have remained much the same. Many men are shocked, indignant and perplexed when their wives throw them out. They don't know what they've done wrong or what their wives expect from them. Some of these points are illustrated in the following case study.

Rosie is 37, and ended the marriage abruptly one day, taking her children and leaving while her husband was at work. 'My husband couldn't believe it, he couldn't begin to understand it. He told everyone I'd had a nervous breakdown.'

What made her do it? 'I'd thought about it for years. It was my private fantasy. I used to think how good it would be not to have to do what he said all the time, not to have a sinking feeling as he came in through the door and started ordering

me and the kids about. He didn't even know he did it, it came so naturally to him. I used to take a deep breath and take it, because I always lost every argument. I'd become a doormat, because it was easier. But inside I was angry and I couldn't tell anyone.'

She says she's ashamed - ashamed she let it happen for so long, ashamed she didn't set out at the start to establish her own rights. 'But I couldn't.' Perhaps she should have talked to him about it, or sought counselling together? 'I did once suggest it. He said I was mad and wouldn't discuss it.'

(adapted from 'When Marriage Ends' by Nicky Hart, Tavistock, London, 1976 and 'The Worm Turned Syndrome' by Polly Toynbee, 'Observer', 10.9.1989)

QUESTIONS

1. The fewer the ties joining family members to each other and to their relatives, the more likely families are to break up. Explain why this might be so. (6)
2. The higher people's expectations, the less likely they are to realise them. Discuss this view in relation to marital breakup. (4)
3. What changes in women's experience of marriage and attitudes towards divorce are suggested by the evidence in Table 1? (6)
4. If men don't change their attitudes towards marriage, then the divorce rate will continue to rise. Discuss. (4)

14 PART — A CRITICAL VIEW OF THE NUCLEAR FAMILY

The nuclear family in Western society is probably more isolated today than at any time in its history. Extended family units are becoming a thing of the past and close-knit communities are tending to break up. This may well place the nuclear family under considerable pressure. This viewpoint is examined in the following article by the anthropologist Edmund Leach. He regards the isolated nuclear family as a major problem in Western society and suggests that a new form of family structure is long overdue.

Psychologists, doctors, schoolmasters and clergymen put over so much soppy propaganda about the virtue of a united family life that most of you probably have the idea that 'the family', in our English sense, is a universal institution, the very foundation of organised society. This isn't so. Human beings, at one time or another, have managed to invent all sorts of different styles of domestic living and we shall have to invent still more in the future. Individual families are linked up with the outside world in many different ways. The external relations of a family can be based on any sort of shared interest - politics, sport, leisure time activities of all kinds - but as a rule much the strongest bonds are those of kinship, neighbourhood and common occupation. It is therefore of the utmost significance that today, in most parts of the country, the householders in any one street will not all be

doing the same job and will not all be related as kin.

This reflects a very great change in our society which has come about mainly as a result of economic developments over the past 50 years. Up until the First World War a major part of the working population, both in the towns and in the countryside, was residentially immobile. The variety of possible occupations open to working class people was small, and although there was a steady drift from the villages to the towns, most people had nothing much to gain by moving around from one town to another. In Lancashire, for example, practically everyone worked in the cotton mills, and there was no point in moving from Rochdale to Oldham or from Oldham to Bury. But today the go-ahead young man moves to the place where he thinks he can earn most, quickest, or he may even get shunted around from place to place by his employers. This change has had radical consequences for the basic structure of society. In the old days, bonds of neighbourhood, kinship and occupation tended to coincide; most people spent their whole lives close to the place where they were born, so they were always surrounded by kinsfolk. Moreover, the girl whom a man married was often a near neighbour, and the two families were quite likely to be related already even before the marriage. It is still possible to find places where this state of affairs persists but the general pattern is fast disappearing.

The effect of this change is as much psychological as social. In the past, kinsfolk and neighbours gave the individual continuous moral support throughout his life. Today the domestic household is isolated. The family looks inward upon itself; there is an intensification of emotional stress between husband and wife, and parents and children. The strain is greater than most of us can bear. Far from being the basis of the good society, the family, with its narrow privacy and tawdry (grubby) secrets, is the source of all our discontents.

We need a change of values here, but it is not at all obvious just what the change should be. History and ethnography (the study of social groups) provide very few examples of societies constructed around a loose assemblage of isolated groups of parents and children. The domestic units are usually much larger and usually based on kinship. But kin groups can only function effectively if most of the members are clustered together in one place, and this requirement conflicts with one of the prime dogmas of capitalist free enterprise: the freedom to move around and sell your labour in the best market.

Our present society is emotionally very uncomfortable. The parents and children huddled together in their loneliness take too much out of each other. The parents fight, the children rebel. Children need to grow up in larger, more relaxed domestic groups centred on the community rather than on mother's kitchen - something like an Israeli kibbutz perhaps or a Chinese commune. Fitting such units into our style of industrial economy could never be easy.

(from 'The Inward-looking Family' by Edmund Leach, 'The Listener',
30.11.1971)

Homeless mother and child - a typical Victorian image. Were the bonds of kinship that strong in the past?

QUESTIONS

1. Give two ways in which families are connected to the outside world. (2)
2. What changes have occurred which have resulted in the family becoming increasingly isolated? (4)
3. What does Leach think are the consequences of isolation for the nuclear family? (5)
4. a) Why does Leach suggest that an extended family unit or some form of commune might solve some of the problems produced by the nuclear family? (5)
   b) Why does he go on to say 'Fitting such units into our style of industrial economy could never be easy'? (4)

15 PART DOMESTIC VIOLENCE

Until recently, domestic violence was largely hidden within the family. However, highly publicised court cases where women have killed their partners after suffering years of violent abuse, high profile TV programmes such as *Brookside* which have featured domestic violence, and the establishment of refuges up and down the country for women and children seeking protection from violent partners have made domestic violence a public issue.

year from women seeking protection from violent partners. However, most violence goes unreported. The women in Dobash and Dobash's sample, drawn from refuges for battered women, suffered 32,000 assaults of which only 517 were reported to the police.

There are many reasons for failing to report domestic violence. These include fear of making the situation worse, the embarrassment of making it public and the feeling that the police either won't take the complaint seriously or can do very little about it. And the reasons why many women stay with violent partners are often similar - fear of reprisals if they leave and the shame that domestic violence and a failed relationship would bring if they were brought to light. In addition, there is always the hope that things will change for the better. Many women do leave their partners only to return. Dobash and Dobash found that 88% of their sample had left at some stage but then returned, often because they could not afford to keep themselves and their children. Most finally left after their children were beaten - this they could not accept.

The vast majority of domestic violence is committed by men against their partners and children. It has been seen as an attempt by men to assert control. This attempt reflects traditional attitudes of the man as head of the household and the woman as subordinate, of 'being a man' and 'keeping the wife in line' and of violence as a normal way of maintaining power within the family unit. In this respect, domestic violence is an expression of male dominance.

(adapted from 'Violence Against Wives' by R. E. Dobash and R. Dobash, Open Books, Wells, 1980)

Trevor and Mandy Jordache from the TV series *Brookside*. Trevor sexually abused their children and beat Mandy. She eventually killed him.

The family is one of the most dangerous social groups in Western society. According to Dobash and Dobash, who studied domestic violence in Scotland, 'For most people, and especially for women and children, the family is the most violent group to which they are likely to belong. Despite fears to the contrary, it is not a stranger but a so-called loved one who is most likely to assault, rape, or murder us.'

It is difficult to estimate the extent of domestic violence. London's Metropolitan Police receive around 100,000 calls a

QUESTIONS

1. Why is so much domestic violence hidden both by those who suffer from it and those who commit it? (7)
2. Judging from the passage, what are the solutions to domestic violence? (7)
3. The nuclear family has often been held up as the ideal by churchmen, politicians and sociologists. Comment on this view in the light of the passage. (6)

16 PART ALTERNATIVES TO THE FAMILY

A number of alternatives to the family have been tried with varying degrees of success. Probably the most famous example is the Israeli kibbutz which is examined in the following passage. A variation on the kibbutz is provided by the 'commune movement' which developed in the West during the 1960s. Communes are self-contained communities which attempt to be self-sufficient - provide for their own needs. They are often formed by people with strongly held political or religious beliefs who wish to create an alternative society and feel they can only do so in the enclosed world of the commune. These beliefs sometimes include the view that the conventional nuclear family is harmful both to adults and children. In some communes marriage is the norm but the rearing of children is seen as the responsibility of the community as a whole. In others there are no marriage ties and all adults are regarded as parents.

Many communes are short-lived. It is difficult to create an alternative society, to avoid the influence of the wider society and to become self-sufficient. In the early 1970s it was estimated that there were one hundred communes in the UK; ten years later the figure was put at fifty.

Estimates vary widely, however. For example, the Communes Network estimated that there were between 544 and 1,360 communes in the UK in the early 1990s.

The following passage looks at childrearing in the Israeli kibbutz - an alternative to the family that lasted for over 50 years.

Children cared for by trained guardians in an Israeli kibbutz.

In Israel about 3% of the population live in about 270 kibbutzim. These settlements vary in size from 100-2,000 members. Most are based on agriculture with some light industry. Property such as buildings, machinery and agricultural produce is communally owned by all members of the kibbutz. Commodities such as clothing and shoes and services such as cooking and laundry are provided by the kibbutz.

Many kibbutzim have a system of collective childrearing. Married couples share a single bedroom/living room. Children spend most of the day and all of the night away from their parents in children's houses. Their socialisation and education is left to specially trained metapelets (child caretakers and educators) - 'In all the countless ways that a parent educates his children - from how they should spend their time, arrange their day, to how they should eat, sit at the table, talk, play alone or with others, and including such extremely intimate matters as their toilet training - the kibbutz, through its metapelets and the peer group, will educate the child.'

Mothers visit their infants in the communal nursery four or five times a day. These visits continue for six months until breastfeeding stops. Then parents spend about two hours a day, after work, with their children. This is seen as 'fun time' rather than socialisation or child training. It is the only time when parents and brothers and sisters come together as a group. As they grow up children move through a series of children's houses, the same age-group staying together until adulthood. The peer group is an important source of security and companionship. Children of the same age-group tend to see each other as brothers and sisters.

Many parents see collective childrearing as protecting their children from 'bad mothering', from family members demanding too much love and attention from each other. However, there remains a strong bond between parents and children. In particular parents provide for many of the child's emotional needs. But the kibbutz provides for their physical needs - clothing from the communal supply, food from the central kitchen and toys which are shared by all the children. In this respect the community rather than parents provide for children who are 'viewed and cared for as children of the kibbutz'.

In one sense collective childrearing is a rejection of the family and of parental roles. It replaces many of the traditional functions of the family. No longer is the family the unit through which the child passes to become a member of society.

In the early days of the kibbutzim (the 1920s-1940s) all able-bodied adults were needed to work the land and establish the settlements. In recent years these demands have been reduced, standards of living have risen and married couples' quarters have increased in size and now include kitchens and additional bedrooms. The early kibbutzim were isolated with little access to the wider society and the mass media. By the early 1990s at Degania, the first kibbutz, most people spent their evenings at home watching TV and around 70% of young people leave - the kibbutz is no longer central to their lives.

Today communal childrearing has all but disappeared. Children now eat and sleep with their parents. Although most parents clearly want this arrangement, not everybody welcomes it. As one kibbutz member angrily remarked, 'We're all locked into our own homes with our own children and our own TV sets'.

(adapted from 'The Children of the Dream' by Bruno Bettelheim, Thames and Hudson, London, 1969 and 'Commune, Sweet Commune' by Cressida Connolly, 'Observer Magazine', 23.5.1993)

QUESTIONS

1. Why are many communes short-lived? (3)
2. Probably the most important function of the family was taken over by the metapelets.
   a) What is this function? (2)
   b) Briefly outline the duties of metapelets. (2)
3. The peer group was more important for children in the kibbutz than for children in the West. Why? (4)
4. Even in the early days of the kibbutz, parents were still important to their children. Why? (3)
5. Why did many parents see collective childrearing as protecting their children from 'bad mothering'? (3)
6. Why do you think collective childrearing ended? (3)

EDUCATION

Education is one of the major growth industries of the past hundred years. State education began in Britain in 1870 with the Forster Education Act by which the state assumed responsibility for elementary education. In 1880 school attendance up to the age of 10 was made compulsory. In 1918 the state took over responsibility for secondary education which was steadily expanded with the raising of the school leaving age. These developments were accompanied by a rapid growth of higher education. From relatively humble beginnings in 1870, the educational system now has its own Minister of State, a clientele of millions and a budget of massive proportions.

This chapter begins with an examination of the role of education in society. It then considers factors which affect the progress and attainment levels of students with particular emphasis on social class, ethnicity and gender. Social relationships in the classroom are then examined and the chapter closes with a review of changes in secondary education in Britain since the mid 1940s.

PART 1 — EDUCATION AND SOCIETY (1)

From one sociological perspective, society has certain requirements or needs which must be met if it is to survive. From this viewpoint the role of education in society can be examined in terms of how it helps to meet these needs. Firstly, society needs a certain degree of social solidarity or social unity. People must feel a sense of belonging to society, a sense of loyalty to the social group. Common norms and values help to provide this. Secondly, every society requires a system for socialising new members. In an industrial society in which occupational status is largely achieved, young people must learn to value individual achievement. Thirdly, every society requires a system for placing people in roles best suited to their talents and abilities. This is particularly true in an industrial society with a highly specialised division of labour. The right people must be matched with the right jobs. Finally, for society to operate effectively its members must possess the necessary skills to perform essential tasks. In an industrial society these skills are highly specialised.

The populations of many societies come from a variety of national and cultural backgrounds. European nations are unusual in this respect since for generations most of their people have been born and bred in a single country. The United States provides an example of a nation with a population drawn from practically every major country in the world. In such societies education has a particularly important role to play. In the United States schools have provided a shared language and a common history for an immigrant population. Students learn about George Washington and Abraham Lincoln, about the War of Independence and the Civil War between North and South. For immigrants, the history of their new society becomes, in part, their history. They begin each school day with an oath of allegiance to the Stars and Stripes - the national flag and symbol of American society.

Schools in all Western societies emphasise individual achievement. Students achieve their status on the basis of ability, talent, determination and effort. Achievement is measured by their performance in examinations.

Education can be seen as a system of sifting, sorting and grading people in terms of their ability. Students leave school having been thoroughly tested. In theory the most talented will achieve the highest qualifications, the least talented will come away with little or nothing to show for their efforts.

State education developed in industrial societies. In Britain at the close of the 19th century industrial processes were becoming more complex and the demand for technical skills

Sorting, grading and allocating to roles

was growing. Industry required a literate and numerate workforce - workers who could read and write and had a basic grounding in mathematics. In 1880 elementary education to the age of 10 was made compulsory. Since then the school leaving age has been steadily increased to the age of 16 in 1973. Throughout the 20th century there has been a growing demand for clerical, technical, professional and managerial skills. The educational system has steadily expanded offering a widening range of academic and vocational courses at all levels.

(adapted from 'Sociology: Themes and Perspectives', 4th edition, by Michael Haralambos and Martin Holborn, Collins Educational, London, 1995)

QUESTIONS

1. With reference to the United States, suggest how education contributes to social solidarity. (5)
2. Education is an agency of secondary socialisation.
   a) What does this mean? (2)
   b) Which major value is transmitted by schools in all Western societies? (2)
   c) How are students encouraged to adopt this value? (3)
3. How does education help to place people in roles best suited to their talents and abilities? (4)
4. What is the relationship between education and the economic system in industrial society? (4)

② PART EDUCATION AND SOCIETY (2)

A very different view of the role of education in society is provided by a Marxist perspective. From this viewpoint workers in Western industrial societies are exploited and oppressed. Firstly, they produce the wealth but part of this wealth is taken away in the form of profits by the owners of private industry. Secondly, as a subject class, the workers are subordinate to the power of the ruling class, those who own private industry. Thirdly, workers get no real satisfaction or fulfilment from their work since, rather than working for themselves and their fellow citizens, they are mainly working for the benefit of the owners of industry. They must therefore be motivated not by work itself and the satisfaction it should bring but by external rewards connected with work such as pay and job status. Fourthly, in terms of social inequality, there is a large gap between top and bottom - wealth and power are concentrated in the hands of the ruling class. If Western industrial societies are to survive, workers must accept this situation and learn to live with it.

The following passage presents a brief summary of the work of Samuel Bowles and Herbert Gintis entitled *Schooling in Capitalist America*. Bowles and Gintis claim that the educational system helps to maintain the structure of Western industrial societies. In particular it helps to produce workers with the kinds of personalities, attitudes and outlooks that will fit them for their exploited status.

In a study based on 237 students in their final year in a New York high school (secondary school) Bowles and Gintis examined the relationship between the students' personality characteristics and the grades they received. They found that students who were creative, independent and aggressive tended to get low grades. These students were inventive, they thought for themselves and liked to do things their own way. They sometimes step on other people's toes and don't like being told what to do. Such characteristics appear to be penalised and discouraged by the school with low grades. Students who received high grades tended to be punctual, dependable and hardworking. They accepted the authority and direction of the teacher and generally did what they were told. They were unlikely to question what the teacher said. Schools appear to encourage and reward these characteristics with high grades.

Schools are organised on the principle of a hierarchy. The teachers are in charge - they give orders and the students obey. Teaching is based on the 'mug and jug' principle. The teacher fills the empty 'mugs' with knowledge. Students have little say in the matter, they have few opportunities to organise their own work in their own way. As a result they get little real satisfaction from schoolwork. They are motivated not by the work itself but

Preparation for work - a Marxist view

by external rewards connected to work such as examination success and the approval of teachers.

Education is a system of social inequality. Students are graded in the school and in external examinations. Some pass, others fail. The education system promotes the view that the inequality it produces is just and reasonable. In theory it provides fair and open competition for all students. Those who obtain high qualifications deserve them, they have earned them by ability and hard work. The belief is created that the educational system is a meritocracy, that success and failure are based on merit.

(adapted from 'Schooling in Capitalist America' by Samuel Bowles and Herbert Gintis, Routledge & Kegan Paul, London, 1976)

QUESTIONS

1. a) According to Bowles and Gintis, what is the relationship between grades and personality characteristics. (2)
   b) How does this help to produce the kind of worker required in Western industrial society? (3)
2. a) According to Bowles and Gintis why do students get little real satisfaction from their work at school? (2)
   b) How are they motivated to work hard? (2)
   c) How does this help to produce the kind of workforce required for private industry? (3)
3. a) What is a meritocracy? (2)
   b) How can it be argued that the education system operates on meritocratic principles? (2)
   c) How does this lead to the acceptance of social inequality? (2)
   d) Why is this acceptance necessary for the survival of Western industrial societies? (2)

PART 3 SOCIAL CLASS AND EDUCATIONAL ATTAINMENT

Many people believe in the idea of equal educational opportunity. This means that everybody should have an equal chance and their educational qualifications should be based on merit, on their ability and effort. Thus if a person is bright and works hard they should do well no matter what their social background. Equality of opportunity for all might be the ideal on which the British educational system is based but it is certainly not the reality. A large body of research has shown that in general, the higher a person's class of origin (the class into which they were born), the greater their chances of achieving high educational qualifications. Social class appears, therefore, to prevent equality of opportunity in education.

The following extract examines the relationship between social class, home background and educational attainment.

Table 1 Social class, IQ and educational attainment

IQ at age 11	Father's occupation	% obtaining higher education of the following kinds:			Total
		Full-time degree eg university	Other full-time eg vocational courses	Part-time eg day release	
130+	Non-manual	37	4	10	51
130+	Manual	18	12	10	40
115-129	Non-manual	17	17	4	38
115-129	Manual	8	7	9	24

(Average IQ is 100.)

(from 'The Sociology of Education' by Olive Banks, Batsford, London, 1971, p55)

Figure 1 Social class and GCSE results, 1988-1994

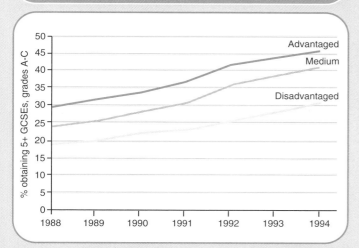

Figure 1 is based on data from Greater London. Local education authorities are divided into three categories:

Advantaged - the 25% with the highest proportion of young people from professional and higher non-manual backgrounds.
Disadvantaged - the 25% with the highest proportion of young people from semi-skilled and unskilled manual backgrounds.
Medium - the remaining 50%.

(adapted from 'Education Divides' by Teresa Smith and Michael Noble, CPAG, London, 1995, p124)

Primary socialisation, the first and probably the most important part of the socialisation process, lays down patterns of behaviour which may last throughout a person's life. Studies by sociologists and psychologists suggest that there are social class differences in childrearing practices which may have important effects on children's educational progress. The argument runs as follows. Compared to the working class, middle class parents place a greater emphasis on high achievement. They expect and demand more from their children and encourage them to continually improve their performance in areas ranging from childhood games to table manners. They give their children greater individual attention and set higher standards for them to attain.

When the child starts school the influence of social class background continues. In general middle class parents are said to place a higher value on education and take a greater interest in their children's progress than working class parents. This is indicated by a large scale study by J.W.B. Douglas which traced the educational careers of 5,000 British children from birth to aged 16. Middle class parents were more likely to visit the school to discuss their children's progress. They were also more likely to want their children to stay on at school beyond the minimum leaving age and to encourage them to do so. Douglas believes that the child's pre-school years are important seeing them as a major influence on the early years of schooling. A child's performance at the start of their educational career is often reflected throughout the secondary school. However, Douglas argues that the most important factor accounting for educational attainment appeared to be the degree of parents' interest in their children's education. In terms of this, he claims that middle class children have a decided advantage over working class children.

(adapted from 'The Home and the School' by J. W. B. Douglas, MacGibbon & Kee, London, 1964 and 'The Sociology of Education' by Olive Banks, Batsford, London, 1971)

QUESTIONS

1. a) Look at Table 1. What percentage of people from (i) non-manual and (ii) manual backgrounds in the 130+ group are studying full time for a degree? (2)
   b) What evidence does the table provide to support the claim that there is a considerable 'wastage' of working class talent? (3)
   c) Why does the table compare manual and non-manual groups with the same IQ in order to examine the influence of social class on educational attainment? (2)
2. a) Briefly summarise the trends shown in Figure 1. (3)
   b) Suggest reasons for this (you may wish to refer to Figure 2, p58 in your answer.) (3)
3. How might the primary socialisation of middle class children give them an advantage over working class children in the educational system? (3)
4. a) What evidence does Douglas provide which suggests that the pre-school years directly affect educational attainment? (2)
   b) What evidence does Douglas give to support his claim that middle class parents are more interested in their children's education than working class parents? (2)

4 PART POVERTY AND EDUCATIONAL ATTAINMENT

In the late 1960s a team led by Ken Coates and Richard Silburn conducted a study of St Ann's, an inner city slum in Nottingham. Their research suggests that the disadvantages of poverty are passed on from one generation to the next. This 'cycle of deprivation' tends to transmit the life chances of parents to their children. The following passage illustrates this process in terms of education. This is followed by evidence from the 1990s which indicates that the growth in relative poverty is reflected in a widening of the gap in educational qualifications between the poor and the rest of society.

Growing up in poverty

St Ann's is a depressing area. Many of the houses are damp, draughty and poorly heated. They are often run down and dilapidated and a quarter have one or more rooms which the occupants consider unusable. The people have a sense of hopelessness and powerlessness and many are resigned to their situation believing that there is little they can do to change it. Few show any signs of optimism or self-confidence.

The children of St Ann's are on average smaller and less hardy than middle class children from the more prosperous suburbs of Nottingham. They have little stamina and are usually on the losing side when their school teams play other schools. Their diet is poor, they have a low resistance to illness and they are often absent from school. Every epidemic which hits the city flourishes in St Ann's. Some of the children arrive at school without breakfast either because their parents have overslept or have gone out to work before them. Many of the children have emotional problems. Up to two fifths came from broken homes and 16% were defined as educationally subnormal.

When starting school many of the children from St Ann's had little idea about how to play with paints, water, sand or clay. Their vocabulary was small and they had little experience of pencils, pictures or books. As a result they lacked much of the grounding required for learning how to read. They showed little ability to discriminate between shapes and therefore had difficulty solving problems involving different shapes. At home they lacked the jigsaw puzzles and educational toys found in most middle class homes.

The children from St Ann's arrived as 'retarded' pupils in the infant school and all too often continued as such into the junior school. A quarter could not read by the time they were seven and less than a tenth were average readers for their age group. Entry to grammar school in the area was based largely on a verbal reasoning test taken at the age of 11. Reading skills had an important influence on test scores. Not surprisingly only 1.5% of St Ann's school population obtained a grammar school place. This compares with 60% for one middle class suburb in Nottingham.

Coates and Silburn argue it would be wrong to blame the teachers for these results. They give the following quotation from a St Ann's headmistress to illustrate the problems of teaching in the area: 'We begin by setting up what we think is a satisfactory environment: we try to give these children emotional security and establish a contact between teacher and child. Any teacher who can write in her daily report "Today William smiled at me" has probably achieved as much as a teacher somewhere else who could write "Today Johnny did five pages of sums".'

(adapted from 'Poverty: The Forgotten Englishman' by Ken Coates and Richard Silburn, Penguin, Harmondsworth, 1970)

Growing up in poverty

Poverty and educational attainment

The 1980s and the first half of the 1990s have seen a steady increase in relative poverty. In particular, the income gap between the poor and the rest of society has steadily widened (see pages 58;90). This is reflected in examination results. Evidence from 1992 to 1995 shows that young people in many low income inner city areas are falling further and further behind those in higher income areas. In some inner city areas a growing proportion of young people are failing to achieve even a grade G at GCSE.

(adapted from 'Times Educational Supplement', 15.12.1995)

QUESTIONS

1. a) Why are the children of St Ann's more frequently ill than children from middle class suburbs? (2)
    b) What effects might frequent illness have on their progress in school? (2)
2. What effects might the feelings of St Ann's residents, as described in the first paragraph, have on their children's performance in school? (3)
3. What evidence does the passage contain which may help to explain why most of the children are poor readers? (3)
4. The effects of poverty continue throughout a child's educational career. What evidence does the passage contain to support this statement? (3)
5. Why does the headmistress believe that a teacher has really achieved something if she can write in her report, 'Today William smiled at me'? (2)
6. How might the idea of a 'cycle of deprivation' help to explain the low attainment levels of St Ann's children? (3)
7. Why are the exam results of young people in many inner city areas falling further behind those of the rest of the country? (2)

SPEECH PATTERNS

PART 5

Picture the neighbourhoods in which the following statements might be made: 'Me ma learnt me to read'; 'My mother taught me how to read.' A picture of an inner city slum is suggested by the first, a middle class suburb by the second. It is generally recognised that there are social class differences in speech patterns. Some sociologists and psychologists claim that these differences have an important effect on children's educational attainment. They see them as one of the reasons why middle class children are more successful in school than working class children. The following passage examines Basil Bernstein's early work on speech patterns and the work of one of his main critics, William Labov.

Two five-year-olds, one from a working class background, the other from a middle class background, are given four pictures on which to base a story. In the first picture several boys are playing football. In the second one of the boys kicks the ball and it breaks a window in a nearby house. The third picture shows a man and a woman looking out of the window. The man is shaking his fist at the boys. The final picture shows the boys running away in the opposite direction. The middle class child clearly and accurately describes and analyses these events. The listener has no need to see the pictures in order to fully understand what they show. However, in order to make sense of the story told by the working class child the listener would need to see the pictures. The child fails to spell out the details of the story, he fails to fully explain the relationship between the boys and the people in the house. Without the pictures his story is unclear and incomplete.

Bernstein uses this example to illustrate some of the differences he believes exist between working and middle class speech patterns. Working class speech is a kind of shorthand speech. In Bernstein's terminology it is a **restricted code**. It uses a smaller vocabulary than middle class speech and makes less use of adjectives and adverbs. As a result it is not well suited for spelling out more subtle, less obvious shades of meaning or for elaborating and developing ideas. Bernstein refers to middle class speech patterns as an **elaborated code**. This type of code spells out many of the meanings taken for granted and left unspoken by the restricted code. It provides the details and background information, the explanations and reasons often left out by a restricted code.

Bernstein claims that speech patterns can affect a child's ability to reason, analyse and think logically. The following example suggests why this might be so. A young child is playing noisily in the kitchen with pots and pans when the telephone rings. A working class mother tells her to 'shut up' or 'be quiet' whereas the middle class mother says, 'Would you keep quiet for a minute; I want to talk on the telephone.' The first message is simple requiring little thought. The child is simply told to keep quiet. The second message is more complex. The child is given a reason for the request, asked to consider the wishes of another person and asked to organise her behaviour according to a time dimension - 'a minute'. Such speech patterns repeated daily over a period of years provide greater mental stimulation for the middle class child and result in more complex patterns of speech.

Bernstein claims that class differences in speech patterns partly explain class differences in educational attainment. Firstly, lessons in school are conducted in an elaborated code. This places the working class child at a disadvantage. Secondly, the restricted code reduces the chances of working class pupils of acquiring some of the skills demanded by the educational system, skills such as describing, analysing and comparing.

A very different view of class differences in speech patterns is provided by the American linguist William Labov. From his research on working class black children in Harlem, New York, Labov claims that their speech patterns are just as elaborated as those of the middle class. They are just as efficient for describing and analysing and just as stimulating for the development of reason and logical thought. Why then do the children do badly at school? Firstly, they speak a different dialect from the teacher.

Harlem, New York. According to Labov, these children have a 'highly verbal culture' and receive a 'great deal of verbal stimulation'.

Secondly, the teacher often criticises their way of speaking - it is not 'correct' English. Partly as a result of this many young children see the classroom as hostile and threatening. They therefore say little so that as little as possible can be held against them. As a result they appear to have a restricted code.

(adapted from 'Language and Social Context' by Basil Bernstein in

'Language and Social Context' edited by P. P. Giglioli, Penguin, Harmondsworth, 1972; 'The Myth of the Deprived Child' by Herbert Ginsburg, Prentice-Hall, Englewood Cliffs, 1972; 'The Logic of Nonstandard English' by William Labov in 'Tinker, Tailor ... the Myth of Cultural Deprivation' edited by N. Keddie, Penguin, Harmondsworth, 1973)

QUESTIONS

1. Briefly outline the differences between a restricted and an elaborated code. (3)
2. Teachers use an elaborated code. Why might this place the working class child at a disadvantage? (4)
3. How might the restricted code reduce the chances of working class pupils of learning the skills and performing the tasks required in school? (3)
4. If Bernstein is correct the working class child enters school with a handicap that is difficult to remove. Explain this statement with reference to the idea of primary socialisation. (4)
5. Why do the children in Labov's research *appear* to have a restricted code? (3)
6. What effect might constant criticism of speech patterns have of a child's progress in school? (3)

PART 6 COMPENSATORY EDUCATION

The arguments presented in Parts 3, 4 and 5 suggest that working class children, particularly those raised in poverty, are lacking the skills, knowledge and experience necessary to be successful in the educational system. Some researchers who accept this view argue that they must be given a helping hand if they are to compete on equal terms with other children. In particular, what they lack must be compensated for. Many believed the answer lay with 'compensatory education'. Only then would children from low income backgrounds have a real chance of making progress at school. The following passage examines compensatory education in the United States where it formed a major part of educational policy during the 1960s and early 70s.

In the early 1960s in the USA, blame was directed at the schools for the widespread failure of children from low income backgrounds. Factors such as school buildings and facilities, teachers' qualifications, pupil-teacher ratios and average expenditure per pupil were held to be responsible. Bring these up to the same high standard for all schools, it was claimed, and social class differences in educational attainment would be reduced or even disappear. In 1966 the publication of the Coleman Report showed that there was no evidence to support these views. The qualifications of teachers, the size of classes, the amount of resources going into the school seemed to make little or no difference to the performance of the pupils.

Attention then shifted from the schools to the pupils. It was they who now required attention. The answer was **compensatory education**. It was based on the idea of positive discrimination, on discrimination in favour of children from deprived backgrounds. Billions of dollars were poured into a massive programme of pre-school education. The aim of programmes like Operation Headstart was 'planned enrichment', the provision of a rich and

Lower East Side, New York. It was to areas like this that Operation Headstart was directed.

stimulating educational environment which would lay the foundation for effective learning in the school system. This would compensate for what was lacking in the backgrounds of low income children. Since it caught them in their early years, its effects should be lasting.

The results of programmes like Operation Headstart were disappointing. They appeared to produce few long term beneficial results. One explanation for this failure was that the programmes tried to do too much and could not hope to compensate for all the deprivations of poverty. What they should do is concentrate on those areas which are crucial to progress in the schools. This view was taken by Bereiter and Englemann who state, 'What is lacking is the use of language to explain, to describe, to instruct, to inquire, to hypothesise, to analyse, to compare, to deduce and to test. And these are the uses that are necessary for academic success.' Bereiter and Englemann devised a series of pre-school programmes to teach language skills to three and four-year-olds. Again the results were disappointing. Many of the children did better during their first few months at school than those not in the programme. However, for most, this progress was shortlived and they soon dropped back to the level of those who had not had training in language skills.

Various explanations have been given for the failure of compensatory education. The schools have been blamed for not building on the foundations laid by the programmes. The programmes themselves have been blamed for being inadequate. The idea that a few hours a week of pre-school education can in any way compensate for the deprivations of poverty has been dismissed as ridiculous. Many sociologists now believe that as long as social class exists there can never be equality of opportunity in the educational system.

(adapted from 'The Myth of the Deprived Child' by Herbert Ginsburg, Prentice-Hall, Englewood Cliffs, 1972 and 'Educational Differences' by Arthur R. Jensen, Methuen, London, 1973)

QUESTIONS

1. Why did the Coleman Report lift blame from schools for the failure of children from low income backgrounds? (4)
2. What is 'positive discrimination'? (3)
3. Why did programmes of compensatory education concentrate on the pre-school years? (4)
4. Why did Bereiter and Englemann see language as a crucial area? (3)
5. Suggest one reason why children who had experienced compensatory education often made progress during their first few months at school but then dropped back. (3)
6. In the light of the failure of past programmes of compensatory education suggest how equality of opportunity in education might be provided. (3)

7 PART — STREAMING

The previous extracts have examined the effects of factors operating outside the school on educational attainment. The following passages look at what goes on inside schools. A number of studies has shown that the internal organisation of schools and, in particular, the way pupils are streamed into ability groups, can have a direct influence on educational attainment. This view will now be examined using information from David Hargreaves' study *Social Relations in a Secondary School*.

Lumley Secondary Modern School for Boys is situated in an industrial town in the North of England. Hargreaves' study focuses on the fourth year boys who were divided into four streams, 4A, 4B, 4C and 4D. The boys were placed in streams on the basis of their performance in school examinations and the teachers' assessment of their ability.

In the eyes of both teachers and boys there is a marked difference of behaviour, attitudes and dress between the higher and lower streams. This was confirmed by Hargreaves' observations. 'A' stream boys conform to the standards of dress approved by the teachers. They wear ties, grey trousers and a sports jacket or sweater and have relatively short hair. Long hair and jeans are typical of lower stream boys (the study was conducted in the mid-1960s). Higher stream boys tend to share the values held by the teachers. They approve of pupils who work hard, who do not copy from others, who pay attention in class, obey teachers and have good manners. Boys who fit this description would be out of place in the lower streams. 'Messing' is the norm there. As one 4C boy observed, 'In this class they're always acting daft just so they can keep up with their mates'. As a general rule, the higher a boy's stream, the less likely he is to be absent from school and the more likely he is to take part in school activities such as playing for a school team.

Boys in the lower streams are given little prestige by those in authority in the school. Many teachers refer to them as 'worthless louts' and 'a waste of time'. The boys' prestige is reduced even further because they attend a second class school, a secondary modern. In Hargreaves' words, 'In the low streams, the boys are deprived of status in that they are **double failures** by their lack of ability or motivation to obtain entry to a Grammar School or to a high stream in the Modern School'.

One solution to being defined as a failure is to reject the system and the people who define you and the values they

Bored and resentful

values of the lower stream subculture. With an audience of their peers they are applauded for what the school terms 'bad behaviour'. As one 4C boy said about a friend, 'I like him 'cos he's always messing about. we get a lot of laughs out of him'. A lower stream boy defined as unsuccessful by the school can be highly regarded in terms of the values of the anti-school peer group. Clint in 4C who was 'cock of the school' is a case in point. His fighting ability brought high status in the eyes of his peer group.

In this way, the boys help to solve their problems of 'status deprivation' (lack of prestige) and 'status frustration' (a sense of frustration and dissatisfaction with their status in the school). They may still be failures in the eyes of the school but by acting in terms of the values of the anti-school peer group they at least have a chance of being successful in somebody's eyes.

Streaming is related to social class. Table 1 shows the percentage of boys from different classes in the top stream (A), the middle stream (C) and the bottom stream (E). Less than 6% of the boys in the school came from non-manual backgrounds.

Table 1 Social class and streaming

					Percentages
Stream	Non-manual & skilled manual	Semi-skilled manual	Unskilled manual	No father or father unemployed	not classified
A	62	17	16	4	1
C	53	13	22	10	2
E	48	13	12	22	5

(adapted from 'Social Relations in a Secondary School' by David H. Hargreaves, Routledge & Kegan Paul, London, 1967)

represent. This solution was adopted by many boys in the lower streams. They reject the values of the school - hard work, high educational attainment, good manners and good behaviour. They reject the people who stand for these values. From the results of a questionnaire, Hargreaves found that only 5% of the boys in 4D have anything favourable to say about their teachers.

Lower stream boys not only reject the values of the school but go one step further and develop values in direct opposition to them. They take the school's values and turn them upside down. Being bad becomes being good. Disrupting lessons, giving cheek to teachers, refusing to do homework, fighting and smoking on school premises is applauded by many boys in the lower streams. By the fourth year two subcultures have developed in Lumley Secondary Modern School. One is the subculture of 4A and 4B, the other the subculture of 4C and 4D.

Most boys choose their friends from members of their own stream. Boys in the lower streams tend to form their own groups in which they can gain status and respect from their friends. In this way the **anti-school peer group** is formed. Boys are given prestige for being successful in terms of the

QUESTIONS

1. Why are boys in the lower streams 'double failures'? (4)
2. a) How did the teachers define the boys in the lower streams? (2)
   b) What effect might this definition have on the boys' educational progress? (4)
3. What effect might the lower stream subculture have on the boys' educational progress? (3)
4. a) What is an 'anti-school peer group'? (2)
   b) How does the anti-school peer group help to solve the lower stream boys' problems of status deprivation and status frustration? (2)
5. a) Summarise the link between social class and streaming shown in Table 1. (1)
   b) How might this link strengthen the negative effects of streaming? (2)

THE SELF-FULFILLING PROPHECY

PART 8

People have a picture of themselves, a self-image or a self-concept. This picture comes in part from the reactions of others towards them. Thus if others respond to a person as if she were bright or dull, she would tend to see herself as such. People can be labelled by others as a certain type of person, as a clown, an idiot, a high achiever and so on. If the label sticks, if everybody sees the person concerned in terms of the label, a self-fulfilling prophecy will tend to develop. The person will be likely to see himself in terms of the label and to act accordingly. Thus if he is defined as a clown, he will tend to behave as a clown. In this way the prophecy is fulfilled - the prediction made about the person comes to pass.

These ideas were applied to education by Robert Rosenthal and Leonora Jacobson. They claim that the way teachers define pupils can have an important effect on the pupils' educational attainment. They outline their research in a Californian school in the following extract. The first paragraph is an introduction to their work for an English readership by E. Stones.

One of the commonest practices in English education is the categorisation of children. In a very large number of schools we have A, B, C and D children. We have children who have been defined as educationally sub-normal and we have 'high flyers'. In recent years another group has been identified: the 'disadvantaged'. In England most of these children are from the schools of decaying inner city areas, often including disproportionate numbers of children from non-English backgrounds. It is important to discover whether these labels set up attitudes in teachers which help to produce the results expected. This effect is called a self-fulfilling prophecy. Thus if a teacher thinks a child is an 'A' child, he is likely to produce 'A' results for that teacher even if he is really a 'C' child in disguise. We have an old saying 'Give a dog a bad name' which is closely related to this problem.

(from 'Readings in Educational Psychology' edited by E. Stones, Methuen, London, 1970, pp414-15)

Our research tries to test the operation of the self-fulfilling prophecy. It was conducted in Oak School, a public elementary (primary) school in a lower class community of a medium sized city. About one sixth of the school population is Mexican. Oak School is a streamed school with fast, medium and slow streams. The Mexican children are heavily over-represented in the slow stream.

It was decided to test the proposition that a favourable expectation by teachers could lead to an increase in intellectual competence (ie brighter children). In order to do this the first step was to test all the children of Oak School with a standard intelligence test. The teachers were led to believe that from the results of this test one could predict intellectual blooming or spurting.

At the beginning of the year following this school-wide IQ testing, each of the 18 teachers was given the names of those children in her classroom who, in the academic year ahead, would show dramatic intellectual growth. These predictions were supposedly made on the basis of those 'special' children's score on the IQ test. For each classroom the names of the special children had in fact been chosen at random and bore no relationship to their score on the IQ test. The difference between the special children and the ordinary children, then, was only in the mind of the teacher.

All the children of Oak School were retested with the same IQ test after one term, after a full academic year and after two full academic years. After the first year of the experiment, a significant expectancy advantage was found and it was especially great for younger children and Mexican children. The advantage of being expected to bloom was evident in the children's IQ scores. After the second year when these children had a different teacher the younger ones lost the advantage of the expectancy effect but the older children maintained it.

We can only speculate as to how teachers brought about an improvement in intellectual competence simply by expecting it. Perhaps by what she said and how and when she said it, by her facial expressions, postures and perhaps by her touch, the teacher may have communicated to the children of the experimental group that she expected improvement in intellectual performance. Such communications together with possible changes in teaching techniques may have helped the children learn by changing their self-concept, their expectations of their own behaviour and their motivation, as well as their cognitive (thinking) style and skills.

(from 'Pygmalion in the Classroom' by R. Rosenthal and L. Jacobson, Holt, Rinehart & Winston, New York, 1968, pp174-81)

QUESTIONS

1. a) How might a teacher's expectations of an 'A' stream student differ from those for a 'D' stream student? (2)
   b) What effect might these expectations have on the progress of the students? (3)
2. How are the expectations of teachers communicated to students? (3)
3. Students from low income and ethnic backgrounds are often defined as 'disadvantaged' or 'underprivileged'.
   a) What effect might these labels have on teachers' expectations of students? (2)
   b) How might these labels help to explain the large numbers of Mexican children in the lower streams? (2)
   c) Why did the Mexican children defined as high ability make *particularly* good progress? (2)
4. If Rosenthal and Jacobson are correct, how might destreaming (mixed ability teaching) help the lower stream students? (3)
5. How might Rosenthal and Jacobson's findings help to explain the failure of programmes of compensatory education? (3)

9 PART — ETHNICITY AND EDUCATIONAL ATTAINMENT

In the 1980s and 1990s the focus of attention moved from social class differences in educational attainment to those of ethnicity and gender. In terms of ethnicity one of the main questions guiding research is whether membership of an ethnic minority group affects a person's educational attainment.

However, it is very difficult to measure the educational attainment of ethnic groups. The Department for Education and Employment statistics on examination results identify gender groups but not ethnic groups. We are left with an assortment of surveys which often differ in terms of time, place, sample size and makeup, ethnic classification and type and level of examination or qualification. This makes it difficult to compare the results of different studies. Some of these difficulties are examined in the following passage.

Table 1 Highest quallification by ethnic group, 16-24 age group, 1988-90 (percentages)

	White	Afro-Caribbean	African Asian	Indian	Pakistani	Bangladeshi	Chinese	African	Other/Mixed
Degree or equivalent	4	1	13	6	2	2	12	5	7
Higher education below degree level	3	2	2	3	1	0	9	4	3
GCE A level or equivalent	26	26	26	27	15	3	24	30	18
GCE O level or equivalent	30	28	20	25	18	16	31	30	31
CSE (not grade 1)	13	17	14	10	9	13	3	3	13
Other	3	3	7	5	5	10	5	8	6
None	20	21	18	22	48	54	15	7	20
Never received any education	0	0	1	0	8	5	0	2	0
Not stated/ not known	1	2	0	2	3	1	2	2	2

A CSE grade 1 is equivalent to an O level pass.
A GCE O level pass is roughly equivalent to GCSE grades A-C.

(adapted from 'Britain's Ethnic Minorities' by T. Jones, Policy Studies Institute, London, 1993, p49 and based on Labour Force Survey data)

Measuring qualifications In Table 1 'GCE O level or equivalent' means a pass in one or more GCE O levels or an equivalent qualification. A very different picture can result from looking at the number and grades of GCEs passed. For example, the Youth Cohort Study found that the proportion of 16-18 year olds passing four or more O levels was 31% for whites, 39% for Asians and 18% for Afro-Caribbeans.

Age groups It is important to look at age groups when measuring ethnic educational attainment. For example, the attainment levels of Afro-Caribbeans are much closer to those of whites in the 16-24 age group (as in Table 1), than in the 16-18 age group. This is because Afro-Caribbeans tend to catch up with whites after the end of compulsory schooling.

Gender Table 1 shows figures for males and females combined. However, there are often important gender differences in attainment within and between ethnic groups. For example, Afro-Caribbean women tend to have higher qualifications than their male counterparts.

Classifying ethnicity Different studies often use different classifications of ethnic groups. For example, in some studies people with Asian backgrounds are distinguished - for instance as Indian, Pakistani and Bangladeshi - while in other studies they are grouped together as Asians.

Social class Compared to the population as a whole, a higher proportion of ethnic group members are working class (see page 73). This is particularly true of Afro-Caribbeans, Pakistanis and Bangladeshis. Before assuming that ethnicity is the cause of ethnic differences in educational attainment, it is important to examine the possible effects of class. For example, one study estimated that at least 50% of the difference in attainment levels between whites and Afro-Caribbeans was due to the effect of social class (Swann Report, 1985).

Sampling The Labour Force Surveys which provided the data for Table 1 were annual surveys from 1988-1990 based on a random sample of 60,000 households which produced information on 150,000 - 160,000 people. Different samples can produce different results and give a very different picture of the educational attainment of ethnic minorities. Compare, for example, the picture of Bangladeshis given in Table 1 with the following. Tower Hamlets has the largest number of bilingual ethnic minority pupils in the country - 60% of the pupil population. Of these Bangladeshis form the largest group. In 1994 they had the highest GCSE results of all ethnic groups in Tower Hamlets. On average they were half a grade above their white counterparts.

(adapted from 'Britain's Ethnic Minorities' by T. Jones, Policy Studies Institute, London, 1993 and 'Times Educational Supplement', 26.5.1995)

QUESTIONS

1. Judging from Table 1, why is it important to distinguish between different Asian groups? (4)
2. Compared to whites and other ethnic groups, Afro-Caribbean, Pakistanis and Bangladeshis are more likely to be working class. How does this help to explain their qualifications as shown in Table 1? (4)
3. Why is it important to take age into account when measuring and explaining the educational attainment of ethnic minorities? (4)
4. a) Compare the picture of Bangladeshi educational attainment given by Table 1 and the information from Tower Hamlets. (4)
   b) Suggest reasons for the differences. (4)

ETHNICITY AND SETTING

PART 10

A number of studies have shown that ethnic minority groups are discriminated against in terms of setting and exam entry. Setting is a form of streaming in which pupils are placed in subject groups in terms of their ability. For example, a pupil may be in set 1 for English and set 3 for maths. Setting often determines whether or not pupils are entered for examinations. For example, a study by the Commission for Racial Equality entitled *Set to Fail?* (1992) of a northern comprehensive school showed that Asian pupils usually needed higher marks than whites to get into the top sets. As a result fewer Asians were entered for GCSEs.

The following passage is based on a detailed study of two comprehensive schools in the Midlands. The study was conducted by Cecile Wright who carried out some 900 hours of classroom observation in each school and formal and informal interviews with teachers and pupils. The examinations referred to are O levels and CSEs. An O level pass is roughly equivalent to GCSE grades A-C; a CSE grade 1 is equivalent to an O level pass. However, compared to O levels, CSEs are lower level examinations.

A comprehensive school, Swiss Cottage, London

The study set out to establish whether ethnicity was a factor influencing the placing of students in streams and sets in two comprehensive schools. Afro-Caribbean pupils entered the schools with reading scores equal to and in one case superior to those of white and Asian students. Yet they were seen as less well-behaved and less cooperative and this led to many being placed in lower ability streams. In one school (school B) nearly 20% of Afro-Caribbeans compared to 7.7% of Asians and no whites were placed in remedial groups. In the other school (school A) Afro-Caribbean students in the lower ability stream had the highest average performance of all the groups in the sample. Even when there was a clear case for re-allocation to a higher stream, teachers were extremely reluctant to make the change. An educational psychologist attached to school B tried to have a bright but discontented Afro-Caribbean girl transferred to the top stream - 'I went into this room where about six teachers who were all hostile (I have never picked up such hostility before) because "over their dead bodies was this child going to be moved into an 'A' stream".'

Afro-Caribbean students encounter, or feel they encounter, racial prejudice and discrimination from teachers. By about the third year in the secondary school they respond with a lack of interest in their work and with disruptive behaviour. As a result they are placed in lower streams and put on to lower level examination courses which do not match their ability. They therefore leave school with fewer qualifications and poorer job prospects. This can be seen from Tables 1 and 2. Table 1 shows the third year examination marks of 12 pupils (4 Afro-Caribbean, 4 Asian and 4 white) and their allocation to examination sets. It shows clearly that ability, as indicated by internal school exams, is not the basis for placing students on O level or CSE courses. Table 2 shows the results of this policy. It shows examination entries for one year in the two schools. Afro-Caribbean students entered the two schools with reading ages on a par with or higher than those attained by the other two groups. They finished up with only one student in each school entered for five or more O levels.

Table 1 School B: individual pupils and allocation to exam sets

		Subject marks (out of 100)				Set placement (O = GCE O level)			
Pupil		English	maths	French	physics	English	maths	French	physics
Afro-Caribbean	A	73	44	58	-	CSE	CSE	CSE	-
	B	62	63	60	59	CSE	CSE	CSE	CSE
	C	64	45	56	72	CSE	CSE	-	CSE
	D	68	37	82	-	CSE	CSE	CSE	-
Asian	E	51	77	-	55	O	O	-	O
	F	60	56	58	-	O	O	O	-
	G	61	62	55.5	-	O	O	O	-
	H	54	55	-	40	O	O	-	O
White	I	61	62	-	62	O	O	-	O
	J	52	57	55	-	O	O	O	-
	K	75	82	77.5	72	O	O	O	O
	L	54	75	64	72	O	O	O	O

Table 2 Examination entries

	Asian	Afro-Caribbean	White
School A	(29)	(19)	(155)
	%	%	%
5 or more CSEs	69	78.9	80
1 or more O levels	58.5	26.3	41.9
5 or more O levels	20.5	5.3	24.5
School B	(92)	(36)	(95)
	%	%	%
5 or more CSEs	65.2	78	57.6
1 or more O levels	46.7	22.2	34.8
5 or more O levels	16.3	2.7	18.5

(Figures in brackets refer to actual numbers of students.)

There is evidence of racism both in the attitudes and practices of the teachers and the policies of the schools. The following examples are taken from observations and interviews in school A. Some teachers regularly made racist remarks such as sending black students 'back to the chocolate factory'. Some were 'amazed' when they discovered black students were bright. Staffroom gossip sometimes labelled Afro-Caribbean students as troublemakers which meant that teachers jumped to conclusions before even meeting students. Black students objected to teachers using racist terms and jokes - 'The jokes are disrespectful' - and to what they saw as racist harassment - 'The teachers are forever picking on the black boys'. They felt this affected their school work - 'We got no time, as you sit down to work they pin something on you'.

Students reacted to this treatment by forming a 30 strong 'all black' group which was anti-school and to some extent anti-white. As one member said, 'We try to get our own back on them. We behave ignorantly towards them, and when teachers talk to us and tell us to do something we don't do it, because we just think about how they treated us.' The evidence presented in the study provides some justification for this reaction.

(adapted from 'School Processes: An Ethnographic Study' by Cecile Wright in J. Eggleston et al 'Education for Some', Trentham, Stoke-on-Trent, 1986)

QUESTIONS

1. According to the extract, why were many Afro-Caribbean pupils placed in lower ability streams? (2)
2. a) From information in Table 1 reallocate students (A-L) to CSE and O level groups for English in terms of their subject marks. Place 4 students in CSE groups (those with the lowest marks) and 8 in 'O' level groups. (2)
   b) In view of this, was the original placement justified? Give reasons for your answer. (3)
3. How might the idea of a self-fulfilling prophecy explain the attainment of Afro-Caribbean students in external examinations? (4)
4. Explain the reaction of black students to their experience of school. (4)
5. Schools reflect the wider society. Discuss with reference to material in the passage. (5)

11 PART ETHNICITY AND EXCLUSION

Exclusion is one of the methods used by schools to deal with pupils regarded as troublesome. Exclusion can be permanent - expulsion - or temporary - suspension. It is difficult to measure the extent of exclusions. A MORI poll in 1993 estimates that they may be twenty times higher than those given in official figures. The following passage looks at the exclusion of Afro-Caribbean pupils.

Figures from the Department for Education (1992) state that Afro-Caribbeans form 8.1% of all permanent exclusions yet only 2% of the school population. Figures from local education authorities from the 1970s to the 1990s give similar proportions. Official figures indicate that all forms of exclusion have risen rapidly since the late 1980s. The Education Reform Act of 1988 required schools to publish examination results and truancy figures. As a result schools became particularly concerned about their public image. So much so that one school in Sheffield 'solved' its truancy problem overnight by excluding all its worst truants.

Why are so many Afro-Caribbean students excluded? There are a number of explanations. The first is racism. Teachers may hold negative stereotypes of Afro-Caribbeans - they may be seen as disruptive and aggressive. The following cases can be used to support the view that racism plays a part in exclusion.

- An Afro-Caribbean boy was permanently excluded because he had two neat lines cut into his hair. He had no record of misbehaviour.
- On his first day in a nursery school in Birmingham a boy of three was surrounded by white children who prodded him and asked, 'Does it wash off?' He became distressed, struck out and was excluded for being 'impossibly violent'.
- An Afro-Caribbean girl in a secondary school was called 'nigger' by a white girl. She retaliated by beating up the white girl. The headteacher and school governors refused to discuss racism and how the incident was provoked. The black girl was permanently excluded.

A second explanation does not see teachers as openly racist. Instead it argues that they often misinterpret the behaviour of Afro-Caribbean pupils which is seen as a threat, as a challenge to their authority. From a two year study of an inner city comprehensive in the Midlands, David Gillborn argues that teachers saw a threat in the actions of Afro-Caribbean pupils where none was intended or existed. He found that 68% of Afro-Caribbean pupils received detention compared to 31% of whites and 50% of Asians. Most whites and Asians got detention for breaking school rules such as smoking. But about half the detentions given to Afro-Caribbeans were for more vague offences such as 'rudeness' and 'nuisance on the stairs'. In general Gillborn found that Afro-Caribbeans were more strictly disciplined than other pupils, a finding white pupils agreed with.

A third explanation states that Afro-Caribbeans are more likely than other groups to experience the frustrations of racism and poverty and to express these frustrations in school. It has been argued that since racism and poverty excludes them from the wider society, Afro-Caribbeans are the very pupils who should *not* be excluded from schools.

Community groups are becoming increasingly concerned about the growing rate of exclusion and are attempting to do something about it. For example, in Croydon the Community Education Panel has an 85% success rate in appeals against exclusion. And some headteachers and staff are beginning to see themselves as a part of the problem. For example, St George's comprehensive in Bristol, where 15% of the pupils are

Afro-Caribbean, has all but ended exclusion. In the words of headteacher Ray Priest, 'You don't exclude children from your home unless there's been a total breakdown. I believe it should be the same at school. We don't get in a sweat if a black child comes in wearing a hat, or with a strange haircut. What we're interested in is the kids learning.'

(adapted from '"Race", Ethnicity and Education' by David Gillborn, Routledge, London, 1990; 'Outcast England: How Schools Exclude Black Children' by Jenny Bourne et al, Institute of Race Relations, London, 1994; 'Observer', 8.1.1995)

Hanging around - exclusion can mean months without schooling.

QUESTIONS

1. In what ways can the case studies used to illustrate the racist explanation be seen as examples of racist behaviour? (6)
2. What effects might the interpretation of Afro-Caribbean behaviour as a threat have on (i) teachers' actions and (ii) pupils' actions. (4, 4)
3. Expulsion can be seen as a failure of headteachers and teaching staff. Discuss. (6)

12 PART GENDER AND EDUCATIONAL ATTAINMENT

The 1980s and 1990s have seen a growing number of studies concerned with gender and education. The following passage compares the educational attainments of male and female students and suggests reasons for differences in their attainment levels.

Figure 1 Highest qualification attained by school leavers

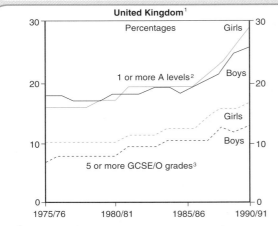

United Kingdom[1]

Percentages

Girls

1 or more A levels[2]

Boys

Girls

Boys

5 or more GCSE/O grades[3]

1975/76   1980/81   1985/86   1990/91

1 Great Britain only for 1980/81, 1982/83 and 1984/85
2 Or 1 or more H grades (Scotland)
3 Includes GSCE/O grades A-C and CSE grade 1 and Scottish equivalent.

(adapted from 'Social Trends', 1994, p50)

Table 1 Male/female GCSE grades A-C, 1988-1994

Males %A-C					Females %A-C					Percentage difference				
1988	1990	1992	1993	1994	1988	1990	1992	1993	1994	1988	1990	1992	1993	1994
All subjects														
39.5	44.9	46.9	47.6	48.8	44.2	50.5	53.9	55.4	56.7	4.7	5.6	7.0	7.8	7.9

(adapted from 'GCSE Inter-Group Statistics, 1988-1994', Associated Examining Board)

Table 2 Male/female A levels, 1980-1994

England						Percentages
	Males			Females		
	1980/81	1990/91	1993/94	1980/81	1990/91	1993/94
3 or more GCE A levels	10	13	14	8	14	15
1 or more GCE A level	16	21	21	15	23	23

(adapted from 'Social Trends', 1996, p68)

Table 3 Full-time enrolments in higher education

United Kingdom									Thousands
	Males					Females			
	1970/71	1975/76	1980/81	1985/86	1992/93	1970/71	1975/76	1980/81	1985/86	1992/93
Universities										
Undergraduates	134	141	157	148	191	59	77	101	108	166
Postgraduates	33	37	34	37	48	10	13	15	17	31
Other										
Undergraduates	}107	123	{120	146	245	}114	123	{95	129	250
Postgraduates			7	7	13			6	7	13
All full-time enrolments	274	301	318	339	496	182	214	217	261	460

Other refers to polytechnics, new universities and other higher education establishments.

(adapted from 'Social Trends', 1995, p54)

Figure 1 shows the highest qualifications of girls and boys when they left school or college. Thus in 1990/91 29% of girls and 25% of boys left with one or more A levels or Scottish Higher grades. Table 1 shows the percentage of male and female students who attained GCSE grades A-C from 1988 (the first year of GCSE) to 1994. Table 2 looks at A level passes and Table 3 provides information about male and female students in higher education.

These measures of educational attainment show that girls' attainment levels are steadily rising, and at GCSE and A level they are now higher than those of boys. What are the reasons for these trends? The short answer is nobody really knows. However, the following suggestions have been made.

Jumping for joy after receiving A level results - she got two As and a B.

Examination results over the past 30 years show that at age 16 girls have done consistently better than boys. A number of reasons have been suggested for this - girls mature earlier than boys, they are more conscientious, their work is neater, they pay more attention to teachers. This is the traditional picture of secondary school girls which many teachers hold. Some sociologists have provided a similar picture, arguing that girls' socialisation encourages conformity and acceptance of authority to a greater extent than that of boys. Whatever the merits of these views, they fail to explain why, until recently, far fewer girls went on to A level and higher education, and why their attainment, particularly in the last few years, has risen so rapidly.

Some of the answers may come from studies conducted by Sue Sharpe of working class girls in secondary schools in the London borough of Ealing. The first study was conducted in the early 1970s. What did the girls see as important? 'Love, marriage, husbands, children, jobs and careers, more or less in that order.' The girls' attitudes to work reflected the general view of women's occupational roles. Office work was the most popular choice, followed by a group of occupations which included teachers, nurses, bank clerks and shop assistants. Many of the chosen jobs did not require A levels. In addition, most girls saw marriage and motherhood as their main roles in life. As a result, many saw little point in continuing their education beyond the age of sixteen.

Sue Sharpe repeated her research in the early 1990s. She found that girls' attitudes had changed. No longer were husbands and children their main priorities. Jobs and careers and being able to support themselves were now their main concerns. As a result, they attached more importance to education than the girls Sharpe had interviewed 20 years earlier.

(adapted from 'Gender and the Politics of the Curriculum' by Sheila I. Riddell, Routledge, London, 1992 and 'Just Like a Girl' 2nd edition by Sue Sharpe, Penguin, Harmondsworth, 1994)

QUESTIONS

1. a) Briefly describe the trends shown in Figure 1 and Tables 1, 2 and 3. (5)
   b) If present trends continue, girls will overtake boys at every level of the educational system. Does the evidence support this view? (5)
2. Primary socialisation has tended to discourage girls from continuing to higher education. Discuss. (5)
3. Why do you think the attitudes of the girls in Sharpe's second study have changed from those in her first study? (5)

13 PART

GENDER AND SCHOOLING

In view of the way girls are treated in schools they do remarkably well in terms of educational attainment. A number of studies have shown that sexism is widespread in the classroom, that teachers, boys and even girls themselves discriminate against girls. The following extract reviews some of the findings of one such study, *Gender and Schooling* by Michelle Stanworth.

Teachers - whether men or women - like boys best. More time, attention, affection and concern is given by teachers of mixed classes to boys than to girls. Boys dominate class discussion while girls, often described by teachers and by boys as 'faceless', are allowed to sit silent at the back of the class. Teachers are less likely to know girls' names, and tend to have low expectations of their job prospects. These are the findings of a study of co-educational A level classes in humanities subjects (at which girls excel) in a further education college.

Interviews with teachers and pupils revealed that both men and women teachers took more interest in their male pupils, asking them more questions in class and giving them more help. Asked which students they were most concerned about, women teachers named boys twice as often as girls. Men named boys 10 times as often as girls. When asked which pupils they were most 'attached' to, teachers named boys three times as often as girls.

Teachers underestimate girls' ambitions. Only one girl was mentioned as likely to get a management job and male teachers could not envisage any occupation other than marriage for two thirds of the girls. One girl, who was getting the top marks in her class in both her main A level subjects, and who wanted a career in the diplomatic service, was described by her woman teacher as likely to become 'the personal assistant to somebody rather important'. The teachers' views were echoed by pupils. 'I can't really imagine where the girls will end up. You can't really imagine they want to be anything. Whereas the boys, they definitely want to get to university and get good jobs,' one boy said.

Both boys and girls, asked to list their class in order of ability, tended to exaggerate the capacity of boys and to downgrade girls. 'It's hard to imagine a girl that's better than me,' one boy said. 'I can if I try but it is unusual.' Several of the girls in his class were getting better marks than he was but he could not know since marks were not made public.

The result of this bias, the author claims, is to give both boys and girls an unjustified reverence for male abilities. When asked who in the class they would least like to be, all the students, boys and girls, named girls. The girls named as unpopular by girls were those who did speak out in class, refusing to accept the silent role played by other girls. They were accused by girls of 'hogging the limelight'. The girls most disliked by boys were the ones who 'sit at the back of the class and might as well be sucking lollipops all day'.

The study leads Ms Stanworth to conclude: 'Girls may follow the same curriculum as boys - may sit side by side with boys in classes taught by the same teachers - and yet emerge from school with the implicit understanding that the world is a man's world, in which women can and should take second place.'

(adapted from 'Study Finds Boys are Teachers' Pets' by Auriol Stevens in 'Observer', 13.2.1983)

QUESTIONS

1. Judging from examination results, girls often succeed despite their teachers. Briefly discuss this statement. (4)
2. Sexism is widespread in the classroom. Provide evidence from the passage to support this view. (4)
3. Even girls are prejudiced against girls. Explain with examples. (4)
4. Schools reinforce girls' primary socialisation. Discuss. (4)
5. Sexual inequality in the classroom reflects the position of women in the wider society. Discuss. (4)

THE TRIPARTITE SYSTEM

14 PART

This part and the one that follows examine the structure of secondary education (the 11-16 age group) in Britain since 1944. The Education Act of 1944 aimed to provide a fair and free system of secondary education for all. It set up the tripartite (three part) system consisting of grammar schools, technical schools and secondary modern schools. The three types of school were supposed to have 'parity of esteem' - their status was intended to be the same. At the age of 11 children were selected for the type of school seen as most appropriate for their particular talents and abilities. Selection was usually on the basis of an intelligence test known as the 11 plus. In theory all students would have an equal opportunity to develop their talents. The following extracts present three views of the tripartite system. The first is by John Vaizey, an educationalist, the second by Rhodes Boyson, a Conservative MP and former headteacher, the third is by Gerald Steinberg, a Labour MP.

The biggest changes in education since the war have taken place in the secondary schools. The grammar schools were made free schools entirely for children of high ability whereas previously they combined clever scholarship winners with children of less ability from the middle classes whose parents could afford the subsidised fees.

In England we have always, until very recently, had different types of schools for different types of children. There they were intended to learn different groups of subjects, because it was thought that children came in layers - clever children (17%) who were able to study classics, mathematics, foreign languages, science and other 'difficult' subjects at grammar schools, not-so-clever children who were to do technical subjects at technical schools (5%) and then the great mass who were to be hewers of wood and drawers of water, able to live life fully doubtless, but not with aid of books.

There is still a great deal of hostility to the secondary modern school. Allocation to a secondary modern school is almost universally regarded as a 'failure' in the 11 plus. Despite the fact that selection at 11 is supposed to be by objective tests of ability and attainment, the grammar school still consists to a large degree of children of the middle class to the exclusion of children from the working class. Because of this the reputation of the secondary modern schools has lagged far behind that of the grammar schools.

(adapted from 'Education for Tomorrow' by John Vaizey, revised edition, Penguin, Harmondsworth, 1966, pp47-49)

There is no doubt that the 11 plus test made considerable mistakes, that very many secondary modern school pupils can undertake academic work and that the arrangements for transfer (from secondary modern to grammar school) within the tripartite system were unsatisfactory. My five years as a secondary modern school head convinced me that the view that secondary schools (in the tripartite system) were equal but different was poppycock. The recent Schools Council Enquiry into Young School Leavers shows that parents see schools largely as places which train their sons and daughters for better

jobs and in this basic requirement the secondary modern schools were and would remain inferior to the grammar schools.

(from 'The Essential Conditions for the Success of a Comprehensive School' by Rhodes Boyson in 'Black Paper 2: The Crisis in Education' edited by C.B. Cox and A.E. Dyson, The Critical Quarterly Society, London, 1969, p57)

I feel passionate on the issue of comprehensive education because, as a youngster, I was a product of the 11 plus examination. In 1955, I failed the exam and still today remember the trauma, grief and unhappiness it caused. I can remember how, as 11-year-olds, we were called into the school hall and a list was read out of who had passed the exam. When my name was not read out, I was devastated. I can remember running out of the school gates, home. Because I had failed the 11 plus, my mother was distraught and I can recall the feeling of failure. It took many years to get over the trauma. I was fortunate to go to a secondary modern school that took GCEs and it was not until I had successfully passed those exams, that the feeling of failure partially disappeared.

(Gerald Steinberg in 'Guardian', 22.1.1996)

QUESTIONS

1. Why did those who set up the tripartite system believe it would give equal educational opportunities to all students? (5)
2. The 11 plus was not intended to be an examination to pass or fail. Why not? (3)
3. Why was selection for a secondary modern school seen as a 'failure' in the 11 plus? (4)
4. What effect might the public's view of secondary modern schools have on the progress of students who attended them? (3)
5. How can it be argued that the tripartite system helped to maintain and perpetuate the class system? (5)

THE COMPREHENSIVE SYSTEM

PART 15

From the beginning the tripartite system had its critics. Their numbers grew over the years and the abolition of the system became official Labour Party policy in the early 1950s. Criticism was wide ranging. The 11 plus was said at best to give a rough idea of a student's performance in GCE exams but nothing about his or her creative, artistic and wider intellectual abilities. To decide a child's educational future at the age of eleven was dismissed as ridiculous. To consign a large section of the population to what was regarded as a second rate institution, the secondary modern school, was condemned as both wasteful and immoral. To suggest that the system gave all students an equal opportunity to develop their talents was regarded as laughable. Added to this, the tripartite system was criticised as socially divisive - it divided the student population into two unequal nations.

Many critics believed that equality of opportunity in secondary education could only come from a single common system of secondary schools for all. Their answer was the comprehensive system. This would end selection at the age of 11. It would provide a broad, basic, high quality course for every student. Children from a broad range of backgrounds would attend the same schools and this social mix would hopefully produce tolerance and understanding. In 1950 there were 10 comprehensive schools in England and Wales, in 1965 - 262, by 1969 - 962. By 1977, 80% of all students in secondary education attended comprehensives.

Like the tripartite system before it, the comprehensive system produced a storm of criticism. The major worry of its critics was that bright children would be held back. They needed special schools (ie grammar schools) to develop their 'special' talents. Only a small proportion of the population, it was claimed, is suitable for this type of education. The following passages consider these criticisms.

A study was conducted of 1,000 boys who failed the 11 plus but were provided with a public school education paid for by their parents. Three quarters passed the GCE examination at O level in five or more subjects. This compares with 56% of all grammar school students. About one third of them passed two subjects at A level and between a fifth and a quarter went on to university.

(adapted from 'The Argument for Comprehensive Schools' by Peter Townsend in 'Education in Great Britain and Ireland' edited by R. Bell, G. Fowler and K. Little, Routledge & Kegan Paul, London, 1973)

Bright children do just as well in comprehensive as in grammar schools, according to the results of a major survey. This government funded study, carried out by the National Children's Bureau, is the first to follow a large nationally representative group of children through different types of secondary school. The research is based on 16,000 children, all born in the same week of 1958, whose progress had been followed by the bureau since birth. They were tested on reading and maths at 11, just before they started secondary school, and again at 16, just before they left.

The results show that children of high ability (their scores were in the top 20% when they were tested at 11) made, on average, the same amount of progress in reading and maths over the five years of secondary education, regardless of whether they went to grammar or comprehensive school. This was true both for bright working class and for bright middle class children. Children of lower intelligence did slightly better if they went to comprehensives rather than to secondary modern schools.

These results cast doubt on the need for the Conservatives' assisted places scheme, which takes some bright children out of comprehensives and puts them in independent schools.

Equally striking is the survey's evidence that comprehensive schools have not had a fair chance to prove themselves. In many areas, comprehensives have co-existed with grammar and direct grant schools, which have 'creamed' (drawn off) the brightest children. Further, there are more comprehensives in working class than in middle class areas.

The study also provides new evidence of the injustices of the selective system. Bright children who ended up in secondary moderns - often because of errors in the 11 plus selection - made less progress than their peers who went to grammar and comprehensive schools. Children who went to grammar schools, despite coming outside the top 20% on the tests at 11, did better than children of equivalent ability who went to other schools.

(from 'Bright Children "Do not Suffer" in Comprehensives' by Peter Wilby, 'Sunday Times', 16.3.1980)

QUESTIONS

1. There was a considerable wastage of talent in the tripartite system. Consider this statement with reference to the first extract. (4)
2. What does the second extract suggest about the claim that bright students will 'suffer' in comprehensives? Assess the evidence in your answer. (4)
3. Why have comprehensives 'not had a fair chance to prove themselves'? Explain the points made in the extract. (4)
4. What points does the second extract make to support the view that selection in secondary education is unjust? (4)
5. Why might the fact that many comprehensives are streamed cast doubt on the claims of some that they provide equality of opportunity? (4)

INDEPENDENT SCHOOLS

16 PART

Independent schools are schools which charge fees for some or all of their pupils. They form the private as opposed to the state sector of the education system. The more famous independent schools, such as Eton, Harrow and Rugby, are known as public schools because, traditionally, they prepared their students for important public office. There are around 200 public schools out of a total of over 2,000 independent schools.

Eton College

In 1995, John Grigg, an 'old boy' of Eton, looked back on his former school. 'It is undeniable that Eton is an ultra-privileged and elitist establishment. Most Eton parents are rich - the fees, getting on for £12,500 a year, are obviously on the high side.'

Public schools have often been seen as a route for privileged young people to the top universities and top jobs and as a means for them to reproduce their parents' wealth and power. There is evidence that public schools are continuing their traditional function of preparing students for public office. Of the 21 members of John Major's first cabinet, 19 attended public schools as did 62% of Conservative MPs in 1992 (see Table 2, page 124).

Independent schools became increasingly popular in Britain during the 1980s and early 1990s. In 1991/92, 7% of all pupils went to independent schools, a percentage that increases with age - 18% of boys and 15% of girls aged 16 and over. Surveys indicate that parents believe that independent schools provide their children with better exam results and better jobs. They put this down to smaller class sizes, firmer discipline, superior teaching and a 'better social environment'.

The 1980 Education Act introduced the assisted places scheme which paid part or all of the fees for 'bright children' whose parents could not afford private education. These 'bright children' were selected by the independent schools. By 1985 there were 17,500 pupils in England and Wales on assisted places, by 1995 around 35,000. The effect on schools varies. For example, in 1995 about 30 boys at Eton were supported by assisted places compared to over half the pupils at Wisbech Grammar in Cambridgeshire.

Wisbech illustrates some of the arguments for and against independent schools and the assisted places scheme. The headteacher of Queens, the only other secondary school in Wisbech, objects to government money being used to subsidise private education and to a private selective school 'creaming' many of the brightest children in the area. In his words, 'I am running a comprehensive but losing half of the above-average ability children to the grammar which has a substantial effect on my statistics and place in the league tables'.

The headteacher of Wisbech sees things in a different light. He emphasises choice and standards. In his words, 'This is a local issue. If you are in a big city you have got lots of choice. It is different in a rural community like this. There are only two schools in Wisbech. I am fed up of hearing of what goes on in the metropolis and in big famous places. People in this town are just as entitled to high standards as those who live in fashionable areas.' And he adds that, 'the amount of money we get in assisted places is the same as the Ministry of Defence spends on providing batmen to maintain high table for senior officers - which is the more important?'

(adapted from 'Sunday Times', 28.3.82; 'Times Educational Supplement', 13.1.1995; 'The Times Magazine', 19.8.1995)

QUESTIONS

1. Neil Kinnock, former leader of the Labour Party, described private education as 'the very cement in the wall that divides British society'.
   a) What does he mean by this? (4)
   b) Provide evidence to support his view. (3)
2. Outline the arguments for and against the assisted places scheme. (7)
3. Discuss the view that private education cannot be abolished in a free society. (6)

THE EDUCATION REFORM ACT

17 PART

The Education Reform Act of 1988 is the most important piece of educational legislation since the 1944 Education Act. It introduced a National Curriculum for all state schools in England and Wales. It reduced the power of local education authorities giving more power to individual schools and their governing bodies. It established grant maintained schools which are independent of local authority control.

Technology - part of the National Curriculum

The National Curriculum For the first time in the history of state education the government has told teachers what to teach. From the ages of 5-16, all pupils in state primary and secondary schools must follow the National Curriculum - subjects whose contents are laid down by law. Pupils are tested in the 'core subjects' - English, maths and science - at the ages of 7, 11 and 14. The idea is to establish national standards against which pupils, teachers and schools can be assessed.

In one respect the National Curriculum can be seen as a move towards equal opportunity. It provides a common curriculum for all pupils. For example, girls are no longer discouraged from taking science because it has traditionally been seen as a 'boys subject'. Science is now compulsory for all pupils. In another respect the National Curriculum can be seen as a move away from equal opportunity. Tests at 11 and 14 are tiered in terms of difficulty. Teachers select and enter pupils for higher and lower level tests in terms of their view of pupils' ability. There is evidence that National Curriculum testing has led to an increase in setting in terms of ability.

Grant maintained schools The Education Reform Act allowed schools to 'opt out' of local authority control and become grant maintained schools. These schools are financed directly by central government and are self governing with headteachers and governors taking decisions about the employment of staff

and the way pupils are selected for entry. The aim is to free schools to specialise, for example in particular subjects and particular types of pupils such as the 'more academically able'. By January 1996, 640 out of 3,614 state secondary schools and 448 out of 18,551 state primary schools in England had become grant maintained.

Competition and choice The Education Reform Act aimed to increase competition between schools and to widen the choice of schools available to parents and their children. Schools are required to publish their National Curriculum test results and their GCSE and A level results. These can then be compared with results in the local area and the country as a whole. This provides a basis for parental choice and, according to the Department for Education, 'the right to choose will encourage schools to aim for the highest possible standards'. The idea is that schools will compete in order to attract pupils and in the process standards of education will rise.

Parents often look closely at examination results when choosing schools. But there are problems with this. A simple league table which ranks schools in terms of results can be very misleading. There is evidence that some of the best schools in Britain do poorly on this kind of league table. These schools, often in run down inner city areas, are achieving extremely good results given the social background of their pupils. They may be doing a far better job than schools well above them in the league table.

A return to selection? Local authority schools are allowed to select 10% of their pupils for special aptitude in areas such as sport, drama and music. In January 1996, the government announced its intention to increase this to 15% and make it possible for schools to select according to pupils' 'general ability'. Grant maintained schools are able to decide their own selection procedures though these must be agreed with the Education Secretary. Some grant maintained schools require interviews with parents and children and tests to assess children's ability. Interviews may lead to selection in terms of social background. For example, Nigel de Gruchy, general secretary of the National Association of Schoolmasters and Union of Women Teachers, fears it will lead to 'selection on social grounds - by accent or the size of the family car'.

Some see the Education Reform Act leading to a new form of tripartite system with grant maintained schools taking the place of grammar schools and local authority state schools becoming similar to secondary modern schools. For example, Simon

Jenkins warns, 'There will be three categories of secondary education in Britain: private schools for the rich, opted out (grant maintained) government schools for the less rich but clever, and local council schools for the poor and rejected'. Time will tell whether he is right.

(adapted from 'Our Children's Education', Department for Education, 1994; 'Sociology in Focus' by Paul Taylor et al, Causeway Press, Ormskirk, 1995; 'Guardian Education', 16.1.1995)

QUESTIONS

1. Outline the advantages and disadvantages of the National Curriculum. (5)
2. Competition between schools will raise standards. Discuss. (5)
3. What are the problems with judging schools in terms of league tables of results? (5)
4. Should schools be allowed to select pupils? (5)

AGE AND GENERATION

Being young and growing old are not simply biological processes. They are also socially constructed. In other words they are influenced by the society in which people live and the culture which they learn. Every society has its own view of age - what it means to be young, middle aged and old. And the way people experience age is strongly influenced by this view. For example, old age in some societies brings respect and prestige whereas in other societies old people have little social standing.

This chapter looks at the social construction of youth and old age in various societies.

PART 1 — INITIATION CEREMONIES

In all societies some of the important stages in a person's life which involve a change in his or her status are marked by ceremonies. These ceremonies are known as rites of passage. They mark the transition or movement from one social status to another. Marriage and death are two such changes of status which are commonly recognised with a ceremony. Often rites of passage are associated with religion, for example church marriages and funeral services in Western society. In many societies, particularly preindustrial societies, the transition from childhood to adulthood is marked by an event known as an initiation ceremony. The following passage examines such ceremonies.

In some societies initiation ceremonies are held at the onset of puberty which in boys is marked by the appearance of facial and bodily hair, in girls by bodily hair and the beginning of menstruation. Puberty is a fairly abrupt event and refers to the beginning of sexual maturity. Adolescence is the period from puberty to sexual maturity. It lasts several years and is a gradual process. In some societies initiation ceremonies occur during or at the close of adolescence.

In many societies girls are initiated to adult status at the onset of menstruation. They are often placed in seclusion and given instruction by older women in matters of sex and marriage and the duties of a wife and mother. Girls often experience hardship which results in changes in their appearance. They may have their ears pierced, skin tattooed, hair cut off or teeth filed. A feast or dance usually ends the period of seclusion and the girl appears in public in the clothes of an adult woman. She now adopts the status of an adult.

Initiation ceremonies for boys usually contain similar elements. This is shown in the following description of an initiation ceremony of the Bakaua tribe of New Guinea in southeast Asia. The boys are taken away from the village and led blindfolded to the ceremonial building which is to be their home for the next three to five months. The details of the ceremony have been kept secret from them and they approach it with feelings of anticipation, wonder, awe, fear and pride. Two sentries guard the boys and terrify them with strange noises and threaten them with a sharp adze (axe-like tool). During their stay the boys must observe certain food taboos - they must not eat everyday food such as pork, mice and lizards or drink fresh water. Male elders instruct the boys in the ways of adults and in the ethics and values of the tribe. The boys are

circumcised during the ceremony. Just before this event the elders frighten them with the booming of bull-roarers (a flat strip of wood tied to a string which makes a roaring sound when whirled round) and the strange rattling of shells and stones hung from the tops of trees. The bull-roarers have a religious significance - they are believed to contain the souls of dead tribesmen.

After the initiation ceremony the boys return to the village wearing ornaments, their faces daubed with paint and finely carved combs in their hair. They are warmly greeted and after a large feast the ceremony comes to a close. The boys have now

Azande boys from Sudan in Africa during their initiation ceremony. They are pictured here in the circumcision camp.

been admitted to adult status. They now have the rights, duties and privileges of adult members of the tribe.

(adapted from 'Primitive Religion' by Robert H. Lowie, George Routledge and Sons, London, 1936 and 'Development in the Individual' by C. S. Ford and F. A. Beach in 'Understanding Society' edited by the Social Sciences Foundation Course Team, Macmillan, London, 1970)

QUESTIONS

1. An initiation ceremony can be seen as an intense, concentrated and very important period of socialisation. Explain this statement using evidence from the extract. (4)
2. Why do initiation ceremonies often involve changes in dress and appearance? (3)
3. Why do you think that there is often a religious element in initiation ceremonies? (3)
4. Why do initiation ceremonies often end in a dance or feast at which the whole community is gathered to welcome the newly initiated young people? (4)
5. a) In the West the status of adolescents is often ambiguous and unclear. Briefly suggest why this is so. (4)
   b) Why is it not so in societies which have initiation ceremonies? (3)

YOUTH IN INDUSTRIAL SOCIETY
PART 2

The following passage examines the changing position of young people in industrial society.

Childhood and adolescence as we know them today can be seen as a creation of modern industrial society. In preindustrial societies children were like miniature adults following in the footsteps of their mothers and fathers. For example, in agricultural societies children often had important duties and responsibilities such as caring for the livestock. In early industrial society child labour was widespread and these 'little adults' often made an important contribution to family finances. From today's viewpoint they were old before their time. During the nineteenth century child labour was banned and compulsory education introduced. The minimum school leaving age has been steadily raised from 10 in 1880 to 16 in 1973. As a result of these changes the length of time between childhood and adulthood has been extended and young people have been increasingly separated from the world of adults.

In preindustrial societies and during the early years of industrialisation, status was largely ascribed. Children usually adopted their parents' occupational roles. Today fewer and fewer children follow in their parents' footsteps when choosing an occupation. Family life therefore fails to present young people with clear role models for the future. As a result they may feel insecure about their status and anxious about their identity. In the family and to some extent in school, a young person's status as a child is ascribed. Yet in the wider society they must achieve their occupational status. In both family and school the young person is part of a group yet in the wider society they must achieve as an individual. Some researchers have argued that the socialisation process in the family and school does not adequately prepare young people for their adult roles. Again the result might be insecurity about status and anxiety about identity.

The transition to adult status in industrial society is not helped by the legal situation. For example a 14-year-old is held to be fully responsible for any crime they commit but cannot leave school or join a trade union until aged 16. At 16 a young person can marry

A 'half-timer' aged 12 in a Lancashire cotton mill in 1920. Half-timers worked half the day and went to school the other half.

and leave home, but cannot do so without parental consent until their eighteenth birthday. At 18 they are legally entitled to vote and buy drinks in a public house but must wait until 21 before standing as a candidate in local or Parliamentary elections. Some researchers have argued that this gradual and piecemeal process of becoming adult results in 'status ambiguity' - confusion and lack of clarity surrounding the status of young people.

The period of time during which young people are financially dependent on the older generation has steadily lengthened in industrial society. As a result the young are subordinated to adult authority well beyond the onset of physical maturity. Some researchers see this development resulting in increasing demands by young people for independence from the adult world and in some cases hostility towards or even an outright rejection of that world.

In industrial society adolescence has been prolonged and adulthood postponed. Young people continue their education for longer and longer periods during which time they are thrown together with their own age group and largely segregated from adults. They share certain experiences, circumstances and problems which separate them from the adult world. As a result the peer group becomes extremely important for many young people providing them with support, security, understanding and a sense of belonging.

(adapted from 'From Generation to Generation' by S. N. Eisenstadt, The Free Press, New York, 1956; 'Power and Privilege' by G.E. Lenski, McGraw-Hill, New York, 1966; 'School Leavers' by T. Veness, Methuen, London, 1962)

QUESTIONS

1. How can the transition to adulthood be seen as relatively easy in preindustrial and early industrial society? (4)
2. Family and school do not adequately prepare young people for adult status in modern industrial society. What evidence does the passage contain to support this statement? (4)
3. Youth in today's society are in limbo - they are neither one thing nor the other. Briefly discuss this statement with reference to the passage. (4)
4. Why are some young people hostile towards the adult world? (4)
5. How does the peer group assist young people in the transition to adulthood? (4)

3 PART — YOUTH AND SOCIAL CLASS

Much of the early writing on youth saw their behaviour as a reflection of their age and as a response to their status as young people. Little mention was made of the fact that young people belong to different social classes. Thus, apart from his age, the lower-working class boy from an inner city area may have little in common with the upper-middle class boy from a well-to-do suburb. A number of researchers have argued that the behaviour of young people must be seen as a reflection not just of age but also of social class.

The terms youth culture or youth subculture are sometimes used to describe the lifestyles of young people, particularly if those lifestyles are different from those of other members of society. The following passage looks at the lifestyle of teddy boys which developed in Britain during the early 1950s. Teddy boys were drawn largely from the working class, particularly the lower-working class. Many lived in run-down inner city areas scheduled for redevelopment. They had few if any educational qualifications and dead-end jobs offering little or no chance for advancement. The lifestyle developed by teddy boys can be seen as a response both to their position as young people in society and to their position in the class system.

In the summer of 1954 a late night train from Southend to London ground to a halt. Someone had pulled the communication cord. Light bulbs were smashed and carriages vandalised. When the train reached Barking the police arrested a gang of youths dressed in Edwardian suits.

In the same year a 16-year-old youth was convicted at Dartford Magistrates Court of robbing a woman 'by putting her in fear'. The Chairman of Magistrates stated:
There are a lot of things and so-called pleasures of the world which demand a lot of money. You tried to get hold of money to pay for ridiculous things like Edwardian suits. They are ridiculous in the eyes of ordinary people. They are flashy cheap and nasty, and stamp the wearer as a particularly undesirable type.'

Again in 1954, two gangs wearing teddy boy clothes fought with bricks and sand-filled socks at a railway station in Kent. 54 youths were arrested and taken in for questioning.

During August Bank Holiday, 1954, the first 'Best Dressed Ted Contest' was held at Canvey Island, Essex. It was won by a 20-year-old greengrocer's assistant. Teddy boys had arrived and were making their presence felt.

The Edwardian suit based on styles current during the reign of Edward VII (1901-1911) was reintroduced in London around 1950. Originally it was adopted by upper class young men. They soon discarded the style when it was taken up by working class youth who adapted it into the teddy boy uniform. The jacket or 'drape' was long, knee length or below, in pea green, deep purple, shocking pink or bright blue with narrow lapels and velvet collar. The drape owed as much to the frock-coat of the Western gunfighter as it did to the jackets of Edwardian times. Drain-pipe trousers emerged below the drape followed by electric pink or green socks and thick crepe-soled shoes known as 'brothel creepers' or 'beetle crushers'. Completing the picture were skinny ties known as 'slim jims' or bootstring ties reminiscent of the Wild West held together by medallions featuring death's heads, cross-bones skulls, eagles or cows heads based on the skulls of Texas longhorns.

Hair was worn long with an ample supply of Brylcreem, swept into a large quiff at the front and combed into a DA or 'duck's arse' at the back. Sideboards or sideburns, named after the American General Burnside, were popular. The picture presented by teddy boys in full regalia was dramatic and quite a shock to the straight world of grown-ups.

Teddy boys adopted American rock and roll as their own. They listened and danced to the music of Bill Haley, Elvis Presley, Eddie Cochran, Jerry Lee Lewis, Carl Perkins and Little Richard. When Bill Haley's *Rock Around the Clock* was shown in British cinemas, teddy boys danced in the aisles and occasionally rioted, slashing seats and ripping them from their mountings.

Dress, music and manner were aggressive. Rival gangs fought for territory, dance halls were wrecked and immigrants attacked. There is evidence that teddy boys started the 1958 'race-riots' in Nottingham and Notting Hill. After the Notting Hill riots nine unskilled working class youths in teddy boy outfits were each sentenced to four years in prison. The violence must not be exaggerated however. Most teddy boys were probably content to strut around in their colourful costumes simply looking tough and aggressive.

Teddy boys outside a London pub

(adapted from 'Cultural Responses of the Teds' by Tony Jefferson in 'Resistance through Rituals' edited by S. Hall and T. Jefferson, Hutchinson, London, 1976; 'Working Class Youth Culture' edited by Geoff Mungham and Geoff Pearson, Routledge & Kegan Paul, London, 1976; 'The Teds' by Chris Steele-Perkins and Richard Smith, Travelling Light/Exit, London, 1979)

QUESTIONS

1. How can the lifestyle of teddy boys be seen to
   a) Express and symbolise the separation of young people from the adult world? (4)
   b) Demonstrate a rejection of the adult world or hostility towards it? (4)
   c) Strengthen peer group solidarity? (4)
2. How can the behaviour of teddy boys be seen as a response to their position in the class system? (8)

4 PART — OLD AGE IN DIFFERENT SOCIETIES

Old age, like youth is socially constructed. The status of old people and their experience of old age varies from society to society. This is illustrated by the following passage.

In many small scale and traditional societies old people are powerful, their status is high and their age brings respect and responsibilities. They are a source of wisdom, their knowledge and experience are valued and their advice is sought after. In the words of an old Chinese proverb, 'My father is all-wise but my father's father is even wiser'.

In many societies authority is allocated on the basis of age. As a general rule, the older people become, the greater their say in public life. Amongst East African people, such as the Masai and Nandi, this idea is built into the organisation of the entire society. The society is divided into **age grades**, for example childhood, junior warriorhood, senior warriorhood, junior elderhood and senior elderhood. People - in this case males - move from one grade to the next gaining in power and prestige as they grow older. Members of the senior grade form a council of elders in which disputes are settled and major decisions affecting the whole society taken. In some age grade societies the elders communicate with the spirits of the ancestors on whose goodwill the wellbeing of everyone depends.

In Western industrial societies older people are encouraged to 'look young' and conceal signs of ageing such as grey hair and wrinkles. In other societies signs of old age are welcomed. For example, among the Venda-speaking people of Southern Africa they indicate approaching contact with the 'real' world of the spirits. In societies where the afterlife is given great significance, the approach of death often enhances rather than reduces a person's status.

Masai warriors being addressed by a village elder (far left).

A respected older woman speaks at a welcome ceremony for visitors - Irim village, Burkina Faso, Africa.

(adapted from 'Other Cultures' by John Beattie, Routledge, London, 1964 and 'Growing Up and Growing Older' by Jane Pilcher, 'Sociology Review', September, 1995)

QUESTIONS

1. a) Compare the status of old people in modern industrial society with those described in the extract. (4)
   b) Suggest reasons for the differences. (4)
2. Suggest a connection between the worship of ancestors and the position of old people in society. (3)
3. The age grade system is often found amongst pastoralists (herders) whose property (eg cattle) is easy to steal and get away with. What advantage might the age grade system have in this situation? (3)
4. a) Why do many older people in the West try to 'look young'? (3)
   b) Describe some of the methods they use. (3)

AGEISM

5 PART

Attitudes and beliefs which present negative stereotypes of old people, and actions which discriminate against them, are known as ageism. In recent years pressure groups such as Age Concern and Help the Aged in the UK and the American Association of Retired Persons in the USA have campaigned against ageism. In the USA, there are laws banning discrimination on the basis of age. Yet despite having laws against racism and sexism, there are no laws against age discrimination in the UK. The following passage looks at some aspects of ageism.

Over 60s training for the London Marathon

A day out in Brighton

■ My husband, a chartered accountant in his fifties, is unemployed. We suspect that age accounts for his inability even to get interviews. Lies and hair-dye are being considered, simply so that he can end his frustration at not being able to use his talents, ability and experience!

■ Now I want to experience being old. Why is age thought about as so disreputable, as a kind of disease? What is wrong with white hair and wrinkles and a life lived without stress and hustle? Why do people want to be mistaken for their daughters' friends and fiancés?

■ Let us reject this idea of old people being a 'burden'. Any number of people on retiring look forward to a change of occupation, to tackling something completely different. Some of these jobs will count as 'gainful' employment, meaning jobs that are paid. Other people will take on voluntary work, not receiving pay and so not 'gainfully' employed, but all the same productively employed in the sense that society benefits from what they do.

(adapted from readers' letters on ageing and ageism in 'New Internationalist', February 1995)

Negative stereotypes of old people are all around us - in everyday conversation, on television, in advertisements and in our beliefs about the meaning of old age. Old people are often pictured as 'past it', 'has beens' and 'over the hill'. And judging from some advertisements for jobs, people are old before they're even 40. 'Salesperson required aged 25-35' suggests that older people lack the drive and energy required for the job. And compulsory retirement ages suggest that older people have nothing useful to contribute in the workplace.

The terms used to refer to old people are often negative and derogatory. They are geriatrics, old fogies, wrinklies, crumblies, boring old farts. And the personality characteristics ascribed to them are often as bad - stubborn, awkward, inflexible, intolerant.

Sometimes the characterisations of old people are less harsh though still negative. They are like children. They are weak and helpless, they need care and attention, they are forgetful. As such old people are often seen as a burden both to their families and to society as a whole.

The media often reinforces these stereotypes. Most references to older people in newspapers and TV news picture them as vulnerable and helpless - as victims of crime, as ill-treated by relatives or staff in old people's homes, as living in poverty and unable to fend for themselves, particularly during winter cold spells. TV soaps and comedies often portray older people as 'dotty old women' like Ethel in *EastEnders* or 'miserable old men' like Percy Sugden in *Coronation Street*. However, *Golden Girls* is a move away from ageist stereotypes - its characters have the same hopes and dreams as everyone else.

(adapted from 'Ageism', Help the Aged, London, 1995)

QUESTIONS

1. Read the letters at the start of the passage. What aspects of ageism are the writers objecting to? (4)
2. The stereotypes of old people reflect their status in society. Discuss using examples from the passage. (5)
3. Why should we be concerned about media representation of old people? (5)
4. There should be laws banning discrimination on the basis of age. Discuss. (6)

PART 6 — AN AGEING POPULATION

Like most of Western Europe the UK has an ageing population. This means that the proportion of older people in the population as a whole is growing (see Chapter 13, Part 5). In 1961 just under 12% of the population were aged 65 and over. By 1994 this had increased to 16% and projections suggest a figure of 23% by 2031 (*Social Trends*, 1996, p39).

Whether an ageing population constitutes a problem depends not so much on the numbers of older people as on their status and social situation. For example, if older people are seen as a burden and a drain on the resources of the welfare state, an ageing population will be defined as a problem. However, this will not be the case if older people are seen as making a valuable contribution to society.

The following passage looks first at some of the problems experienced by older people in the UK. It then looks at the positive side of old age and at the possibility of 'grey power' transforming the position of older people in society.

Counting the pennies

Poverty Mrs Austin is a 76 year old disabled widow who lives on her retirement pension and income support. She budgets strictly and watches every penny. Even so she can't afford to have her gas fire on at night. She has nothing to fall back on in an emergency. In her words, 'You worry every week wondering if you're going to have enough'.

In 1991/92, 40% of single pensioners and 28% of pensioner couples had less than half the average income. The Council of Europe defines poverty as below 50% of average national income.

Loneliness and isolation Mrs Austin lives alone. Problems with her feet mean she cannot go out without help. She used to use the Freedom Ride, a special bus service which would pick her up and drop her off at her door. But council cuts have ended this service. Her relatives live some distance away, rarely visit and don't have time to take her out. The only time she gets out is once a week to a pensioners' lunch club at a local school. Mrs Austin is a lively and sociable person. If she could afford it, she would take a taxi to visit friends. In her words, 'I'm just stuck here. I feel like climbing the walls sometimes - last week I had two days where I never saw a soul - nobody came, nobody rang up, they never ring up, I can't get out, I'm stuck here.'

In 1993, 28% of people aged 65-74 lived alone and 50% of those over 75. This compares with 14% for the population as a whole over 16. Living alone does not necessarily mean that old people are isolated and lonely but this is often the case.

Crime Doris is an elderly widow. She used to go regularly to dances where she met up with her friends, had a chat and enjoyed an evening out. She looked forward to her nights out as they provided a welcome change in her daily routine and got her out of her flat.

Pensioners' Day of Action in London

After learning about an attack on a young woman in her neighbourhood, Doris no longer felt safe enough to go out alone at night. She now only occasionally goes to dances when she can afford to take a taxi, which isn't very often. The feeling of fear which Doris now has, seriously affects the quality of her life.

Stories of old people robbed of their life savings or viciously beaten by muggers regularly hit the headlines. This creates the impression that old people are most at risk from crime. Yet young people aged 16-30 are much more likely to be the victims of crime. Despite this, many older people are very concerned about the threat of crime. The 1991 Attitudes to Ageing survey showed that 45% of people aged 55 and over are worried about becoming a victim of crime. And this fear can seriously affect their lifestyle.

Health The vast majority of older people remain fit and healthy enough to run their own lives. This can be seen from the fact that in 1993 only 5% were in residential or nursing care. However, many older people do have special health needs. The increasing emphasis on community care (see Chapter 7, Part 6)

has made the role of unpaid carers, such as family and friends, particularly important. There are an estimated 6.8 million carers in Britain of which 5.4 million are looking after someone age 65 or over. Many, however, need help themselves. A survey of members of the Carers' National Association showed that 65% feel that their health has suffered as a result of caring and 47% had experienced financial difficulties.

Old age - a positive view A Eurobarometer survey (1993) of older people in the European Union found that two thirds had a fairly active life. The most common pastime was watching television - as for the population as a whole - closely followed by seeing and looking after relatives and friends. 70% liked shopping, 40% enjoyed gardening and DIY and 50% took a regular walk or exercise. And there is evidence that older people are becoming more active in politics. In Britain the 20,000 strong Pensioners Rights Campaign is putting pressure on government to raise state pensions, abolish VAT on fuel and spend more on care for the elderly. However, it is dwarfed by the American Association of Retired Persons which has 34 million members and considerable political clout. Time will tell whether it has the power to transform the position and status of older people in US society.

(adapted from 'Hardship Britain' by Ruth Cohen et al, CPAG, London, 1992, pp12-15; 'Sociology in Focus' by Paul Taylor et al, Causeway Press, Ormskirk, 1995; 'Topic Sheets', Help the Aged, London, 1995)

QUESTIONS

1. Look at the problems which older people experience. In each case discuss whether they are problems of old age as such, or of the way older people are treated in British society. (10)
2. Why do you think we hear so little about the positive side of old age? (5)
3. 'Grey power' will eventually transform the position of older people in society. Discuss. (5)

GENNDER

Women produce children; women are wives and mothers; women do the cooking, sewing, mending and washing; they take care of men and are subject to male authority; they are largely excluded from positions of high status and power. To some degree these generalisations apply to all known human societies. In every society there are men's jobs and women's jobs, in other words there are gender roles. In terms of the rewards of prestige, wealth and power attached to gender roles women nearly always come off worse.

This chapter begins with an examination of the role of women in small scale preindustrial societies. It then looks at the changing status of women during industralisation. The focus then moves to the 20th century with an examination of women's fight for equal rights, their position in the labour market and changes in their attitudes and outlook.

The chapter shows clearly that gender is a social construction. The roles of men and women are not fixed by their biological makeup. There is nothing natural or inevitable about behaving as a man or a woman. Culture rather than biology shapes gender.

PART 1 — GENDER, BIOLOGY AND CULTURE

In many societies it is regarded as natural for a woman to raise children and perform domestic tasks. She is seen to be biologically equipped for such jobs and her role is simply an expression of her female nature. Some social scientists have adopted a similar argument claiming that gender roles are linked to the biology of men and women. Thus the American anthropologist George Peter Murdock argues that biological differences such as the greater physical strength of men and the fact that women bear children lead to the sexual division of labour in society. From a survey of 224 societies Murdock finds that tasks such as hunting, lumbering and mining are usually part of the male role while cooking, gathering wild vegetables, water carrying and making and repairing clothes are usually assigned to women. He claims that, 'Man with his superior physical strength can better undertake the more strenuous tasks, such as lumbering, mining, quarrying, land clearance and housebuilding. Not handicapped, as is woman by the physiological burdens of pregnancy and nursing, he can range further afield to hunt, to fish, to herd and to trade. Woman is at no disadvantage, however, in lighter tasks which can be performed in or near the home, eg the gathering of vegetable products, the fetching of water, the preparation of food and the manufacture of clothing and utensils.'

The view that gender roles are shaped by biology has been strongly criticised. Many sociologists argue that the roles of men and women are determined by culture and therefore learned as part of the socialisation process. If this is the case then there is nothing 'natural' about their roles. Some support for this viewpoint is provided by the following extracts which give brief descriptions of gender roles in three societies.

The Kgatla of South Africa

The women and girls till the fields, build and repair the walls of the huts, granaries and courtyards, prepare food and make beer, look after the chickens, fetch water, earth and wood, collect wild plants, and do all the other housework.

The women fill in their time with one or other of the many tasks that village life may entail. A new coating of plaster may be needed on the walls, or there are cracks that must be mended, and for these purposes loads of earth must first be dug, carried in baskets and worked into a suitable mud.

Men, on the other hand, have no regular daily work in the villages. The herding of livestock is done by the boys, who take the animals out in the morning to graze and bring them back again in the afternoon. Specialists like the doctors and thatchers will generally have something to do almost every day, but the rest seem to work spasmodically, and frequently spend days on end merely lounging about.

(adapted from 'Married Life in an African Tribe' by Isaac Schapera, Penguin, Harmondsworth, 1971, pp141-2)

The Manus of New Guinea

For a year mother and baby are shut up together in the house. For that year the child still belongs to its mother. But as soon as the child's legs are strong enough to stand upon and its small arms adept at clutching, the father begins to take the child from its mother. Now that the child is in no need of such frequent suckling, he expects his wife to get to work. The plea that her child needs her would be ignored. The father is delighted to play with the child, to toss it in the air, tickle it beneath its armpits, softly blow on its bare smooth skin.

On the eve of the birth of a new baby, the child's transfer of dependence to its father is almost complete. While the mother is occupied with the new baby, the older child stays with its father. He feeds it, bathes it, plays with it all day.

(adapted from 'Growing Up in New Guinea' by Margaret Mead, Routledge, London, 1931, pp57-9)

The Tchambuli of New Guinea

The women go around with shaven heads, unadorned,

determinedly busy about their affairs. Adult males in Tchambuli society are skittish (highly strung and fickle), wary of each other, interested in art, in the theatre, in a thousand petty bits of insult and gossip. The men wear lovely ornaments, they do the shopping, they carve and paint and dance. Men whose hair is long enough wear curls, and the others make false curls out of rattan rings.

(adapted from 'Male and Female' by Margaret Mead, Penguin, Harmondsworth, 1962, pp106-7)

A man from New Guinea in traditional dress

QUESTIONS

1. Because of their superior physical strength men do the heavy work. What evidence do the extracts provide to contradict this view? (4)
2. There are certain 'feminine characteristics' which are a 'natural' part of a woman's makeup. What evidence do the extracts contain to challenge this view? (5)
3. Some psychologists have argued that in order to develop into a normal, well-balanced adult a child needs a close, warm and continuous relationship with its mother. How can this view be questioned given the fact that the children described in the extracts grow into well-balanced adults? (4)
4. How can the evidence in the extracts be used to argue that gender roles are shaped by culture rather than biology? (7)

PART 2 — WOMEN AND INDUSTRIALISATION

As the previous extract indicates the role of women can vary considerably from society to society. It can also change significantly over a period of time within a single society. This is shown in the following passage which summarises Ann Oakley's analysis of the changing status of women in British society from the eve of the industrial revolution in 1750 to the 1970s.

In preindustrial Britain the family was the basic unit of production. Agriculture and textiles were the main industries and women were essential for both. In the production of cloth, the husband did the weaving while his wife spun and dyed the yarn. On the farm women were in charge of dairy produce - they made the butter and cheese. Most of the housework - cooking, cleaning, washing, mending and childcare - was performed by unmarried children.

During the early years of industrialisation (1750-1841) the factory steadily replaced the family as the unit of production. Women were employed in factories where they often continued their traditional work in textiles. However a series of factory acts, beginning in 1819, gradually restricted child labour. Someone now had to care for and supervise children, a role which fell to women. The restriction of women to the home had begun.

Women were seen by many men as a threat to their employment. As early as 1841 committees of male workers called for 'the gradual withdrawal of all female labour from the factory'. In 1842 the Mines Act banned the employment of women as miners. Women were excluded from trade unions, men made contracts with their employers to prevent them from hiring women and laws were passed restricting female employment in a number of industries. Tied down by dependent children and increasingly barred from the workplace the restriction of women to the home continued.

Victorian beliefs about a 'woman's place' reinforced this process. No less a figure than Queen Victoria announced, 'Let a woman be what God intended, a helpmate for man, but with totally different duties and vocations'. Articles in the *Saturday Review* illustrate the ideal of womanhood. In 1859 - 'Married life is a woman's profession, and to this life her training - that of dependence - is modelled'. And in 1865, 'No woman can or ought to know very much of the mass of meanness and wickedness and misery that is loose in the wide world. She could not learn it without losing the bloom and freshness which it is her mission in life to preserve'.

Slowly but surely women were being locked into the mother-housewife role and confined to the home. In 1851, one in four married women were employed, by 1911 this figure was reduced to one in ten. From 1914 to 1950 the employment of married women grew slowly but the mother-housewife role remained their primary responsibility. During these years women received many legal and political rights, for example the vote in 1928, but these had little effect on their main role in life. Even by 1970 when about half of all married women were employed, most saw their occupational role as secondary to their duties as a wife and mother and their responsibility for the home.

Oakley concludes that industrialisation had the following effects on the role of women. First, the 'separation of men from the daily routines of domestic life'. Second, the 'economic dependence of women and children on men'. Third, the 'isolation of housework and childcare from other work'. The result is that the mother-housewife role became 'the primary role for all women'.

(adapted from 'Housewife' by Ann Oakley, Allen Lane, London, 1974 and 'The Place of Women in Society' by K. Hudson, Ginn, London, 1970)

CUPID'S HARNESS.

Most women naturally look forward to matrimony as their proper sphere in life, but they should constantly bear in mind that a fair, rosy face, bright eyes, and a healthy, well-developed form, are the best passports to a happy marriage. All those wasting disorders, weaknesses, and functional irregularities peculiar to their sex, destroy beauty and attractiveness and make life miserable. An unfailing specific for these maladies is to be found in Dr. Pierce's Favorite Prescription. It is the only medicine for women, sold by druggists, **under a positive guarantee** from the manufacturers, that it will give satisfaction in every case, or money will be refunded. This guarantee has been printed on the bottle-wrappers, and faithfully carried out for many years. $1.00 per Bottle, or six Bottles for $5.00.

Copyright, 1888, by WORLD'S DISPENSARY MEDICAL ASSOCIATION. Proprietors.

An American advertiser's view of Victorian womanhood

QUESTIONS

1. How did industrialisation lead to the 'separation of men from the daily routines of domestic life'? (5)
2. How did industrialisation lead to the 'economic dependence of women and children on men'? (5)
3. How and why were women increasingly restricted to the home during the last century? (6)
4. Suggest why the mother-housewife role continued as the primary role for women despite the growing numbers of married women entering the workforce. (4)

WOMEN'S RIGHTS

Women's battle for equal rights has a long history. And many believe it is far from won. This part looks at the legislation which resulted from women's struggle for equality in Britain during the 20th century.

The vote By 1900, 70% of men but not a single woman had won the right to vote. During the early 20th century the National Union of Women's Suffrage Societies and the Women's Social and Political Union campaigned for votes for women. Known as suffragettes, they used a variety of tactics - mass meetings, demonstrations, chaining themselves to railings outside Parliament, smashing shop windows in the West End of London, bombing and arson. In 1918 women over 30 and men over 21 were given the right to vote. In 1928 this right was extended to women over 21. As far as the Prime Minister Stanley

Baldwin was concerned, women were now equal under the law, they were now full citizens. In 1928 he announced, 'The inequality of women, if there be such a thing, will not now depend on any creation of the law. It will never again be possible to blame the state for any position of inequality. Women will have, with us, the fullest rights. The ground and justification for the old agitation is gone and gone for ever.'

Many women felt that gaining the vote would bring major changes to their lives. In 1919 Nancy Astor became the first woman MP, 8 women were elected MPs in 1923 and 14 in

A postcard, 1908

A suffragette banner, 1912

responsibility. In a noteworthy case that went to the House of Lords, Julie Hayward, a cook at the Camell Laird shipyard, successfully compared her pay to that of a painter, a carpenter and a thermal insulation engineer - men earning £30 a week more than she was. However, in the words of the Equal Opportunities Commission, the Equal Value Amendment is 'uniquely unworkable'. Between 1984 and 1993 there were 139 cases, just 23 of which were successful. Unless backed by the Commission or a trade union employees cannot afford the thousands of pounds which it costs to take a case to an industrial tribunal. And cases often take years as the following example illustrates.

Dr Pamela Enderby is a speech and language therapist. 98% of speech therapists are women. She noted that clinical psychologists and pharmacists, most of whom are men, earned considerably more than speech therapists. In 1985 she made an equal value claim with these professions against her employer Frenchay Health Authority. The case has been grinding through the courts ever since. In 1993 it finally reached the European Court which found in her favour and in December 1995 the case was sent to an 'independent expert' for consideration. Such experts take an average of 11 months to deliver their reports.

1929. However, it was not until the 1960s with the development of the Women's Liberation Movement that women's rights returned to the political arena.

Equal pay When men and women have the same jobs and do the same work, men have often been paid more than women. The Equal Pay Act of 1970 was intended to end this practice. Despite its good intentions the Act has been difficult to enforce. To claim equal pay a woman has to show she is doing 'like work' to a man and the burden of proving it falls on her. Also the Act made little difference to the two-thirds of the female workforce in 'women's jobs' - occupations such as caring, cleaning and hairdressing where the workforce is largely female and wages for all workers have been set at 'women's rates'.

Equal value The Equal Value Amendment to the Equal Pay Act was passed in 1984. It was seen as a solution to the inequalities in pay between male and female occupations. It stated that women could claim equal pay if they could show that their work is of equal value to a man's on measures such as skill and

Ford machinists strike for equal pay, Dagenham, 1984

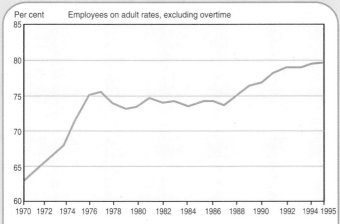

Figure 1 Women's hourly pay as a percentage of men's, 1970-1995

Per cent   Employees on adult rates, excluding overtime

(adapted from 'Employment Gazette', October 1995, p387 and 'Labour Market Trends', November 1995, p407)

Sex discrimination The Sex Discrimination Act became law in December 1975. It banned discrimination on the basis of sex in employment, for example in recruitment, training, promotion, redundancy and dismissal. It also applied to a range of other areas including education, accommodation, transport, entertainment and the provision of goods and services. For example, women often pay more than men for similar goods and services. In 1995 a 50ml facial scrub for men at the Body Shop cost £2.20, a similar product for women cost £4.85. In many hairdressing salons women are charged more for a cut and blow dry than men. If it can be shown that the costs to the provider of the goods and services are the same for both men and women, then a case could be made for discrimination. However, such cases are difficult to prove. Even more difficult are cases involving appointment and promotion. How, for example, is a person to know, let alone prove, that discrimination has affected their job prospects. And this person can be male as well as female. The Equal Opportunities

Commission, which investigates possible cases of discrimination, is receiving an increasing number of complaints from men who have been turned down for jobs as nannies, receptionists, clerks and shop assistants.

Taxation During the 1980s and 1990s women's groups have continued to campaign for equal rights. Compared with the 1970s, more recent legislation has focused on fairly specific areas. Taxation provides an example. Under the 1918 Finance Act married women were classified along with 'incapacitated persons and idiots' as people unable to deal with their own taxes. Husbands were solely responsible for filling in tax forms, they were entitled to a married man's allowance and to receive all tax allowances and rebates on their wives' earned or investment income. The 1952 Income Tax Act confirmed that a wife's income should be considered to belong to her husband. It was not until 1990 that wives could be taxed independently from their husbands.

(adapted from 'The Politics of Women's Rights' by April Carter, Longman, London, 1988; 'A Law that is Not Equal to the Task' by Kirsty Milne, 'New Statesman & Society', 22.10.1993; 'Times', 14.9.1995; 'Britain and the World' by Tony and Steve Lancaster, Causeway Press, Ormskirk, 1995)

QUESTIONS

1. a) What is the postcard suggesting about votes for women? (2)
   b) What is the banner suggesting about votes for women? (3)
2. Comment on Stanley Baldwin's statement about women's rights. (5)
3. Why is it difficult to enforce laws on equal pay and sex discrimination? (5)
4. What views of married women underlie the various laws on taxation? (5)

4 PART SOCIALISATION AND THE ROLE OF WOMEN

As Chapters 1 and 2 indicated, behaviour patterns learned during the early years of life may well have a lasting effect. The following extract, taken from an article written by Jacqueline Penrose in 1982, supports this view. It argues that children are prepared from birth for their adult roles as men and women. It is followed by a report on children's toys during Christmas 1995 which reinforces this point.

Learning to be men and women

In a high street toyshop I picked up a catalogue. It states - and I think rightly - that 'babies are ready to start to learn about the world right from the start ... The right toys will provide the stimulation they need'.

And they learn that certain types of toys are suitable only for boys, and others for girls. There's Judy and Velvet, her pony:

'This pretty pair are tipped for the top'. What boy would be caught dead with that? There are 'dolls' for boys: 'The Cosmic Command defence forces. These brave heroes...' And Tommy Gunn, 'a man of many roles. He is trained as a medic, but can use a gun'.

For the girls: 'Sweet Baby. Advice for young mothers from Auntie Brenda. Dear Auntie Brenda - I want to be sure to keep my baby

(from 'The Girl Who Always Says Yes' by Jacqueline Penrose, 'Guardian', 6.4.1982)

Power Rangers and Barbie

Power Rangers were Britain's bestselling toy in 1995. It seemed that every four to eight-year-old boy was demanding them for Christmas. Power Rangers are Californian high-school kids who, through the power of the mighty Zordon, can morph into superheroes with a gift for martial arts which they employ against the evil Rita Repulsa. If Rita gets really tricky, the Rangers morph on to a second level - as battling Dinozords.

For Christmas 1995, everyone's favourite was Tommy, the White Power Ranger. Unfortunately Tommy, complete with the deadly Saba - his talking battle-blade which controls his personal vehicle, the Tigerzord - has morphed right out of the shop window. Even at £39.99 a throw, everyone has sold out of Tommy.

Every girl in America owns an average of eight Barbies. Over 500 million have been sold worldwide. And for Christmas 1995, Barbie was the bestselling girls' toy in the UK. Sun Jewel Barbie, the new fuschia-bikinied and diamond-necklaced model, is the bestselling Barbie ever. Other new models include 'Dance 'n' Twirl', a radio-controlled Barbie who flounces across the dance floor and a horse and carriage set to take Barbie and Ken (her boyfriend) to the ball. According to Michelle Norton, PR person for Mattel Toys who created Barbie, 'She's a wonderful role model for little girls. She does everything they want to do and dream of. She's got lovely fashions and a boyfriend. It's a friendship sort of thing.' And it has to be - sex is out as Ken lacks the appropriate parts.

(adapted from 'Observer', 30.10.1994; 'Times Educational Supplement', 22.12.1995; 'Observer', 24.12.1995)

warm this winter, but it is also very important that she has pretty clothes'. And there's Rachel Ballerina, 'of great beauty and grace but she is also a young lady with a tremendous interest in fashion'.

Even when children themselves want to experiment with a wider range of toys, this hard sell makes it very difficult. So does the packaging. I saw a large chemistry set in the window, a boy and a girl shown on the box. The boy was eight inches high, the girl only two. Before the Renaissance artists would make the most important figure in a picture the largest; children's own work follows the same principle and they can recognise it when they meet it on a box. This toy is for boys.

In another shop I picked up a selection of children's birthday cards, which will be chosen by adults, presumably to conform to their notions of what children are like - or ought to be like. First, for the newborn boy. His cot is trimmed with blue. Inside it says: 'A baby boy - You must be proud: and very happy, too'. The baby girl is dressed in pink, with a ribbon in her hair. Inside: 'Bet she's even sweeter than you ever dreamed she'd be'. Sons one is proud of, daughters are sweet.

For the four-year-olds: the girls' card shows a girl in a flounced pink dress, flowers in her hat. She pushes a pram and carries a handbag. The four-year-old boy is dressed in jeans and trainers, and he is fishing. At eight the girl is wearing a dress (with a tiny waist) made entirely of pink roses. There are roses in her long fair hair - but she does nothing. Inside it says: 'For a sweet young Miss who is eight today and growing up in such a lovely way'. The eight-year-old boy is on a racing bike, in a T-shirt, jeans and trainers.

Such examples abound. They show that girls are still expected to be sweet, demure, pretty and passive, destined only for domesticity and motherhood. They are reminded of it wherever they look. It is not a matter of choice. Hard luck if they are born with a creative, dynamic intelligence. Parents and teachers need to be more aware of the problem if this unjust and arbitrary division of people into active and passive roles is to stop.

QUESTIONS

1. Using evidence from the extracts suggest how women *learn* to be 'feminine' and men to be 'masculine'. (5)
2. What evidence suggests that girls are socialised for the mother-housewife role? (5)
3. In schools boys are more likely than girls to select science subjects. How do the extracts help to explain this? (3)
4. The top jobs in society often involve taking decisions and managing and directing the activities of others. They are 'active' roles. Using evidence from the extracts suggest why men outnumber women in these occupations. (3)
5. Why does Jacqueline Penrose argue that the ways in which girls and boys are divided and distinguished are unjust? (4)

5 PART — WOMEN IN THE LABOUR FORCE

Women are entering the labour force in ever increasing numbers. Since 1970 they have taken nearly 90% of the new jobs in the UK and by 1995 they made up 44% of the labour force. The following passage looks at the position of women in the labour market.

Figure 1 Gender and employment, 1961-1995

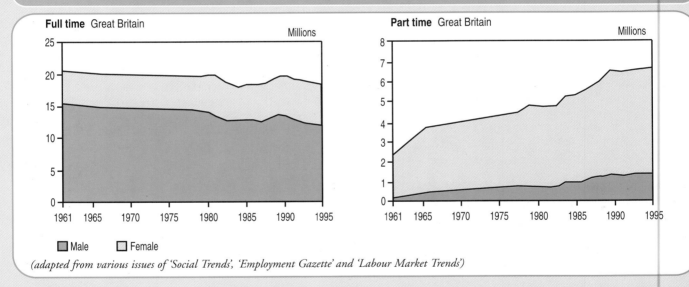

(adapted from various issues of 'Social Trends', 'Employment Gazette' and 'Labour Market Trends')

In recent years there has been a steady growth in the number of part-time jobs. Between 1987 and 1995 the number of women in part-time employment increased by 12% to 5.2 million and for men the increase was over 50% to 1.2 million. Over the same period the number of women in full-time employment rose by 8% whereas the number of men went down by 2%.

Surveys indicate that marriage and children influence a woman's choice of full or part-time work. Of the women working part time who said they did not want a full-time job (see Table 1), married women with children were most likely to give this answer and unmarried women without children least likely.

Table 1 Reasons for taking a part-time job

Great Britain, 1995, percentages	Men	Women
Did not want full-time job	36	80
Could not find full-time job	27	11
Student or at school	33	8
Ill or disabled	3	1

(adapted from Labour Force Survey 54, 'Employment Gazette', October 1995)

Figure 2 Gender and occupation, employees 1995

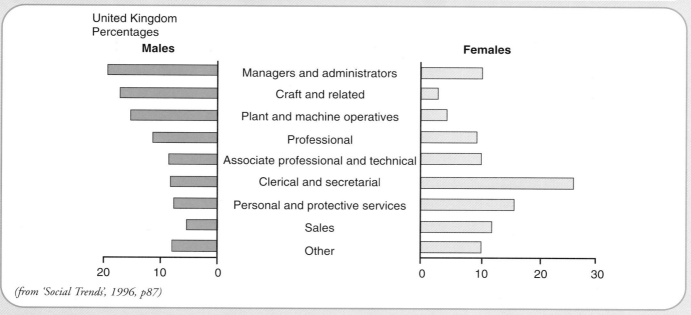

United Kingdom
Percentages

Males   **Females**

Managers and administrators
Craft and related
Plant and machine operatives
Professional
Associate professional and technical
Clerical and secretarial
Personal and protective services
Sales
Other

(from 'Social Trends', 1996, p87)

Men and women are not spread evenly throughout the labour market as Figure 2 shows. Women tend to be concentrated in occupations traditionally seen as 'women's jobs'. They are typically employed as clerks, secretaries, keyboard operators, hairdressers, shop assistants, cleaners, child minders and waitresses. For example, in 1995, 75% of clerical and secretarial jobs were filled by women, over 65% of personal service occupations and over 60% of sales jobs. Women outnumber men 4 to 1 in health (eg nurses) and 2 to 1 in education (eg teachers). However, women are moving into traditionally male occupations. For example, around 30% of solicitors in England and Wales in 1994 were women compared with 12% in 1984. And they are also moving up in traditionally male occupations. For example, 7% of the officers in the UK armed forces were women in 1995 compared with 4% in 1975.

As a general rule women are less likely to be found in senior positions. This applies even to those occupations in which women outnumber men. For example, women made up 81% of teachers in nursery and primary schools in England, Wales and Northern Ireland in 1992, yet only 57% of head and deputy head teachers. And in occupations where women are in the minority, they are even less likely to be in positions of power and authority. For example, despite making up around 13% of the police force in the UK, women had to wait until 1995 before one of their number was appointed to the rank of chief constable.

Compared to men, women tend to work in jobs which are low in terms of status, skill, pay and power, with few if any promotion prospects. This applies particularly to part-time jobs where women outnumber men by over 4 to 1. (See Figure 1, Part 3 for a comparison of men's and women's pay.) Some of the reasons for gender inequality in the labour market are examined in Part 6.

(adapted from 'Social Focus on Women', Central Statistical Office, HMSO, London, 1995 and 'Social Trends', 1996)

School dinners

QUESTIONS

1. Briefly summarise the trends shown in Figure 1. (4)
2. Suggest reasons for the differences between men and women shown in Table 1. (3)
3. a) How can many 'women's jobs' be seen as extensions of the mother/housewife role? (4)
   b) Why are these jobs often low in status and pay? (3)
4. a) What evidence does the passage contain to indicate that women's position in the labour market is improving? (3)
   b) What evidence indicates that they still have a long way to go to gain equality with men? (3)

PART 6 — GENDER INEQUALITY IN THE LABOUR MARKET

As Parts 3 and 5 have shown, women are not equal in the labour market. On a range of measures - job status, skill, pay, seniority and power - women's position in the workplace is generally below that of men. This part looks at some of the reasons why.

The bank

Lesley Wayne started as a teagirl at 16 for one of the major high street banks. Twenty-two years later she 'crawled' (her word) into middle management and is one of the three managers in a large branch. She is one of a tiny minority - although 57% of the bank's employees are women they make up only 6% of its managers.

It has been an uphill struggle. In her words, 'When I started in the late 1960s, men were paid more for the same job. When a woman married it was presumed she would leave. Women worked in the back office and were only allowed to go on the counters on Saturday mornings as a sort of treat or reward.

I got stuck in my twenties for six years on a junior clerical level - I'd married and the bank labelled me with the career potential assessment of a married woman - that meant a secretary for life. I went through a grievance procedure for 18 months to get myself reassessed because only then was there any chance of getting the training I needed.'

Ms Wayne had her child when she was in management and could afford a reliable childminder. She has successfully combined her workplace and domestic roles but she reckons a second child would have made things 'extremely difficult'. She believes that if government and business are really concerned about improving women's position in the workplace 'they should make childcare widely available at affordable prices'.

The airline

Val Gooding manages British Airways' 9,500 cabin crew staff, 18 years after joining the company as a telephone reservations agent. She looks back over her career.

'One of the biggest barriers to women in this company is they don't have enough confidence to come forward for jobs. During my first 10 years I was in relatively junior positions and never imagined I could do what I'm doing now.

The presumption was that I would stay in customer service jobs. There were no credible role models in senior positions so I just didn't believe it was possible. There was always this feeling of all boys together and that women aren't quite as capable. British industry is still male-dominated. But it's easier for women now because there are role models. That's good for men too because they see women are just as competent.'

British Airways cabin staff

The civil service

Like most organisations, the civil service is dominated by men - the higher the grade, the fewer women there are. Although there have been changes since the days when married women were barred from work - the marriage bar ended in 1972 - the past still shapes the present. From her study of women in the civil service, Cynthia Cockburn reports, 'I met one senior woman who, though she had long been in a stable partnership and had reared children, had decided from the start to cohabit rather than marry, so as not to risk being penalised in her service career. Another had put off the announcement of her engagement until after her promotion was confirmed, "just to be safe". It was usually taken, often without asking the woman in question, that a married women would not be prepared to be geographically mobile. Her husband's job was presumed to take preference.'

In Whitehall, home of the top civil servants, men rule the roost. Data from 14 ministries in 1994 shows that there were only 69 women among the 686 civil servants on the top four grades. The Health Department, then headed by a woman, Virginia Bottomley, had the best record for promoting women - they had a quarter of the top 64 posts.

Former grade 3 civil servant Pamela Meadow, looks back on her days at Whitehall. 'Standing back,' she says, 'the culture of Whitehall remains very male-dominated at higher levels. The more senior you are in the civil service, the more you lose control over your hours. Men are prepared to tolerate the late hours of Whitehall. Women quite like to see their children.'

Part-time work

In 1995, nearly 40% of women in the labour force worked part time. Table 1 in Part 5 shows that 80% of these women 'did not want a full-time job'. But is this really a matter of choice? The view that women should accept the main responsibility for housework and rearing children is still widespread. Often childcare facilities are unavailable or too expensive. Part-time jobs are the main growth area in the labour market (see Figure 1, Part 5) and are seen as particularly suitable for women. Given all this, many women may have little 'choice' when selecting part-time employment.

Many employers assume that women will leave work to produce and raise children. This means they will be reluctant to invest money in expensive training programmes for female workers and will make sure they are easily replaceable. This results in women being placed in low skill jobs which can be learned quickly. These jobs are poorly paid.

The following case study from 1993 illustrates some of the worst aspects of part-time work.

Amanda Peters works 32-and-a-half hours a week for four different employers and collects £76.98 for her efforts. Mrs Peters is 38 and lives in Birmingham. She works as a part-time cook in two pubs, as a sales assistant in a greengrocer's shop and as a cleaner. She is married with two young children. Although her husband works, the family could not afford to repay the mortgage on the council house they bought or meet their fuel bills if she did not seek out as much work as possible.

In a diary of her working week, she wrote: 'My jobs are low grade with low grade wages, which unfortunately seems to be the only type of job that a married woman with a family can get'. She does five lunch and evening sessions a week as a pub cook. 'But I don't just cook, I serve the customers, wash up, clean the cooker and mop the floors.'

Every Monday and Friday evening is spent cleaning an office for £1.50 an hour. 'I have two-and-a-half hours to polish and dust six offices, clean and disinfect two toilets and a kitchen, sweep, mop and polish the showroom floor,' she writes.

Two mornings a week Mrs Peters works in a greengrocer's for £2.68 an hour. 'For five-and-a-half hours I serve, restock and clean with just a half-hour break for lunch.' Thursdays are her 'days off' when she does all the shopping, ironing and cleaning. 'I wonder what the hell I've done to deserve this lot,' she says. 'I am totally exhausted, but I still have to run a home and care for a husband and two children.'

The glass ceiling

Many women come up against a 'glass ceiling', an invisible barrier which limits their progress up the occupational ladder. There are many reasons for this, some of which have already been given. Others include beliefs that men are more ambitious and will be prepared to work longer hours to further their careers. Men are often seen to have the qualities required for management - toughness, assertiveness, aggression - simply because they are men. Sometimes there is a reluctance to place women in positions of power over men because they are thought to lack the required 'authority' and male subordinates may resent a female boss. Women are advancing rapidly in

A typical 'woman's job'

professional jobs which require individual skills, for example law, medicine and teaching, but not in managerial jobs which involve control over people.

The glass ceiling may account for the fact that three times as many women as men are setting up their own businesses.

Occupational segregation

Large parts of the labour market are divided into 'men's jobs' and 'women's jobs'. This is known as occupational segregation. 'Women's jobs' can often be seen as extensions of the mother-housewife role and as reflecting qualities which women are supposed to have. For example, nurses, shop assistants, personal secretaries, nursery and primary school teachers are typically women. Such occupations reflect the stereotype of the caring female and are often an extension of the traditional domestic duties of the housewife and mother. One reason suggested for the low pay and low status of 'women's jobs' is that the status of women and housework is low. As a result 'women's jobs' are valued less and therefore paid less.

Traditionally women have been paid less than men, even when they did the same jobs. This reflected the view of man the breadwinner and woman the homeworker. If women were employed, it was often assumed they worked for 'pin money', to buy 'little extras' for the home and family. Survey after survey has shown that for the vast majority of working wives their earnings are an essential part of the family wage.

The Equal Pay Act (see Part 3) has gone some way to reducing pay inequality between women and men. However, occupational segregation makes things difficult because in 'women's jobs' women set the standard for wages. Higher paid men are usually absent so cannot be used for comparison. And as Part 3 shows, the Equal Value Amendment Act which states that women can claim equal pay if their work is of equal value to a man's, is largely unworkable.

(adapted from 'In the Way of Women' by Cynthia Cockburn, Macmillan, London, 1991; 'Observer', 2.1.1994, 12.3.1995; 'Guardian', 29.10.1991; 'Independent on Sunday', 16.5.1993)

QUESTIONS

1. Read the three case studies - the bank, the airline and the civil service.
   a) What evidence do they contain of discrimination against women? (3)
   b) Judging from the case studies, what steps should be taken to provide equal opportunity for women? (3)
2. a) Why do so many women work part time? (2)
   b) Outline some of the problems of combining part-time work with the mother/housewife role. (2)
3. The glass ceiling is partly a reflection of gender stereotypes and male prejudice. Discuss. (6)
4. How does occupational segregation help to explain why many women earn less than men? (4)

7 PART — CHANGING WOMEN

A survey of 2,000 18-34 year olds in Britain entitled *Freedom's Children* found that women were becoming increasingly masculine in their outlook. The 1990s woman is seeking what used to be seen as male pleasures - risk, excitement and living on the edge. Young women are no longer putting their energies into domesticity - they are as likely to be rock climbing, travelling the world or bungee jumping. They admire women who are assertive and in control. They look to Tank Girl in comics and films and Courtney Love in music - women who no longer feel the need to be submissive.

The following passage looks at evidence which supports this view.

Crime

The scar on the young woman's face was a neat, livid line running from her ear to her mouth. She wore it with pride. It was part of her initiation into one of the women's gangs which have recently emerged on the streets of Brooklyn in New York. In the early 1990s girls in their early teens began joining America's male inner city gangs. Now more and more are forming all female gangs. Typically their crimes are stealing jewellery, clothes and money. Some have become increasingly violent resulting in the death of their victims.

British newspapers have provided similar reports from the UK. In 1993 headlines announced the mugging of film star and model Elizabeth Hurley by a gang of teenage girls in London. There is evidence which can be used to support the impression

Members of the East Coast Baby Dolls gang in Los Angeles

given by these headlines. From 1984 to 1994 the number of women found guilty of an offence involving violence nearly doubled. And from 1988-1994 the number of 14-17 year old girls found guilty of breaking the law rose by 36% while among boys of the same age the figure fell by 10%.

However, caution is needed in interpreting these figures. Crime statistics often tell us little about the actual extent of crime (see Chapter 16, Parts 2 and 3). And headlines about girl gangs terrorising city streets do not reflect the vast majority of female crime.

Women boxers

Sport

Traditionally women played badminton, tennis, hockey and netball. Increasingly they are taking up sports such as soccer, rugby and martial arts. According to one 26-year-old secretary, 'I like doing martial arts because they make me feel powerful, in control. If I can control my body, I'm more likely to change my life.'

Women are now moving into boxing, something unheard of a generation ago. In 1995 there were 150 women in Britain fighting competitively, almost double the number in 1990. According to Persi Dixon of the Women's International Boxing Federation, 'In a time when gender roles are changing so much, there is no blueprint of what men's and women's roles are'.

Drink

Babycham, a bubbly champagne-like drink, was invented in the 1950s. At last women could go to the pub and ask for a drink which was not seen as a man's drink. 'I'd love a Babycham' said pretty women on countless posters and commercials and millions of women lapped it up. In its heyday it sold a million bottles a week and any man who bought one ran the risk of having his manhood questioned.

The stigma attached to women in pubs, especially women drinking 'men's drinks' has largely disappeared. Women now drink beer - and in pint glasses. Babycham's sales have slumped. In the 1990s a TV advertising campaign attempted to sell Babycham to men. It had little success.

Boddingtons hope for more success with their new

Early 1970s

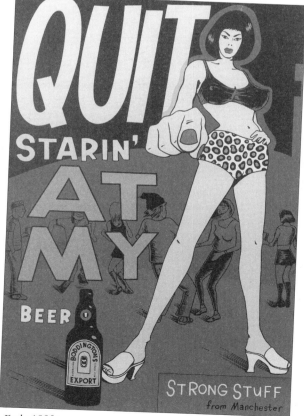

Early 1990s

superhero, Tankard Girl. She is mean and moody and heads the advertising campaign launched in 1995 for Boddingtons Export. According to the marketing people, 'This is a younger campaign pitched at women'.

(adapted from 'Freedom's Children', Demos, London, 1995; 'Observer', 10.9.1995, 24.9.1995, 12.11.1995; 'Sunday Times', 24.9.1995)

Magazines

April, 1955

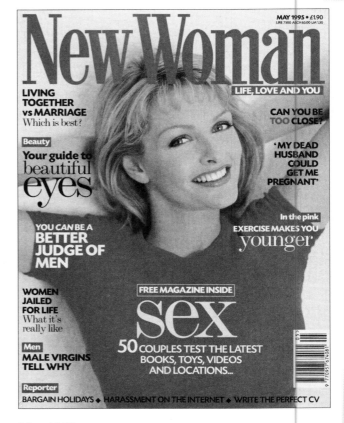

May, 1995

QUESTION

What does each of the sections - crime, sport, drink and magazines - indicate about changes in women's attitudes, values and self-concepts?

POPULATION

The study of population is known as demography. It involves the measurement of births, deaths and migration which account for changes in population size. Demography also involves an examination of the factors which underlie changes in population. If, for example, the number of births in a society rises rapidly, demographers will try to explain this change in terms of the possible influence of social, political and economic factors. They will also be concerned with the consequences of population change. Thus they will consider the effects on society of a rapid rise in births.

This chapter concentrates on the population of Britain over the past 150 years. It begins however with a brief examination of population in the Third World - the developing countries of Asia, Africa and Latin America.

World population is growing at what many consider an alarming rate. Much of this growth is occurring in Third World countries due mainly to a dramatic decline in the death rate. This decline in mortality has been largely due to a successful fight against infectious and contagious diseases such as malaria, cholera, smallpox, tuberculosis and dysentery. With little change in the numbers of babies being born but with a rapid decline in the numbers of people dying each year, the size of the population increases. This can be seen from the size of India's population which in 1951 stood at 361 million, in 1960 - 429 million, in 1970 - 539 million, in 1980 - 659 million, in 1984 - 746 million and in 1994 - 914 million. In an attempt to reduce population growth many Third World countries have introduced programmes of birth control. The following extract considers one such programme in India.

PART 1 — POPULATION AND THE THIRD WORLD

A project known as the Khanna Study was India's first major programme of birth control. It was conducted in seven villages with a total population of 8,000 people. The programme, financed by the Rockefeller Foundation in the USA and the Indian government, lasted six years and cost a million dollars. It was a failure. Some of the reasons why people 'failed' to accept family planning are given in the following extract. It is a summary of some of the main findings of a book by Mahmood Mamdani who conducted research in Manupur, one of the villages in the Khanna Study.

One of the foundation stones of the Khanna Study was the belief that people were having more children than they actually wanted - because they were still working on the assumption (thankfully no longer true) that half their children would die in infancy. But from months of talking to the villagers of Manupur, Mamdani concludes that 'an overwhelming majority of the people in the Khanna Study area have a large number of children not because they overestimate their infant mortality rates (the proportion of infants dying between birth and one year) but because they *want* large families. More important, they want them because they *need* them'.

The majority of people in Manupur need children because they are poor. The work of staying alive is hard work - and they cannot afford to buy labour-saving machines or to pay other people for the help they need.

From a very early age, the children of Manupur make a vital contribution to the family wellbeing. They look after cattle; they help with sowing crops, weeding and harvesting; they bring in the family's water supply and take the food out to the fields at midday (jobs which can take several hours); they help with household jobs - sewing, cleaning, cooking and washing. For one who labours in the field, the day centres around work. Time for relaxation or for tending to personal needs is usually found between different types of work. Without children to help, the workload can become unbearable and more stress and suffering is often the result.

A man and his wife who pray for many children can hardly be expected to respond enthusiastically to family planning

Youngsters in an Indian village collecting cow dung to be used as manure

programmes. What is more, children are often the only 'insurance' for the poor. Without children, there is no help or support in illness or old age - and illness is frequent and old age can begin at 40.

The land dominates life in Manupur. 95% of the people earn their living directly or indirectly from agriculture. The poor, the majority, are those with the least land. And the less land a farmer has, the more labour per acre he needs - for he cannot afford labour saving machines like tube wells or cutting machines or tractors which are in any case uneconomical for very small plots.

So the farmers who need labour most are the ones least able to afford it. And children are the only answer. Farmer after farmer in Manupur told Mamdani that the cost of having children was almost negligible compared with the benefits they bring.

(adapted from 'The Myth of Population Control', 'New Internationalist', May 1974, pp18-19)

QUESTIONS

1. What is the connection between farming, poverty and family size? (7)
2. Why are children in Manupur seen as 'insurance' by their parents? (3)
3. How might a welfare state on the British lines encourage the people of Manupur to have fewer children? (2)
4. What does the reference to religion in the extract suggest about the importance of children to the people of Manupur? (2)
5. Freely available contraceptives and knowledge about their use are not enough, in themselves, to reduce the birth rate. Discuss this statement with reference to the passage. (6)

2 PART — THE DEATH RATE IN ENGLAND AND WALES

The death rate refers to the number of deaths per thousand of the population per year. In England and Wales the death rate fell steadily during the 19th century. In 1770 it is estimated at 32 per 1,000, by 1870 it had fallen to 20 per 1,000. The fall continued until 1920 when the rate levelled off and has remained largely unchanged to the present day. Changes in the death rate are shown in Figure 1. The passage that follows considers some of the possible reasons for the decline in the death rate in England and Wales.

Figure 1 The death rate in England and Wales, 1700-1994

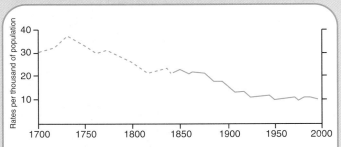

Registration of births, marriages and deaths began in 1847. Recent historical research suggests that death rates recorded during the early years of registration under-estimate the actual figures.

(adapted from 'Population Trends' 5, HMSO, London, 1976, and 'Social Trends', 1986 and 1996)

During the 19th century medical science was primitive compared with today's standards. A vast range of 'cures' were available but few were effective. Some simply relieved pain, such as drugs derived from opium. A variety of purgatives effectively emptied the bowels but didn't cure anything. At best few medicines did anything other than give patients the impression that something was being done for their ailments.

Surgery offered even less hope. Anaesthetics were not available until the close of the 19th century and deaths following surgery were common. Surgeons sometimes commented that the operation was successful but the patient died.

Sanitation, particularly during the first half of the 19th century, was appalling by today's standards. The following description of a street in Bethnal Green in London's East End given by Dr Southwood Smith in 1838 provides a flavour of the times: 'Along the centre of the street is an open, sunk gutter, in which filth of every kind is allowed to accumulate and putrefy. A mud bank on each side commonly keeps the contents of the gutter in their situation; but sometimes, and especially in wet weather, the gutter overflows; its contents are poured into the neighbouring houses and the street is rendered nearly impassable. The privies (toilets) are close upon the footpath of the street, being separated from it only by a parting of wood. The street is wholly without drainage of any kind. Fever constantly breaks out in it and extends from house to house.'

Improvements in sanitation dating from the last half of the 19th century were probably far more significant in reducing the death rate than the slow advance of medical science. The provision of piped water and effective sewage disposal systems (in 1865 the new London sewage system was officially opened by the Prince of Wales) plus improvements in hygiene in the home, such as flush toilets, led to a significant decrease in diseases such as typhoid, cholera and dysentery.

However, improved nutrition probably had the greatest effect on the death rate. Recent evidence from developing countries in the Third World shows a close link between diet and death rates. In particular, the more nutritious the food, the lower the infant and child death rates. From 1770 to 1870 infant mortality in England fell from over 200 per 1,000 to just over 100 per 1,000. During this period the virulence of common infectious diseases such as scarlet fever diminished - they were much less likely to kill. This may well have been due to the fact that people were better fed and so more able to ward off the worst effects of such diseases. (See Chapter 19, Part 2.)

From the late 19th century onwards medical science began to reduce the death rate. During the early years of this century increasing attention was given to maternity and child welfare and local authorities began to assume responsibility for the health of children in schools. In later years inoculations were available against many of the common infectious diseases. Their main effect appears to be in the areas of infant and child mortality. However, the major fall in infant and child death rates occurred during the first half of the 20th century. The most effective drugs - sulphonamides and antibiotics - and the establishment of widespread immunisation date from the 1940s and 50s. (See Chapter 19, Part 2.)

(adapted from 'People Populating' by Derek Llewellyn-Jones, Faber, London, 1975, pp190-194 and 'Population' by Roger Gomm in 'Fundamentals of Sociology' edited by P. McNeill and C. Townley, Hutchinson, London, 1981, p327)

The 'Water King of Southwark' reigning over the polluted River Thames (cartoon by George Cruikshank, 1828). The inhabitants of Southwark had to boil their water and skim off the scum to make it drinkable.

QUESTIONS

1. **Briefly summarise the changes in the death rate shown in Figure 1. (3)**
2. **Assess the effect of medical science on the death rate in**
   a) the 19th century (3)
   b) the 20th century. (3)
3. **There has been a significant decline in absolute poverty during the first half of the 20th century. What effect might this have had on the death rate? (5)**
4. **With reference to the information in the passage, suggest why the death rate for members of the working class has been consistently higher than the rate for members of other social classes. (6)**

Advertisements such as this reflect the growing concern for children's health at the turn of the century.

③ PART 3 — BIRTH AND FERTILITY RATES IN ENGLAND AND WALES (I)

This passage considers the main trends in birth and fertility rates in England and Wales over the past 100 years. It also examines some of the reasons put forward for changes in these rates. The birth rate refers to the number of live births per thousand of the population per year. The fertility rate refers to the number of live births per thousand women of childbearing age (15-44) per year.

In Britain, as in other Western industrial societies, there has been a steady decline in the birth rate over the past 100 years. This is mainly due to a decline in fertility - women are producing fewer children - and as a result the average size of families has grown smaller.

Figure 1 The birth rate in England and Wales 1700-1994

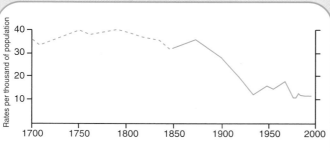

(adapted from 'Population Trends' 5 and 82, HMSO, London, 1976 and 1995)

There seems to be a link between the fall in the death rate and the fall in the fertility rate. In preindustrial Europe there was an extremely high rate of infant and child mortality and only about 50% of children survived to adolescence. This meant that a family which produced six children (the average for the time) could expect only three or four to reach adulthood. Today almost all children survive beyond adolescence. A present-day couple therefore needs a fertility rate of only half their preindustrial counterparts to produce families of the same size. In Britain birth and fertility rates declined significantly between 1870 and 1920, a period when the death rate, especially for infants and children, also fell steadily.

The 1870s mark the beginning of the decline in fertility in Britain. It began in the upper and middle classes - in the families of military and naval officers, lawyers and doctors, with dentists, teachers and clerks not far behind. The years 1850-70 saw a rapid expansion of middle class occupations and a growing demand for the status symbols of a middle class lifestyle - large houses, expensive food and wine, servants, carriages and holidays abroad. The prosperity of these years was followed by the so-called 'Great Depression' of 1870-90. Although it was not particularly serious in economic terms, many people at the time thought it was. Rather than put their standard of living at risk, many middle class families decided to cut down on what was becoming an increasingly expensive item - children.

The growing expense of children was partly due to the fact that education was becoming increasingly lengthy and costly. Qualifications were becoming more important for entering professions such as medicine and law and for a career in the army and civil service. Fees for public schools for the rich and private schools for the nearly rich cut deeply into many family budgets.

At the very time when infant and child mortality was steadily falling, children were becoming more expensive. The combination of these factors probably led many parents to decide to limit the size of their families. Developments in contraceptive techniques helped to provide the means for doing this. During the second half of the nineteenth century the discovery of vulcanisation (a process which increases the elasticity and strength of rubber) led to the condom (contraceptive sheath) being manufactured in rubber. Around 1880 the vaginal diaphragm and cervical cap appeared. Increasing publicity was given to birth control. In 1877 Charles Bradlaugh and Annie Besant were prosecuted for encouraging the publication of Charles Knowlton's *Fruits of Philosophy* which

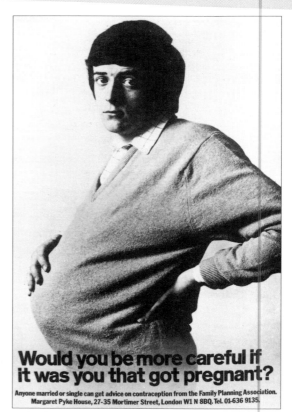

A Family Planning Association poster from 1971

described methods of contraception. Within three months 125,000 copies had been sold. The 20th century has seen the development of increasingly effective methods of birth control, such as the coil and the pill, which was introduced in the early 1960s. There has also been a more general acceptance of the idea of family planning. The Family Planning Association was started in 1930 and in the same year the Church of England accepted the use of artificial techniques of birth control. However, it is important not to exaggerate the effect of advances in birth control techniques. Research has shown that the decline in births in the 1930s in Britain and the Western world was achieved mainly by withdrawal ('coitus interruptus'), abstinence (refraining from sexual intercourse), late marriage and probably widespread illegal abortion.

Decline in working class fertility was somewhat slower than in the middle classes. The financial benefits of children were steadily reduced throughout the 19th century. A series of Factory Acts limited child labour. In 1880 school attendance was made compulsory up to the age of 10, in 1893 up to the age of 11 and in 1899 up to the age of 12. The process has continued during the 20th century with the school leaving age being raised to 16 in 1973. The development of the welfare state with measures such as old age pensions and unemployment benefits meant that parents had less need to rely on their children for support. As Rowntree's three studies of York (1899, 1936, 1950) indicated, the extent of absolute poverty declined significantly during the first 50 years of the 20th century (see Chapter 6, Parts 2 and 3). Rising working class living standards meant that parents were less likely to look to their children for financial assistance.

Despite the economic advantages of smaller families, old attitudes die hard. Willmott and Young recount the following incident from their study in the early 1950s of Bethnal Green, a traditional working class community in the East End of London. A woman was persuaded by a social worker to have a contraceptive cap fitted. Two months later she was pregnant again. Asked what had happened she said, 'My husband wouldn't have it. He threw it on the fire.' Apparently he saw the device as a threat to his masculinity.

However attitudes do change. During the 20th century working class fertility steadily declined though it remained significantly higher than that of the middle class. By the late 1960s class differences in family size were not significant though working class fertility still remained slightly higher than that of the middle class.

(adapted from 'Human Societies' edited by Geoffrey Hurd, Routledge & Kegan Paul, London, 1973; 'Population' by Roger Gomm in 'Fundamentals of Sociology' edited by P. McNeill and C. Townley, Hutchinson, London, 1981; 'Population' by Roland Pressat, Penguin, Harmondsworth, 1973)

QUESTIONS

1. Briefly outline the changes in the birth rate shown in Figure 1. (4)
2. Infant and child mortality rates for the working class have always been higher than those for the middle class. How might this help to explain social class differences in fertility? (4)
3. What evidence does the extract contain to suggest that advances in contraceptive techniques may have had little effect on the birth rate until recent years? (4)
4. The decline in fertility is due mainly to economic factors. Briefly outline the evidence to support this view with reference to
   a) the middle class (4)
   b) the working class. (4)

4 PART BIRTH AND FERTILITY RATES IN ENGLAND AND WALES (2)

Although the overall trend in birth and fertility rates is downward, there have been a number of fluctuations in the rates. This part examines the ups and downs in the birth rate during the 20th century and looks at some of the reasons suggested for these fluctuations.

Figure 1 The birth rate in England and Wales 1900-1994

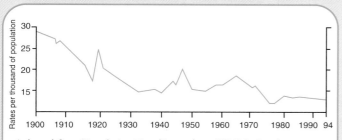

(adapted from 'Population Trends' 1 and 82, HMSO, London, 1975 and 1995; 'Annual Abstract of Statistics' 1982; 'Social Trends', 1986)

The two World Wars - 1914-18 and 1939-45 - were followed by sharp but shortlived rises in the birth rate. This appears to be mainly due to postponed births. The separation of men from home and families prevented many marriages and births within existing marriages.

The rapid increase in the birth rate shortly after World War 1 was followed by a steady decline. Part of this was due to a return to peace-time conditions, part to the fact that the large number of men killed in World War 1 meant that there were not enough husbands to go around and part to the severe economic depression during the early 1930s. With up to 20% of the working population unemployed, many marriages were postponed, the proportion of people getting married fell and fertility declined. The increase in the birth rate from the mid-1930s to 1947 was probably due in part to people getting married at an earlier age and a higher proportion of people getting married rather than any change in completed family size.

Fluctuations in the birth rate refer to irregular ups and downs which don't alter the overall trend. Often these are due to decisions about *when* to have children rather than how many to have. For example, the rise in the birth rate from 1954 to 1964 appears to be due to a change in timing. Previously many women had continued to work for a number of years after marriage before having children. However from 1954 to 1964 many women decided to have their children soon after marriage. This coincided with births by older women who had put off starting a family. The result was a 'baby boom' with births being crammed together in a fairly short time period. As a result of this babies were relatively thin on the ground during the late 1960s and early 70s. However despite such fluctuations, the overall trend in the birth rate is downwards.

Table 1 shows fertility rates - live births per thousand women aged 15-44 per year - from 1961 to 1994. It shows an overall decline in fertility from 1961 to 1981 then a levelling out from 1981 to 1994. It also shows that women are having children at a later age. Despite the levelling out of the overall fertility rate, the rate for women under 30 has carried on falling as they continue to put off childbearing.

If the 1994 fertility rate remains the same women will have an average of 1.75 children. This is around 10% below the figure needed for the long term replacement of the population.

Table 1 Fertility rates 1961-1994

Great Britain					Births per 1,000 women		
	15-19	20-24	25-29	30-34	35-39	40-44	All ages
1961	36.9	173.3	178.2	104.3	49.0	15.1	90.0
1971	50.3	153.8	154.1	77.8	33.1	8.7	83.7
1981	28.3	106.0	129.3	68.4	21.6	4.8	61.5
1986	30.2	92.6	123.4	77.2	24.2	4.7	60.4
1991	33.0	88.7	119.1	85.9	31.6	5.2	63.3
1993	31.0	81.7	113.7	86.3	33.5	6.0	62.1
1994	28.9	78.3	111.6	88.0	35.1	6.2	61.4

(adapted from 'Social Trends', 1996, p60)

Figures 2 and 3 provide an indication of the possible effects on the fertility rate of contraceptive methods - the introduction of the birth control pill in 1963 - and legal abortion - the 1967 Abortion Act.

Figure 2 Live births 1961-1994

(adapted from 'An Introduction to Population Geography' by W. F. Hornby and M. Jones, Cambridge University Press, Cambridge, 1980, p58 and 'Social Trends', 1986 and 1996)

Figure 3 Abortions 1969-1994

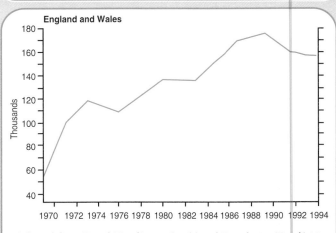

(adapted from 'Social Trends', 1986, p44 and 'Population Trends' 82, HMSO, London, 1995)

Why are women having fewer children? Part of the reason is that they are getting married at a later age and also having children later in the marriage. There has also been a steady rise in the number of women who have never had a child. Only 12% of the women born in 1947 were childless by the age of 45. It is expected that around 20% of women born after 1957 will be childless when they reach 45.

What accounts for these trends? The reasons are complex and relate to changes in society generally and in the position of women in society in particular (see Chapter 12). Evidence from Britain and Europe indicates that women's increased participation in the labour market not only delays marriage and childbearing but also appears to reduce the number of children women want when married. And the higher women move up the occupational ladder the fewer children - if any - they have. Increasing numbers of women in professional and managerial occupations appear to be giving up childbearing for the sake of their careers. Women seem to be placing more emphasis on the independence, fulfilment and material rewards offered by life outside the home and less on the dependence of motherhood and domesticity inside the home.

(adapted from 'Human Societies' edited by Geoffrey Hurd, Routledge & Kegan Paul, London, 1973; 'Births and Family Formation Patterns' by David Pearce, 'Population Trends' 1, HMSO, London, 1975; 'Population' by Roger Gomm in 'Fundamentals of Sociology' edited by P. McNeill and C. Townley, Hutchinson, London, 1981; 'Social Trends' 1982 and 1996; 'Sociology Update' by Martyn Denscombe, Olympus Books, Leicester, 1995)

QUESTIONS

1. a) Identify the two sharpest rises in the birth rate shown in Figure 1. (2)
   b) What explanation can be provided for these rises? (2)
2. a) With reference to Figure 1, distinguish between overall trends and fluctuations in the birth rate. (2)
   b) Why is it important to make this distinction? (2)
3. What evidence does the passage contain to suggest that economic factors can affect the birth rate? (3)
4. Briefly summarise the trends shown in Table 1. (3)
5. What do Figures 2 and 3 indicate - if anything - about the possible effects of the pill and legal abortion on fertility rates? (3)
6. Women may have chosen to have fewer children. Suggest reasons for this possible choice. (3)

⑤ PART THE AGE STRUCTURE OF THE POPULATION

The population of Western industrial societies has steadily grown older. This process is known as the 'ageing of the population'. Compared to Third World and preindustrial societies, Western countries have a small proportion of children, a high proportion of old people and a fairly large intermediate group sometimes known as the 'working age group' made up of people from 15-64 years of age. The following population pyramids illustrate the ageing of the population of England and Wales. They are followed by a passage which examines some of the reasons for changes in the age structure of the population. Some of the consequences of these changes are examined in Chapter 11, Part 6.

Figure 1 England and Wales: population pyramids for 1881 and 1931

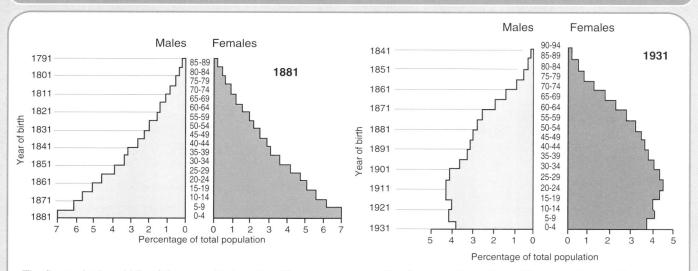

The figures in the middle of the pyramid show the different age groups. The figures at the bottom of the pyramid show the age groups as a percentage of the population as a whole. Thus in 1981, the age group 0-4 years made up just over 6% of the population. The figures on the left hand side give the approximate year of birth for the age groups in the pyramid.

Figure 2 England and Wales: population pyramid for 1981

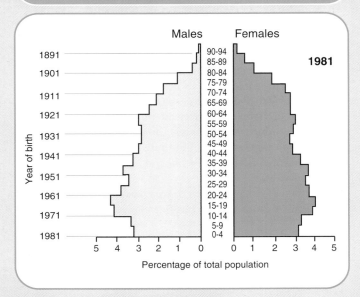

Table 1 Life expectancy

United Kingdom				Years
	1901	1931	1961	1993
Males				
At birth	45.5	57.7	67.8	73.6
At age				
1 year	54.6	62.4	69.5	74.1
10 years	60.4	65.2	69.9	74.2
20 years	61.7	66.3	70.3	74.5
40 years	66.1	69.3	71.4	75.4
60 years	73.3	74.3	74.9	77.8
80 years	84.9	84.7	85.2	86.4
Females				
At birth	49.0	61.6	73.6	78.9
At age				
1 year	56.8	65.3	75.1	79.3
10 years	62.7	67.9	75.4	79.5
20 years	64.1	69.0	75.6	79.6
40 years	68.3	71.9	76.3	80.1
60 years	74.6	76.1	78.8	81.9
80 years	85.3	85.4	86.3	88.3

(adapted from 'Social Trends', 1996, p130)

Common sense suggests that the main reason for the ageing of the population is that old people are living longer. However, this has not had a major influence on the age structure of the population. In fact the life expectancy of a person aged 60 has increased by only six years since the beginning of the 20th century. The reduction in mortality has led to an increase in the life expectancy of every age group, not just the elderly. In the 20th century the main decline in mortality has been for infants and children. This would lead, if it continued at the same rate, to a rejuvenation of the population. The population would grow younger as increasing numbers of infants and children survived. Why then is the population ageing? The main factor is a decline in fertility. Women are producing fewer children. This means that the proportion of young people in the population grows smaller and the proportion of older people increases. The result is an ageing population.

Although the average life expectancy of a person aged 60 has only increased by six years in the 20th century, a lot more people are reaching their sixtieth birthday. The decline in infant and child mortality has resulted in a much higher proportion of young people eventually reaching old age. In 1961 just under 12% of the United Kingdom's population were aged 65 or over, by 1994 this had increased to 16%. In contrast, the population under 16 years of age fell from 25% in 1961 to 21% in 1994.

Table 1 looks at life expectancy for different age and gender groups from 1901 to 1993. Figure 2 shows the reduction in infant mortality - deaths under one year of age. Death rates for children between the ages of one and fifteen in the UK more than halved between 1971 and 1994.

Figure 3 Infant mortality

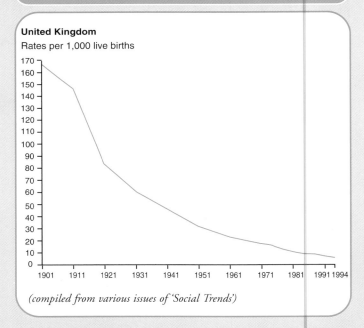

(compiled from various issues of 'Social Trends')

(adapted from 'Human Societies' by Geoffrey Hurd, Routledge & Kegan Paul, London, 1973 and 'Social Trends', 1996)

QUESTIONS

1. a) What percentage of the population (to the nearest whole number) does the youngest age group (0-4 years) form in (i) 1881 and (ii) 1981? (2)
   b) What percentage of the population (to the nearest whole number) does the age group 60-64 form in (i) 1881 and (ii) 1981? (2)
2. The changing shape of the population pyramids indicates an ageing population. Show that this is the case with reference to information from the pyramids. (6)
3. a) Summarise the trends shown in Table 1 and Figure 3. (5)
   b) Use this information to show how an ageing population occurs. (5)

MIGRATION

PART 6

Changes in population size are caused not just by births and deaths but also by international migration - movements of people in and out of the country. In terms of official definitions an immigrant is a person who enters a country with the intention of living there for a year or more - having lived outside the country for at least a year. An emigrant is a person who leaves a country with the intention of living abroad for a year or more - having lived in the country for at least a year. The migration statistics in the following passage are based on these definitions.

Figure 1 Net migration, United Kingdom 1901-1993

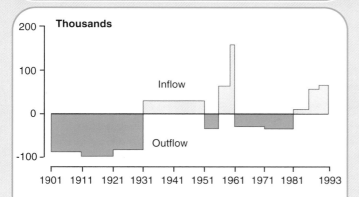

Net migration is the difference between immigration (inflow) and emigration (outflow). It may be positive (+) in which case more people enter than leave the country or negative (-) in which case more people leave than enter.

(compiled from various issues of 'Social Trends')

The traditional picture of a migrant is someone leaving their homeland to start a new life in a far away country. This still happens but today many migrants are simply moving from one country to another for a limited period. They may be students, lecturers, politicians, business people or workers on a contract abroad, many of whom have every intention of returning home after a few years. When they do return they will be immigrants in terms of the official definition. From 1990 to 1993, 33% of immigrants to the UK were people born in the UK and 47% of emigrants from the UK were born abroad (see Table 1).

Table 1 Average annual migration, 1990-1993

United Kingdom			Thousands
Non-British	**Inflow**	**Outflow**	**Balance**
European Community	46	42	4
Old Commonwealth	26	18	8
New Commonwealth	57	15	42
Other foreign	76	42	33
All non-British citizens	205	117	88
British citizens	103	132	-29
All countries	308	250	58

(adapted from 'Social Trends', 1996, p45)

Table 2 Main reason for migration, 1990 - 1993

United Kingdom			Thousands
	Inflow	**Outflow**	**Balance**
Work related	44	62	-18
Accompany/join	79	64	15
Formal study	46	10	36
Other	36	39	-3
No reason stated	34	52	-18
All reasons	240	227	13

'Accompany/join' refers to mainly husbands and wives rejoining their partners.
'Other' includes people looking for work.

(adapted from 'Social Trends', 1996, p45)

From 1901 to 1931 there was a net outflow of people from the UK averaging 80,000 a year (ie there were 80,000 more emigrants than immigrants a year). From 1931 to 1951 there was a net inflow due mainly to refugees from Europe. There was a return to net outflow from 1951 to 1956. From 1956 to 1961 there was a net inflow due mainly to immigrants from the New Commonwealth, particularly from the West Indies and the Indian subcontinent (the New Commonwealth includes all Commonwealth countries apart from Canada, Australia and New Zealand which together are known as the Old Commonwealth). From 1961 to 1982 there has been a net outflow with Britain returning to its traditional role as an exporter of people. From 1981-1993 there was a net inflow of migrants averaging some 36,000 a year.

With the exception of people expelled from a country, such as Jews from Nazi Germany and Asians from Kenya (in 1968) and Uganda (in 1972), people come to Britain for much the same reason as they leave. They hope for a better job, an improved standard of living, they may have family ties, they may be restless or dissatisfied with their own country. Some of these reasons probably also account for migrants returning to their country of origin. Figures for Afro-Caribbean migration suggest that the experience of Britain was not what many had hoped for. From 1970 to 1980 53,000 migrated to the UK but 54,000 returned to the Caribbean.

Asians expelled from Kenya in 1968 arrive at Heathrow Airport.

Table 2 gives reasons for migration in and out of the UK. It is important to note, however, that many people do not give a reason other than migration itself.

(adapted from 'Population' by Charles Gibson, Basil Blackwell, London, 1980; 'International Migration: Recent Trends' in 'Population Trends' 18, HMSO, London, 1979; 'Social Trends', 1996)

QUESTIONS

1. Use evidence from Figure 1 and Table 1 to consider the view that Britain has been 'swamped' by immigrants. (6)
2. During periods of economic expansion most European countries have encouraged immigration. Suggest reasons why. (4)
3. Suggest two reasons why Afro-Caribbeans who return to the West Indies might have been dissatisfied with their experience of British society. (6)
4. Why do you think that many people give the only reason for their migration as migration? (4)

POPULATION CHANGES - UNITED KINGDOM

This part brings together the factors which affect population size - births, deaths and migration. It also looks at projections for changes in population size.

The population of the United Kingdom has grown from just over 38 million in 1901 to 58.4 million in 1994. Figure 1 illustrates this growth and includes a projection, based on 1992 figures, of future population size. Figure 3 shows the factors - births, deaths and migration - which have produced these changes in population size. Natural increase refers to the growth in population caused by an excess of births over deaths. Figure 2 looks at the numbers of live births from 1945-1980 and compares them with various projections made at different times.

Figure 1 Population size and projections - United Kingdom

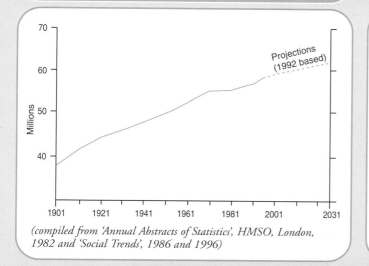

(compiled from 'Annual Abstracts of Statistics', HMSO, London, 1982 and 'Social Trends', 1986 and 1996)

Figure 2 Actual and projected live births in England and Wales

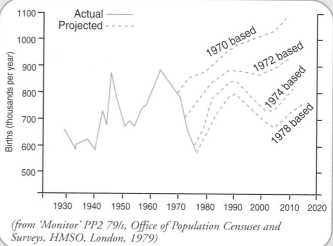

(from 'Monitor' PP2 79/s, Office of Population Censuses and Surveys, HMSO, London, 1979)

Figure 3 Population changes and projections - United Kingdom

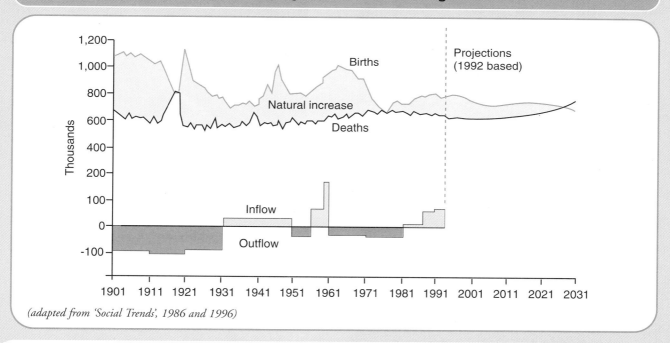

(adapted from 'Social Trends', 1986 and 1996)

QUESTIONS

1. Briefly outline the changes in population size shown in Figure 1. (2)
2. Assess the effect of migration on changes in population size (Figure 3). (5)
3. On the basis of Figure 3, why did the population of the United Kingdom increase during the 20th century? (5)
4. From the evidence in Figure 2, how much confidence should be placed on projections of population changes? Present information from the figure to support your answer. (4)
5. Briefly suggest why governments need to make projections about changes in the population. (4)

THE SOCIAL EFFECTS OF THE FALL IN MORTALITY

Death, as the following extract shows, is no longer at the centre of human life.

At the end of the seventeenth century, the life of the average family man, married for the first time at 27, could be summed up thus: born into a family of five children, he had seen only two or three of them reach the age of 15; he himself had had five children of whom only two or three were alive at his death.

This man, living on average until 52, will have seen about nine people die in his immediate family (not counting uncles, nephews and first cousins), among whom would have been one grandparent (the three others being dead before his birth), both his parents and three of his children.

Nowadays, the situation of the average man of 50 is as follows: born into a family of three, at 26 he married a girl of 24. The only deaths he has seen have been those of his four grandparents. And he still has one chance in two of living a further 26 years.

In the past, in one out of every two cases, the death of young children occurred before that of their father, and half the remaining children saw their father die before they were fully grown. The average age of the children at the death of their first parent was 14.

In the future, the 'average' man will be 55 or 60 when his father dies. This means that the funds of the family inheritance will almost constantly be in the hands of men and women over 60; about half the private wealth of a nation will be in the hands of people over 70.

(Fourastie, quoted in 'Population' by R. Pressat, Penguin, Harmondsworth, 1973, pp51-2)

QUESTION

Discuss the possible effects of these changes on society and on the lives of individuals. (20)

CHILDREN AT THEIR FATHER'S GRAVE

Ah yes, around tombs there must gather the orphan-hearts yet undefiled:

The grave-grass of many a father is fresher for tears of a child.

The children with infinite yearning have brought him the garden's best worth,

As though in the dead they were turning to flowers and freshness of earth.

URBANISATION AND COMMUNITY

Towns and cities are a recent development. For 99.9% of its history the human race lived in hunting and gathering bands. These bands led a nomadic existence, moving from place to place, with little in the way of shelter other than tents and brush huts. Jericho, one of the oldest known cities, was built around 10,000 years ago and by 1500 BC towns and cities were spread from Turkey in the west to India in the east.

A town can only exist if there is sufficient food to feed its inhabitants. A hunting and gathering economy does not produce enough food to support a large urban population. In certain areas it has proved possible for small, settled populations to 'live off the land'. For example a permanent population living in stone houses was established in Syria about 10,000 years ago in an area of high natural production - wild grains, fish and animals. However, it was the invention of agriculture which provided the foundation for urban life. Farmers were able to produce enough food both for their own needs and to support urban populations.

The establishment of towns and cities is not, however, the same thing as an urbanised society. A society only becomes urbanised when the majority of its population lives in towns and cities. Britain was the first country to urbanise. The following passage examines this process.

URBANISATION IN BRITAIN

In eighteenth century Britain (1700-1800) most people lived in rural areas and the economy was mainly agricultural. In 1750 the proportion of the population living in communities of 5,000 or more was probably not over 16%. By 1851 this proportion had risen to over 50%, by 1900 to 75%. The growth of towns and cities was due to two main factors - migration and natural increase. Migration from rural to urban areas was extensive. In 1851 less than half the inhabitants of Manchester, Liverpool and Glasgow had been born in those cities. Natural increase (the excess of births over deaths) also contributed to the growth of urban populations. The migrants tended to be young adults with a higher than average proportion of people in the child bearing age group. The combined effects of migration and natural increase can be seen from the following figures. In 1811 the population of Liverpool was 115,000. By 1851 it had risen to 453,000, an increase of 338,000 of whom 222,000 were migrants.

The move to urban areas was due to a 'push' from the countryside and a 'pull' from the towns. The enclosure movement (enclosing small, scattered landholdings into larger, compact units), new farming techniques (new crops, new systems of crop rotation and selective breeding of sheep and cattle) and the increasing use of new types of agricultural machinery (seed drills, new types of ploughs and threshing machines) led to increased output and a reduction in the labour requirements for agriculture. This provided the food for a rapidly growing urban population and the labour for an industrialising nation. Small farmers and agricultural labourers were

'pushed' off the land - the proportion of the workforce employed in agriculture declined from 33% in 1831, to 15% in 1871, to 7.6% in 1911.

The 'pull' from the towns was due to industrialisation and the expansion of trade and commerce. The growth of the big cities such as Liverpool and Glasgow was due partly to the development of overseas trade. However the bulk of urbanisation was due to industrialisation. It was the application of power - first water power and then steam power in the 1780s - to machinery that changed the unit of production from the family workshop to the factory. Workforces were concentrated around factories in the towns. Typical of these

George Cruikshank's (1829) view of urbanisation - farm animals, haystacks and trees flee from the march of bricks and mortar.

Gustav Doré's engraving of Wentworth Street, Whitechapel, London in the 1870s

noxious by its dampness and closeness, is greatly preferable to the back room: the latter has only one small window, which though on a level with the outer ground, is near the roof of the cellar; it is often patched with boards or paper, and in its best state is so much covered with mud as to admit very little either of air or light. In this cell, the beds of the whole family, sometimes consisting of seven or eight, are placed. The floor of this room is often unpaved: the beds are fixed on the damp earth. But the floor, even when paved, is always damp. In such places, where a candle is required even at noon-day, to examine patients, I have seen the sick without bed-steads, lying on rags; they can seldom afford straw.'

Particularly during the first half of the nineteenth century, urban life for the mass of the working class was characterised by overcrowding in inadequate housing on unpaved and unlit streets with open sewers, high death rates and widespread poverty. It was not until the second half of the nineteenth century that some of the basic amenities of urban living began to appear (see Chapter 13, Part 2; Chapter 19, Part 2).

(adapted from 'An Economic and Social History of Britain since 1700' by M.W. Flinn, Macmillan, London, 1963; 'The First Industrial Revolution' by Phyllis Deane, Cambridge University Press, Cambridge, 1965; 'The First Industrial Nation' by Peter Mathias, Methuen, London, 1969)

QUESTIONS

1. When did Britain become an urbanised society? (1)
2. a) What is migration? (2)
   b) What is natural increase? (2)
   c) How much of the growth in Liverpool's population between 1811 and 1851 was due to (i) migration, (ii) natural increase? (2)
3. a) What are 'push' and 'pull' factors? (4)
   b) Briefly outline the 'push' and 'pull' factors that contributed to urbanisation in Britain. (6)
4. Using evidence from the passage suggest why the death rate in urban areas was high particularly during the first half of the nineteenth century. (3)

developments were the cotton towns in southeast Lancashire, the woollen towns in Yorkshire, metal-working and engineering in the Midlands' towns and the iron and coal towns of South Wales. The increasing demand for labour and the relatively high wages 'pulled' migrants from rural areas into the towns and cities.

Urban life for the new industrial working class was harsh by today's standards. This is how Dr Ferriar described cellar dwellings in Manchester in 1796.

'Each consists of two rooms under ground, the front apartment of which is used as a kitchen, and though frequently

② PART THE 'LOSS OF COMMUNITY'

Sociology as an academic discipline was born in the nineteenth century. Its founding fathers grew up in a rapidly changing society. They were impressed, concerned and sometimes frightened by what they saw as massive social upheavals caused by industrialisation and urbanisation. They wished to understand and explain this process. Some of their ideas are examined in the following passage.

For many of the early sociologists the change in their societies was not simply a change in locations from rural to urban settlements. It was a change in social relationships. They saw the whole texture and fabric of the new urban life as fundamentally different. There was a change from the close-knit, 'natural' life of the village to the fragmented impersonal, 'artificial' existence of the city. There was a 'loss of community'.

The German sociologist Ferdinand Tonnies (1855-1936) spelt this out in his distinction between the **gemeinschaft** relationships of traditional society and the **gesellschaft**

Social unrest was widespread in the early years of the 19th century. This picture shows the Peterloo Massacre of 1819. A crowd of 60 - 80,000 people gathered in Manchester to protest about taxes and lack of representation in Parliament. The meeting turned into a riot. Troops were called in and 13 people were killed and hundreds wounded.

fewer aspects of culture are shared and life is centred on the individual rather than the community. Although Durkheim welcomed this change, feeling it would provide more freedom for people to live their own lives, he feared its consequences. In particular he saw the rapid social change of the nineteenth century producing a situation of **anomie** or normlessness. Traditional norms and social controls were breaking down and had yet to be replaced by new ones. As a result individuals were becoming increasingly rootless, isolated and dissatisfied. Anomie and the breakdown of traditional social controls was seen in the rising rate of suicide, crime and social disorder in urban society.

In America sociologists were making similar contrasts between traditional rural and modern urban life. In his famous essay 'Urbanism as a Way of Life' (1938), Louis Wirth argues that city dwellers tend to be nervous and insecure, they are lost in the crowd and life lacks the depth and meaning of traditional rural society. Relationships with others at work, in shops and on the street are short-lived, shallow, practical and rational.

More recently these sweeping statements about the 'loss of community' have been questioned. Firstly, there is considerable doubt about the rosy picture of rural life presented by some

relationships of industrial society. Gemeinschaft means community and refers to social relationships based on close personal ties centred on the family, the neighbourhood and the church. People have a sense of belonging to the community in which they have been born and raised. By comparison, gesellschaft relationships lack depth and warmth, they are superficial, impersonal and calculating. People relate to each other in terms of their roles as shopkeeper, policeman and teacher, not as members of the same community who have grown up together and shared many of the same experiences.

Emile Durkheim (1858-1917) saw a similar change when he distinguished between the **mechanical solidarity** of traditional society and the **organic solidarity** of modern industrial society. Traditional society is based on mechanical solidarity. Its unity comes from a shared culture, it is based on tradition and face-to-face relationships. People are united in a social group because they are basically similar. Modern industrial society is held together by organic solidarity. Its parts are different but each is necessary for the functioning of society - just like the different parts in a petrol engine. Industrial society has a specialised division of labour with each occupational group dependent on others. People are becoming increasingly different,

Presenting a prize at an English village fete - a rosy picture of a rural community

sociologists. Raymond Williams points out that the peasantry in preindustrial England often lived in poverty, exploited and oppressed by local landowners. He sees the harmony and solidarity of village life as little more than 'a mutuality of the oppressed' - people clung together because they were all stuck in the same rut.

Secondly, the picture of isolation and 'lack of community' in the city has been questioned by a range of studies. Writing in the 1950s about Bethnal Green, a working class borough in the East End of London, Young and Willmott state, 'There is a sense of community, that is a feeling of solidarity between people who occupy the common territory which springs from the fact that people and their families have lived there for a long time'. Bethnal Green in the 1950s was a place where 'everybody knew everybody else', where people were born, raised and died on the same or adjoining streets, where relationships between kin and neighbours were often close, supportive and longstanding (see Chapter 9, Part 5). In *The Urban Villagers*, the American sociologist Herbert Gans describes similar 'village-like' working class and ethnic communities in Boston and New York.

The idea of a 'loss of community' is based in part on an idealised and romantic picture of village life. More recent research has shown that close-knit communities can be found in both rural and urban settlements.

(adapted from 'Urban Sociology' by Martin Slattery, Causeway Press, Ormskirk, 1985)

QUESTIONS

1. Briefly explain the idea of 'loss of community'. (5)
2. The picture of 'traditional society' provided by Ferdinand Tonnies suggests a much more pleasant way of life than that of urban/industrial society. In what ways does it appear more pleasant? (5)
3. Durkheim both welcomed and feared what he saw as the change from mechanical to organic solidarity. Why? (5)
4. How does Raymond Williams' view of preindustrial England differ from Tonnies' picture of traditional society? (2)
5. The discovery of 'urban villages' casts doubt on the idea of a 'loss of community'. Explain why. (3)

3 PART — INTERNAL MIGRATION AND DE-URBANISATION

Official statistics on the extent of urbanisation are difficult to interpret. A number of different definitions of an urban area are used in government statistics and by different government departments. However, whichever definition is used the same general trends appear. These trends are examined in the following passage.

In the 19th century the pattern of migration was from the countryside to the town. In 1885 E.G. Ravenstein published his *Laws of Migration* based on a study of the 1881 census. He stated that

- most movements were over short distances
- any long distance moves usually ended in a large urban centre
- the urban population was less likely to move than the rural population.

In the 20th century the pattern of migration changed. There has been a movement away from larger urban centres, particularly from inner city areas. For example, the population of Liverpool declined from 789,000 in 1951 to 474,000 in 1994. There is now more movement between towns and from town to countryside. In England, East Anglia, a largely rural area, has been the region with the fastest population growth - from 1.38 million in 1951 to 2.11 million in 1994. This growth has been due mainly to **internal migration** - migration from other parts of the country. The movement of population from urban to rural areas is sometimes known as **de-urbanisation**.

Changes in industry account for many of the changes in migration patterns. The older industrial areas such as the North West are losing population as traditional manufacturing

industries such as shipbuilding, heavy engineering and textiles decline. New industries able to utilise electricity and oil are not tied to traditional industrial areas near the coalfields as they often were in the 19th century. There has been a movement of population to the South and the East where job opportunities are greater. Those areas are closer to European markets and have seen the fastest growth in service industries where most of the new jobs have been created in the last 25 years. (See Chapter 15, Part 2.)

The same push/pull factors largely account for the movement from large to small towns and to rural areas. During the past 25 years the decline in manufacturing jobs has been greatest in Britain's largest cities. This decline has been particularly rapid in inner city areas which is part of the reason for the 'flight from the inner cities'. In contrast manufacturing employment has fallen little if at all in small towns and has actually increased in rural areas.

Movement from the inner cities has also been a matter of choice. For those who can afford to move, the suburbs are seen to offer better housing and amenities and a cleaner, healthier and safer environment. The pull to suburbia has been matched by a push from the inner cities. Since the late 1970s, the income gap between rich and poor has steadily widened (see Chapter 6, Part 4). In many inner city areas poverty and deprivation are widespread and the crime rate is high (see Table 1). Those who can afford it 'escape' to the suburbs, to smaller towns and to rural areas. On the basis of 1991 census data, it has been estimated that the fastest population growth will occur in the Home Counties districts north of London. Buckinghamshire and South and East Cambridgeshire lead the way with a projected population growth of 13.5% in the 10 years leading up to 2001.

Movement from the inner cities is not all one way. Certain areas have been 'gentrified' - taken over by the middle classes who have refurbished Victorian and Edwardian houses. Other areas have been redeveloped with housing designed for higher income groups. Waterfront development has proved particularly attractive with London's Docklands Development on the Thames and Preston's Riversway on the River Ribble. Movement back into urban areas is sometimes known as **re-urbanisation**.

Living standards for most people have risen steadily since 1945. Many people can now afford to move to retirement homes in areas of their choice. Towns on the South coast such as Torquay, Bournemouth and Brighton are favourite spots as are areas such as Dorset and Devon. The surroundings are pleasant and the climate relatively mild. Such migrants may move considerable distances.

Table 2 and Figure 1 show how the distribution of the population of England and Wales has changed during various periods in the 20th century. These changes are due mainly to migration rather than regional differences in birth and death rates.

Brighton pier

(adapted from various issues of 'Annual Abstract of Statistics', 'Population Trends' and 'Regional Trends')

Table 1 Areas of high and low deprivation

The 10 least deprived were:

1	Mid Sussex	6	Chelmsford
2	Aylesbury Vale	7	S. Northants
3	East Herts	8	Chiltern
4	Huntingdonshire	9	Hart
5	Wokingham	10	Waverley

The 10 most deprived were:

1	Newham	6	Liverpool
2	Southwark	7	Tower Hamlets
3	Hackney	8	Lambeth
4	Islington	9	Sandwell
5	Birmingham	10	Haringey

The Index of Local Conditions was compiled by the Department of the Environment using data from the 1991 Census. It measures relative levels of deprivation in England's 366 local authority districts. Indicators used include unemployment, housing, cars, education, health, crime, derelict land, numbers of children in low-earning households and in unsuitable accommodation.

(from 'Observer', 5.6.1994)

Table 2 Regions of England - percentage of population, 1911 and 1994

	1911	1994
North	8.1	6.3
North West	16.8	13.1
Yorkshire & Humberside	11.6	10.3
West Midlands	9.7	10.8
East Midlands	7.3	8.4
East Anglia	3.5	4.3
South West	8.4	9.8
South East	34.5	36.7

(compiled from 'Annual Abstract of Statistics', 1996, p23)

Figure 1 Population change, England and Wales, 1961-1994

Percentage increase, 1961-1994	Area	1994 population (millions)	Percentage decrease 1961-1994
+11.7%	England and Wales	51.6m	
	Greater London	7.0m	-12.7%
	Inner London	2.7m	-23.5%
	Outer London	4.3m	-4.2%
	Metropolitan areas	11.2m	-4.3%
	Main metropolitan cities	3.5m	-17.9%
+3.3%	Other metroplitan districts	7.7m	
+26.1%	**Non-metropolitan districts**	33.5m	
+1%	Non-metropolitan cities	4.7m	
+14.8%	Industrial districts	6.9m	
+54.8%	New Towns	2.4m	
+30.4%	Resorts and retirement areas	3.7m	
+39.9%	Mixed urban/rural districts	10.1m	
+32.8%	Remoter, mainly rural areas	5.6m	

60 50 40 30 20 10 0
Percentage increase

0 -10 -20 -30
Percentage decrease

Examples of areas in Figure 1 are:
Metropolitan areas - West Midlands, Greater Manchester, Merseyside.
Main metropolitan cities - Birmingham, Manchester, Liverpool.
Other metropolitan districts are the districts which make up the metropolitan areas minus the main metropolitan cities, eg Merseyside without Liverpool.

Non-metropolitan districts are made up of the following:
Non-metropolitan cities - Cambridge, Durham, York.
Industrial districts - Darlington, Scunthorpe, Rhondda Valley.
New Towns - Milton Keynes, Harlow, Welwyn.
Resorts and retirement areas - Torbay, Bournemouth, Southend-on-Sea.
Mixed urban rural districts - North Bedfordshire, East Hampshire, Ribble Valley.
Remoter, mainly rural areas - Fenland, North Cornwall, Forest of Dean.

(compiled from 'Annual Abstract of Statistics', 1996, p23)

QUESTIONS

1. Briefly summarise the differences between migration patterns in the 19th and 20th centuries. (7)
2. Why are inner city populations declining? (7)
3. Explain the main population changes shown in Table 2 and Figure 1. (6)

4 PART   THE INNER CITY

Recession, industrial decline, high unemployment, a growth in poverty and public spending cuts have affected the nation as a whole, but the harshest effects have been felt by those living in the inner cities. The problems of the inner city were focused by the riots of 1981, 1985 and 1995. They have been intensified by the growth in poverty over the past 25 years. But, as the following passage shows, they are not new.

The inner city has a long history. It has existed since the birth of the industrial town. This is how Engels described Manchester Old Town in 1844.

Everywhere, half or wholly ruined buildings, rarely a wooden or stone floor to be seen in the houses, almost uniformly broken, ill-fitting windows and doors, and a state of filth. Everywhere heaps of debris, refuse and offal; standing pools for gutters, and a stench which alone would make it impossible for a human being, in

any degree civilised, to live in such a district.

Over 130 years later the Liverpool Inner Area Study provided a remarkably similar description of Liverpool's inner city.

In 1975, eleven per cent of land in the study area was lying vacant, much of it the cleared sites of terraced houses. For those who have to live with the day to day reality of large, rubble-strewn sites the impact is immediate, unsavoury and depressing. Packs of half wild dogs scavenge among bags of abandoned household refuse. Pools of water collect where badly fitted cellars have subsided. Children build fires with cardboard cartons and the abandoned timber from demolished houses and play among the piles of brick, rubble and broken glass. Half bricks provide a ready and almost endless supply of ammunition for the frequent destruction of the windows of surrounding houses. Mattresses, furniture, gas cookers, prams and even cars that have outlived their usefulness are dumped.

Mattresses, prams and cars are not the only things dumped. The inner cities are a dumping ground for people. From his study of Hackney in London, Paul Harrison writes,

> The inner city is a sump for the disadvantaged of every kind, a place to which those with the fewest resources sink, and from which those who gain any freedom of choice escape. It is a place of deprivation, of toil and struggle and isolation, a knacker's yard for society's casualties, a breaker's yard where the pressure of need grinds people against each other and wears them down.

Inner cities are urban areas with the highest concentrations of bad housing, unemployment, poverty and crime. They are the sites of the older, declining industries - clothing, textiles, shipbuilding and docking. The decline in these industries has led to the shedding of labour and a relative fall in wage rates.

The result is rising unemployment and lower incomes. Housing is a mixture of old Victorian terraces now reaching the end of their useful life and more modern council estates, often of the worst possible design. Inner city areas have higher than average concentrations of unskilled and semi-skilled manual workers and high levels of unemployment. People live there because they cannot afford to live anywhere else.

Something of the pressures and problems of inner city life can be seen from the following quotations taken from Paul Harrison's study of Hackney. A woman describes the problems of low income.

> 'When we have to break into the rent money to pay the milk, that really gets us arguing, and once we start, we're down on each other's throats all night. It isn't fair that we have to suffer like this. We don't ask much out of life, just a little money to buy food and decent clothes.'

An unemployed man talks about the future.

> 'I got no plans, I just take it as it comes. What's the worth of thinking ahead? The only time you can think ahead is if you've got money. If you made plans, you'd only be disappointed. They wouldn't work out any way.'

An old age pensioner talks about her fears of burglary.

> 'After my last break-in I had a special chain and alarm bell fitted, but I still think about burglars all the time. I lie in bed at night and worry. I think, what if they got in? If my alarm bell went off at night, I'd die of fright. My son set it off once by mistake, and I nearly had a heart attack.'

Paul Harrison argues that the problems of the inner city are not primarily caused by the city itself or by the people who live there. Their lives are shaped by events outside the inner city, by economic and political processes beyond their control. Inner city life is lived by people at the bottom of the class structure, people who are powerless to change their situation, people the rest of the country has turned its back on and would prefer to forget. Class is the problem and the only real solution is more equality, a redistribution of income and wealth. People need money to escape from inner city life. Harrison concludes,

> But I doubt whether any policy aimed at particular deprived areas can solve the inner-

city problem, because the local problem is the symptom of national diseases. Improve one particular location, and another inner-city area would burst forth elsewhere. Dress and heal the open sore in Hackney, and another will erupt in Tottenham or Leyton. As long as British society continues to generate an underclass on low incomes with insecure jobs or no jobs, and without adequate education, new inner-city areas will continue to arise wherever housing is significantly worse than average.

(adapted from 'Inside the Inner City', [revised edition] by Paul Harrison, Penguin, Harmondsworth, 1985 and 'Urban Sociology' by Martin Slattery, Causeway Press, Ormskirk, 1985)

QUESTIONS

1. Inner cities are 'dumps' in more ways than one. Briefly explain this statement. (5)
2. Why is unemployment particularly high in the inner cities? (5)
3. Why is life in the inner cities stressful? (5)
4. The problems of the inner cities cannot be solved by the people who live there. Why not? (5)

WORK AND LEISURE

This chapter goes from what many people see as one extreme to the other - from work to leisure. It begins by looking at production technology - the technology used to produce goods - and examines its influence on people's experience of work. Changing employment patterns are reviewed, for example the movement of jobs from the manufacturing to the service sector and the move from full-time to part-time work. The future of work is considered with particular reference to the development of computer technology.

Most people's lives are divided between work and leisure. But, for a sizeable minority, there is a third alternative - unemployment. The problem of defining and measuring unemployment is examined along with the social characteristics of the unemployed and the effects of unemployment on their lives.

The chapter goes on to consider the possibility that the work people do shapes their leisure activities. It also examines the influence of social class on leisure. The chapter closes with a view of the future of leisure by the famous futurologist and science fiction writer, Arthur C. Clarke.

PRODUCTION TECHNOLOGY

This part looks at the main trends in production technology in preindustrial and industrial society. Production technology is the technology used to produce goods.

Craft production

Before the industrial revolution, which began in Britain in the second half of the 18th century, goods were produced by craftsmen and women in their homes and in small workshops. This type of production is sometimes known as cottage industry as goods were often produced in cottages as shown in the picture.

Around 1720, Daniel Defoe (author of *Robinson Crusoe*) journeyed to Halifax in the West Riding of Yorkshire. This is what he saw.

'People made cloth in practically every house in Halifax. They keep a cow or two and sow corn to feed their chickens. The houses were full of lusty fellows, some at the dye-vat; some at the loom, others dressing the cloths; the women and children carding, or spinning; all employed from the youngest to the oldest. The finished cloth was taken to the market to be sold.'

Mechanisation

Mechanisation is the use of machinery to produce goods. The industrial revolution replaced human labour power with new machines and new ways of powering them. It was the application of first water power and then steam power to machines that moved production from the family workshop to the factory. Richard Arkwright provides an example of one of the new factory owners. He was a highly successful businessman whose mills made him a fortune. In 1780 he introduced steam power into his factories putting his workers

on 12 hour shifts in order to operate the machinery 24 hours a day. By 1782 he was employing over 5,000 workers in his mills.

Mass production Mechanisation made large scale mass production possible. Mass production is the production of large quantities of identical products. As production technology improved larger and larger quantities could be produced. For example, in 1840 it took 20 men and boys one day to turn out 20,000 screws on a lathe. By 1875 automatic lathes minded by one man could make 120,000 screws a day.

Assembly production Mechanisation also made assembly production possible. Standardised parts were machine made and then assembled into the finished product. Samuel Colt provides one of the earliest examples. In his American factory he

Spinning in a cottage in the early 1700s

A Colt .45 six-shot revolver

Ford Motor company assembly line

mass produced and assembled the parts for revolvers, the most famous of which was the Colt .45. Identical revolvers were bought by cowboys in stores across the USA.

The assembly line Parts of a product were often put together on an assembly line. Henry Ford's motor car assembly line provides the most famous example. The cars were moved from worker to worker - at first by hand and then by machine power when the line became mechanised. Each worker carried out one or more simple tasks such as tightening a wheelnut.

Automation

Mechanisation is taken a step further by automation. Automated production has traditionally been used in the oil and chemical industries. The raw materials enter the production process, the various stages of manufacture are automatically controlled by machines, and the finished product emerges 'untouched by human hand'.

Computer technology The introduction of computer technology means that increasingly complex production processes can be automated. Fiat proudly boasts that its cars are 'hand-built by robots'. Workers producing and assembling parts for cars are steadily being made redundant by computer technology. The heart of this technology is a silicon chip, the size of a shirt button or smaller. It has the power to control detailed and complex operations. The following description provides an example of a computer controlled production process.

When it is finished early next year, a highly computerised plant in Somerset will be run by one white coated supervisor, who will rarely get his hands dirty and spend most of his time sitting in front of a computer console. He will be helped by just four other workers.

A conventional factory of the same size would require several more machinery operators. It would also need clerical staff, warehousemen and people who push pieces of metal from one machine to another. All these people are absent from the Somerset plant. Thanks to computer technology, its staff of 5 will do the work of 20. With the new equipment, the five will make

£1 million worth of goods per year; an average of £200,000 per person. For the rest of the company's 2,000 employees the comparable figure is £17,000.

Initially the machines in the workshop will turn out parts for just one product - bomb release mechanisms for the Tornado

Renault assembly line using robots

military aeroplane. But the machines operate according to computer programs which can be varied by tapping a few buttons on a keyboard. So the equipment is flexible enough to make thousands of other components that could be fitted to products as diverse as engines and pressure valves.

(adapted from 'Britain Advances in Computerised Factories' by P. Marsh, 'New Scientist', 19.3.1981; 'A Social and Economic History of Industrial Britain' by J. Robottom, Longman, Harlow, 1986; 'British Economic and Social History 1700-1870' by P. Sauvain, Stanley Thornes, Cheltenham, 1987)

QUESTIONS

1. Why did mechanisation lead to the move from home and small workshop production to factory production? (4)
2. How did mechanisation make (i) mass production and (ii) assembly production possible? (5, 5)
3. Automation and computer technology often lead to a reduction in the workforce employed in production. Suggest reasons why. (6)

PART 2 — THE CHANGING WORKFORCE

Changes in the workforce often reflect changes in production technology. However, this is not the only reason for changes in employment patterns. During the second part of the 20th century there has been a rapid growth in the service sector - insurance, banking, health, education, hotels and catering. This reflects changes in what people want and what they can afford. This part looks at changes in employment patterns.

The primary sector

Haymaking in Berkshire in 1906

Baling hay on a modern farm

The primary sector of the economy includes agriculture, fishing, forestry, mining and quarrying. In all these areas there has been a steady reduction in the workforce. Mechanisation is one of the main reasons for this reduction. Figure 1 shows the decline in employment in agriculture from 1861 to 1995. Look at the picture of harvesting in 1906 and compare it with the picture of harvesting today on a mechanised farm. These pictures provide a graphic illustration of the replacement of human power with machine power.

Mechanisation has also contributed to the decline of the workforce employed in mining. There are a number of other reasons for this decline. For example, in the case of coal mining competition from other energy sources - gas, oil and nuclear power - and from cheaply produced coal from abroad. However, mechanisation in the form of coal cutting machines and conveyor belts to transport the coal has replaced the picks, shovels and manpower of large numbers of miners. In Britain the numbers employed in mining and quarrying dropped from 3.3 million in 1961 to 67,000 in 1995.

Figure 1 Employment in agriculture, UK 1861-1995

(adapted from 'British Social and Economic History 1850 to the Present Day' by P. Sauvain, Stanley Thornes, Cheltenham, 1977, p9 and 'Annual Abstract of Statistics', 1996, p127)

The secondary sector

The secondary sector of the economy is made up of manufacturing industry. Employment in this sector has steadily declined, particularly since the 1970s. In 1971 employees in manufacturing made up 36% of all employees in Britain, by 1995 this was reduced to 18%. This decline has been greatest in the old 'smokestack' industries such as iron and steel and traditional industries such as textiles, shipbuilding and motor vehicles. This has been due to a variety of factors including foreign competition and increasing mechanisation and automation.

One of the few growth areas for employment in the secondary sector is computer manufacture. Ironically, it is computer technology which has contributed to the reduction of the workforce in manufacturing as a whole.

The tertiary sector

The tertiary or service sector is made up of a range of 'service industries' including banking, insurance, education, health and welfare, hotels and catering, shops, garages, transport and post and telecommunications. The tertiary sector is the major growth area for employment. In 1971 employees in services made up 56% of all employees in Britain, by 1995 this had increased to 75.7%. However, in some service industries this trend has been reversed in recent years. For example, in banking the workforce has been reduced in the first half of the 1990s due in part to the increasing use of computer technology.

Most of the new jobs in the tertiary sector are part time and filled by women. Many of these jobs are low in pay, status and skill. For example, the growing leisure and tourism industries - hotels, catering, sport and recreation - employ mainly sales, clerical, cleaning and unskilled staff.

In summary, the expansion of the tertiary sector has led to a growing number of part-time jobs for women, whereas the primary and secondary sectors have been shedding full-time jobs for men.

(adapted from various issues of 'Social Trends' and 'Annual Abstract of Statistics')

Smokestacks at East Moors steelworks Cardiff, about to be demolished. A man who has spent all his working life as a steel worker at East Moors is now employed to demolish it.

QUESTIONS

1. Summarise and give reasons for the trend shown in Figure 1. (3)
2. a) Briefly explain why job losses have occurred in traditional manufacturing industries. (3)
   b) Amongst manual workers the largest job losses have occurred in the unskilled manual group. Suggest why this is so. (4)
3. Should we welcome the increase in jobs in the tertiary sector? (5)
4. Why are women more likely to be part-time workers than men? (5)

3 PART — CHANGING WORK PATTERNS

There have been important changes in work patterns during the second half of the 20th century. As shown in Figure 1, there has been a steady decline in full-time jobs which has been more than matched by an increase in part-time jobs. Changes in patterns of work are examined in the following passage.

The workforce

Figure 1 Employment patterns, Great Britain, 1961-1995

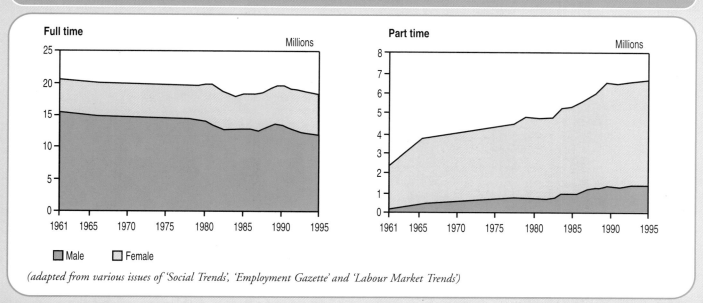

(adapted from various issues of 'Social Trends', 'Employment Gazette' and 'Labour Market Trends')

The workforce is made up of people in employment plus those claiming unemployment benefit. In Britain in 1995 the workforce numbered 28 million of which 15.7 million were men and 12.3 million women. From 1970 to 1995 women have taken nearly 90% of the new jobs in the UK.

Part-time work

Most new jobs created are part time. And, as Figure 1 shows, most of them have been filled by women. It has been estimated that if the trend shown in Figure 1 continues then 45% of all workers will be part time by 2003. Some workers, particularly women, welcome this trend. A Labour Force Survey showed that 80% of women, but only 36% of men, took a part-time job because they did not want full-time employment (see Table 1, p188). For many women part-time working enables them to fit

work in with other responsibilities such as caring for children, elderly relatives and housework. They find it gives them flexibility and freedom. However, for many workers, particularly men, part-time work is a last resort as full-time jobs disappear.

From the point of view of employers, part-time work means greater flexibility, efficiency and profitability. This is illustrated by new working practices introduced by the Burton Group (Burton Menswear, Dorothy Perkins, Top Shop, Top Man, Evans, Principles and Debenhams). In 1993 the Burton Group decided it had too many shop assistants hanging around doing nothing during slack trading times. It made 2,800 full-time staff redundant and then took on 7,000 part-time staff. According to the company, 'We wanted staff in the shops when the customers were there'. Part-time employment gave them the flexibility they required.

Temporary work

Temporary employment is employment which is not permanent - it can be for a day, a month, a year or longer, it can be full time or part time. Temporary employment was the fastest growing type of employment in the first half of the 1990s. In 1995 there were over 1.5 million temporary workers in the UK, an increase of one third in 5 years. Over half of temporary workers are women. Table 1 gives the results of a Labour Force Survey inquiry into reasons for taking temporary employment.

Table 1 Reasons for temporary employment

Main reasons for taking a temporary main job Percentages	All	Men	Women
Could not find a permanent job	40	47	35
Did not want a permanent job	32	24	39
Had a contract which included a period of training	5	7	4
Some other reason	22	22	22

(from 'Labour Market Trends', January 1996, LFS6)

Temporary work covers a range of working practices. It includes **seasonal work** in agriculture - fruit and vegetable picking, in the leisure industry - during the tourist season, and at Christmas when the demand for Father Christmases rockets. It includes **casual labour** when workers are employed as and when required. Supply teachers in schools and some dockworkers provide examples of casual labour. Temporary work also includes people employed on fixed-term contracts. For example, at the BBC about one third of journalists and production staff are on **fixed-term contracts** of one year or less.

For employers, temporary employment offers greater flexibility, efficiency and competitiveness. In recent years the fastest growth of temporary employment has been in manufacturing. Increasing numbers of manufacturers are adopting 'just-in-time' policies which means large stocks are no longer held in storage. Instead products are made just in time to meet demand. Firms such as Black and Decker and Raleigh bicycles now rely on temporary workers to meet fluctuating demand for their products.

However, what's good for employers isn't always good for employees. Anne works in a hospital in southern England. She has been on short-term contracts for the past 6 years. She began on monthly contracts. Although she worked on the same ward for two years, 'I never knew if I would be working from month to month'. She is now working on a two year contract but there's no guarantee it will be renewed. Ann feels insecure, anxious and unable to plan her future. In her words, 'It's not the money that's the problem, as I earn as much as permanent nurses. It's the fear that next year I may be earning nothing.'

For some temporary employees, however, money is the problem. Casual dockworkers for example, are sometimes employed at rates which are up to 50% lower than those with permanent jobs.

Self-employment

Throughout the 1970s there were around 2.2 million self-employed workers in Britain, some 8% of the workforce. By 1995 there were over 3.2 million, some 13% of the workforce. Roughly two-thirds are one-person businesses. The growth in self-employment began during the recession of the early 1980s which resulted in high levels of unemployment. Some who lost their jobs used their redundancy payments to set up their own businesses. Some saw self-employment as the only way out of unemployment. And they were encouraged to become self-employed by employers and government.

In a recession employers are reluctant to take on staff in case there is no work for them in 6 months or a year's time. Often they prefer to contract work out to the self-employed. Contracting out became increasingly popular during the 1980s and 1990s (see Figure 2). It is a way of getting work done without the responsibility, and the additional cost, of employing people.

Governments have encouraged self-employment. For example, the Enterprise Allowance Scheme, set up in 1983, provided £40 a week for one year to help people establish their own businesses.

Homeworking and teleworking

Homeworkers as their name suggests work from home. Many are teleworkers using personal computers, e-mail and other electronic communication methods in their work. Their numbers have grown slowly but steadily. In 1995, 631,000 worked at home as their main job. More than half were self-employed. The main occupations of teleworkers are translation and research, writing, editing, journalism, data entry and typing. Many are employed on short-term contracts.

From an employer's point of view homeworking has the advantages of flexibility and reduced costs, it can solve travel problems and allow them to employ staff with childcare responsibilities. And these are often seen as advantages by homeworkers. However, some homeworkers experience social isolation, they find they don't get enough work and their pay is low. In other words, they see themselves as cheap labour to be used at their employer's convenience. A survey entitled *Home Truths*, published in 1994, looked at 175 homeworkers in 10 areas of the country. Over 90% were women, three-quarters had school children, and they worked on average for £1.28 an hour. The survey found that some were working for as little as 30p an hour.

Job sharing

In 1995 0.7% of employees shared jobs - 1.2% of women and 0.2% of men. Job sharing is a form of part-time work where two or more people share the same full-time job. It can provide advantages for both employers and employees. Job sharers working for Hewlett Packard, for example, guarantee that if one of them is away, the other will fill in for them. The employer gets full cover at little extra cost. Other advantages stated by employers are increased flexibility, less absenteeism and the availability of a wider range of skills. Job sharing allows employees to combine paid work with other activities ranging

Teleworking

Homeworking

from childcare and looking after elderly relatives to taking courses, doing voluntary community work and enjoying hobbies.

Annualised hours

Growing numbers of companies are employing workers on annualised hours contracts. This means that the number of hours an employee has to work are calculated over a full year. For example, rather than 40 hours per week, employees are contracted to 2,000 hours a year. Longer hours are worked during certain times of the year and shorter hours at other times. Hours worked depend on changes in demand for the company's goods or services.

Annualised hours contracts suit companies whose workload varies. It usually avoids paying costly overtime rates and paying workers when they have little or no work to do. For some employees it can mean more money for less hours - they get paid for the annual hours even if they don't work them. For others, who relied on many hours of overtime, it can lead to a reduction in pay. And for all employees, working extra hours at short notice can be inconvenient, especially if they have to cancel evenings out, barbecues and so on.

Flexible working

The changing work patterns examined in this part are a move away from the traditional pattern of employment - the full-time, long-term job. Work practices are becoming increasingly flexible and present trends suggest they will become even more so. Figure 2 is based on a survey of organisations in 1995. It shows

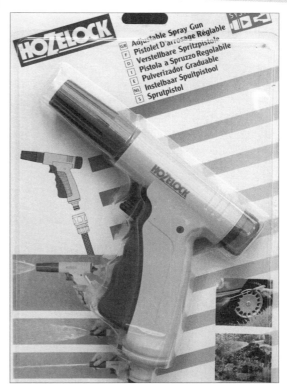

Hozelock makes hose pipes and sprinkler systems. Its workers have annualised hours contracts.

the percentage using flexible working practices and whether they have increased or decreased their use. For example 66% used temporary labour with 61% increasing and 5% decreasing its use.

(adapted from various issues of 'Employment Gazette' and 'Labour Market Trends'; 'Economics' 2nd edition by Alain Anderton, Causeway Press, Ormskirk, 1995; 'Observer', 17.4.1994; 'Guardian', 25.10.1993, 13.9.1994, 22.4.1995, 3.2.1996)

Figure 2 Flexible working practices, UK 1995

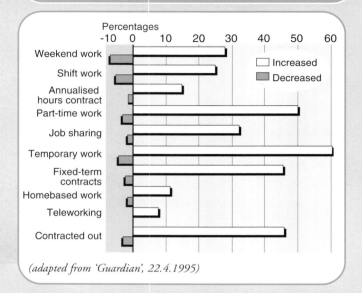

(adapted from 'Guardian', 22.4.1995)

QUESTIONS

1. Summarise the trends shown in Figure 1. (2)
2. a) How might part-time work benefit both employers and employees? (3)
   b) Many employees are not happy with part-time work. Why not? (3)
3. On balance temporary work benefits the employer rather than the employee. Discuss. (4)
4. a) Show how self-employment, homeworking, job sharing and annualised hours provide flexibility for contractors and employers. (3)
   b) Why are annualised hours particularly suitable for a company like Hozelock? (2)
5. Flexible working practices will probably increase. Briefly summarise the evidence in the passage which supports this view. (3)

PART 4 — THE FUTURE OF WORK

In recent years a growing number of books and articles have been published predicting the end of work as we know it. Most look forward to an age in which intelligent machines take over much of the work now done by human beings. For some this heralds a golden age of leisure. Others give a dire warning of millions of people thrown out of work to rot on a human scrapheap.

The following passage is based on an article entitled 'The End of Work?' by Jeremy Rifkin, president of the Foundation of Economic Trends in the USA.

For the first time in history human labour is being systematically eliminated. With new forms of computer based information, communication and production technologies and new forms of business organisation and working practices, millions of workers are being forced into temporary jobs and unemployment.

The production of goods and the delivery of services is becoming increasingly automated. We can now look forward to the workerless factory in which robots produce goods of a quality beyond the ability of mere human beings. In the words of the economist Wassily Leontief, 'The role of humans as the most important factor of production is bound to diminish in the same way that the role of horses in agricultural production was first diminished and then eliminated by the introduction of tractors'.

The steady decline of workers in manufacturing is matched by a steady increase in production. Automation produces more goods with fewer workers. And the same is happening in the service sector. Banks are shedding employees with automatic cash points and financial transactions along the information superhighway. Secretaries and clerks are being replaced by personal computers, electronic mail and fax machines. In retailing the use of electronic bar codes and scanners has greatly increased the efficiency of cashiers and so reduced their numbers. Some fast-food drive-through restaurants are replacing human order takers with touch-sensitive menu screens. And the rise of electronic home shopping may well replace shops as we know them.

Intelligent machines are even replacing professional jobs. Synthesizers are taking over from human musicians in clubs and theatres and even replacing orchestras in opera houses. And a

There are however alternatives. Job sharing and a shorter working week could increase employment. And millions of new jobs could be created which cannot be performed by 'thinking machines'. There are countless people who require help and support from others - the mentally ill, the elderly, the sick and the disabled. And there are numerous socially useful jobs that need doing - building homes for the homeless, clearing derelict land in towns and cities, providing nursery education for preschool children and so on. If a 'social wage' were provided for these services, then many people could be usefully employed and, in the words of the song, 'the world would be a better place'.

Ending on a positive note, in the words of Jeremy Rifkin, 'For the first time in human history, large numbers of human beings could be liberated from long hours of labour to pursue leisure and community activities'.

robot that will perform hip replacement surgery is now being developed in California.

What will become of all the workers displaced by the new technology. Some argue that the emergence of an underclass is pointing the way to the future. They foresee a growing mass at the base of society - unwanted, unneeded, unwashed and unhappy. Summarising the attitude of future employers, Nathan Gardels writes, 'We don't want what they have and they can't buy what we sell'. This growing underclass living on welfare will become increasingly discontented and threaten social stability. Mass unemployment may well lead to mass violence.

On a more optimistic note some argue that new technology will produce new jobs. They point to the fact that when cars replaced horse drawn transport millions of new jobs were created. But the new products and services of the computer age require far fewer workers to produce and operate them than those they replaced.

(adapted from 'The End of Work?' by Jeremy Rifkin, 'New Statesman and Society', 9.6.1995)

QUESTIONS

1. Why does Rifkin argue that computer technology, unlike previous forms of technology, will eliminate large numbers of workers? (7)
2. Why should we be concerned about the possibility of millions being thrown out of work? (6)
3. Today a person's status and identity are largely shaped by their occupation. How might this change in the future? In particular, what might people use as a basis for their status and identity? (7)

5 PART — ASSEMBLY LINE PRODUCTION

Production technology - the technology used to produce goods - can have an important influence on the behaviour and attitudes of workers and the amount of satisfaction they derive from their work. The following extract, taken from Arthur Hailey's novel *Wheels*, looks at the assembly of motor cars on a production line. It reflects the findings of a number of sociologists who have studied assembly line production.

But neither pay nor good fringe benefits could change the grim, dispiriting nature of the work. Most of it was physically hard, but the greatest toll was mental - hour after hour, day after day of deadening monotony. And the nature of their jobs

robbed individuals of pride. A man on a production line lacked a sense of achievement; he never made a car, he merely made, or put together, pieces - adding a washer to a bolt, fastening a metal strip, inserting screws. And always it was the identical washer or strip or screws, over and over and over and over and over and over and over again, while working conditions - including an overlay of noise - made communication difficult, friendly association between individuals impossible. As years went by, many, while hating, endured. Some had mental breakdowns. Almost no one liked his work.

Thus, a production line worker's ambition, like that of a prisoner, was centred on escape. Both a temporary breakdown of the line and absenteeism provided partial escape; so did a strike. All brought excitement, a break in monotony.

(adapted from 'Wheels' by Arthur Hailey, Souvenir Press, London)

QUESTIONS

1. Identify three reasons given in the passage for the dispiriting effect of assembly line work. (3)
2. With some reference to the extract, suggest why assembly line workers often feel powerless. (4)
3. a) Identify the three ways noted in the passage which allow 'partial escape' from the problems of working on the line. (3)
   b) Briefly suggest why these methods of escape provide at least short-term relief for the workers. (3)
4. Why do pay and 'good fringe benefits' appear so important to assembly line workers? (3)
5. Why do you think that relationships between assembly line workers and management are often hostile? (4)

6 PART — TECHNOLOGY AND JOB SATISFACTION

The American sociologist Robert Blauner claims that workers will experience satisfaction from their work if 1) they feel they are able to control their work 2) they find a sense of purpose and meaning in their work 3) they feel a part of a social group at work and 4) they become involved and are able to express themselves in their work. These ways of experiencing satisfaction from work are largely unavailable to the assembly line workers described in Part 5. Blauner argues that this is due to the production technology used in the assembling of motor cars.

Blauner looks at four types of production technology. First, craft technology which is typical of preindustrial production. Second, mechanisation and machine technology which brought about the industrial revolution. Third, assembly line production which became increasingly typical as industrialisation developed. And fourth, automation which represents the later stages of industrialisation. Blauner argues that the relatively high level of satisfaction resulting from craft technology largely disappears with mechanisation and assembly line production. However, he believes that automation restores much of the satisfaction lost in the earlier years of industrialisation.

Craft technology

Blauner uses printing as an example of craft technology. His study was conducted before mechanical typesetting was widely used and before computer typesetting was invented.

The essential feature of a craft technology is the lack of standardisation of the product. Printers turn out new editions of newspapers, new magazines and new books every day. Since

Mechanisation

Machine minding The textile industry is typical of the early stages of industrialisation. Most textile workers in Blauner's study were machine minders. They looked after a dozen or so machines, feeding them with yarn and mending breaks in the yarn. The traditional craft skills of weaving are, in Blauner's words, 'built into the machine'.

Textile workers are tied to their machines with little freedom of movement. Their tasks are routine and repetitive, requiring little skill, judgement or initiative. The pace and rhythm of their work is largely controlled by machines. Their contribution to the finished product is small - most do little more than tend machines.

Craft printers in 1902

Weaving shed, Harle Syke Mill, Burnley, 1905

the product they work on is constantly changing, it has been more difficult to standardise the work process.

In a craft technology, the worker sets his own pace of work because he must be able to take special pains when the process requires it. Since operations aren't standardised and craftsmen are responsible for a high quality product they need time to perfect their work. When hand compositors are working up a page form they must insert an unspecified number of empty metal lines or spaces on various columns of the page so that the lines of type are spread evenly. When pressmen make ready the presses and page forms for final printing, they must make a large number of elaborate and unpredictable adjustments. A printing craftsman not only sets his own work rhythm, he is free from pressure on the job.

The freedom to determine techniques of work, to choose one's tools and to vary the sequence of operations is part of the nature and traditions of craftsmanship. Because each job is somewhat different from previous jobs, problems continually arise which require a craftsman to make decisions. Traditional skill thus involves the frequent use of judgement and initiative, aspects of a job which give the worker a feeling of control over his environment.

Craftsmen generally have considerable freedom of physical movement since they do not work on conveyor belts or other machines which control their pace and demand their presence. Printers can usually walk anywhere they want, not only on the shop floor but also to editorial offices and other parts of the plant.

Craft technology does not involve the elaborate subdivision of work characteristic of mass production. A craftsman may no longer be a 'jack-of-all-trades' who makes the entire product himself; still his work is always quite varied and he continues to work on a large segment of the product. His craft training is very broad rather than narrowly specialised.

Assembly line production Blauner saw satisfaction from work reaching its lowest ebb with assembly line production (see Part 5). Most of the workers in his study found work on the line dull and monotonous. They had little control over their work - the speed of the line determines the pace of work and allows them little freedom of movement. Their tasks are broken down into simple, repetitive operations requiring little skill or judgement. As a result they find it difficult to identify with the final product - their only contribution might be tightening wheel nuts or fitting hub caps. Tied to the line, they have little opportunity to socialise with other workers.

Automation

Blauner is optimistic about automation believing it would reverse the trend towards decreasing job satisfaction in manufacturing industry. He gives the following picture of work in an automated factory. Workers have considerable control over the production process - they monitor and check dials which measure factors such as temperature and pressure and make the necessary adjustments. They are responsible for the production process, making decisions which require 'considerable discretion and initiative'. Work also involves the maintenance and repair of expensive and complicated

Electricity generating plant

machinery by skilled technicians. They move around the factory working in teams. Blauner argues that work in an automated plant has variety, skill, responsibility and control.

Criticisms of Blauner

Blauner sees production technology as the main factor affecting job satisfaction. A number of studies have supported his view that production technology does affect job satisfaction. However, it may not be the most important factor. For example, a study by Goldthorpe and Lockwood of workers in Luton found that skilled maintenance workers in a largely automated chemical plant experienced greater job satisfaction than machine operators or assembly line workers. But, in terms of their more general attitudes to work, their **work orientation**, the attitudes of all the workers were very similar. They defined work as a means to an end, as a means for obtaining money to raise their living standards. If the money is good and the job is secure, then they were satisfied with their work whatever the production technology.

Questionnaires

Both Blauner and Goldthorpe and Lockwood relied heavily on data from questionnaires to measure job satisfaction and work orientation. What do people mean when they say they are satisfied with their work? Are they referring to pay, social relationships at work, the status of the job, the work process itself and so on? Do their views reflect their age, gender, length of time in the job, their experience of previous jobs or of unemployment? And the way questions are worded, as Blauner admits, 'may favour one response rather than another'. In addition, 'the meaning of the question may not always be the same to the worker as it is to the interviewer'.

Questionnaire data must be regarded with caution, particularly with ideas as vague and wide ranging as job satisfaction and work orientation.

(adapted from 'Alienation and Freedom' by Robert Blauner, University of Chicago Press, 1964 and 'The Affluent Worker in the Class Structure' by J.H. Goldthorpe, D. Lockwood et al, University of Cambridge Press, Cambridge, 1969)

QUESTIONS

1. Briefly explain how job satisfaction is related to production technology. (6)
2. Blauner placed too much emphasis on production technology as a factor affecting job satisfaction. Discuss. (6)
3. Questionnaire data must be treated with caution. Discuss. (8)

PART 7 — ALIENATION

From a Marxist point of view workers employed in capitalist society cannot experience any real sense of satisfaction from their work. They are employed by privately owned companies geared to making profit. Much of the wealth produced by the workers is taken from them in the form of profit by the owners of private industry. Work becomes wage labour, a means of earning money to survive. As a result the worker is *alienated*, cut off from his or her work, unable to derive real satisfaction or fulfilment from work. In a capitalist society they will be alienated no matter what form of production technology they work with.

Marxist views on alienation are examined in the following passages.

The village blacksmith shop was abandoned, the roadside shoe shop was deserted, the tailor left his bench, and all together these mechanics (skilled workers) turned away from their country homes and wended their way to the cities wherein the large factories had been erected. The gates were unlocked in the morning to allow them to enter, and after their daily task was done the gates were closed after them in the evening.

Silently and thoughtfully, these men went to their homes. They no longer carried the keys of the workshop, for workshop, tools and keys belonged not to them, but to their master.

Thrown together in this way, in these large hives of industry, men became acquainted with each other, and frequently discussed the question of labour's rights and wrongs.

Terrance Powderly,
Grand Master Workman, Knights of Labour,
Thirty Years of Labour, 1889

(quoted in 'Schooling in Capitalist America' by Samuel Bowles and Herbert Gintis, Routledge & Kegan Paul, London, 1976, pp56-7)

Karl Marx believed that only in a communist society could a person experience true satisfaction and fulfilment from work. In a communist society industry is owned by the people rather than by private individuals. The wealth produced by workers is shared by everybody on the basis of 'to each according to their need'. People therefore work for society as a whole and, since they are members of society, they also work for themselves. In doing so they satisfy their own needs and also the needs of others. Work in a communist society allows people to express their basic human needs - care and humanity for others. As a result workers experience a deep satisfaction from their labour and alienation is a thing of the past.

In capitalist societies such as the USA and the countries of Western Europe, much of industry is privately owned. The owners invest capital (money) in companies in return for a share of the profits. Marx believed that this system resulted in the exploitation of workers. Wealth was produced by their labour but a part of this wealth was taken from them by the owners of industry in the form of profit. People cannot find real satisfaction by working in a system which is based on their own exploitation. In Marx's words, 'the alienated character of work for the worker appears in the fact that it is not his work but work for someone else, that in work he does not belong to himself but to another person'. As a result the worker 'does not fulfil himself in his work but denies himself, has a feeling of misery, not of wellbeing, does not develop freely a physical and mental energy, but is physically exhausted and mentally debased. The worker therefore feels himself at home only during his leisure, whereas at work he feels homeless.'

I MAKE CIRCUIT BOARDS FOR...

...ME IN HIS FACTORY. WE MAKE CIRCUIT BOARDS MAKE A PROFIT FOR...

...ME BECAUSE I OWN A SHARE OF BOTH OF THEM.

I JUST MAKE MONEY MAKE MONEY...

(adapted from 'Karl Marx: Selected Writings in Sociology and Social Philosophy' edited by T. B. Bottomore and M. Rubel, Penguin, Harmondsworth, 1963)

QUESTIONS

1. a) Who is 'the master' mentioned in the first extract? (2)
   b) Why is he referred to as 'the master'? (4)
2. Why do Marxists regard workers in capitalist society as 'wage slaves'? (5)
3. Why do Marxists argue that both craft workers and assembly line workers are alienated if they work in private industry? (4)
4. How might communism end the alienation of the worker? (5)

DESKILLING

PART 8

Deskilling means reducing the skill required to perform a task. Since the early 1970s there has been a large amount of research and debate about the question of deskilling. The following passage provides a brief introduction to this area.

In 1974 the American sociologist Harry Braverman published his ideas about deskilling. Writing from a Marxist point of view he argued that the main concern of capitalism is profit. Profits can be increased by reducing labour costs - by reducing the numbers of workers employed, by paying them less and by making them work harder. This can be done in various ways including (1) introducing new technology which replaces workers by machines (2) reducing the skill needed for work (deskilling) - unskilled workers are cheaper to employ than skilled workers (3) increasing management control in order to get more work from the workforce. Deskilled workers are easier to control because they can be easily replaced and their tasks can

be designed from above by management. Skilled workers have more power - they have greater control over their work, they cannot be easily replaced and so they can bargain more effectively with management.

Braverman argues that the history of capitalism is a history of deskilling, of building workers' skills into machines and cheapening labour by systematically reducing the skill levels required for work. The result is the 'degradation of work' - workers are degraded, they lose skills, creativity and control over their work.

Many researchers reject Braverman's view of an evil capitalist

Computer typesetting

'We must take more account of the job satisfaction element in the future of word processing. On a shared logic system such as ours, the operators are keying in bits and pieces of data dictated to them without ever seeing the finished results of their work in hard copy. We cannot regard typists as automatons; somewhere along the line technology must be applied to making the work interesting as well as efficient.'

The cooperation of the workforce is needed for efficiency. To gain this programmes of 'job enrichment' have been created with the aim of increasing interest and involvement in work. They include enlarging jobs (increasing the number of operations performed by each worker) rotating jobs (moving workers from one job to another), increasing worker participation in decisions which affect their work and 'quality circles' (small groups of workers who meet to discuss and solve production problems). At one extreme job enrichment has been seen as a con-trick to encourage workers to accept 'wage-slavery', at the other extreme it has been seen as a means of really improving the quality of workers' lives.

(adapted from 'Labour and Monopoly Capitalism' by Harry Braverman, Monthly Review Press, New York, 1974 and 'Work' by Paul Thompson in 'Developments in Sociology' Vol 2 edited by Michael Haralambos, Causeway Press, Ormskirk, 1986)

system steadily deskilling workers, grinding them underfoot and squeezing profits at their expense. However they do recognise that deskilling does occur, especially with the introduction of computer technology. More than any other form of technology it has the capacity for (1) deskilling work and (2) replacing workers. Thus computerised typesetting has made the traditional craft of compositing obsolete. As one worker said, 'It took me six years, perhaps eight, to learn how to be a good comp and operator. You could take any competent typist from out on the street and I maintain that within two months she would be doing my job.'

But computer technology does not necessarily lead to deskilling. Some workers learn new and higher level skills. A process of 'reskilling' can occur. There are examples of workers programming machines themselves and so raising the level of skill in their jobs. Nor does computer technology necessarily lead to greater efficiency. If the interest is taken out of work the result is often high labour turnover and absenteeism. Some managers are aware of this problem as the following quotation from a manager in charge of word processing at Cadbury Schweppes shows.

QUESTIONS

1. What does the term 'deskilling' mean? (2)
2. How might deskilling lead to higher profits? (4)
3. Why is computer technology a greater threat to jobs and skills than previous forms of technology? (4)
4. Simply introducing computer technology does not necessarily lead to increased efficiency. Explain with reference to the passage. (4)
5. Briefly explain how job enrichment can be seen as
   a) a con-trick (3)
   b) a means of improving the quality of workers' lives. (3)

PART 9 — INDUSTRIAL SABOTAGE

Industrial sabotage may be defined as any action aimed at the destruction of the workplace, the plant or machinery used at work or the goods produced. The following extract looks at examples of industrial sabotage.

They had to throw away half a mile of Blackpool rock last year, for, instead of the customary motif running through its length, it carried the terse injunction 'Fuck Off'. A worker dismissed by a sweet factory had effectively demonstrated his annoyance by sabotaging the product of his labour. In the Christmas rush in a

Knightsbridge store, the machine which shuttled change backwards and forwards suddenly ground to a halt. A frustrated salesman had demobilised it by ramming a cream bun down its gullet. In our researches we have been told by Woolworth's sales girls how they clank half a dozen buttons on the till simultaneously to win a few minutes' rest from 'ringing up'. Railwaymen have described how they block lines with trucks to delay shunting operations for a few hours. Materials are hidden in factories, conveyor belts jammed with sticks, cogs stopped with wire and ropes, lorries 'accidentally' backed into ditches. Electricians labour to put in weak fuses, textile workers 'knife' through carpets and farmworkers cooperate to choke agricultural machinery with tree branches.

(adapted from 'Industrial Sabotage: Motives and Meanings' by Laurie Taylor and Paul Walton in 'Images of Deviance' edited by S. Cohen, Penguin, Harmondsworth, 1971, p219)

QUESTIONS

1. How might a Marxist explain industrial sabotage in capitalist society? (4)
2. Suggest why the jamming of conveyor belts by assembly line workers is a typical example of industrial sabotage. (4)
3. a) How might a person feel after having committed an act of industrial sabotage? (3)
   b) With some reference to the extract briefly explain why they might feel this way. (4)
4. Suggest two ways, other than industrial sabotage, by which people can express dissatisfaction with their experience of work. Briefly explain your choices. (5)

10 PART — UNEMPLOYMENT AND THE MEANING OF WORK

What does work mean to people? Obviously it varies from person to person and from occupation to occupation. It may also vary according to whether a person is young, middle-aged or approaching retirement, whether or not they have dependent children, whether or not they are self-employed and so on. Despite this variation, the experience of unemployment suggests that there is a broad measure of agreement about the meaning of work. Many of the effects of unemployment seem common to all groups of unemployed people. These are examined in the following passage.

The spare time produced by unemployment is spent in bed, watching television, listening to the radio, reading and gardening. Pastimes become cheaper and less commercial - people don't have the money for expensive hobbies and nights out. Gradually 'luxuries' like holidays, a car and evenings in the pub have to be abandoned. Even such do-it-yourself hobbies like home decorating (which in the past saved money) become too expensive. The enforced 'leisure' brought about by unemployment does not compensate for the loss of work.

Unemployment is tedious and depressing. Mental and physical health suffer. People are isolated - they have less contact with friends than when they were working.

Then there is the stigma - the shame and disgrace - of unemployment. Public opinion polls show that most people see unemployment as the result of economic conditions and government policy. Yet this does not prevent individuals from feeling that unemployment is their own fault for being unqualified, too lazy, too choosy or unable to impress an employer. Even if they don't believe this, they often feel that others see them in this way.

Loss of work means a drop in social status and self-esteem. Often the unemployed feel useless and worse - a burden on the community. Practically every time they meet somebody the first question is, 'Have you found a job yet?' Admitting failure is painful. This is another reason why the unemployed often withdraw from mixing with friends and neighbours.

The severity of the effects of unemployment usually increases the longer people are out of work. Those recently unemployed tend to see themselves as 'between jobs' and 'looking for work'

Unemployed men in a Department of Health and Social Security office

rather than as part of the long-term, 'hard-core' unemployed.

The middle class unemployed often have savings and golden handshakes to soften the blow but they have further to fall than redundant manual workers. Unemployment is less common and in some ways less easy to live with in middle class communities, so much so that some people hide their situation from friends, neighbours and even their own families.

(adapted from 'Leisure' by Kenneth Roberts in 'Developments in Sociology' Volume 2, edited by Michael Haralambos, Causeway Press, Ormskirk, 1986)

QUESTIONS

1. The experience of unemployment shows what work means to people. With reference to the passage briefly outline the meaning of work. (5)
2. a) Why do people have less contact with friends when they are unemployed? (2)
   b) How might this affect them? (2)
3. With reference to the passage suggest why the growth in long-term unemployment in particular is a cause for concern. (4)
4. Why do many unemployed people feel 'useless'? (4)
5. How might the class position of the unemployed affect their experience of unemployment? (3)

11 PART THE EXTENT OF UNEMPLOYMENT

There is no agreement about the definition of unemployment. Even the government uses two different definitions. As a result official statistics on unemployment give two different totals. The following passage looks at some of the problems of defining and measuring unemployment.

Offical statistics on unemployment are based on two definitions - claimant unemployment and ILO unemployment.

Claimant unemployment This is a count of the number of people who claim unemployment related benefits. It excludes anyone who is not eligible to claim such benefits and those who, for whatever reason, do not claim the benefits to which they are entitled.

International Labour Organisation (ILO) unemployment This counts as unemployed those aged 16 and over who are without a job, are available to start work in the next two weeks, who have been seeking a job in the last four weeks or are waiting to start a job already obtained. It excludes people who want to work but, for whatever reason, have not looked for a job in the last four weeks.

Around a million people in each measure of unemployment are not included in the other. For example, in November 1995 the number of female unemployed claimants was 525,471 (4.3% of the workforce) but the ILO count was 847,000 (6.9% of the workforce). Despite such differences, as Figure 1 shows, both measures show broadly the same levels of and trends in unemployment.

As Figure 1 shows, the ILO count includes a higher number of unemployed women than the claimant count. This is because many women who are living with a partner and want work are not eligible for unemployment related income support once their unemployment benefit has finished. This is either because their partner is working or claiming, or because of the level of

Figure 1 ILO and claimant unemployment

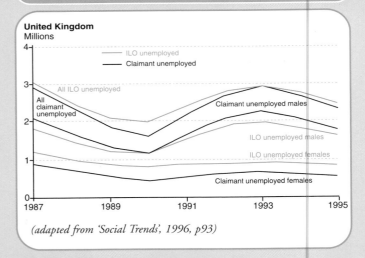

(adapted from 'Social Trends', 1996, p93)

their own or their partner's savings.

Table 1 shows people who want a job but are not included as unemployed in the ILO count. They are excluded because they either had not looked for work in the past four weeks and/or they were not available to start work in the next two weeks. Their reasons are given in the table. 'Discouraged workers' are people whose reason for not seeking work was the belief that no work was available.

Table 1 Wanting work but excluded from ILO count

Great Britain, Spring 1995, thousands				Age groups			
	All persons	Men	Women	16-24	25-34	35-49	50-59/64
Wants a job	**2,230**	**836**	**1,394**	**583**	**554**	**592**	**501**
Discouraged workers	**95**	54	41	-	12	13	62
Long-term sick/disabled	**519**	324	195	23	59	182	255
Looking after family/home	**779**	54	725	125	343	251	60
Students	**419**	217	201	349	44	23	-
Temporarily sick/disabled	**132**	74	57	15	29	44	43
Other	**287**	112	174	62	67	79	78

- equals less than 10,000

(adapted from 'Labour Market Trends' December 1995, LFS 63)

The Unemployment Unit (UU) is an independent research organisation which provides an alternative definition and measurement of unemployment. It gives an unemployment total which is around one million higher than the claimant and ILO counts. For example, in January 1996 the claimant count for unemployment was 2,310,500 (8.3% of the workforce) whereas the UU count was 3,376,500 (11.3% of the workforce).

The Unemployment Unit broadens the ILO definition of unemployment. It includes those who want work and are available to start in two weeks, but have not looked for work in the past four weeks. Many of these are women and older men and those identified in Table 1 as 'discouraged workers'.

Reducing official unemployment While the Unemployment Unit argues that government figures underestimate the extent of unemployment, other researchers see them as an overestimate. They argue that various groups should be excluded from official statistics. These include 1) claimants who are not really looking for jobs; 2) those who have jobs 'on the side' and are claiming benefit illegally; 3) 'job changers' who are out of work for four weeks or less; 4) those who have obtained a job and are waiting to start work.

The politics of unemployment Unemployment is a political issue. Governments are judged on their unemployment record which can win or lose votes. From 1979 to 1994 British governments have changed the basis of the claimant count 31 times. In nearly every case this has led to a reduction in the numbers eligible for benefits and therefore a reduction in claimant unemployment. Critics have seen these changes as an attempt by governments to artificially reduce unemployment levels in order to improve their public image.

(adapted from various issues of 'Employment Gazette', 'Labour Market Trends', 'Labour Research' and 'Unemployment Unit Statistical Briefings')

QUESTIONS

1. What are the similarities and differences shown in Figure 1 between the ILO and claimant unemployment rates and trends? (5)
2. Many of those excluded from the ILO count (see Table 1) are included in the UU count. Make out a case for including them in the ILO count. (5)
3. Look at the groups that some researchers wish to exclude from those officially defined as unemployed. Which groups would be difficult to exclude and why? (5)
4. Why have governments been criticised for changing the basis of the claimant count? (5)

WHO ARE THE UNEMPLOYED?

Unemployment is not spread evenly across the country or across social groups. The following passage provides a geographical and social map of unemployment.

Social Class

As Table 1 shows, unemployment levels are linked to social class. The lower a person's social class, the higher their chances of becoming unemployed. As previous parts have shown, the decline in the workforce in the primary and secondary sectors of the economy has steadily reduced the demand for manual workers, ie those in the lower levels of the class system.

However, the most rapid increase in unemployment in the first half of the 1990s was in white collar occupations, particularly amongst professionals and managers. Many companies are 'delayering' - removing layers of management. For example, Eastman Kodak has reduced its levels of management from 13 to 4 and British Telecom got rid of 80,000 managers between 1989 and 1993. Employment in banking reflects the pattern for much of the service sector. There was a steady rise in the numbers of banking staff throughout the 1970s and 80s reaching a peak of 444,800 in 1990. The early 1990s saw a steady decline to 371,000 in 1994. This is due to a number of factors including 'downsizing' - a policy of employing fewer people to do the same work, the increasing use of computer technology and contracting more work out.

Table 1 Unemployment and social class

Class	Level 1994 (thousands)	Rate 1994 (%)	Increase 1990-94 (thousands)	(%)
Professional	55	3.8	40	267
Intermediate	350	4.6	182	106
Skilled non-manual	400	6.7	135	51
Skilled manual	670	11.8	340	101
Partly skilled	550	13.5	255	85
Unskilled	230	14.7	97	73

(adapted from 'Times', 17.8.1994)

Gender and age

Table 2 shows unemployment by gender and age. Female unemployment rates are lower than those of males. This makes sense in terms of the trends outlined in Part 3 - a decrease in full-time jobs, particularly those filled by men, and an increase in part-time jobs, most of which have been filled by women. However, the statistics in Table 2, as with all statistics on unemployment, must be treated with caution. For example, many women who want a job are not included in official statistics.

In terms of age, the trend in recent years is to employ people in the 25-50 age group rather than younger or older people. Table 2 reflects this trend for the younger age group but not for the oldest group. However, as the following figures indicate, this is because many older people have left the workforce rather than becoming officially unemployed. In 1994, one in four men aged 55 to 59 and nearly half the men aged 60-64 were no longer in paid employment. Thirty years earlier the figures were 5% (55 to 59) and 10% (60 to 64). In recent years many men over 55 have taken early retirement, either by choice or because they have been forced to when faced with the alternative of redundancy.

Table 2 Unemployment rates: by gender and age, United Kingdom, 1995

			Percentages
Males		**Females**	
16-19	19.6	16-19	14.8
20-29	14.0	20-29	9.2
30-39	8.3	30-39	6.5
40-49	7.1	40-49	5.0
50-64	9.2	50-59	4.2
All males aged 16 and over	10.1	All females aged 16 and over	6.8

(adapted from 'Social Trends', 1996, p94)

Ethnicity

Figure 1 shows the unemployment rates of certain ethnic groups. Ethnic unemployment is particularly acute in inner city areas. For example, in Inner London in 1995, 61% of young black men aged 16 to 24 were unemployed compared with 22% of whites in the same age group. Part of the reason for the high rates of ethnic unemployment is the age and class composition of ethnic groups. Compared to the white majority, members of the ethnic groups in Figure 1 are more likely to be younger and working class. However, part of the reason for high levels of ethnic unemployment is racism, as Chapter 5 has shown.

Figure 1 Unemployment rates by ethnic group, Spring 1994

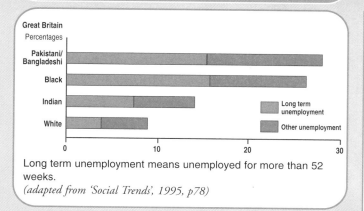

Long term unemployment means unemployed for more than 52 weeks.

(adapted from 'Social Trends', 1995, p78)

Table 3 Unemployment rates by region, United Kingdom, 1994

	Percentages
North	11.7
North West	10.2
West Midlands	9.9
Yorkshire & Humberside	9.8
South East	9.6
East Midlands	8.3
South West	7.5
East Anglia	7.4
Wales	9.4
Scotland	9.9
Northern Ireland	11.5

(adapted from 'Social Trends', 1995, p77)

Regions

Table 3 shows unemployment rates in the regions of the United Kingdom. Regional rates reflect the varying fortunes of different sectors of British industry. For example, regions which are largely dependent on heavy manufacturing industry, like shipbuilding and steelmaking, and on primary sector industry such as coalmining, have suffered most.

Within regions, the highest unemployment rates are in Inner London - in 1995 the rate in Hackney was nearly 30% and in Newham, just under 25%. Outside London, the highest rate was in Knowsley in Liverpool at nearly 19%. Most of the lower rates are found in mainly rural counties with Oxfordshire having the lowest rate - 3.5% in 1995.

(adapted from various issues of 'Social Trends', 'Employment Gazette', 'Labour Market Trends'; 'Independent on Sunday', 24.10.1993; 'Independent', 22.2.1996; statistics on employment in banking from British Bankers' Association Statistical Unit)

QUESTIONS

1. Look at Table 1.
   a) Which class has the highest rate of unemployment? (2)
   b) Which class has the highest percentage increase in unemployment? (2)
2. There are indications that the growth in jobs in the service sector is ending. What evidence in the passage supports this statement? (4)
3. When there is a decreasing demand for workers, employers first stop recruiting and then make their most recent employees redundant. Which age group will be hardest hit? Give reasons. (5)
4. Using information from every section in the passage, explain the high unemployment rate of young blacks in London. (7)

13 PART WORK, LEISURE AND FAMILY LIFE

In the early 1950s a study of the relationship between the work, leisure and family life of coal miners was conducted by Dennis, Henriques and Slaughter in the mining town of Featherstone in Yorkshire. Like a number of similar studies their research indicated that the nature of work influences leisure activities and family life. However a word of caution is necessary. Featherstone is a mining town in which miners form an occupational community. Miners who are less concentrated in occupational communities, such as those in Nottinghamshire, may well have a rather different lifestyle which is less influenced by the nature of their work. In addition, the Featherstone study was conducted in the early 1950s in a traditional working class town. The miners' lifestyle may be due as much to traditional working class subculture as to mining itself.

The second part of the following passage is a case study from the 1990s of a senior Local Authority Officer in the West Midlands. It illustrates a very different link between work, leisure and family life.

Miners at Armthorpe welfare club

Despite improvements in working conditions, coal miners believe that 'pitwork can never be other than an unpleasant dirty, dangerous and difficult job'. Many dislike and are even hostile towards their work. Nevertheless, men are proud of their status as miners. The strength and skill required for the job are seen as a reflection of the miner's manhood and they are held in high regard in the community.

Mining is a dangerous occupation with a high rate of injury and death. One man's mistake can lead to the death of others. As a result miners develop a sense of unity, of group solidarity, with their first loyalty being to their workmates. A miner's wages are partly determined by the productivity of his work group. This encourages everybody to pull their weight and cooperate as members of a team. Miners share experiences which to some extent set them apart from other workers. They work in extreme and demanding conditions which produce a high level of stress.

The leisure activities of the miners in Featherstone revolve around drinking in pubs and workingmen's clubs with their workmates. Leisure is vigorous, boisterous and frivolous with little thought given to tomorrow. In the company of their workmates miners live for the moment, 'let off steam' and spend much of their time drinking and gambling.

Miners' wives rarely work outside the home due partly to the traditional belief that a wife's place is in the home and partly to the lack of job opportunities for women in the area. Their role is mainly domestic and many are proud of their performance as housewives. Dennis, Henriques and Slaughter write, 'Housewives boast of their attention to the needs of their husbands, and of how they have never been late with a meal, never confronted a returning worker with a cold meal, never had to ask his help with household duties.' Husbands, for their part, feel that it's a 'poor do' if they do not receive this kind of attention. After work they return home to be fed, to get cleaned up, changed and rested and then they are 'off out' with their mates.

(adapted from 'Coal is our Life' by N. Dennis, F. Henriques and C. Slaughter, Eyre and Spottiswoode, London, 1956)

Tom Burton is a senior Local Government Officer in the West Midlands. He manages two busy departments and presents reports to the local council. His contract requires him to work the hours 'necessary to do the job'. This often means working evenings and weekends. The following extract from his diary covers the busy run up to Christmas.

Monday Budget meeting 6pm-8pm. Meeting overran. Too tired to eat.

Tuesday Traffic Subcommittee meeting 6pm-7pm. Home in time to play a game of scrabble with the children before their bedtime.

Wednesday Full council meeting 7pm-10pm. Dashed home for a quick meal and shower before the meeting.

Thursday Reminded Ellen (his wife) to arrive promptly at the Mayoress's 'At Home', 2.30pm-4.30pm. She's expected to circulate and make the guests feel welcome. A free evening so caught up on reading technical journals.

Friday Gave a talk in the evening to the local Architectural Society about conservation areas.

Saturday Looked round local shopping centre as shopkeepers had been complaining about inadequate parking. Ellen and the kids came along to do Christmas shopping. Ben (his son) helped to take photographs of the car parks.

Sunday Had a lie in and a walk after lunch. In-laws came for tea.

Monday Got home at 7pm. Meal in oven - still edible.

Tuesday Highways and Transportation Committee meeting 7pm-9pm. Got home at 9.30pm. Said goodnight to the kids and watched TV.

Wednesday Annual Parish Councils meeting 7pm-9.30pm. Spent most of the time listening to complaints about dog fouling and litter which are not part of my area of responsibility.

Thursday Planning Committee Meeting, 7pm-9.30pm, to discuss a new supermarket proposal. Had a drink in the local pub with the Planning Chairman and Chief Executive.

Friday Free evening at last! Caught up with news about the children's week and enjoyed a family meal.

Saturday 3.30pm, Christmas lights switched on by the Mayoress. Walked through town in the procession and went to the reception at the Kings Arms Hotel. Tea, mince pies and cream cakes, followed by Father Christmas. Rather boring, but it's all part of the job.

Sunday A lie in and lunch with the family. Went to local car boot sale as residents had been complaining about noise and parking. Took camcorder to video the situation. Ellen and kids came along. Discussed whether we both needed to go to the Mayor's sherry reception next week. Didn't want to go but decided we ought to.

(adapted from unpublished MA thesis)

QUESTIONS

1. How does the miner's work influence a) his leisure activities b) the way he sees his wife's role? (5, 5)
2. How does the Local Government Officer's work influence a) his leisure activities b) his relationship with his wife and children? (5, 5)

14 PART — WORK AND PATTERNS OF LEISURE

The British sociologist Stanley Parker argues that leisure activities are 'conditioned by various factors associated with the way people work'. He suggests that the amount of autonomy people have at work (the amount of freedom to take decisions and organise their work), the degree of involvement they find in work and level of satisfaction they derive from work are directly related to their leisure activities. Parker bases his findings on a series of interviews he conducted with bank clerks, child care officers and youth employment officers plus published material on a range of occupations studied by sociologists (including the study of coal miners outlined in Part 13). He sees the relationship between work and leisure falling into three main patterns: the *extension pattern*, the *neutrality pattern* and the *opposition pattern*.

Parker admits that 'considerably more research needs to be done' to confirm his findings. His caution is justified since more recent research indicates that the connection between work and leisure is not as close as his study suggests.

In the **extension pattern** work extends into leisure. Work and leisure activities are similar and work is a central life interest rather than family and leisure. People who follow this pattern have relatively little time for leisure activities as such. Studies of managers in the USA give a picture of all work and no play with a working week of over 60 hours. Non-work time was often spent reading trade journals or keeping fit with the aim of improving performance at work. Even when leisure was used purely for relaxation, nearly three-quarters of the managers in one survey stated that they saw 'leisure time as a refresher to enable you to do better work'. The extension pattern is associated with occupations providing high levels of autonomy, involvement and job satisfaction. Such occupations include those of managers, business people, doctors, teachers, social workers and some skilled manual workers.

In the **neutrality pattern** a fairly clear distinction is made between work and leisure. Activities in the two areas differ and family life and leisure, rather than work, form the central life interest. The neutrality pattern is associated with occupations providing a medium to low degree of autonomy, which require the use of only some of the individual's abilities and where satisfaction is with pay and conditions rather than work itself. Hours of leisure are long compared to the extension pattern and are used mainly for relaxation. Leisure is often family-centred involving activities such as the family outing. Occupations typically associated with the neutrality pattern include clerical jobs and semi-skilled manual jobs.

In the **opposition pattern** work is sharply distinguished from leisure. Activities in the two areas are very different and leisure forms the central life interest. Hours of leisure are long and used mainly to recuperate from and compensate for work. The opposition pattern is associated with occupations providing a low degree of autonomy, which require the use of only a limited range of abilities and which often produce a feeling of hostility towards work. The opposition pattern is typical of unskilled manual work, mining and distant water fishing.

(adapted from 'Work and Leisure' by Stanley Parker in 'The Sociology of Industry' edited by S.R. Parker, R. K. Brown, J. Child and M. A. Smith, George Allen & Unwin, London, 1967)

QUESTIONS

1. Which patterns do the following activities fall into? Briefly explain your answers.
   a) Having a few drinks to escape from work. (2)
   b) Wining and dining clients at a restaurant. (2)
   c) Taking the children to the zoo. (2)
2. Suggest why many teachers and social workers extend work into leisure. (3)
3. Considering the types of occupations in the neutrality pattern, suggest why work is not extended into leisure. (3)
4. Why do people whose leisure falls into the opposition pattern need to recuperate from and compensate for work? (3)
5. A survey by John Child and Brenda MacMillan of 964 British managers showed that they worked some 20 hours a week less than American managers. They used their relatively long hours of leisure for relaxation and enjoyment. Playing and watching sport, home improvement and hobbies such as photography were major leisure time activities.
   a) How can this evidence be used to question Parker's argument? (2)
   b) How can the concept of culture be used to explain the differences between British and American managers? (3)

PART 15 — LEISURE AND SOCIAL CLASS

The way people spend their leisure time is influenced by a range of factors including their class, gender, age, ethnicity, employment situation and marital status. This part looks at the influence of social class on leisure.

Leisure can be expensive. A day out in 1996 at Alton Towers, which bills itself as 'Britain's Number 1 Theme Park' costs £17.50 for adults and £13.50 for children. For a family of four this adds up to £62 which doesn't include transport, food and drink. And leisure often requires appropriate clothes and footwear, especially for young people. Names like Nike, Umbro, Adidas, Ellesse and Reebok don't come cheap. But being without them can make a real difference to people's enjoyment of leisure. The following interview with young people from low income families about what to wear on non-uniform day in school gives some idea of the importance of leisure clothes.

Interviewer	'Do you think it's important to be in fashion?'
Jenny	'Well yes. If you're not you might get picked on. People make fun of you and you get really embarrassed.'
Kate	'Like if someone should come into school in right dear Adidas trainers and someone come in in right cheap trainers.'
Janet	'Like Lorraine. Just because she's got a pair of cheap trainers called "Pony" she sometimes gets beat up.'

Poverty and leisure Poverty often excludes people from leisure activities. A study by the Child Poverty Action Group of people in Bradford living on state benefits gives the following picture.

Social life was virtually non-existent. 'We haven't had a night out for years' was a typical comment. One young woman stated, 'Being on benefit forces you into a ghetto. You've no freedom to buy a newspaper or have a night out.' People complained of not having enough money to invite friends round for a meal - 'It's very shameful when you can't treat your

Alton Towers

guests good and feed them well'. Celebrations like Christmas and birthdays present real problems. In the words of one mother, 'We've got Christmas coming up. For me that's not enjoyment, it's a nightmare. I look in the shops, looking at prices and it's a bloody nightmare.' And for most, holidays are out of the question. Children often have to miss out on school trips and outings with their friends - 'We can't afford to send the children on school trips, so they stay at home for the day'.

Home-based leisure Most leisure time is spent at home. For example, people from all social classes spend more time watching TV than any other leisure activity. Table 1 gives the hours per week spent by members of different social classes on various home-based leisure activities.

Leisure away from home Table 2 shows the most popular leisure activities away from home for members of different social classes.

Table 1 Social class and home-based leisure, 1993-94

Great Britain					Hours per week
	Social class				**All**
	AB	**C1**	**C2**	**DE**	**persons**
Watching TV	13.5	15.4	17.5	20.2	17.1
Listening to the radio	9.2	8.7	11.6	10.9	10.3
Listening to CDs, tapes or records	4.3	4.0	3.4	4.4	4.0
Reading books	5.1	4.3	3.2	3.4	3.8
Reading newspapers	3.6	3.3	3.4	3.2	3.3
Caring for pets	2.6	3.1	3.2	3.5	3.1
Gardening	2.4	2.0	2.2	1.8	2.1
Cooking for pleasure	1.8	1.8	1.8	2.0	1.9
Watching videos of TV programmes	1.6	1.4	1.7	1.9	1.7
DIY or house repair	1.6	1.6	1.7	1.4	1.6
Sewing and knitting	0.9	1.3	1.4	1.5	1.3
Reading specialised magazines	1.2	1.1	1.0	0.8	1.0

Class A: Higher managerial, administrative and professional
Class B: Intermediate managerial, administrative and professional
Class C1: Supervisory or clerical, and junior managerial, administrative, or professional
Class C2: Skilled manual workers
Class D: Semi and unskilled manual workers
Class E: State pensioners or widows (no other earners), casual or lowest grade workers, or long term unemployed

(adapted from 'Social Trends', 1995, p216)

Table 2 Social class and leisure away from home, 1993-94

Great Britain					Percentages
	Social class				**All**
	AB	**C1**	**C2**	**DE**	**persons**
Visit a public house	67	70	65	59	65
Meal in a restaurant (not fast food)	81	74	56	44	61
Drive for pleasure	50	53	45	39	46
Meal in a fast food restaurant	48	49	39	37	42
Library	57	46	32	31	39
Cinema	46	39	29	24	33
Short break holiday	41	34	28	19	29
Disco or night club	21	25	25	28	25
Historic building	41	29	19	12	23
Spectator sports event	25	24	23	18	22
Theatre	33	24	16	10	19
Museum or art gallery	34	23	14	10	19
Fun fair	12	13	15	16	14
Exhibition	24	17	10	8	14
Theme park	12	10	12	9	11
Bingo	3	6	11	17	10
Visit a betting shop	5	8	13	11	10
Camping or caravaning	9	9	10	7	9
Pop or rock concert	8	9	8	6	8
Classical concert or the opera	15	9	3	3	7
Attend an evening class	11	6	4	4	6
Circus	1	1	3	4	2

(adapted from 'Social Trends', 1995, p220)

The commercialisation of leisure Leisure is big business. For example, the Rank Organisation is involved in the film industry, the manufacture of hi-fi and video equipment, dancehalls, bowling and bingo and owns hotels, marinas and Butlins. Package holidays are a multi-million pound industry. No sooner are we over Christmas than holiday companies bombard us with ads on TV and in newspapers and magazines for the forthcoming holiday season.

People buy leisure. In this sense leisure is a commodity - something that is bought and sold. And the more money people have the greater their choice of leisure and the more they can consume.

For many people the leisure they purchase is important for their identity - their sense of who they are. The restaurants they eat in, the holidays they take, the films they watch, the hi-fi equipment they own, the clothes they wear and the drinks they consume announce to themselves and others who they are.

(adapted from various issues of 'Social Trends'; 'Hardship Britain', CPAG, London, 1992; 'Family Fortunes', CPAG, London, 1994)

QUESTIONS

1. How might peer group pressure influence young people's views of leisure clothes? (5)
2. How does poverty exclude people from normal leisure activities? (5)
3. Examine Tables 1 and 2. To what extent does class influence leisure activities? (4)
4. How does leisure contribute to a person's picture of who they are? (6)

16 PART — THE FUTURE OF LEISURE

With the development of computer technology the optimists look forward to a golden age of leisure. The 5 day, 40 hour week will be a thing of the past. Save for the occasional spell of work, people will have the freedom to enjoy a life of leisure. This will not of course happen overnight. People will have to be educated for leisure and there needs to be a large investment in sport and leisure facilities.

But, as this chapter has indicated, unemployment is not the same as leisure. There are few if any signs that the unemployed regard their situation as leisure. Work appears to provide a status, identity and sense of personal worth that leisure cannot offer.

The pessimists are forecasting an age of enforced unemployment for a large section of the population. Part of the workforce will enjoy the fruits of the new technology while the rest will be unemployed, their skills unwanted and unneeded. The following rather pessimistic note is sounded by the famous science fiction writer Arthur C. Clarke, author of *2001*.

The future of work and leisure?

In the world of the future, the sort of mindless labour that has occupied 99% of mankind for much more than 99% of its existence, will, of course, be largely taken over by machines. Yet most people are bored to death without work - even work that they don't like. In a workless world, therefore, only the highly educated will be able to flourish, or perhaps even survive. The rest are likely to destroy themselves and their environment out of sheer frustration. This is no vision of the distant future; it is already happening, most of all in the decaying cities. So perhaps we should not despise TV soap operas if, during the turbulent transition period between our culture and real civilisation, they serve as yet another opium for the masses. The drug, at any rate, is cheap and harmless, serving to kill time for those many people who like it better dead.

(quoted in 'Society Today' p1, in 'New Society', 29.11.1979)

QUESTIONS

1. What does Arthur C. Clarke mean by 'mindless labour'? (3)
2. Why are most people bored without work? (3)
3. Why does Arthur C. Clarke see education as essential for survival in a workless world? (3)
4. What events in the 'decaying cities' is Clarke referring to? (3)
5. Why does Clarke suggest that TV soap operas may have an important role to play in the 'transition period'? (4)
6. Briefly suggest what Arthur C. Clarke might mean by 'real civilisation'. (4)

CRIME AND DEVIANCE

Deviance refers to those acts which do not conform to the norms and values of a particular society. Crime refers to those activities which break the law and are subject to punishment applied by officials appointed by the state. All crime is deviant yet many deviant acts are not defined as criminal. For example, attempted suicide and alcoholism are often seen as deviant but they are not crimes in Britain today.

The chapter begins with a description of the culture of the Kalahari Bushmen showing that what is defined as normality and deviance varies from one society to another. It then looks at the problem of using crime statistics to measure the extent of crime and to identify those who commit it. Explanations of criminal behaviour are examined in terms of the relationship between crime and social class. The focus then changes. Rather than asking why people commit crime, the question becomes why certain people and certain acts come to be defined as deviant or criminal. The chapter closes with an examination of the relationship between ethnicity and crime and gender and crime.

PART 1 — DEVIANCE AND CULTURE

Crime and deviance are culturally defined. As culture changes, so do definitions of deviant and criminal activities. At certain times in Western society it was considered deviant for women to use make-up and consume alcoholic drinks in public. Today this is no longer the case. In the same way definitions of crime change over time. Sexual relations between people of the same sex were once a criminal offence in Britain. Since 1969 homosexual acts between consenting adults in private have no longer been illegal.

Different cultures have different norms and values. As a result what is considered normal and deviant will vary from one society to another. This can be seen from a comparison of our own society with that of the Bushmen of the Kalahari Desert in southern Africa. Their traditional way of life is briefly described in the following passage.

The Bushmen live in small family bands rarely numbering more than twenty people. They have a hunting and gathering economy - the men hunt and the women gather edible roots and berries. The Bushmen are nomadic - they roam from place to place in search of food and water. They have few possessions and build small dome shaped huts made of grass.

Bushmen dress in the skins of animals. Men wear only a leather loincloth, women a small leather apron and a cape made from a whole animal hide. Sometimes they wear sandals but mostly their feet are bare. Bushmen waste nothing. When they kill an antelope most of the meat is dried to preserve it and sooner or later every last bit is eaten down to the gristle inside the ears and sometimes even the hide. Blood from the kill is collected in a shallow hole lined with skin then scooped out in handfuls and drunk. Bones are cracked open for marrow and worked into arrow points to kill more antelope.

Bushmen are polygynous - a man may have two or more wives. He is allowed to have as many wives as he can afford - which depends on how well he hunts. Co-wives are often sisters. Girls marry young -

around 8 or 9 years old - to a husband in his teens. However, sexual intercourse is not permitted until the wife reaches puberty. The husband always goes to live with his wife's family. Divorce is a straightforward matter - the couple simply announce their divorce and separate.

Many Bushmen women have decorative scars on their foreheads and thighs. The cuts are made while they are young

Bushman hunter

Bushman family

with a knife or an axe blade, then charcoal is rubbed in. One woman explained that it was worth the pain - she had been extremely ugly and the scars had improved her looks.

Bushmen rarely fight with each other and go to great lengths to avoid quarrels and disagreement. In particular they try to prevent jealousy and for this reason the few possessions they have are constantly circulating round the group. No one keeps a good knife for long, even though they may really want it, because they will become the object of envy. Their culture insists that food, water and material possessions are shared. Without this they may not survive the famines and droughts of the Kalahari Desert.

(adapted from 'The Harmless People' by Elizabeth M. Thomas, Penguin, Harmondsworth, 1969)

QUESTIONS

1. What norms of dress in Bushmen society would be viewed as deviant in Western society? (3)
2. The Bushmen would consider some of our eating habits extremely wasteful. Briefly suggest why. (2)
3. If English parents behaved like Bushmen parents they might well be taken to court by the National Society for the Prevention of Cruelty to Children. Why? (2)
4. What aspects of marriage and divorce among the Bushmen would be defined as illegal in the UK? Briefly explain why they would break the law. (5)
5. Why would many of our norms and values regarding property be considered immoral and deviant by the Bushmen? Give examples in your answer. (4)
6. Briefly outline why certain aspects of Bushmen culture make sense in a desert environment. (4)

2 PART — OFFICIAL CRIME STATISTICS

Each year the Home Office publishes statistics on crime for England and Wales. They are compiled from information provided by local police forces. How accurate are these statistics? The following passage attempts to answer this question.

Figure 1 shows the total number of crimes in England and Wales recorded by the police from 1876 to 1995. Since the mid-1950s, apart from minor short-term falls, the crime rate has risen sharply. However, as this passage shows, the statistics on which Figure 1 is based cannot be accepted at face value.

Figure 1 Crimes recorded by the police 1876-1995

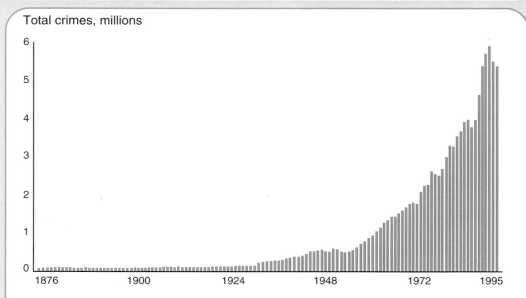

Total crimes, millions

(adapted from 'Criminal Statistics' by M. Maguire in M. Maguire et al (eds) 'The Oxford Handbook of Criminology', Clarendon Press, Oxford, 1994, p258 and 'Guardian' 27.3.96)

Figure 2 Reasons for not reporting crime

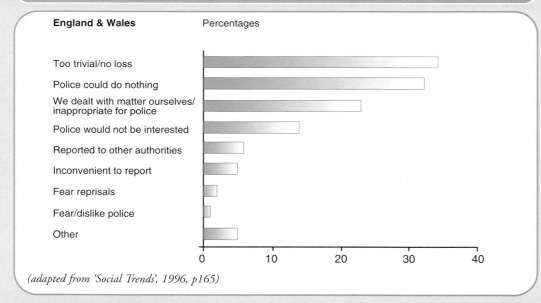

England & Wales   Percentages

Too trivial/no loss

Police could do nothing

We dealt with matter ourselves/inappropriate for police

Police would not be interested

Reported to other authorities

Inconvenient to report

Fear reprisals

Fear/dislike police

Other

(adapted from 'Social Trends', 1996, p165)

Reasons for not reporting crime Over 80% of crime recorded by the police comes from reports by the public. But there are many occasions when crime is not reported to the police. People might be too ashamed or too shocked to report an offence, as in cases of rape. They might be too frightened to approach the police for fear of reprisal, as in cases of assault. They may feel the crime is too trivial to bother the police, as in cases of vandalism where a window is smashed or a garden fence broken. They may wish to protect the offender, as in cases of domestic violence where a woman does not report she has been beaten by her partner. They may think it's not worth reporting a crime as there's little the police can do about it, as in cases of burglary or bicycle theft. They may feel nobody will believe them, as in cases of child abuse. And finally, they may not even know they've been a victim of crime, as in cases of cheque card fraud where money is stolen from a person's bank account without their knowledge.

Figure 2 shows reasons for not reporting crime from the 1994 British Crime Survey, a large scale survey based on a sample of 14,500 people.

Changes in reporting crime One of the reasons for the apparent increase in certain crimes is simply that people are more willing to report them to the police. Take rape, for example. The total of offences reported to the police rose from 1,200 in 1980 to 5,039 in 1994. At least part of this increase is due to a greater willingness to report cases. A number of reasons have been suggested for this. Increased police sensitivity - police officers are now specially trained to deal with rape victims; changes in attitudes - victims are less likely to feel that they'll be blamed for the offence; more publicity such as media coverage of so-called 'date rape' in the 1990s.

Part of the increase in reporting crime is due to the increase in insurance cover. In 1983, 45% of theft and damage incidents were covered by insurance, in 1991 50%. In order to claim on insurance, such cases must be reported to the police. This accounts for the high rate of reporting for car crime - it is estimated that 98% of cases are reported.

Police recording practices Only about 40% of the offences reported to the police are actually recorded by them. Often crimes are not recorded because they are seen as too trivial. Variations in crime rates between different areas may be due to differences in police recording practices. For example, in 1981 Nottinghamshire appeared to be the most criminal county in the country. However, this was due to the fact that the Nottinghamshire force was much more likely to record crimes involving £10 or less than other police forces.

If several offences are committed, the police often record only the most serious. This not only reduces the number of crimes recorded but also makes certain crimes appear less significant. For example, domestic violence often takes place over long periods of time yet only one particular incident might be officially recorded.

Police priorities The number and type of offences discovered by the police themselves will depend on their priorities. These will determine the crimes they decide to target. Rises and falls in particular crimes may therefore reflect police priorities rather than any change in the level of those crimes. Mary Tuck, former head of research at the Home Office, gives the following example.

'The *Daily Mail* once had a headline: SEXUAL OFFENCES UP 10 PER CENT. So I did a breakdown. 10% meant 1,300 extra offences. Of these, 50% were between consenting males. Of these, 30% were in Slough. I thought, what's suddenly happening in Slough? Then I find all these extra offences are from one particular public lavatory, which accounts for the whole bloody lot of them. So you do have to handle figures with care.'

Crimes without victims People often report crimes to the police because they are victims of those crimes - they have been burgled, assaulted and so on. But many crimes are so-called 'crimes without victims'. Tax fraud provides an example. In cases of false declaration of income to the Inland Revenue or false VAT returns to Customs and Excise, there is no victim as such. Tax fraud is often difficult to detect. And, when discovered, it is often dealt with 'administratively' rather than reported to the police. This means, for example, that the Inland Revenue will come to an arrangement with the individual concerned for the repayment of tax. The police will not be involved. As a result official statistics underestimate the extent of crimes without victims.

Cautions and convictions Statistics compiled by the police give an official account of the extent of crime. Statistics compiled from police cautions (people who are cautioned for an offence but not charged) and from court records provide an official account of those responsible for crime. These figures show that, compared to the population as a whole, those cautioned or convicted are more likely to be male, young and working class. But, only 1 in 10 offences recorded by the police results in a caution or a conviction. And only 2% of known crime ends in a conviction. Given this, it is very unlikely that those who are officially responsible for committing crime are representative of those who actually commit criminal offences.

(adapted from 'Criminal Statistics' by M. Maguire in M. Maguire et al (eds) 'The Oxford Handbook of Criminology', Clarendon Press, Oxford, 1994 and 'Independent', 10.10.1993)

QUESTIONS

1. Why might people *not* report the following crimes to the police?
   a) child abuse b) assault in the school playground
   c) theft of garden tools d) violence between a married or cohabiting couple. (8)
2. A rise in the number of arrests for prostitution in a particular police authority does not necessarily mean a rise in prostitution. Explain why not. (4)
3. At least part of the rising crime rate may be due to a greater willingness to report crime. Explain with examples. (4)
4. Why should we be cautious of the picture of the 'typical criminal' provided by official statistics? (4)

3 PART — ALTERNATIVE CRIME STATISTICS

As Part 2 has shown, there are serious problems with official crime statistics. In response to these problems a number of alternative ways of measuring crime have been developed. Two such measures - victim studies and self-report studies - are examined in the following passage.

Victim studies

The British Crime Survey (BCS) has been carried out five times from 1982 to 1994 with the aim of measuring crime in England and Wales in the year before the survey. The 1994 BCS was based on a representative sample of 14,500 people aged 16 and over. They were asked if they had been victims of particular crimes and whether or not they had told the police about them. Figure 1 summarises part of the results of the 1994 survey. It shows, for example, that in 1993 there were over 7 million 'acquisitive crimes', over 3 million of which were not reported to the police.

The BCS does not claim to provide a complete picture of crime. However, for the offences it covers, it does claim to give a more accurate figure than police statistics and to provide a more accurate indication of trends in crime. For example, from 1981 to 1993 BCS figures show a 77% rise in crime compared with police figures of 111%.

There are, however, problems with victim studies. As the BCS researchers admit, many crimes such as fraud, crimes against businesses and drug offences cannot be covered in a household survey. They also point to the problems of faulty memories and people's reluctance to talk about their experience as victims.

Figure 1 The 1994 British Crime Survey

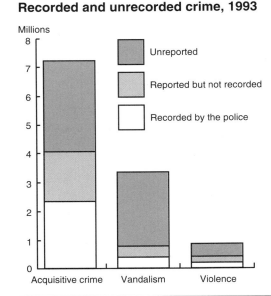

Recorded and unrecorded crime, 1993

Millions

Legend:
- Unreported
- Reported but not recorded
- Recorded by the police

(x-axis categories: Acquisitive crime, Vandalism, Violence)

Acquisitive crime	Burglary; all vehicle and bicycle theft from the person.
Vandalism	Against household property and vehicles.
Violence	Wounding and robbery.

(adapted from 'Research Findings' 14, Home Office Research and Statistics Department, September 1994)

countries. Compared to official statistics, they revealed a much higher level of middle class delinquency.

There are, however, problems with self-report studies. People are usually asked about a limited range of crimes, for example burglary and street crimes rather than domestic violence or fraud. And there is the problem of whether or not they are telling the truth. They may be too ashamed, too distrustful or too frightened to admit to certain crimes. Or they may boast about crimes they have not committed. Various tests have been carried out to check the results ranging from lie detector tests to questioning respondents' friends about the crimes they claim to have committed. These checks suggest that about 80% of those who reply are telling the truth. Despite the problems with self-report studies, they do reveal more offenders than those indicated by police cautions and court convictions.

Sociological research

Although sociological studies do not usually provide alternatives to official statistics, they do offer considerable evidence to question the official view of the typical offender. For example, a number of studies have shown that young working class males are more likely than any other group to be observed by the police, more likely to be stopped, questioned and arrested, more likely to be sent for trial, to be found guilty and to be given a jail sentence. And as a result they are more likely to become an official statistic.

(adapted from 'Research Findings' 14, Home Office Research and Statistics Department, September 1994 and 'Sociology in Focus' by Paul Taylor et al, Causeway Press, Ormskirk, 1995)

For example, many people don't want to talk about their experience as a victim of a sexual assault or domestic violence. In most victim studies 20-25% of those asked to take part refuse - the response rate in the 1994 BCS was 77%. Their refusal may well affect the results. However, for the types of crime it measures, most researchers believe that the BCS provides more accurate figures than those based on police records.

Self-report studies

Self-report studies are based on questionnaires or interviews which ask people to report the crimes they have committed. The results suggest that most of us have committed one or more crimes at some stage in our lives. They also cast doubt on the picture of the 'typical criminal' presented by official statistics. Stephen Box examined 40 self-report studies on delinquency (the crimes of young people) from a number of different

Stop-and-search

QUESTIONS

1. What are the problems with police statistics indicated by Figure 1? (4)
2. Why are victim studies not suitable for gathering information about certain types of crime? (4)
3. a) Self-report studies provide a valuable alternative to official statistics. Suggest why. (4)
   b) What types of crime might people be unlikely to admit to in self-report studies? (3)
4. Why do the police focus their attention on young working class males? (5)

4 PART — WHITE COLLAR CRIME

Edwin Sutherland who pioneered the study of white collar crime defines it as 'crime committed by persons of respectability and high social status in the course of their occupations'. It includes factory owners breaking health and safety laws, council officials taking bribes from building firms in return for contracts, lawyers fabricating evidence for the benefit of their clients and accountants 'cooking the books' and embezzling money from their employers.

The following passage begins with three case studies, then takes a more general look at white collar crime.

Bribery

Gordon Foxley retired from the Ministry of Defence in 1984. For the next ten years he led a life of luxury - a £450,000 six-bedroom mansion backing on to Henley golf course in Oxfordshire plus eight other properties, two with swimming pools, a Rolls Royce, a Jaguar and several Range Rovers. In December 1993 he was sentenced to 12 months imprisonment for bribery offences.

Foxley had received millions of pounds in backhanders for awarding Ministry of Defence arms contracts to firms in Italy, Norway and Germany. Most of this money is believed to be still hidden in Swiss bank accounts in Geneva. In Blackburn, in Lancashire, 450 workers at the Royal Ordnance factory blame Foxley for the loss of their jobs. They made fuses. Foxley, in return for bribes, gave the contracts for fuses to overseas firms.

(adapted from 'Independent', 27.5.1994)

Insider dealing

In 1988 Mecca Leisure planned to make a bid of £580 million to take over Pleasurama. Samuel Montagu, a merchant bank in the City of London was advising Mecca. One of its employees told a friend working for Morgan Grenfell, another merchant bank, about the intended takeover. The friend then passed on this information to an employee of Lazard Investors. This person immediately purchased 15,000 Pleasurama shares. When news of Mecca's intended takeover was made public, Pleasurama shares jumped from 34p to 260p giving a profit of £9,000 on the 15,000 shares purchased. This only came to light because the compliance officer at Morgan Grenfell tape recorded the telephone calls of those involved.

The dealings described above are

Gordon Foxley   Foxley's house in Henley

illegal. They are known as insider dealing and involve the use of confidential information for personal gain.

(adapted from 'Observer', 21.8.1988)

Safety at work

Nearly every coal miner in Logan County, West Virginia can name a friend or family member who is suffering from or has been killed by black lung. Black lung is caused by coal dust. Reducing the dust to a safe level in the mines is an expensive business. However, levels are fixed by law and federal inspectors are employed to enforce the law.

According to the United Mine Workers of America (the miners' union) more than 500 companies at 847 mines had tampered with the filters of pumps designed to test for dust content in the air. Last week 33 coal companies and 41 executives pleaded guilty to falsifying test results. They face fines of up to $7 million.

'The system is so easy to beat, it's a joke,' says Larry Bledsoe, a retired miner from Logan County. He says that testing devices were regularly placed in areas free of dust, far from where the miners worked. Some devices were even kept inside plastic bags and lunch boxes to ensure clean samples.

(adapted from 'Time', 4.11.1991)

An American miner suffering from black lung breathing oxygen

White collar crime

White collar crimes are difficult to detect. Many are 'crimes without victims'. In cases of bribery, both parties involved see themselves as gaining from the arrangement, both are liable to prosecution and neither, therefore, is likely to report the offence. Many white collar crimes, even if detected, do not come to court and so escape public attention. In the case of embezzlement, banks or building societies may come to a private arrangement with the staff concerned. Offenders may be sacked and given time to pay back the money they have stolen. They escape prosecution which avoids publicity and preserves public confidence in the good name of their former employer. Violations of health and safety laws rarely result in prosecution. Usually inspectors simply notify a firm that a particular matter 'requires attention'. Misconduct by professionals such as doctors or lawyers is often dealt with behind closed doors by their professional associations. Usually they are reprimanded, in exceptional cases their licence to practice is withdrawn. In most instances the public never hears about the offence and the good name of the profession is maintained. In cases of tax evasion the offence often results in nothing more than an 'official demand' for payment. The matter is neatly summarised by Willie Sutton, an American bank robber, who stated, 'Others accused of defrauding the government of thousands of dollars merely get a letter from a committee in Washington asking them to come in and talk it over. Maybe it's justice but it's puzzling to a guy like me.'

When suspected white collar criminals are apprehended and brought to court they are treated rather differently from other defendants. Sutherland gives the following reasons for this. Firstly, judges have a similar social background to many white collar criminals. They tend not to think of politicians, businessmen and professionals as 'criminal types'. They often hand out lenient sentences feeling that only light pressure is needed for reform. Secondly, compared to the burglar and the mugger, white collar criminals are not considered to be a danger to the public. They are therefore more likely to be fined or put on probation. In this way they escape prison and the stigma it brings and can more easily return to normal life. Thirdly, the victims of white collar crimes are not seen to be harmed as seriously as the victims of many other crimes. If an accountant has been defrauding a building society the loss to each individual depositor may be tiny. Fourthly, the media tends not to portray white collar crime as serious. Indeed it is sometimes presented in a sympathetic light. For example when VAT inspectors 'raid' a business person's home they can appear as the 'villains of the piece'. Sutherland suggests that mass media portrayal of white collar crime is influenced by the fact the media are owned by business people who may themselves break the law.

(adapted from '"Is White Collar Crime" Crime?' by Edwin H. Sutherland in 'The Sociology of Crime and Delinquency' edited by M.E. Wolfgang, L. Savitz and N. Johnston, John Wiley and Sons, New York, 1962 and 'Sociology of Deviant Behaviour' by Marshall B. Clinard, Holt, Rinehart & Winston, New York, 1974)

QUESTIONS

1. Many white collar crimes are described as 'crimes without victims'. Is this a fair description of the crimes in the three case studies? (5)
2. Why is white collar crime often difficult to detect? (5)
3. Why are many white collar crimes dealt with 'out of court'? (4)
4. Why are many white collar criminals treated fairly leniently by the courts? (6)

WORKING CLASS CRIME

PART 5

A number of sociological theories have been developed to explain working class crime. The following passage examines one such theory put forward by the American sociologist Albert Cohen.

Before Cohen developed his theory one of the standard explanations for working class crime went as follows. In Western society a high value is placed on individual achievement and materialism. The successful person reaches the top of their chosen career, lives in a large, detached house, drives an expensive car and has a substantial bank balance. However, relatively few members of the working class have the opportunity to achieve this kind of success. Many have few educational qualifications and work in dead-end jobs with little or no opportunity for promotion and advancement. Their way to the top is largely blocked. As a result there is greater pressure placed on them to find alternative ways of becoming successful. Crime offers one such way. A bank robbery can provide all the trappings of success.

This theory does help to explain certain crimes such as burglary and robbery which can result in material gain. But consider the following example taken from a study of a teenage gang in Glasgow.

The lads burst into the reading room in a public library. Dan and Bill began setting fire to the newspapers on display while Tim and some of the others pushed books off tables and emptied the shelves of encyclopedias and reference books. Dave tried to set fire to the newspapers which old age pensioners were reading. On the way out the boys punched and kicked an attendant in a green uniform. This was a source of great amusement and they could hardly run for laughing.

It is difficult to see how this incident can be explained by the theory outlined above. It involved no material gain - the boys stole neither money nor property. Official statistics suggest that this type of crime is committed mainly by young working class males. Albert Cohen offers the following explanation.

Many crimes appear, at first sight, to be motiveless - there seems to be no sensible or practical reason for them. Even when theft is involved, the articles are sometimes of little or no value to the thieves. A group of teenagers may steal light-bulbs from a shop and run down a busy street smashing them as they go. Cohen sees this type of activity as stealing 'for the hell of it'. There is an enjoyment of the discomfort it produces for others, a delight in defying the rules of society. It involves spite and malice, contempt and ridicule, challenge and defiance.

Cohen begins his explanation in much the same way as the theory which began this passage. With low educational qualifications, dead-end jobs, or no jobs at all, the road to the top is blocked for many working class boys. In terms of society's standards their status is low and as a result they experience **status frustration** - they are frustrated and dissatisfied with their status. Rather than

Vandalism

turning to crime in an effort to be successful in material terms, they look to crime as a means of gaining status and prestige. Thus the successful thief gains respect from other members of his group, the joy rider is highly regarded by his peers, the good fighter is admired by his friends. A **delinquent subculture** has been created which turns many of the norms and values of the wider society upside down. Bad becomes good. In terms of this subculture a person can achieve something, he can be successful, at least in the eyes of his peers. The main motive for crime now becomes prestige rather than material gain. In this way the problem of status frustration is at least partly solved. At the same time crime offers the chance to hit back at the wider society which has denied many working class boys the opportunity to become successful.

(adapted from 'Delinquent Boys' by Albert K. Cohen, The Free Press, Glencoe, 1955 and 'A Glasgow Gang Observed' by James Patrick, Eyre Methuen, London, 1973, p77)

QUESTIONS

1. Why does the explanation of working class crime given in the first paragraph fail to explain the behaviour of the Glasgow boys? (4)

2. Briefly suggest how the types of crime described by Cohen can be seen as 'the D stream's revenge'? (4)

3. a) What is status frustration? (2)
   b) Why are working class boys more likely to experience status frustration than middle class boys? (3)
   c) How does the delinquent subculture help to solve the problem of status frustration? (3)
   d) In view of your previous answer, suggest why the types of crimes discussed by Cohen are often committed by groups or gangs. (4)

6 PART — LABELLING THEORY (1)

A large body of sociological research has been concerned with explaining why people commit criminal acts. Cohen's explanation of working class crime in Part 5 is an example of this approach. Labelling theory starts from a different viewpoint. It asks how and why certain people and certain acts come to be defined as deviant or criminal.

Defining an act as deviant or criminal is not a simple, straightforward process. Take the act of nudity in Western society. Nudity in the bedroom between husband and wife is usually considered normal. Should a stranger enter the room then continued nudity in his or her presence would be seen as deviant. Yet in some situations such as nudist camps or certain holiday beaches nudity in the presence of strangers would be considered perfectly normal by those present. A spectator at a cricket match who 'streaked' across the pitch might be viewed as a 'bit of a lad' but dressed in a mackintosh and exposing himself on a street corner he would probably be regarded as 'some kind of pervert'. He might be arrested for indecent exposure and charged with a criminal offence.

Thus there is nothing normal, deviant or criminal about the act of nudity. It all depends on how others interpret, define and label the act. Whether or not it is defined as deviant will depend on who commits the act, when and where it is committed, who observes it and the interaction between the various people involved.

Lords cricket ground

A Spanish beach

This type of reasoning led to the development of **labelling theory** by the American sociologist Howard Becker. He argues that deviance and crime are simply acts which are labelled as such. In his words, 'The deviant is one to whom the label has successfully been applied; deviant behaviour is behaviour that people so label'. This leads to questions which previous approaches to crime and deviance had not fully considered. In particular, why is there a tendency for certain types of people and certain kinds of activities to be labelled as deviant? To answer this question we must examine those who define others as deviant. Thus with respect to crime we must look at the ways in which police, probation officers and the courts define crime and criminals.

In an important study of probation officers in California, Aaron V. Cicourel tried to discover why some boys but not others were defined as delinquents. It was the probation officer's job to decide whether or not to charge boys who had been arrested, with a criminal offence. Cicourel found that this decision was influenced by the officers' view of the 'typical delinquent'. In terms of this view a delinquent was likely to come from a broken home, have a poor school record, reject authority, belong to an ethnic minority group, come from a low income background and live in an inner city area. If a boy's background corresponds to this picture he is more likely to be charged with a criminal offence, and, if found guilty, labelled as a delinquent. By comparison, the middle class white boy is more likely to be warned and released without charge. He does not fit the picture of the 'typical delinquent'. In addition his parents with their 'respectable' background are often able to convince the probation officer that their child's act was not really delinquent

and was excusable - he was ill; under strain; he got in with a bad crowd; it's not his usual behaviour; he's really sorry for what he's done; he's got a bright future to look forward to; and so on.

In this respect a delinquent is a person who is defined as such. It's not so much what he's done but the way others define both him and his actions. Whether or not a person is labelled as deviant depends on the interactions and negotiation that takes place between those involved.

(adapted from 'Sociology: Themes and Perspectives', 4th edition by M. Haralambos and M. Holborn, Collins Educational, London, 1995)

QUESTIONS

1. Briefly state why the definition of an act as deviant is not simple and straightforward. Refer to the pictures in your answer. (5)
2. A person kills another person. Examine the various ways in which this action might be defined. (5)
3. You are caught taking goods out of a supermarket without having paid for them. How might you avoid being seen as a thief? (5)
4. In view of Cicourel's study it is not surprising that official statistics show that most delinquents come from working class backgrounds. With reference to the passage explain why this is so. (5)

LABELLING THEORY (2)

The previous passage looked at how and why certain people are defined as deviant. This passage considers the effects that such labelling may have on their lives.

A label defines an individual as a certain kind of person. It is a 'master status' in the sense that it overshadows all the other statuses possessed by an individual. If a person is labelled as criminal, mentally ill or gay such labels tend to override his status as father, husband, worker, friend and neighbour. The deviant label becomes the dominant status. Others tend to respond to him in terms of the label and assume that he has the characteristics associated with the label. Thus if a person is labelled a thief, behaviour which was once seen as normal - a late night, a new video recorder, a change of car - may well be seen in a new light.

A person's self-concept, the way they see themselves, comes largely from the way others respond to them. Labelling may well produce a self-fulfilling prophecy - people will tend to see themselves in terms of the label and act accordingly (see Chapter 10, Part 8 for a discussion of the self-fulfilling prophecy). There

are a number of possible stages in this process.

First, a person is publicly labelled as deviant. This may lead to rejection by family and friends, they may lose their job and be forced out of the neighbourhood. This may encourage further deviance. For example, drug addicts may turn to crime to support their habit since employers may refuse to give them a job. Those labelled as deviant may seek out others in the same situation. They provide understanding and support since they share the same problems. Within this group a deviant subculture may develop in which a deviant lifestyle is a major concern. This can be seen in certain gay communities particularly in the United States. The self-fulfilling prophecy has now come to pass. Those forced into 'deviant communities' now see themselves as different from the wider society and act accordingly.

This process is not inevitable. Drug addicts do give up their

A street fair in the gay district of San Francisco

habit and re-enter conventional society; ex-convicts do get jobs and return to mainstream society. However, once labelled, there is pressure on the individual to follow the route described in the previous paragraph - there is pressure for the label to stick.

(adapted from 'Sociology: Themes and Perspectives', 4th edition, by M. Haralambos and M. Holborn, Collins Education, London, 1995)

QUESTIONS

1. Why is a label sometimes described as a 'master status'? (3)
2. How might labelling theory help us to understand some of the problems faced by ex-convicts? (4)
3. One pupil has been labelled as a troublemaker. Another is seen as well-behaved. Both do the following things:
   - arrive late for a lesson
   - talk when they are supposed to be working in silence
   - fail to hand in their homework.
   a) Bearing in mind the way the pupils are seen, how might teachers interpret the behaviour of each? (4)
   b) What effect might the teachers' reactions have on the progress of the two pupils in school? (4)
4. People in 'deviant' communities' sometimes re-define their deviance as a problem of the wider society. Thus gays often argue that the so-called 'problem of homosexuality' is a problem created by heterosexuals (non-gays).
   a) What do they mean by this? (2)
   b) What justification is there for this argument? (3)

PART 8 — MORAL PANICS

If we believe everything the media tells us, then there are times when the moral fibre and social fabric of the nation are seriously threatened. Muggers, child abusers, drug addicts, football hooligans and even lone parents have been singled out as threats to our way of life. At times, concern about these groups appears to reach the level of panic. Sociologists use the phrase *moral panic* to describe this level of public concern.

Child abuse In the USA in the 1980s, billboards on roadsides advised motorists to GUARD YOUR PAPOOSE FROM SEXUAL ABUSE! A free *Spiderman* comic was distributed to all children revealing that Spiderman had been sexually abused as a child. A robot called Officer Mac called on schools telling pupils how to avoid being sexually molested. Bookshops were full of titles on the same topic - for infants, *Red Flag, Green Flag People*, a colouring book warning about 'dangerous strangers'; for older children, *My Very Own Book About Me* teaching how to avoid sexual abuse without fear or embarrassment.

Child abuse also became a national concern in Britain during the 1980s. There were highly publicised cases of children being removed from parents suspected of abusing them. Judging from stories in newspapers and magazines and broadcasts on radio and TV it appeared that child abuse had reached crisis proportions. And then, all of a sudden, it ceased to be newsworthy. The panic was over.

Football hooliganism Moral panics usually have the following elements. Football hooliganism, which became a moral panic in the 1980s, will be used to illustrate them.

- An activity or group is identified as a threat to society.
- The group is stereotyped and stigmatised - football hooligans are 'animals', 'savages', 'morons'.
- The cause of the 'problem' is presented at best in terms of simplistic half-truths, at worst in terms of plain untruths - football hooliganism is due to a decline in moral standards, to a lack of discipline, to drink and so on.
- The 'problem' is exaggerated, blown up out of all proportion and the media stirs up public indignation. During the European Championship of 1988 headlines referring to the behaviour of football supporters included, 'World War III' (*Sun*) and 'Yobs Plot War' (*Star*). Demands were made for 'action' against the hooligans, for the police and courts to 'get tough'.
- The powers that be often stamp down hard in response to public demand - stiffer sentences for hooligans, fines for football clubs whose supporters misbehave.
- And this response can make worse the very problem it was designed to stamp out, a process known as the amplification of deviance. According to some fans, they became more violent in response to what they saw as increasing and unjustified police violence.

A golden age Moral panics are often based on the view that the problem is new, that it didn't exist in the past. People look

Switzerland 2 England 1, Basle 1981

Ages - lepers were accused of poisoning the wells after being bribed by Jews. This led to the slaughter of Jews across Europe.

Closing off debate Moral panics often look for simple solutions and people to blame. Thus the panic over ecstasy in the mid 1990s blamed 'the evil pushers' (*Sun*) and saw the solution as 'an even tougher crackdown on the pushers' (*Mirror*). Caught up in a moral crusade, the media has little time or inclination to consider alternative and often unpopular solutions. Think about the following view put forward by Mary Tuck, former head of research at the Home Office. Asked whether she would decriminalise drugs, she replied:

'Oh, without doubt. It's precisely the same question as with prohibition (the prevention by law of the manufacture and sale of alcoholic drinks) in the 1920s. Look at America. You create a gang culture in which all exchange is at the point of the gun. The natural pricing mechanism of the market is destroyed. You have prostitution, burglary, house-breaking, all to finance the artificially high price of the commodity. You destroy South American countries, you create an intolerable burden of enforcement costs which no society can afford. In America, the inner cities are totally destroyed and handed over to criminals, all to protect the price of crack and heroin.'

(adapted from 'Hooligan: A History of Respectable Fears' by G. Pearson, Macmillan, London, 1983; 'A Panic over Child Abuse' by N. Tucker, 'New Society', 18.10.1985; 'Independent on Sunday', 10.10.1993; 'Moral Panic' by S. Platt, 'New Statesman & Society', 24.11.1995)

back to a 'golden age', the 'good old days' when it was 'safe to walk the streets' and 'people knew right from wrong'. But there is nothing new about many of the 'problems' and the moral panics which surround them. In *Hooligan: A History of Respectable Fears*, Geoffrey Pearson looks at moral panics based on violent street crime from Victorian times to the 1970s. He finds that 'for generations Britain has been plagued by the same fears and problems' yet each generation thinks they're new. In 1843 Lord Ashley stated in the House of Commons, 'The morals of children are tenfold worse than formerly'. His statement has been echoed down the ages to the present as each generation compares the morality of its day to a mythical golden age of yesterday.

Scapegoating Moral panics often lead to scapegoating (see Chapter 5, Part 11). Certain groups are selected and blamed for the panic of the moment - Jews for the problems of Nazi Germany, gay men for AIDS, teenage mothers for the rise in lone parent families, ethnic minorities for street crime and so on. The ideal scapegoat is a) different b) unpopular c) in the minority and d) relatively defenceless. For example, lepers and Jews were blamed for the Black Death in Europe in the Middle

QUESTIONS

1. Moral panics are often based on fear. Discuss using examples. (4)
2. How can moral panics amplify (create more) deviance? (4)
3. Explain, using examples, why particular groups are scapegoated in moral panics. (4)
4. Why do people often look back to a 'golden age'? (4)
5. Why are solutions, such as that put forward by Mary Tuck, often ignored during moral panics? (4)

9 PART CRIME AND ETHNICITY

In recent years the media has given considerable attention to the subject of ethnicity and crime. It has focused on what has been seen as the link between 'street crime', ethnicity and the inner city. The following passage looks at some aspects of this question.

In July 1995 Sir Paul Condon, Commissioner of the Metropolitan Police, claimed that most street robberies or muggings in London were committed by young black men. He stated: 'It is a fact that very many of the perpetrators of mugging are very young black people who have been excluded from school and/or are unemployed.' Metropolitan Police statistics indicate that in some areas of London more than 80% of muggings were committed by blacks. Here are some of the reactions to Sir Paul's statement.

- A spokesman for the Black Police Association said: 'This will reaffirm the racist belief that all black people are criminals. We know that white people are disproportionately involved in burglary yet there is no mention of this as being a *white* problem.'

- Black MPs were angry. Bernie Grant MP said: 'People will just think that every young black person is a mugger because the Metropolitan Police Commissioner says so.'

Paul Boateng MP added: 'You can produce the same facts that show that the overwhelming majority of city fraud is committed by white, middle-aged, upper class males. Are we going to have specific initiatives geared towards that sector of the community?'

- Jock Young, Professor of Criminology at Middlesex University states: 'It's terribly easy to get the wrong end of the stick. This is a poverty issue, not a race issue. Mugging is carried out by young alienated inner city males, poor males. Therefore where you have a large black population which is poor you are bound to get a high proportion of street robberies occurring. So in London it would be blacks, and in Glasgow it would be whites. The racial thing is a red herring.'

Unemployment statistics support Jock Young's view. In 1995, 61% of black males aged 16-24 in London were unemployed compared to 22% of white males in the same age group. Probation officers in London state that nearly all the young muggers they deal with are unemployed.

Stop-and-search
Between April 1993 and April 1994, 42% of those stopped and searched by the police in London were from ethnic minorities - about twice their proportion of the population. According to Chief Superintendent David Gilbertson, 'Most people stopped and searched are from lower social classes - they are young, they are unemployed and unfortunately black people are disproportionately affected'.

Between 30% and 40% of all arrests come from stop-and-search. The police stop people they believe are behaving 'suspiciously'. The behaviour of young blacks often appears suspicious to white policemen. Paul Harrison provides the following account of why people are stopped from his study of Hackney, an inner city area in London. Four policemen give their reasons.

PC Rod Bateman 'Anything out of the ordinary. It's the sixth sense you pick up.'

PC Colin Dryden 'They say the hairs on the back of your neck stick up. I'd stop someone acting suspiciously in house doorways, near cars, or at bus-stops.'

PC Paul Wilson 'Any younger blacks in a Jewish street, that would draw my attention.'

PC Simon Herrema 'In the early hours of the morning, we'd stop almost anyone walking the streets doing anything out of the ordinary. If we see a couple of young lads, white or black, driving a car at 2 in the morning, it's always worth while stopping them.'

Paul Harrison gives the following summary of the relationship between young blacks and white policemen.
'It is an unfortunate fact of cultural diversity that many young Afro-Caribbeans, innocent or otherwise, behave in a way that makes those hairs stand up on white policemen's necks. They tend to hang around in the street more. More of them are out partying in the small hours. Many run away on principle when they see a police officer - which most police also take as a sign of guilt, as they cannot understand why any law-abiding person could possibly wish to avoid meeting them. But this is not simply a matter of cultural mis-interpretation. For while in many cases these signs are innocent, they are also, often, the places, the times and the patterns of behaviour that do, regardless of race, fit in with actual or imminent crime.'

Crime statistics and ethnicity A final note - last time the Home Office produced crime statistics on ethnicity and crime, in 1989, it admitted that, 'the available statistics have limited value as measures of ethnic criminality'.

(adapted from 'Inside the Inner City' by Paul Harrison, Penguin, Harmondsworth, 1985 and 'Guardian', 8.8.1995)

1. Why do many blacks object to Paul Condon's linking of mugging and ethnicity? (4)
2. Why does Jock Young argue that ethnicity as such has nothing to do with mugging? (4)
3. How might labelling theory help to explain the high proportion of blacks arrested for street crimes? (6)
4. Mugging represents a very small proportion of all known crime. Why is it frequently reported in the newspapers? (6)

10 PART CRIME AND GENDER

Before the 1980s sociologists paid little or no attention to female crime. Even today we know far more about male crime. Much of the evidence about female crime is based on official statistics and, as Parts 2 and 3 have shown, such evidence must be treated with caution.

Official statistics

Official statistics for England and Wales present the following picture of women and crime. First, women commit far fewer offences than men. Figure 1 compares males and females cautioned for or found guilty of offences. Second, the types of crime committed by males and females tend to be different. Table 1 shows that 58.6% of all women convicted by the courts were found guilty of theft and handling stolen goods. The comparable figure for men is 36.8%. Third, the crime rate for women is increasing more rapidly than the rate for men. For example, from 1988 to 1993 female crime increased by 12%, four times the rate of increase for men.

Figure 1 Known offenders

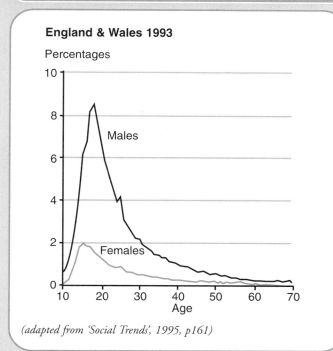

England & Wales 1993

Percentages

(adapted from 'Social Trends', 1995, p161)

Table 1 Convictions for criminal offences

England and Wales 1993

Offences	Males Nos (000)	Males %	Females Nos (000)	Females %
Violence against the person	35.5	91.3	3.4	8.7
Sexual offences	4.3	98.0	0.1	2.0
Burglary	39.2	97.5	1.0	2.5
Robbery	4.8	94.1	0.3	5.9
Theft and handling stolen goods	99.5	81.8	22.1	18.2
Fraud and forgery	13.6	77.7	3.9	22.3
Criminal damage	8.6	91.5	0.8	8.5
Drug offence	19.9	90.9	2.0	9.1
Other (excluding motoring)	34.2	90.5	3.6	9.5
Motoring	10.3	95.4	0.5	4.6
Total	**269.9**	**87.7**	**37.7**	**12.3**

(from Home Office, 1993)

How accurate is the picture of female crime based on official statistics? The short answer is we don't know. However, self-report studies reflect two of the conclusions drawn from official statistics - women commit fewer crimes than men and their crimes tend to be different from those of men.

Women, men and crime

Assuming that women do commit fewer crimes than men, what are the reasons for this? Differences in socialisation have often been suggested - compared to men, women are socialised to be more passive and conformist, they are more strictly supervised and given less freedom. In a male dominated society this control continues into adult life. Women are locked into domestic labour - housework and childcare - which reinforces their early socialisation and gives them less time and opportunity

Gang members, Los Angeles

to commit crimes. And criminal activity can seriously threaten their status as a 'good wife and mother'.

According to official statistics women tend to commit 'women's crimes'. The most common is theft and handling stolen goods - mainly shoplifting, followed by fraud - mainly welfare benefit fraud. These crimes have been seen as extensions or variations on traditional female roles - when times are hard shopping for the family becomes shoplifting for the family and family welfare benefits are supplemented by welfare fraud.

Assuming once again that official statistics provide a fairly accurate picture of female crime, why are women's crime rates rising more rapidly than those of men? One suggestion is that the rise in relative poverty since the 1980s has placed greater pressure on women to turn to crime to supplement family income. A second suggestion sees the explanation in changes in women's attitudes and outlook. It argues that women are becoming more like men in terms of both their legal and illegal behaviour (see Chapter 12, Part 7). This is reflected in the rapid growth of burglaries, robberies and crimes of violence committed by women. For example, from 1984 to 1994 the number of women cautioned for or found guilty of an offence involving violence nearly doubled. However, even in 1994, the actual number of violent crimes committed by women was small, numbering only 9,400.

Women and the justice system

There is some evidence that women are treated more leniently by the criminal justice system. For example, in England and Wales in 1993, for all males charged with offences

82% were found guilty and 18% were cautioned, while 60% of females were found guilty and 40% cautioned. If women are convicted they are less likely to go to prison and, if sent to prison, they tend to receive shorter sentences.

Research has indicated that if a woman has domestic responsibilities these are often used to explain, and to some degree excuse her crime, and this influences her treatment by the courts. The following quotes from magistrates illustrate these points.

- A married woman, and especially a mother, is the keystone of the family and is subject to great strains and tensions, particularly if in a 'one-parent family' situation or when the husband is unemployed. This could push a woman into crime particularly, in my opinion, shoplifting or attempting to obtain benefits to which she would not be entitled.

- Trying and sentencing a mother has its problems for me because I look at her situation, taking into account the effect upon her family.

- In cases where women have in their care babies or young children I feel that magistrates explore every possible sentence other than imprisonment.

This picture of leniency does not, however, extend to all women. Prostitutes, for example, have long complained about their treatment by the police and the courts. They don't fit the stereotype of the struggling mother, though in fact many are. In the eyes of the powers that be they are doubly deviant - they have committed a crime and have failed to conform to the mother/housewife role. Women appear to be treated more harshly when they deviate from the social norms of female

Protestors at Greenham Common, 1983

sexuality. For example, sexually promiscuous girls are more likely to be taken into care or given custodial sentences than boys. Other women who have complained about their treatment by the justice system include suffragettes campaigning for votes for women, women protesting against the nuclear weapons at the US base at Greenham Common in the early 1980s, black and Irish women and lesbians. To some extent all these groups fall outside the standard stereotype of women.

The traditional picture of leniency may be less applicable in the 1990s. For example, in 1994, the number of women imprisoned rose by nearly a quarter to 3,000.

And finally, the view that many women are treated leniently is called into doubt by a comparison with men who have committed white collar crime and domestic violence. Many consider their punishment, or lack of it, as far more lenient than the treatment of female offenders.

(adapted from 'Offending Woman' by Anne Worrall, Routledge, London, 1990; 'Masculinity, Femininity and Crime' by Madeleine Leonard, 'Sociology Review', September, 1995; 'Observer', 25.8.1995)

QUESTIONS

1. a) Compare the extent of male and female crime shown in Figure 1 and Table 1. (4)
   b) Describe the main differences between male and female crime indicated by Table 1. (4)
   c) Briefly suggest reasons for these differences. (2)
2. a) Why are some women treated leniently by the criminal justice system? (5)
   b) Why might each of the groups of women who complain of injustice be treated more severely? (5)

RELIGION

Religion may be defined as a belief in some form of supernatural power which influences or controls the lives of human beings and the world of nature. This chapter examines the role of religion in society from a number of different viewpoints. It also considers the claim that religion is steadily declining in importance in modern industrial society.

RELIGION AND SOCIETY

PART 1

Religion has often been seen as a means of strengthening and reinforcing social norms and values. In doing so it contributes to order and stability in society. Religious ceremonies have been seen as a means of uniting a social group and so producing social solidarity. Religion is different from all other aspects of society because it involves a belief in supernatural power. Because of this many sociologists argue that it can make a unique and vital contribution to the wellbeing of society. These points are examined in the following passage.

Supernatural power means literally power above and beyond the forces of nature. It is, for example, the power of the Christian God who is believed to be omniscient - all knowing, and omnipotent - all powerful. Such power is beyond the normal powers which are found in the world of nature and the society of human beings. It is a special kind of power which does not obey the normal rules which operate in the natural world. Thus the Christian God has no beginning and no end. He does not experience birth and death like men and women. He is supernatural, he lives on another plane.

A belief in supernatural power is the basis of religion. It sets religion apart from the everyday world.

Religion involves the creation of the sacred. When something is made sacred or sanctified it is set apart, given a special meaning and treated with reverence, awe, respect and sometimes fear. Thus the beliefs of the Christian religion and its symbols such as the cross and communion wine are sacred. Mistreatment of the sacred, such as vandalising a church, causes deep revulsion and shock for those who believe.

Religion includes a set of beliefs and practices which the faithful are required to hold and follow. Thus the Christian religion includes the Ten Commandments which among other things instruct its members to honour their parents, not to commit adultery, not to steal and not to kill. These commandments are backed by supernatural power. Those who follow them may be rewarded with an afterlife of eternal happiness in a land flowing with milk and honey. Those who break them may suffer an afterlife of eternal damnation. Religious beliefs can therefore have considerable control over the behaviour of people in society. (See Chapter 2, Part 2.)

The influence of religion on social life can also be seen from religious rituals and ceremonies. Many sociologists argue that such events can unify people in society. They produce social unity or social solidarity. In a religious ritual a social group comes together to express its faith in common values and beliefs. People often recite prayers and sing songs which spell out these shared beliefs. In doing so they experience a sense of collective identity and a feeling of belonging. This unity is backed by the power of religion which gives the gathering a sense of awe and reverence. The atmosphere is highly

charged, emotions are touched and the ceremony is raised above the level of a normal social event. By participating in a religious ritual people feel a part of something larger than themselves and become aware of the moral bonds which unite them.

(adapted in part from 'Sociology' by Leonard Broom and Philip Selznick, 6th edition, Harper & Row, New York, 1977)

Gustav Doré's vision of hell

QUESTIONS

1. a) The norms and values of society are often similar to religious beliefs. If this is the case, how can religion strengthen and reinforce social norms and values? (4)
   b) How does this contribute to order and stability in society? (3)
2. a) What beliefs of the Christian religion reinforce the norms and values of marriage and family life? (3)
   b) A church marriage sanctifies the union between two people. How might this strengthen the marriage? (3)
3. How does a religious ritual help to unite a group of people? (3)
4. Religion does not always contribute to order and unity in society. In fact it can do just the opposite. Briefly discuss this view using at least one example to support it. (4)

PART 2 RELIGION AND SOCIAL ORDER

In every society certain events and situations produce stress, worry and anxiety. If these emotions were not kept in check, social order might be threatened. Imagine a society in which people were constantly tense and anxious - it is difficult to see how things could run smoothly. The anthropologist Bronislaw Malinowski argues that one of the main functions of religion is to check and reduce emotions which threaten to disrupt society. He also believes that religion strengthens social solidarity or unity in society. Religious ceremonies involve people coming together to worship as a community. Joining together in a common faith and often in mutual support helps to unite a social group.

Malinowski spent several years studying the people of the Trobriand Islands which are off the coast of New Guinea in southeast Asia. The Trobriands consist of a number of small atolls - ring shaped coral reefs surrounding a lagoon. The waters of the lagoon are calm since they are protected from the open sea by a barrier reef which acts as a breakwater. The islanders fish in the lagoon by dropping poison into the water. The fish are stunned, they float to the surface and are scooped into canoes. In Malinowski's words, within the lagoon, 'fishing is done in an easy and absolutely reliable manner by the method of poisoning, yielding abundant results without danger and uncertainty'.

The same is not true of fishing in the open sea. Tropical storms are common. They may overturn or break up the frail outrigger canoes resulting in injury or loss of life. In the lagoon the islanders can always predict a reasonable catch. Sometimes they return empty-handed from an expedition beyond the barrier reef. They have to rely mainly on luck, hoping that their nets strike a shoal of fish.

Before fishing in the open sea the islanders perform a religious ceremony. However, no religious ritual is associated with fishing in the lagoon.

(adapted from 'Magic, Science and Religion and Other Essays' by Bronislaw Malinowski, Anchor Books, New York, 1954)

Fishing in calm waters off the coast of New Guinea in an outrigger canoe

257

QUESTIONS

1. Why is religion associated with fishing in the open sea but not in the lagoon? (6)
2. Malinowski claims that in all societies religion is associated with one or more of the 'life crises', that is birth, puberty, marriage and death.
   a) How might the emotions that death produces disrupt normal social relationships? (4)
   b) How might religion check and reduce these emotions? (5)
   c) How might a funeral ceremony strengthen social solidarity? (5)

PART 3 — RELIGION - THE OPIUM OF THE PEOPLE

Karl Marx described religion as 'the opium of the people'. Opium is a narcotic drug which gives a feeling of wellbeing. It produces feelings which distort reality. Marx believed that religion gives a false picture of society. It prevents people from seeing the truth. It provides an illusion of happiness and offers an imaginary escape from problems.

Marx believed that religion helps to keep the poor and oppressed in their place. He saw it placing 'imaginary flowers on their chains'. This kept their chains hidden and made them easier to wear. By offering comfort and support religion made their suffering more bearable. By appearing to give solutions to their problems, religion tended to prevent them from taking practical steps to solve those problems. In particular, it discouraged them from trying to overthrow their oppressors.

The following passage provides evidence which can be used to support Marx's views. It describes the religious music of many black Americans who have been a downtrodden minority in United States' society.

Throughout the USA black churches have resounded with the sound of gospel music. In Detroit the Reverend C.L. Franklin, father of the famous soul singer Aretha Franklin and pastor of the Bethel Baptist Church, has raised congregations to fever pitch with his preaching and gospel singing. So intense is the feeling that he arouses that nurses are regularly on hand to tend members of his flock overcome with emotion. People leave the church feeling cleansed, their burdens lifted, recharged and ready to face the problems of a new week.

At a Madison Square Garden gospel concert in New York City, Mahalia Jackson, the Queen of Gospel, sings *Just Over The Hill*, a song about going to heaven. As she sinks to her knees, singing with intensity and jubilation, women in the audience shriek and faint. Gospel music, in the words of one of its singers, 'stirs the emotions'.

A member of the Ward Sisters, a famous black gospel group states, 'For people who work hard and make little money, gospel music offers a promise that things will be better in the life to come'. According to Thomas A. Dorsey, one of the founders of modern gospel music, 'Make it anything other than good news and it ceases to be gospel'. Many gospel songs ring with joy, excitement, anticipation and conviction about

The Stars of Faith

reaching the 'blessed homeland' and 'waking up in glory'. Life on earth might be hard and painful with little hope for improvement but life after death is nothing but good news.

God not only promises eternal salvation and perfect happiness, he also provides support and direction for life on earth. Typical lines from gospel songs include, 'Take your burdens to the Lord and leave them there', 'God will carry you through', 'Since I gave to Jesus my poor broken heart, he has never left me alone', and 'What would I do if it wasn't for the Lord'. The songs often say as much to the singers as their audiences. The gospel singer Dorothy Love refused to sell her song *I've Got Jesus And That's Enough* to a rock and roll song company. Her reason: 'That's my whole story. I'd be selling out everything I am'.

(adapted from 'The Gospel Sound' by Tony Heilbut, Simon and Schuster, New York, 1971 and 'Right On: From Blues to Soul in Black America' by Michael Haralambos, Causeway Press, Ormskirk, 1995)

In the late 1950s and early 1960s some black preachers came out of their churches and on to the streets. Led by the Reverend Martin Luther King, the Southern Christian Leadership Council, an organisation of black churches in the southern states of the USA, directed mass protest against racial discrimination. Partly due to its campaign, the American government passed civil rights laws which declared discrimination on the basis of skin colour to be illegal.

(adapted from 'The Negro in Twentieth Century America' edited by J.H. Franklin and I. Starr, Vintage Books, New York, 1967)

QUESTIONS

1. Why does Marx compare opium with religion? (4)
2. a) What are the emotional effects produced by gospel music? (3)
   b) What are the messages contained in the words of gospel music? (3)
   c) How might the emotional effects and the message of gospel music help to keep blacks at the bottom of the stratification system? (6)
3. Explain how the evidence in the second passage can be used to argue that Marx's theory of religion does not always apply. (4)

PART 4 — SECULARISATION

At first glance the future of religion in Britain and in many other Western societies is not bright. Dwindling congregations, churches up for sale and in a state of disrepair, increasing numbers of people married in registry offices and fewer children attending Sunday school suggest a steady decline in the influence of religion. Evidence such as this has led a number of researchers to argue that Western societies are undergoing a process of secularisation which means they are becoming increasingly secular or non-religious.

Those who argue that secularisation is occurring claim 1) that participation in organised religion is declining, for example fewer people attend church, 2) that religion has less influence on society as a whole, for example the churches are no longer responsible for educating the young and 3) that people are no longer guided by religious beliefs in their everyday lives, for example the will of God is not an important consideration affecting their decisions.

However, it is very difficult to measure the strength of religious belief. Simply because church attendance has declined does not necessarily mean that people are any the less religious. They may well have turned to 'privatised religion', preferring to worship in the privacy of their own homes. Also, because the state has taken over many of the social welfare responsibilities of the church, such as caring for the poor, does not necessarily mean that religion has lost influence in society. It may well be that the strength of Christian beliefs, such as the importance of caring for the poor, has led the state to take over these responsibilities. The evidence can therefore be interpreted in a number of ways and the case for secularisation is far from proven.

The first passage is based on the work of the British sociologist Bryan Wilson. He is one of the strongest supporters of the view that secularisation is occurring in Western societies.

The case for secularisation

The signs of a decline in religion became increasingly clear after World War II which ended in 1945. War memorials lost many of the religious symbols with which they were traditionally adorned. Indeed they were often not put up at all. In 1947 the BBC, which had traditionally stood firm on the side of the Church of England, abandoned its policy of not broadcasting opinions hostile to Christianity.

Except for ceremonies like the coronation and the opening of Parliament, the church is rarely seen or heard on the national stage. At the close of the last century a Prime Minister's correspondence gave serious attention to church opinion. But the last Prime Minister who appeared to pay any attention to the church's opinion was Margaret Thatcher in the 1980s who ticked them off for 'interfering' in politics. No longer do people look to the pulpit for guidance and information. They are more likely to turn to television, books, newspapers and magazines. Control of social welfare has long since passed to armies of specialists employed by the state who educate, counsel, cure, rehabilitate and care for the poor and the aged.

Religion seems less and less to guide people's thoughts and direct their actions. They no longer appear to ask 'What is God's will?' so much as 'What shall I do to get on?' They seem less concerned about death and the afterlife than about happiness here and now. The church's traditional disapproval of divorce, artificial techniques of birth control, sexual relationships outside marriage and homosexuality appears to have little impact. If anything, changing attitudes in society about these and other matters have changed the church's views. More and more the church seems to follow rather than lead.

The decline in the church's influence on people's beliefs and actions is reflected in participation in organised religious activities. Membership of the Church of England has steadily declined along with attendance at services, baptisms, confirmations, church marriages and Sunday school.

Former churches in Preston converted into an antiques centre,

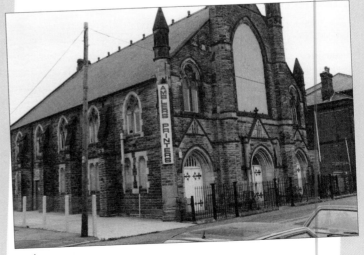

a radio station,

a printers.

Table 1 Church membership

United Kingdom	1970	1980	Millions 1994
Trinitarian churches			
Roman Catholic	2.7	2.4	2.0
Anglican	2.6	2.2	1.8
Presbyterian	1.8	1.4	1.1
Methodist	0.7	0.5	0.4
Baptist	0.3	0.2	0.2
Other free churches	0.5	0.5	0.7
Orthodox	0.2	0.2	0.3
All Trinitarian churches	8.8	7.4	6.5
Non-Trinitarian churches			
Mormons	0.1	0.1	0.2
Jehovah's Witnesses	0.1	0.1	0.1
Other Non-Trinitarian	0.1	0.2	0.2
All Non-Trinitarian churches	0.3	0.4	0.5
Other religions			
Muslims	0.1	0.3	0.6
Sikhs	0.1	0.2	0.3
Hindus	0.1	0.1	0.1
Jews	0.1	0.1	0.1
Others	0.0	0.1	0.1
All other religions	0.4	0.8	1.2

(adapted from 'Social Trends', 1996, p225)

However it would probably be a mistake to conclude that religion is doomed. There is, and probably always will be, a deeply committed minority of religious people. However for the vast majority religion is becoming simply an 'optional extra'.

(adapted in part from 'How Religious Are We?' by Bryan Wilson, 'New Society', 27.10.1977)

The case against secularisation

It is not religious belief that is declining, instead it is organised religion. A decline in participation in church activities does not necessarily say anything about the strength of religious belief. With nearly 70% of people in Britain claiming to believe in God, this is hardly evidence for a secular society. 'The size of congregations is meaningless', says Laurence Brown, director of the Alister Hardy Centre in Oxford which investigates religious experiences. Surveys indicate that about half of all adults in Britain have had some kind of religious experience.

Table 2 Religious belief

Great Britain	percentages
Believe in God	69
Believe God is personally concerned	37
Believe the Bible is the 'actual' or 'inspired' Word of God	44
% believing in:	
Life after death	55
Heaven	54
Hell	28
The Devil	28
Religious miracles	45

(adapted from R. Jowell et al, 'British Social Attitudes', Dartmouth, Aldershot, 1992)

Although membership of the traditional Christian churches is declining, membership of the 'new' churches, such as the Pentecostals, has grown steadily over the past 15 years. And, as Table 1 shows, membership of non-Christian religions in the UK is growing rapidly. To these must be added the many religious and semi-religious movements which are outside mainstream religion. Variously called sects, cults and new religious movements, they include Krishna Consciousness, the Children of God, Transcendental Meditation and so-called 'pagan religions' such as witchcraft. To some this is evidence of **resacrilisation** - a revival of religious beliefs and practices, a renewal of interest in the sacred.

If new religious buildings are anything to go by, then it's the non-Christian religions that are leading this revival. Compare the former churches in Preston with the new Hindu temple in

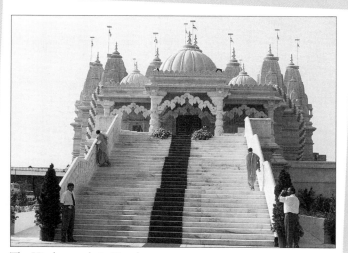

The Hindu temple in Neasden

Neasden in north London. The three-year, multi-million pound project was funded entirely by Britain's Hindu community. The temple, which accommodates 2,000 worshippers, is made from 3,000 tons of Bulgarian limestone and 2,000 tons of Italian marble, which was shipped to India to be hand-carved by village craftsmen before making the journey to London. Built by hundreds of volunteer workers, it is a monument to the faith and hard work of thousands who gave money and sponsored fundraising activities.

(adapted from 'Observer', 16.4.1995 and 'Telegraph', 19.8.1995)

QUESTIONS

1. What evidence does the first passage contain to suggest that religion is becoming less effective as a mechanism of social control? (3)
2. a) What are the occupational groups referred to by the phrase 'armies of specialists'? (2)
   b) What functions has the church lost to these specialists? (2)
3. a) Briefly summarise the trends shown in Table 1. (2)
   b) How do the pictures from Preston support these trends? (2)
4. Why is it important to examine religious beliefs as well as participation in organised religion? (4)
5. The problem with measuring secularisation is that we don't really know what it means to people when they participate in organised religion and when they say they believe in God. Discuss. (5)

THE MASS MEDIA

The mass media refers to television, radio, newspapers, magazines, books, advertisements, films, recorded music, in fact any means of communication which reaches large numbers of people. The chapter begins by examining the concentration of ownership of the media into fewer and fewer hands. It then looks at the influence of newspapers on people's political attitudes and behaviour. Theories of media effects - the effects the media has on its audience - are then examined. The chapter closes by looking at ways in which women are represented by the media.

1 PART — OWNERSHIP AND CONTROL

Large parts of the British media are owned and controlled by a small number of people. Does this matter? Does it limit the range of views expressed by the media? Are the media simply the mouthpieces of the owners? This part examines these questions.

Concentration of ownership

Ownership of the media is increasingly concentrated. When satellite television was introduced into Britain in 1989 there were two competing companies - BSB and Sky. In 1990 Rupert Murdoch's News International took over BSB. BSkyB now has a monopoly in the delivery of satellite TV to Britain. Takeovers within the ITV network provide further evidence of the concentration of ownership. In the early 1990s there were four major takeovers - Yorkshire TV of Tyne Tees, Carlton of Central, Meridian of Anglia and Granada of London Weekend Television.

Ownership of the press in the 1990s is more concentrated in Britain than anywhere else in the Western world. For example in 1994, 85% of daily and Sunday newspaper circulation was controlled by just seven companies of which five owned 9 out of every 10 newspapers. News International alone accounted for over one third of all newspapers sold in Britain. Most regional and local newspapers and even many of the free papers are owned by large corporations.

Cross-ownership of the media is increasing. This means that the same company owns different sections of the media such as radio and television stations and newspapers. For example, Viscount Rothermere, owner of the *Daily Mail*, controls a network of local, regional and national media in cable, radio, television, magazines and newspapers.

Table 1 shows News International's main media holdings in the UK.

Rupert Murdoch

Table 1 News International

Newspapers	Circulation
Sun	4,104,278
Times	631,449
Today	614,459
News of the World	4,854,766
Sunday Times	1,262,772

These figures (Jan 1995) give News International a 37% share of daily and 39% of Sunday paper sales

Book Publishing	Harper Collins
Magazines	Shoppers Friend
	Times Educational Supplement
	Times Higher Education Supplement
	Times Educational Supplement Scotland
	TV Hits (UK) (45% interest)
	Inside Soap (45% interest)
Satellite Television	British Sky Broadcasting (40% interest)

(adapted from 'New Statesman & Society', 24.3.1995)

Democracy and the media

In George Orwell's novel *Nineteen Eighty-Four*, the Ministry of Truth, which controlled information broadcast to the masses, based its policy on the slogan 'ignorance is strength'. Orwell was writing about a totalitarian society. In a democracy people participate in their own government and to do this effectively they need access to information. For example, in order to decide which political party to vote for, they need information about the policies of the various parties. In modern industrial society, much of this information comes from the mass media.

Does the increasing concentration of ownership in the media restrict people's access to information? And does it lead to a narrowing of opinion given that at least some owners wish to see their own views reflected in their media output?

In 1948 Lord Beaverbrook, owner of the *Daily Express* stated: 'I run the *Daily Express* purely for the purpose of making propaganda, and with no other motive'. Harold Evans, former editor of the *Times*, claims he was sacked for not toeing the line and for failing to reflect the views of its owner, Rupert Murdoch. When Murdoch bought the *Times*, he signed documents guaranteeing editorial independence. When Evans reminded him of this, Murdoch is quoted as replying, 'They're not worth the paper they're written on'. The *Sunday Times* used to be a politically independent paper with a strong tradition of investigative journalism. After Murdoch bought it, it swung sharply to the right. In the words of its former political editor, Hugo Young: 'Very little space is any longer available for the discussion of poverty, inequality, injustice or anything which might be recognised as a moral issue'.

If the viewpoints of owners are reflected in the media, then evidence from newspapers suggests that most owners support the Conservative Party. Table 2 shows the political parties supported by the major national daily and Sunday newspapers at the time of the 1992 general election.

Table 2 Newspapers and party support

Title	Party support	Circulation	Title	Party support	Circulation
Daily Express	Con	1,525,000	*Independent on Sunday*	None	402,000
Daily Mail	Con	1,575,000	*Mail on Sunday*	Con	1,941,000
Daily Mirror	Lab	3,581,000	*News of the World*	Con	4,788,000
Daily Star	None	806,000	*Observer*	Lab	541,000
Daily Telegraph	Con	1,038,000	*The People*	Lab	2,165,000
Financial Times	Lab	290,000	*Sunday Express*	Con	1,666,000
Guardian	Lab	429,000	*Sunday Mirror*	Lab	2,775,000
Independent	None	390,000	*Sport*	None	301,000
Sun	Con	3,571,000	*Sunday Telegraph*	Con	558,000
Times	Con	386,000	*Sunday Times*	Con	1,167,000
Today	Con	533,000			

This table shows the party preference and circulation of newspapers at the time of the 1992 general election.

(adapted from 'British Politics in Focus' edited by David Roberts, Causeway Press, Ormskirk, 1995, p569)

The market

Is it the views of owners which shape the content and politics of the media? What about the consumers, those who buy the newspapers and decide which programmes to watch and listen to on TV and radio? Don't they shape the content of the media? This is Rupert Murdoch's view. He, like all media owners, is in business to make a profit. But he wouldn't make a profit if he didn't give consumers what they wanted. Following this argument the media reflects the views of its readers, listeners and viewers.

But there is another argument. Consumers choose within the limits available to them. With the concentration of ownership, that choice is becoming increasingly narrow and restricted. In the words of Granville Williams, an effective democracy must 'ensure that the printed word and the visual image, in the interests of diversity of opinion and pluralism, should not be unduly monopolised. No single party should be allowed to dominate the press, radio or television, and no private owner should be allowed an unacceptable degree of control over channels of communication.'

(adapted from 'New Times' by Granville Williams in 'New Statesman & Society', 24.3.1995 and 'British Politics in Focus' edited by David Roberts, Causeway Press, Ormskirk, 1995)

QUESTIONS

1. a) What does the Ministry of Truth's slogan 'ignorance is strength' mean? (3)
   b) Why is access to information essential for democracy? (3)
2. Should we be concerned about the growing concentration of ownership of the media? (4)
3. a) Summarise the information in Table 2. (2)
   b) The lack of support for the Liberal Democrats by national newspapers in the 1992 election is bad for democracy. Discuss. (4)
4. At the end of the day people get the newspapers they deserve. Discuss. (4)

POLITICS AND THE PRESS

Part 1 showed that the majority of newspapers supported the Conservative Party in the 1992 general election. On the day of the election the *Sun*'s headline read, 'If Kinnock wins today will the last person to leave Britain please turn out the lights' (Kinnock was then leader of the Labour Party). The following day the *Sun* greeted the Conservative victory with the headline 'IT'S THE SUN WOT WON IT'. Is there any justification for this claim? The following passage looks at this question.

The *Sun* claiming credit for the Conservative victory in the 1992 election

Table 1 Voting in the 1992 election

Party	Electorate	*Sun* readers
Conservative	43%	45%
Labour	35%	36%
Liberal Democrat	18%	15%

(based on figures in 'Guardian', 7.3.1994)

By the end of 1993 the voting intentions of *Sun* readers again reflected the electorate as a whole.

Table 2 Voting intentions, 1993

Party	Electorate	*Sun* readers
Conservative	29%	29%
Labour	46%	48%
Liberal Democrat	22%	19%

(based on figures in 'Guardian', 7.3.1994)

After the Conservative victory of 1992, Lord McAlpine, former Conservative Treasurer, described the newspaper editors who supported the party as 'heroes'. 'Never, in the past nine elections,' he said, 'have they come out so strongly in favour of the Conservatives'. And Neil Kinnock, the defeated leader of the Labour Party, blamed the tabloid press for winning a victory the Conservatives couldn't have won for themselves.

In 1992 the nation voted on much the same lines as the *Sun*'s readers as Table 1 shows.

There are various ways of interpreting Tables 1 and 2. First *Sun* readers reflected public opinion as a whole, and the *Sun* had little influence on their political views. Second, the *Sun*'s readers were influenced by their newspaper both in 1992 and 1993. The *Sun* withdrew much of its support from the Conservatives in 1993 and in January 1994 headlined its previous support for John Major with the words 'WHAT FOOLS WE WERE'. Third, rather than the *Sun* influencing its readers, its readers and the public as a whole influenced the *Sun*. In other words the *Sun* was simply reflecting public opinion.

The run-up to the general election

The majority of *Sun* readers are usually Labour voters. But they swung heavily to the Conservatives in the run-up to the 1992 election. Readers of the Labour supporting *Daily Mirror*, on the other hand, showed no swing to the Conservatives. Table 3 shows the percentage swing to the Conservatives of readers of different newspapers during the 1992 election campaign.

Table 3 Readers' swing to Conservatives

Conservative papers		Labour papers	
Sun	8%	Daily Mirror	0%
Daily Express	8%	Guardian	0%
Daily Telegraph	8%	(The Guardian is not a traditional Labour paper but it supported the Labour Party in 1992.)	
Daily Mail	14%		

(based on figures in 'Guardian', 30.10.1995)

What does Table 3 show? *Sun* and *Daily Mirror* readers are mainly working class. The *Sun* gave strong support to the Conservatives in 1992, the *Mirror* to Labour. Since the social background of their readers is similar, it could be argued that their newspapers made the difference. Thus, Martin Linton, who has conducted a major study of the influence of newspapers on the 1992 election result draws the following conclusion. 'The

widely-held assumption that traditionally Conservative newspapers have no influence in elections because they are merely preaching to the converted turns out to be quite wrong.'

Or does it? As Tables 1 and 2 indicate, it may be that *Sun* readers reflect the electorate as a whole. Maybe their commitment to the Labour Party is less strong than *Mirror* readers. The fact that they read the *Sun*, a Conservative newspaper, suggests this. If this is the case, they will be more likely to swing with changes in public opinion, and this swing will have little to do with the newspaper they read.

(adapted from 'Guardian', 7.3.1994; 30.10.1995)

QUESTIONS

1. Summarise the information in Tables 1 and 2. (4)
2. Which of the three explanations for the evidence in Tables 1 and 2 do you prefer? Give reasons for your answer. (6)
3. Summarise the information in Table 3. (4)
4. Which of the two explanations for the evidence in Table 3 do you prefer? Give reasons for your answer. (6)

PART 3 — MEDIA EFFECTS

Media effects refer to the effects the media has on people's attitudes and behaviour. But how can the effects of the media be separated from all the other factors which influence people - their family, friends, education, religion, class, gender, ethnicity and so on. The answer is with great difficulty, if at all.

This part looks at some of the theories which try to explain media effects. It begins with one of the most dramatic media effects of all time - the invasion of the world by Martians.

Orson Welles broadcasting *War of the Worlds*

The Martians are coming 'The girls huddled around their radios trembling and weeping in each other's arms. They separated themselves from their friends only to take their turn at the telephone to make long distance calls to their parents, saying goodbye for what they thought might be the last time. Terror-stricken girls, hoping to escape from the Mars invaders, rushed to the basement of the dormitory.'

With these words an American college student recalls the reaction of herself and her friends to a radio broadcast in 1938. The broadcast was a radio play by Orson Welles based on H.G. Wells's *War of the Worlds*, a novel about an invasion from Mars. It was so realistic that hundreds of thousands of people, who missed the announcement that it was only a play, were convinced the Martians had invaded. Many panicked at the news that millions had been killed by Martian death rays.

Hypodermic syringe theory The broadcast about the Martian invasion had a direct and immediate effect on hundreds of thousands of people. The hypodermic syringe theory takes a similar view of media effects in general - they are simple and direct. It pictures media effects as an injection into the veins of the audience, an injection that is usually harmful but occasionally beneficial. For example, violence on television leads to violence in real life.

Hypodermic syringe theory is one of the earliest theories of media effects. Few researchers accept it today, but its simplicity appeals to many members of the public.

Audience interaction theory Hypodermic syringe theory saw the audience as victims of the media - they were injected and there was little they could do about it. Audience interaction theory - of which there are many versions - sees people interacting with the media, interpreting its output in various ways, and making decisions about whether to accept or reject media messages. The following example illustrates this approach.

169 people were interviewed a year after the miners' strike of 1984/85. Television news programmes had focused on violent incidents during the strike - clashes between picketing miners and police. Those selected for interview included miners and police who had been involved in the strike, plus a range of people from different parts of the country and with different social backgrounds. The researchers found that people interpreted the media's version of the strike in terms of their experiences and previously held attitudes and beliefs. 54% of those interviewed believed that the picketing was mostly violent. This reflected media coverage of the strike. However, none of those who had direct knowledge of the strike - the miners and police - believed that picketing was mostly violent. They rejected the impression given by the media. According to them, strikers and police spent most of their time sitting round doing nothing.

Studies like this show that media effects are not simple and direct. They are interpreted in various ways in terms of people's experiences and beliefs.

Cultural effects theory This theory assumes that the media has important effects on the audience but these effects are not as simple and dramatic as those indicated by the hypodermic syringe theory. Instead the effects are seen as a slow, steady buildup of ideas and attitudes. For example, if we are 'drip-fed' over a long period of time with certain media images of women, disabled people, ethnic minorities and so on, those images will tend to stick.

However, cultural effects theory does recognise that audiences don't just accept media images and messages. People interpret them in terms of their beliefs, experiences and social background. For example, media effects will depend in part on the age, gender, ethnicity and social class of members of the

Pickets and police at Orgreave Coke Works - a typical media image of the 1984/85 miners' strike

audience. Cultural effects theory is examined in Part 4 in terms of media images of women.

(adapted from 'The Sociology of the Mass Media' by David Glover in 'Sociology: New Directions' edited by M. Haralambos, Causeway Press, Ormskirk, 1985 and 'Getting the Message' by Greg Philo in 'Getting the Message: News, Truth and Power' edited by J. Eldridge, Routledge, London, 1993)

QUESTIONS

1. a) Why is the hypodermic syringe theory so called? (3)
   b) Show how it can be used to explain violence in society. (3)
   c) Why do you think many 'ordinary' people believe the theory is correct? (3)
2. How does audience interaction theory differ from hypodermic syringe theory? (3)
3. a) Why is the idea of a drip-feed often used to illustrate cultural effects theory? (3)
   b) How might cultural effects theory see the effect of media images of women on women's attitudes and behaviour? (5)

REPRESENTATIONS OF WOMEN

Media representations refer to the way the media represents, pictures and presents people, groups and activities. This part looks at examples of media representations of women (see also Chapter 2, Part 5).

Page 3 girls

- 'Birthday Suit! From time to time some self-appointed critic stamps his tiny foot and declares that the *Sun* is obsessed with sex. It is not the *Sun*, but its critics who are obsessed. The *Sun*, like most of its readers, likes pretty girls. And if they are as pretty as today's Birthday Suit girl, 20-year-old Stephanie Rahm, who cares whether they are dressed or not?

  (Text accompanying first Page 3 girl, November 17, 1970)

- 'The editor did it while I was away. I was just as shocked as anyone else but it became a national institution - a statement of youthfulness and freshness.'

  (Rupert Murdoch, owner of the *Sun*)

- 'Is it that people want that porn, or that dirty-minded newspaper owners and editors who actually despise their own readers think that's all they're fit for?'

  (Clare Short MP, who in 1986 introduced a bill to ban newspaper nudes.)

- 'I'm convinced that these pictures of naked women with coy "temptress" expressions only serve to confirm the attitude that rape victims ask for it.'

  (One of more than 5,000 letters from women received by Short.)

Advertising

What a nice bit of fluff!

• DANNI, 22 of Herts, wanted to wear her new fluffy jacket today. We like girls without coating so we hesitated fur a moment - until we saw it was double breasted!

Scotch miss

• TASTY Emma Caesari, 24, is used to making chaps feel light-headed - she was once a cocktail waitress. So why not spend a happy hour savouring the London lass's delights - while your ima-gin-ation runs wild.

Tracy's gym tonic

• TASTY Tracey Coleman, 23, stays in trim by working out in the gym. And the bare-robics classes certainly keep our Sheffield sweetie in peek condition!

Former Page 3 girl Linda Lusardi

Pictures of women plaster the environment. Legs, breasts, hands, bottoms and smiles are displayed on advertising hoardings, in magazines, calendars and TV commercials. They belong to Ms Perfection and are used to sell a variety of objects - car tyres, lawnmowers, deodorants, diamonds, videos and hair dyes.

A survey of women's reactions to car advertisements found that many women feel patronised and insulted. Published in 1996 and based on a sample of over 700 women, the survey noted that Renault's commercial for its Clio small car was singled out for criticism. The ad features Papa and his daughter Nicole who is portrayed as a spoilt child who drives a Clio bought by her indulgent father. Some women objected to an advertisement showing a woman with her hair blowing out of the sun roof of a Ford Fiesta which was described as, 'your 16-valve hairdryer'. Another objection was the impression given by some manufacturers that all women wanted was a powder-blue coupé with a vanity mirror.

(adapted from 'A Woman's Place' by D. Souhami, Penguin, Harmondsworth, 1986; 'Guardian', 13.11.1995; 'Times', 10.2.1996)

QUESTIONS

1. a) What images of women are portrayed by the Page 3 girls? (2)
   b) Are Page 3 girls a harmless 'bit of fun'? (6)
2. Why do many women feel patronised and insulted by advertisements for cars? (4)
3. Look at the pictures. What images of women do they present? (4)
4. Given that we still live in a patriarchal or male dominated society, media representations of women are to be expected. Discuss. (4)

HEALTH AND SOCIETY

S ociology is the study of society and social relationships. This chapter looks at health from a sociological perspective. It asks how people's health is shaped by the society in which they live and the social relationships in which they participate.

1 PART — HEALTH AND SOCIAL RELATIONSHIPS

This part begins with a description of the treatment of illness by a shaman - religious healer - in traditional Inuit (Eskimo) society. It suggests that social relationships are an important factor in health. This is followed by evidence from Western society which reinforces this point by suggesting that social relationships can keep people healthy or make them ill.

Inuit women beating fish skin to make into 'fish leather'

An Inuit shaman

A woman named Nanoraq, the wife of Makik, lay very ill, with pains all over her body. The patient, who was so ill that she could hardly stand upright, was placed on a bench. All the inhabitants of the village were summoned, and Angutingmarik, the shaman, inquired of his spirits as to the cause of the disease. He walked slowly up and down the floor for a long time, swinging his arms backwards and forwards with mittens on, talking in groans and sighs, in varying tones, sometimes breathing deeply as if under extreme pressure.

Shaman: 'I ask you, my helping spirit, whence comes the sickness from which this person is suffering?'

Patient: 'The sickness is due to my own fault. I have but ill fulfilled my duties. My thoughts have been bad and my actions evil.'

Shaman: 'That is not all. There are yet further offences, which have brought about this disease.'

Patient: 'Oh, I did comb my hair once when after giving birth to a child I ought not to have combed my hair; and I hid away the combings that none might see.'

Listeners: 'Let her be released from that. Oh, such a trifling thing; let her be released.'

Shaman: 'We wish her to get well again. Let all these obstacles be removed. Let her get well! And yet I see, and yet I espy things done which were forbidden.'

Patient: 'Oh, I ate part of a goose at a time when I was not allowed to eat such meat.'

Listeners: 'Never mind that. Let her be released from that, let her get well.'

Shaman: 'She is not released. It may perhaps prove impossible to release her from these burdens. What is it that I begin to see now? It must be blood, unless it is human filth. But it is outside the house, on the ground. It looks like blood. It is frozen, and covered with loose snow. Someone has tried to hide it.'

Patient: 'Yes, that was in the autumn. I had a miscarriage, and tried to conceal it, I tried to keep it secret.'

Listeners: 'This is certainly a great and serious offence. But let her be released nevertheless. Let her be released!'

Shaman: 'There are more sins yet. There is more to come. She grows cleaner with every confession, but there is more to come. There is more yet about forbidden food.'

Patient: 'Can it be because I once stole some salmon and ate it at a time when salmon was forbidden me?'

Listeners: 'Let her foolishness, let her misdeeds be taken from her. Let her get well.'

Shaman: 'Return to life, I see you now returning in good health among the living.'

The patient was by this time so exhausted that she could hardly sit upright, and the listeners left the house believing that all the sins and offences now confessed had taken the sting out of her illness, so that she would now soon be well again.

(adapted from 'An Eskimo Shaman Purifies A Sick Person' by K. Rasmussen in 'Reader in Comparative Religion' edited by W. A. Lessa and E. Z. Vogt, Harper & Row, New York, 1965)

Social relationships and health

In many small scale, preindustrial societies, illness is believed to be caused either by the actions of the person who is ill or by their relationships with other people. For example, the Azande of Sudan believe that illness is the result of witchcraft directed at the sufferer by a person who 'wishes them ill'. And among the Nuer, another Sudanese tribe, sickness is explained by actions such as sexual infidelity - being unfaithful to your marital partner.

Zambian traditional healer and patient

These beliefs are often dismissed in the West as irrational nonsense. Yet there is growing evidence from Western societies that illness is linked to personal crises and problems with social relationships. For example, a study entitled *Broken Heart* shows that in the year following the death of their wives, widowers had an increased risk of dying themselves. When compared to a control group of men of similar age and occupation, newly widowed men were 40% more likely to die from a number of causes, the most frequent being heart disease. After one year the widowers returned to the same level of mortality as the control group. The authors conclude that the stress of losing their wives was a serious risk factor for heart disease and that there may be some truth in the old belief that people die of a broken heart.

A number of studies have shown a link between increased risk of illness and death and situations which produce stress. These include separation and divorce, the death of a marital partner or close relative, adultery, job change, unemployment, migration and retirement.

Stress is not necessarily harmful to health. People often react positively to a stressful situation, acting with determination to change or improve it. However, if exposure to stress is intense and prolonged, then its effects can be harmful. Figure 1 shows how stress may result in illness.

Figure 1 Stress and illness

Stressful experience - eg loss of job.

Recognition of consequences - loss of job means loss of income to pay bills and mortgage/rent, status as breadwinner, contact with workmates, everyday routine.

Stress - excessive secretion of adrenalin and release of dangerous volume of corticosteroids.

Organic state - increased susceptibility to disease through damage to lymphatic system which produces antibodies.

Environmental exposure - to a disease agent such as influenza virus.

Body's response - weakened immune system means less resistance to disease.

Symptoms - flu.

(adapted from 'The Sociology of Health and Medicine' by N. Hart, Causeway Press, Ormskirk, 1985)

QUESTIONS

1. a) What evidence does the passage contain to indicate that the Inuit woman's illness might be the result of stress? (4)
   b) How might her treatment reduce the level of stress? (4)
2. Social relationships can keep people healthy or make them ill. Explain using the example of widowers. (6)
3. How might (i) divorce and (ii) retirement threaten people's health? (3, 3)

HEALTH AND SOCIETY

2 PART Project Piaxtla is a community health programme run by villagers in Mexico. Their children were dying at an alarming rate from diarrhoea and malnutrition. The cause of the problem - poor, landless farmers had to give up half their harvest to the rich landowner. Recognising the problem, the villagers succeeded in gaining over half of the best farming land in the area for their own use. They now had more to eat, their children put on weight, and the death rate of the under-fives dropped from 34% to 6%. The improvement in their health and life expectancy was due to changes in society - a change in land ownership - rather than any improvement in medical facilities. In the words of David Werner who observed Project Piaxtla, 'Most children can survive without medicine, none without food'.

This point is supported by the following passage which looks at changes in British society and their relationship to health during the 19th and early 20th centuries.

Nutrition

Breakfast for Manchester cotton workers in 1833 consisted of tea or coffee with a little bread and occasionally oatmeal porridge. Lunch was usually boiled potatoes with melted lard or butter, sometimes with a few pieces of fried bacon. Eighty years later, in 1913, breakfast for Lancashire cotton workers consisted of tea or coffee, bread, bacon and eggs and lunch of potatoes and beef.

In 1863, Dr Edward Smith investigating the diet of agricultural workers and low paid industrial workers stated, 'The average quantity of food supplied is too little for health and strength'. Table 1 compares typical weekly food purchases for a semi-skilled worker, his wife and three children in 1841 and 1904.

Table 1 Weekly food purchases

1841		1904	
Bread	20 lb	Bread and flour	29.9 lb
Meat	5 lb	Meat	
Potatoes	40 lb	(bought by weight)	5.3 lb
Sugar	1 lb	Other meat (incl. fish)	
Butter	1 lb	Bacon	1.1 lb
Tea	0.2 lb	Eggs	
Porter	7 pints	Fresh milk	7.7 pints
(beer brewed from malt)		Cheese	0.7 lb
		Butter	1.5 lb
Cost	**10s 4d**	Potatoes	15.8 lb
		Vegetables and fruit	
		Currants and raisins	0.5 lb
		Rice, tapioca and	
		oatmeal	2.6 lb
		Tea	0.5 lb
		Coffee and cocoa	0.2 lb
		Sugar	4.6 lb
		Jam, marmalade,	
		treacle syrup	
		Pickles and condiments	
		Other items	
		Cost	**17s 10d**

(adapted from 'A Social and Economic History of Industrial Britain' by J. Robottom, Longman, Harlow, 1986, pp157, 166)

The quality and quantity of food improved steadily during the second half of the 19th century. Wages kept ahead of prices and cheap imports of wheat and meat led to a reduction in the price of basic foods. Fish became part of most people's diet and by 1914 fish and chip shops were common in working class areas.

In 1887, Mr W.H. Sykes, headmaster of Wapping Road School, Bradford, sent a pupil to buy a pot of jam and a batch of loaves.

Green Lane School kitchen, Bradford

Headteacher weighing children in Bradford for Dr Crowley's experiment

A junior member of staff was asked to brew tea and the world's first free school meal was served. During morning prayers a child had fainted and Mr Sykes diagnosed starvation. In 1902 Bradford started the world's first municipal school meals service. In 1914 the government made free school meals 'for the needy' compulsory. Table 2 shows a week's menu from Bradford in 1908.

The importance of school meals can be seen from Figure 1. It shows the results of an experiment conducted in 1907 by Doctor Ralph Crowley, Bradford's School Medical Officer. 109 children were given free school breakfasts and dinners during term time and compared with 69 children who were not fed by the school. Both groups were weighed each week. The solid line on the graph shows the average weight gains and losses of the children provided with school meals; the broken line shows the average weight gain of the children who were not fed by the school.

Table 2 School meals, Bradford 1908

Monday	Lentil and tomato soup. Currant roly-poly pudding.
Tuesday	Meat pudding (stewed beef and boiled suet pudding). Ground rice pudding.
Wednesday	Yorkshire pudding, gravy, peas. Rice and sultanas.
Thursday	Scotch barley broth. Currant pastry or fruit tart.
Friday	Stewed fish, parsley sauce, peas, mashed potatoes. Cornflour blancmange.

(All these meals included bread.)

(from 'Britain Since 1800: Towards the Welfare State' by H. Martin, Macmillan, Basingstoke, 1988, p47)

Figure 1 School meals and children's weight, Bradford 1907

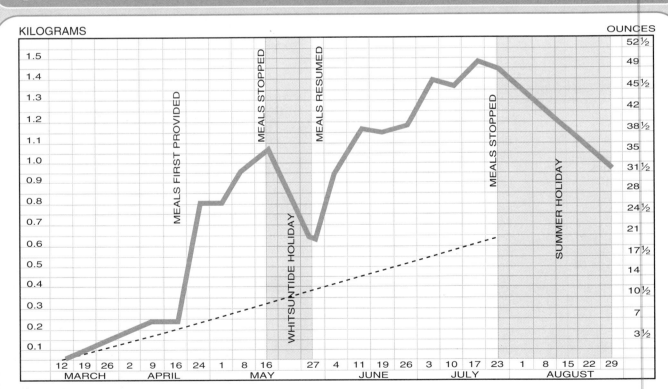

(adapted from 'Take A Bite Into … A Cross Curricular Resource Pack For School', Bradford Education, Bradford, 1994)

Infective diseases

One of the clearest and simplest ways of measuring the health of a population is mortality. Mortality statistics show people's age at death and allow us to calculate death rates and average life expectancy. As Chapter 13, Part 2 shows, the death rate has declined steadily during the last two centuries. Life expectancy at birth has increased from around 40 years in the first half of the 19th century to over 75 years by the early 1990s.

It is estimated that more than 60% of the decline in mortality was due to a reduction in infective conditions - tuberculosis (the single most important cause of death from infective disease), measles, scarlet fever, pneumonia, bronchitis and whooping cough. All these diseases tell the same story - a steady decline beginning well before the introduction of effective treatment. The number of cases left by the time vaccination or effective drugs became available was relatively small. This can be seen in the case of tuberculosis from Figure 2.

Figure 2 Tuberculosis in England and Wales, 1840-1970

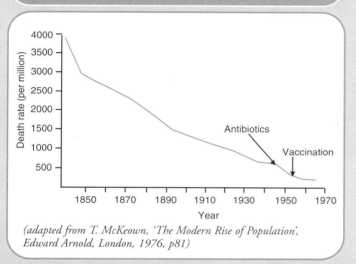

(adapted from T. McKeown, 'The Modern Rise of Population', Edward Arnold, London, 1976, p81)

The evidence indicates that the fall in the death rate was due mainly to changes in society rather than improvements in medicine. A number of researchers believe that improvements in nutrition are the main cause of improvements in health. For example, McKeown, a doctor who studied the relationship between social conditions and health in Britain, argues that being well fed is the most effective form of disease prevention. He concludes that the high mortality of preindustrial Britain was due either directly to starvation or to a lowering of resistance to infection brought about by undernourishment.

McKeown also singles out public hygiene as a major cause of improvements in health.

Public hygiene

Cholera and typhoid were major killers in the 19th century. They are bacteria spread mainly by water which has been contaminated by the excreta of people suffering from or carrying these diseases. Cholera came to Britain in 1832 killing half the people who caught it. Its main symptoms were continual diarrhoea and vomiting - those who died usually did

so within a week of acute dehydration. By the time the epidemic died down in 1834, it had killed over 50,000 people. At the time people thought that all diseases were caused and spread by the 'deadly effects of foul air'.

There is no doubt that many towns stank. This is how Doctor Howard described Manchester in 1842.

'Whole streets are unpaved and, without drains or main sewers, are worn into deep ruts and holes in which water constantly stagnates, and are so covered with refuse and excrementious matter as to be almost impassable from depth of mud, and intolerable from stench. In the narrow lanes, confined courts and alleys are to be seen privies (toilets) in the most disgusting state of filth, open cesspools, obstructed drains, ditches full of stagnant water, dunghills, pigsties, etc. from which the most abominable odours are emitted.'

Sewers being built, 1862

Queueing to collect water from a tap, London, 1862

Some local authorities responded to the 'deadly effects of foul air' by installing drains and sewers to clean up their towns and cities. In 1848 the government made town councils responsible for cleansing streets, laying sewers and supplying drinking water. In some towns the results were striking - for example, Macclesfield reduced its death rate from 45 per 1,000 in 1847, to 26 per 1,000 in 1858. But despite such improvements, there was a cholera epidemic in 1848 which killed over 100,000 people. And in 1853, Croydon, which had just installed a new sewerage system, had its worst outbreak of typhoid.

Sewers did carry the waste away but often recycled it into the drinking water. This is how the *Times* described how London was drained in 1859. 'All the sewers in London on both sides of the river discharged themselves into the Thames. Upwards of 200,000 gallons (900,000 litres) of sewage has been daily added to the Thames at low water.' And the River Thames was one of the main water supplies for the people of London.

The last outbreak of cholera occurred in London in 1866 with the deaths of around 14,000 people, After 1866 local authorities treated sewage before they piped it into rivers and supplies of drinking water steadily improved. As a result cholera and typhoid died out in Britain.

(adapted from 'The Sociology of Health and Medicine' by N. Hart, Causeway Press, Ormskirk, 1985; 'A Social and Economic History of Britain' by J. Robottom, Longman, Harlow, 1986; 'Britain Since 1800: Towards the Welfare State' by H. Martin, Macmillan, Basingstoke, 1988; 'Observer', 20.1.1994; 'Who Killed Primary Healthcare?' by D. Werner, 'New Internationalist', October, 1995).

QUESTIONS

1. Compare the diets in Table 1. Which is more healthy and why? (4)
2. Why were school meals important for reducing the death rate? Refer to Figure 1 in your answer. (4)
3. Show how Figure 2 indicates that the reduction in tuberculosis was due to changes in society rather than improvements in medicine. (3)
4. Why did towns and cities install drains and sewers? (5)
5. Why might the people pictured queuing for water in London be in danger of catching cholera or typhoid? (4)

SOCIAL CLASS AND HEALTH

The link between social class and health is supported by a large body of evidence from both the 19th and 20th centuries. Class inequalities in life expectancy and health are wide and may well be widening. This part examines the evidence and some of the explanations for social class differences in health.

Table 1 was published in 1824. It shows the average age of death of three occupational groups in Manchester.

Table 1 Occupation and average age of death

Occupation	Average age of death
Professional persons and gentry and their families	38
Tradesmen and their families	20
Mechanics, labourers, and their families	17

(adapted from 'A Social and Economic History of Industrial Britain' by J. Robottom, Longman, Harlow, 1986, p142)

Table 2 Social class and mortality

Great Britain 1979-80 and 1982-83	Males (aged 20-64)	Females (aged 20-64)
Social Class I	66	69
Social Class II	76	78
Social Class IIIN	94	87
Social Class IIIM	106	100
Social Class IV	116	110
Social Class V	165	134
All classes	100	100
Ratio V/I	2.5	1.9

(adapted from 'Sociology of Health and Health Care' edited by S. Taylor and D. Field, Blackwell, Oxford, 1993, p59)

Table 2 shows the relationship between social class and death. The average mortality rate for all social classes is 100. Any figure below 100 shows a lower than average mortality rate, any figure above 100, a higher than average mortality rate. The figures for each social class show the mortality of that class as a percentage of the mortality of the population as a whole.

Table 2 shows that men in Class V are 2.5 times more likely to die before retirement age than men in Class I. Similar patterns of class inequality are revealed by disability, long-standing illness, infant mortality and health-related absence from work. In general the higher your position in the class system, the more likely you are to lead a long and healthy life.

274

A number of explanations have been given for the link between social class and health. Two will now be briefly examined.

Materialist theory

Materialist theory argues that the material differences between social classes determine class differences in health. These include income, housing, diet, local environment and working conditions. These factors are usually related as Chapter 4 Social Stratification shows. For example, low income is often linked to inadequate diet and poor housing conditions. Materialist theory was used in Part 2 to explain the decline in the death rate in the 19th century with particular reference to diet and public hygiene.

Working conditions provide an example of a materialist explanation. The Health and Safety Executive estimates that 2 million people in Britain suffer from a work-related illness, resulting in the loss of 29 million working days each year. People in manual occupations are at far greater risk than others, particularly those in contact with machinery, chemicals and industrial wastes. Occupational diseases often develop gradually. They include a range of cancers (largely due to contact with dangerous chemicals) and respiratory diseases (as a result of breathing in various kinds of dust). In the early 1990s there were around 190,000 officially recorded occupational

Removing asbestos cladding from pipes

injuries, of which some 30,000 were major injuries. It is estimated that only 30% of injuries at work are reported.

Most sociologists conclude that material circumstances are the main determinant of class inequalities in health.

Cultural/behavioural theories

These theories argue that class inequalities in health are linked to class differences in behaviour, attitudes, values and lifestyles. Where materialist theory would argue that class differences in diet are due to differences in income - for example, the poor cannot afford an adequate diet - cultural/behavioural theories might argue that they are due to class differences in taste. Thus the diet of the poor is due to their choice of food rather than their low income.

Smoking provides an illustration of cultural/behavioural theories. Not only do men and women in Class V smoke more than those in Class I, they are also less likely to give up smoking. As a result they are 'more likely to die from lung cancer. This behaviour has been explained in terms of cultural differences between classes. For example, the working class has been described as fatalistic which means accepting the situation in the belief that there is little they can do to change it. By comparison, the middle class are said to have a more purposive approach to life, based on the belief that situations can be changed by individual effort. If these characterisations of the classes are correct - and there are many researchers who don't accept this - then they can be used to explain why members of the working class are less likely to give up smoking.

While not dismissing cultural/behavioural theories completely, most sociologists would see them as much less important for explaining class inequalities in health than materialist theory. Some have argued that the two types of explanation should be combined. This can be illustrated with the example of smoking. The material circumstances of working class life lead to greater anxiety and stress. Smoking is a way of coping with this situation. It therefore becomes more established as part of the lifestyle of many members of the working class.

Are class inequalities in health widening?

Throughout the 1980s the income gap between the classes steadily widened. At the start of the 1980s the income of the richest 20% of the population was 4 times as large as that of the poorest 20%. By 1991 it was almost 6 times as large. During this period the income of the poorest 10% went down in real terms (see Chapter 4, Part 7). From the point of view of materialist theory, this should lead to a widening of health inequalities between the social classes. A large scale study of health in northern England from 1981-1991 showed that this was indeed the case. The study was based on the counties of Cleveland, Cumbria, Durham, Northumberland and Tyne and Wear. 1981 and 1991 census data was used to rank the electoral wards in these counties in terms of material deprivation which was measured in terms of unemployment, car ownership, housing tenure (owned or rented) and household overcrowding. Health was measured in terms of mortality.

The results show that mortality differences between the richest fifth and the poorest fifth widened from 1981 to 1991. They also show that in the poorest areas the mortality rates among men aged 15-44 rose substantially. This reverses the long-term trend of reducing mortality rates. These findings are mirrored by similar evidence from Glasgow. Commenting on the study, Richard Wilkinson writes that the high mortality rates of the poor 'dwarfs almost every other health problem ... If risks as great as these resulted from exposure to toxic materials then offices would be closed down and populations evacuated from contaminated areas.'

Table 3 summarises the results of the northern England study. It compares the most deprived fifth of electoral wards with the least deprived fifth in terms of mortality for different age groups. The figures are based on a mortality rate for England and Wales in 1981-83 of 100. Figures above 100 show higher than average mortality, figures below show lower than average.

(adapted from 'The Sociology of Health and Medicine' by N. Hart, Causeway Press, Ormskirk, 1985; 'Sociology of Health and Health Care' edited by S. Taylor and D. Field, Blackwell, Oxford, 1993; 'Divided We Fall' by R.G. Wilkinson, 'British Medical Journal', 30.4.1994; 'Widening Inequality of Health in Northern England, 1981-91', by P. Phillimore, A. Beattie and P. Townsend, 'British Medical Journal', 30.4.1994)

Table 3 Changes in mortality in Northern region

		Mortality ratios for most deprived wards		Mortality ratios for least deprived wards	
	Age group	1981-3 (total population 900,501)	1989-91 (total population 829,453)	1981-3 (total population 415,024)	1989-92 (total population 433,517)
All persons	0-64	136	124	87	70
	0-14	116	99	80	60
Males	0-64	137	123	85	66
	15-44	117	131	84	69
	45-54	137	137	79	66
	55-64	144	120	90	67
	65-74	124	113	94	75
Females	0-64	136	125	91	76
	15-44	117	106	90	76
	45-54	127	119	84	67
	55-64	146	138	95	81
	65-74	123	127	95	82

(adapted from 'British Medical Journal', 30.4.1994, p1127)

QUESTIONS

1. Briefly summarise the relationship between social class and mortality shown in Tables 1 and 2. (5)
2. How can materialist and cultural/behavioural theories be combined to explain class differences in health? (6)
3. Give two examples of widening health inequality between the most and least deprived wards from Table 3. (4)
4. Show how materialist theory can be used to explain the findings shown in Table 3. (5)

4 PART MALNUTRITION IN BRITAIN

In 1994 the Department of Health set up the Low Income Project Team to investigate the evidence on diet, low income and ill-health. An unpublished report based on the team's findings was leaked to the *Observer* newspaper in January 1996. The following passage is based on the *Observer's* health correspondent Judy Jones' summary of the report.

Mounting poverty during the last 16 years has produced malnutrition in Britain on a scale unseen since the Great Depression of the 1930s. Millions of people have insufficient money to afford a healthy diet. Malnutrition means a lack of the nutrients vital for good health and long life. 'Malnutrition is an emotive word', said a member of the Low Income Project Team. 'But yes, given the low levels of vital nutrients, vitamins and minerals that are found in the diet of the poor, that's exactly what it is.'

In Britain the average household spends about 17% of its income on food. In September 1994, Sainsburys compiled a low income shopping basket for a family of four costing £11.66 a week per person. In the same year, the average two-child family living on benefits received £113.05 a week. So the Sainsburys' basket would take 40% of their income. Given their other outgoings such as rent and clothing, they couldn't afford it.

And even if they could afford the food basket, it would cost them money they didn't have to go and get it. Between 1980 and 1992 the number of food shops in Britain decreased by 35% and the number of superstores on the outskirts of town increased fourfold. According to the report, this has left 'whole communities with inadequate access to the constituents of a healthy diet'. Without cars, or money for transport, many poor people live in what the experts call 'fresh food deserts'.

Unable to afford an adequate diet, many poor parents regularly go without proper meals, snacking instead on 'tea and toast', so that their children can eat. This has been shown in survey after survey. Table 1 gives some indication of the problems of low income parents.

There is general agreement within the medical profession that eating a balanced diet containing plenty of fibre, fresh fruit and vegetables reduces the risk of developing some common cancers and heart diseases by up to 40%. Several studies have shown that as income goes down, so does the consumption of fresh fruit and vegetables - because of insufficient money rather than ignorance. Rates of cancer and heart disease in Britain are amongst the highest in the world. According to John Middleton, Director of Public Health for Sandwell, the third most deprived English borough outside London, 'Poor families are still eating high-fat diets as a matter of basic survival. They don't have enough money, nor the access to good fresh food in large enough quantities.'

What's the solution? In John Middleton's words, 'benefit levels must rise'. State benefits do not provide enough money for people to afford a healthy diet. The report suggests that the state should provide money to help people to grow food locally. This goes back to the 'Dig for Victory' campaign of the Second World War. In addition sellers of fruit and vegetables should be given tax incentives to encourage them to set up shop in low income areas. According to the report, 'Undoubtedly what many people want is the chance to shop like other citizens'.

Self-help may be part of the solution. Alarmed at the situation in Sandwell a group of residents formed the Sandwell Food

Table 1   The parents' anguish

'I normally buy four packets of bread, but if I'm running out of money we just buy two. So those who have six slices, I tell them to take four ... those taking four, I tell them to take three - and I don't eat. Sometimes I lie to them ... they say "Mummy don't, we know you're trying to keep us alive, but don't starve yourself, let's share it"... they're very good children, they understand.'
Parent on income support. Two dependent children.

'He gets hot nourishing food inside him [with his free school meals] - he gets meat I can't afford to buy, veg I can't afford to buy, he gets a pudding ... School holidays are a nightmare, trying to give him that extra meal a day is impossible.'
Parent on income support. One son.

'I buy apples and bananas every fortnight ... It's horrible when she has a banana and then says "Can I have an apple?" and you've got to stop her because it's got to last.'
Parent on income support. One daughter.

'The main thing is price, because sometimes you get it 2p cheaper. If you calculate, 1p is nothing, 5p is nothing, but at the end of the day it might come to 50p - and that stands for two bottles of milk.'
Parent on income support. Four children, two dependent on her.

A World War Two poster. Are we going backwards?

Cooperative. With a grant from the local health authority they provide cut-price fresh fruit and vegetables for more than 500 low income families. A van tours the council estates once a week. In the early days people would peer in, point at the celery and ask: 'What on earth's *that*?' The Sandwell scheme is one of more than 80 food cooperatives around the country set up to bring fresh food to poor people.

(adapted from 'The Bad Food Trap' by Judy Jones, 'Observer', 2.1.1996)

QUESTIONS

1. The poor simply cannot afford a healthy diet. What evidence supports this view? (6)
2. Why is malnutrition an emotive term? (4)
3. Self-help is no real solution to the problem of inadequate diet. Discuss. (4)
4. Which theory - materialist or cultural/behavioural (see Part 3) - best explains the malnutrition of the poor? Give reasons. (6)

5 PART — THE SICK ROLE

In Western societies, doctors have almost complete control over medical care. They have the right to define health and to treat illness and the authority to state officially whether people are sick or well.

The following passage looks at the sick role and the way in which it is defined and regulated by doctors. It shows that being ill is not just a physical experience, it is also the performance of a social role.

The sick role

The American sociologist Talcott Parsons argues that for society to operate effectively people must perform social roles, for example their roles as workers or students. Parsons sees sickness as a threat to society since it can lead people to withdraw from their normal roles and responsibilities. Given the seriousness of this threat, any withdrawal must be regulated. If it is not, people may use sickness as an excuse for getting out of their social obligations.

This is where doctors come in. They act as agents of social control, ensuring that the adoption of the sick role is justified. They weed out those who seek to misuse the sick role - the 'skivers', 'malingerers', 'deadbeats' and hypochondriacs. Doctors have the power to diagnose (identify) and treat disease and to allow or disallow people to adopt the sick role. Their patients have the duty to seek medical guidance and submit their body to medical inspection.

Parsons identifies four aspects of the sick role - two rights and two responsibilities.

Rights 1) Patients have the right to some form of exemption from normal social activities, eg time off work.

2) They are freed from personal responsibility for the illness - it's not their fault. They have a right to be taken care of.

Duties 1) They must see being ill as undesirable and strive to get better and resume their normal social roles.

2) They must seek professional help and cooperate with the treatment.

Blaming the sick

The sick role does not always operate in the way Parsons describes. There are situations where people are seen to be responsible for their illness. For example, alcoholics are sometimes blamed for their condition. And some doctors have argued that people with smoking-related diseases should be given low priority on National Health Service waiting lists because they have 'brought it upon themselves'.

Some diseases carry a stigma - a mark of shame and disgrace

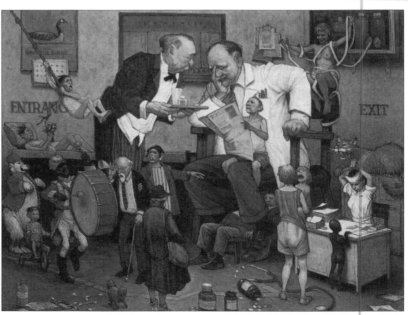

Who takes care of the doctor? From a painting entitled 'The Family Practitioner' by José Perez.

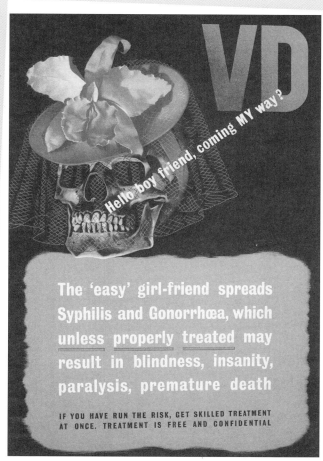

A World War Two poster

God delivers a warning !

- which may lead to sufferers being seen as less deserving of sympathy and treatment. For example, at various times epilepsy, leprosy and syphilis have been stigmatised and people with these conditions denied care and even persecuted.

The stigma sometimes associated with AIDS can be seen from the following quotations.

- 'If AIDS is not an act of God with consequences just as frightful as fire and brimstone, then just what the hell is it?' (John Junor, former editor of the 'Sunday Express')

- 'AIDS victims swirl in a cesspit of their own making.' (James Anderton, former Chief Constable of Manchester)

- 'The most sinister decline in our standards of behaviour is the tolerance of unnatural sexual behaviour, ie homosexuality. But the laws of nature are not so easily bent because the consequence is the current invasion of AIDS. It is a plague.' (P. Drabble in 'The Field', March 1987)

If an illness is stigmatised, people may deny they suffer from it. They may keep their condition secret from others and avoid consulting a doctor and adopting the sick role. They may feel others will blame them for their illness and see them as unclean or dangerous.

(adapted from 'The Sociology of Health and Medicine' by N. Hart, Causeway Press, Ormskirk, 1985 and 'The Social Construction of AIDS' by R. Pattman in 'Discovering Sociology' edited by P. Langley, Causeway Press, Ormskirk, 1988)

QUESTIONS

1. a) In what ways may illness threaten society? (3)
   b) How might doctors reduce this threat? (3)
2. How might the stigmatisation of illness prevent the sick role from being performed? (4)
3. Suggest why certain illnesses are stigmatised. (4)
4. What impression does the poster give of syphilis and gonorrhoea and of the people who are seen to spread these diseases? (3)
5. What does the cartoon say about the cause and treatment of AIDS? (3)

INDEX